19

Honor and Shame
in the Gospel of Matthew

Also by Jerome H. Neyrey
from Westminster John Knox Press

Paul, in Other Words
A Cultural Reading of His Letters

with Bruce J. Malina
Portraits of Paul
An Archaeology of Ancient Personality

Honor and Shame
in the Gospel of Matthew

Jerome H. Neyrey

Westminster John Knox Press
Louisville, Kentucky

Scripture quotations from the Revised Standard Version of the Bible are copyright
1946, 1952, © 1971, 1973 by the Division of Christian Education of the National
Council of the Churches of Christ in the U.S.A. and are used by permission.

Book design by Douglas & Gayle Ltd.
Cover design by Pam Poll
Cover illustration: Rembrandt, The Denial of Peter. *Courtesy of SuperStock*

First edition
Published by Westminster John Knox Press
Louisville, Kentucky

This book is printed on acid-free paper that meets the
American National Standards Institute Z39.48 standard. ∞

PRINTED IN THE UNITED STATES OF AMERICA
98 99 00 01 02 03 04 05 06 07 — 10 9 8 7 6 5 4 3 2 1

Library of Congress Cataloging-in-Publication Data

Neyrey, Jerome H., 1940–
    Honor and shame in the Gospel of Matthew / Jerome H. Neyrey.
        p.   cm.
    Includes bibliographical references and indexes.
    ISBN 0-664-25643-0
    1. Bible. N.T. Matthew—Socio-rhetorical criticism.   2. Honor in
the Bible.   3. Shame in the Bible.   I. Title.
BS2575.6.H634N48   1998
226.2'06—dc21   98-7521

Contents

Abbreviations

AB	Anchor Bible
ABD	*Anchor Bible Dictionary*
AJP	*American Journal of Philology*
ANRW	*Aufstieg und Niedergang der römischen Welt*
Ant.	Josephus, *Antiquities of the Jews*
ARN	*The Fathers according to Rabbi Nathan*, trans. Judah Goldin, New Haven, Conn., 1955
ATR	*Anglican Theological Review*
BAGD	W. Bauer, W. F. Arndt, F. W. Gingrich, and F. Danker*, Greek-English Lexicon of the New Testament*, 2d ed., Chicago, 1979
BARev	*Biblical Archaeology Review*
BETL	Bibliotheca ephemeridum theologicarum lovaniensium
BI	*Biblical Interpretation*
Bib	*Biblica*
BJRL	*Bulletin of the John Rylands University Library of Manchester*
BTB	*Biblical Theology Bulletin*
BVC	*Bible et vie chrétienne*
BZ	*Biblische Zeitschrift*
BZNT	Beihefte zur ZNW
CBQ	*Catholic Biblical Quarterly*
CBQMS	CBQ Monograph Series
CP	*Classical Philology*
ConBNT	Coniectanea biblica—New Testament series
CQ	*Classical Quarterly*
CurTM	*Currents in Theology and Ministry*
CW	*Classical World*
DR	*Downside Review*
EBib	*Études bibliques*
EvQ	*Evangelical Quarterly*
ExpT	*Expository Times*
GR	*Greece and Rome*
HDR	Harvard Dissertations in Religion
HeyJ	*Heythrop Journal*
HR	*History of Religion*
HSCPh	Harvard Studies in Classical Philology
HTR	*Harvard Theological Review*
HUCA	*Hebrew Union College Annual*

IBS	*Irish Biblical Studies*
IDB	*Interpreter's Dictionary of the Bible*
IESS	*International Encyclopedia of the Social Sciences*
Inst. Orat.	Quintilian, *Institutiones Oratoriae*
Int	*Interpretation*
JAAR	*Journal of the American Academy of Religion*
JBL	*Journal of Biblical Literature*
JECS	*Journal of Early Christian Studies*
JHS	*Journal of Hellenic Studies*
JQR	*Jewish Quarterly Review*
JRS	*Journal of Roman Studies*
JSJ	*Journal for the Study of Judaism*
JSNT	*Journal for the Study of the New Testament*
JSNTSup	JSNT Supplement
JSOT	*Journal for the Study of the Old Testament*
JSOTSup	JSOP Supplement
JTS	*Journal of Theological Studies*
J.W.	Josephus, *Jewish War*
LSJ	H. Liddell, R. Scott, and H. Jones, *A Greek-English Lexicon*, Oxford, 1940
LXX	Septuagint
MM	J. Moulton and G. Milligan, *The Vocabulary of the Greek Testament*
Neot	*Neotestamentica*
NTS	*New Testament Studies*
NovT	*Novum Testamentum*
NovTSup	NovT Supplement
NTSMS	NTS Monograph Series
PEQ	*Palestine Exploration Quarterly*
QR	*Quarterly Review*
RAC	*Reallexikon für Antike und Christentum*
RB	*Revue biblique*
ResQ	*Restoration Quarterly*
RevExp	*Review and Expositor*
Rhet.	Aristotle, *Rhetoric*
Rhet. Her.	*Rhetoric to Herennius*
RSRev	*Religious Studies Review*
SBLDS	SBL Dissertation Series
SBLSBS	Studies in Biblical Theology
SBLSP	*Society of Biblical Literature Seminar Papers*
SBT	Studies in Biblical Theology
SE	*Studia Evangelica*
SNTSMS	Society for New Testament Studies Monograph Series
ST	*Studia Theologica*

Str-B	H. Strack and P. Billerbeck, *Kommentar zum Neuen Testament aus Talmud und Midrasch*
TAPA	*Transactions of the American Philological Association*
TBT	*The Bible Today*
TDNT	*Theological Dictionary of the New Testament*
TGF	A. Nauck, ed., *Tragicorum Graecorum Fragmenta*
ThR	*Theologische Rundschau*
TJT	*Toronto Journal of Theology*
TS	*Theological Studies*
TU	Texte und Untersuchungen
TZ	*Theologische Zeitschrift*
VT	*Vetus Testamentum*
WUNT	Wissenschaftliche Untersuchungen zum Neuen Testament
ZNW	*Zeitschrift für die neutestamentliche Wissenschaft*

Texts Cited, Translations, and Abbreviations

Note: The translation of the Bible used in this book is the Revised Standard Version. All texts and translations of Greek and Roman authors come from the Loeb Classical Library, with one exception. George A. Kennedy's rendering of Aristotle's *Rhetoric* is used because of its clear understanding of epideictic rhetoric and its sensitivity to technical rhetorical terms.

Four texts of the rules for an encomium are used here: Aelius Theon (James Butts, "The 'Progymnasmata' of Theon: A New Text with Translation and Commentary" [diss., Claremont Graduate School, 1987]), Apthonius of Ephesus (trans. Ray Nadeau, *Speech Monographs* 19 [1952]: 264–285); Hermogenes of Tarsus (trans. C. S. Baldwin, *Medieval Rhetoric and Poetic* [New York: Macmillan, 1928], 23–38), and Menander Rhetor (trans. D. A. Russell and N. G. Wilson, *Menander Rhetor* [Oxford: Clarendon Press, 1981]).

Introduction

1.0 Topic and Focus

The New Testament frequently praises God's majesty and power. These acknowledgments may simply express respect, such as "To the only wise God be glory for evermore" (Rom. 16:27), or more complex declarations of praise for God's power and benefaction, such as: "Worthy art thou, our Lord and God to receive glory and honor and power. For thou didst create all things, and by thy will they existed and were created" (Rev. 4:11). In addition, we find other formulaic acknowledgments of God's exalted status, uniqueness, and glory, such as the doxology in 1 Timothy: " . . . blessed and only Sovereign, the King of kings and Lord of lords, who alone has immortality and dwells in unapproachable light, whom no man has ever seen or can see. To him be honor and eternal dominion" (6:15–16). Indeed the New Testament sparkles with such paeans of praise, honor, and glory to God (Eph. 3:21; Phil. 4:20; 1 Tim. 1:17; 2 Tim. 4:18; Heb. 13:21; 1 Peter 4:11; 2 Peter 3:18; and Jude 24; see Neyrey 1993:94–101). People in the ancient world knew intuitively from their cultural milieu how to praise and honor another, especially the Deity.

The same is true concerning Jesus. The Christian scriptures contain but few doxologies or hymns of praise to Jesus, since the articulation of his exalted status and role was still in the process of development. Nevertheless, notable praise is rendered to the Lamb, who alone can open the scroll and break its seals: "Worthy art thou to take the scroll and to open its seals, for thou wast slain and by thy blood didst ransom men for God from every tribe and tongue and people and nation, and hast made them a kingdom and priests to our God, and they shall reign on earth" (Rev. 5:9–10). "Worthiness" is an adequate synonym for "praise," "honor," and "glory." Yet praise of Jesus should not be limited to doxologies or hymns. The Gospels, and Matthew in particular, praise Jesus in a literary mode quite different from the hymnic or confessional celebrations of "worth" or "praise, glory, and honor." Although written in light of Jesus' vindication and elevation to an exalted status after his death, the Gospels touch upon the nobility of his earthly life and hold up for admiration and imitation his virtuous deeds. This book focuses on the praise of Jesus of Nazareth as presented in narrative form by the evangelist Matthew.

Like the stylized doxologies which honor the Sovereign God, the Gospels follow in great measure conventional formulae for praise articulated in the epideictic rhetoric of praise and in the rules for the encomium. Our task, then, is to clarify what praise, honor, and glory mean to Matthew and his audience. To do this we must familiarize ourselves with (1) the traditional literary forms according to which such praise was regularly bestowed and (2) the conventional grounds for awarding honor and praise in Matthew's world.

2.0 "Let Us Now Praise Famous Men . . ."

Along with forensic and deliberative rhetoric, ancient Greece and Rome developed a special type of rhetoric for expressing praise and honor, namely, epideictic rhetoric. In addition to formal speeches of praise, the Greco-Roman world expressed praise in other genres such as encomiums, biographies, and funeral orations. In recent years, Greek "lives" or biography have attracted scholars' attention for understanding the genre of the Gospels. Scholars studied the formal conventions of typical biographies and compared them with the narrative about Jesus (Talbert 1974, 1978; Shuler 1982; Burridge 1992). Scholarly opinion has shifted between outright rejection of gospels as biography (Aune 1987:16–36, 46–76) and limited acceptance of biographical elements in the Gospels (Barr and Wentling 1984:63–88; Robbins 1984). Because of biblical interest in history and historiography, many are reluctant to see biography as a formal antecedent of the Gospels. Yet ancient biographies were conventionally structured according to formal criteria for praise; and in most cases their rhetorical purpose was that of praise. But we do not have from the Greco-Roman world instructions on how to write a biography, so we resort to comparison among the Lives written by Plutarch, Suetonius, and others. Only by painstaking examination of many examples can we begin to learn the cultural significance of elements such as omens at a hero's birth or funeral games at his death. With the encomium, however, we fare much better.

Elaborate and precise rules for writing an encomium are found in the educational handbooks called the *progymnasmata*. The advantage of these rules lies in the formal and self-conscious categories they contain for praising a person. The handbooks provide detailed instruction on what to say concerning each section of a hero's life (birth, education and training, public life, and death). Nothing is left to chance, as students are taught both the form of the encomium and the prevailing criteria for praise. These rules, moreover, consciously articulate what biographies and lives express more intuitively; in encomiums the formal structure is bold and clear. The advantage of studying the encomium lies precisely in discovering the clear, conventional rules for expressing praise and honor. Our study of the encomium will no doubt support scholarly arguments that Matthew's Gospel has some formal relationship to ancient biography.

It is premature to classify Matthew's narrative as an "encomium" or "encomiastic biography." Sufficient for us to examine the ancient rhetoric of praise and then draw what conclusions seem evident. Now, however, we must turn to the rhetoric of praise and especially the rules for an encomium to discover the formal structure according to which the ancients regularly praised someone (origins and birth, education and training, deeds of body, soul, and fortune, and death), and conventional criteria for praise at these stages of a typical life.

The encomium was not an exclusively Greco-Roman literary or rhetorical phenomenon, as Sirach 44–50 indicates (Lee 1986). A distinctive section of Sirach begins with the topic statement, "Let us now praise famous men" (44:1). The author then rehearses the glorious events in the lives of Israelite heroes such as Enoch, Noah, Abraham, Moses, Aaron—a list which includes warriors, kings, prophets, and high priests. The rhetorical aim of Sirach 44–50 is unabashedly praise, glory, and honor, that is, the positive evaluation of these persons and a burnishing of their great reputation and fame. Although it recounts important deeds in their lives, it is neither history nor biography. Before Sirach begins his celebration of these heroes, he offers a brief sketch of what he means by "praise," which provides us with important clues to the topic. He notes that they all enjoyed ascribed honor, that is, God allotted them their glory and fame: "The Lord apportioned to them great glory" (44:1). Sirach immediately illustrates the abstract term "glory" in terms of the noble roles and statuses which the heroes enjoyed: they "ruled in their kingdoms" and "were renown for their power" (v. 3); that is, some were kings and warriors. To others God ascribed the role of sage and prophet, also very high status positions: some were renowned for "giving counsel and proclaiming prophecies" (v. 3) and others were famous "in understanding of learning" and "wise in their words of instruction" (v. 4). Others achieved their fame by "composing musical tunes and setting forth verses in writing" (v. 5). In part their worthiness was a function of their wealth, for they were "rich men furnished with resources" (v. 6) who could live a royal or aristocratic lifestyle.

Honor is nothing unless acknowledged by others. Hence, Sirach notes that in their own lifetime Israel's heroes enjoyed great respect and honor. "All these were honored in their generations and were the glory of their times" (v. 7). Most of the heroes "left a name, so that all declare their praise" (v. 8). Yet not all were honored in their lifetime; and so Sirach sets as his task the present glorification of all of these past heroes. He builds a literary monument to their fame which will last forever. For, if his encomium is successful, he will have created a new and lasting public forum where the heroes will be continually remembered and acclaimed: "Peoples will declare their wisdom, and the congregation proclaim their praise" (v. 15).

This section of Sirach (chaps. 44–50) and its thematic introduction are clear evidence that praise, honor, and glory were important cultural elements, not just in the Greco-Roman, but also in the Judean world. We call attention, not only to the topic, "the praise of famous men," but also to the preliminary articulation of what "praise" means, and the formal celebration of the merits of ancestral heroes. This document was surely read and heard by many, and so it either reinforced already existing notions of praise or introduced them to its audience. Although we will concentrate on Greco-Roman articulations of honor and praise, Sirach provides proof that the conventions of praise were by no means confined to the cultural world of the Greeks and Romans.

3.0 Theses and Hypotheses

This book examines Matthew's Gospel in terms of honor and shame. It is becoming an accepted fact that honor and shame were pivotal values in antiquity that structured the daily lives of peoples around the Mediterranean, including Jesus and his disciples. Readers of Matthew who take the historical-critical task seriously may want to read that document according to its appropriate cultural context, which necessarily includes appreciation of honor and shame. Hence, use of the cultural values of honor and shame for interpretation of a text such as Matthew is not an optional enterprise. One simply cannot read Matthew correctly without basic information about the pivotal values of his world.

The Gospel of Matthew was not an arbitrary choice for this book. Nor is it the unwilling victim of this analysis, a guinea pig on which to experiment. We are not forcing Matthew to conform to some abstract and arbitrary model. We argue instead that Matthew the evangelist was trained in the conventional educational manner as found in the *progymnasmata*, such that he both knew the rhetoric of praise and blame and employed many of the genres taught in the rhetorical handbooks concerning praise. In the typical process of formal education in antiquity, those who learned to write Greek with the kind of proficiency demonstrated by Matthew were ordinarily trained in the compositional skills listed in the *progymnasmata*, that is, the handbooks of rhetorical education. These handbooks were the "preliminary exercises . . . the elementary stage of instruction in schools of rhetoric" (Russell 1980:883). En route to formal studies in rhetoric, students were initially taught to write and organize their remarks on traditional topics in terms of highly conventional genres. The *progymnasmata* taught them to become proficient in writing: (1) myths, (2) chreia and proverbs, (3) refutation and confirmation, (4) commonplaces on virtues and vices, (5) encomium and vituperation, (6) comparison, (7) character imitation, (8) description, (9) theses for or against something, and (10) legislation, for or against a law. Thus students learned compositional skills corresponding to the three types of rhetoric: deliberative for use in legislative assemblies, forensic for use in courtrooms, and epideictic or the rhetoric of praise for celebratory occasions.

For those who study the Gospels, two of these progymnastic exercises are highly significant, the chreia and especially the encomium. The rules for composing an encomium (and vituperation) instructed students how to praise (and blame) someone. Nothing in the exercise of praise was left to chance, for students were instructed concerning the form of a speech of praise, as well as the specific content of each element of that form. They learned to organize their praise according to the conventional manner of presenting a person's life from birth to death and in light of specific rules for developing praise at each stage of this life. Thus students were socialized as to what was praiseworthy in their culture, both the criteria for praise and the formal expressions of it. The content of praise and the form in which it is expressed embody what I will shortly describe as the "general code" of honor and shame.

Although Matthew may have been raised speaking Greek, he surely went to school to learn to write that language as well as he did. And his Gospel indicates a sophisticated mastery of the art of praise. The very existence of a document such as Matthew presumes a degree of literacy that could only be achieved by some formal education, which was most likely based on the mastery of conventional rhetorical materials, both the rhetoric of praise and blame and the forms taught in the rhetorical handbooks, the *progymnasmata*. Although the ancients distinguished three kinds of rhetoric, Matthew's Gospel reflects the exercises and perspectives associated with the rhetoric of praise and blame. As we shall see, Matthew follows very closely the guidelines for an encomium, whether it is an "encomiastic biography" or some other genre.

4.0 In Brief, What Is Honor?

"Honor" is the generalized term which refers to the worth or value of persons both in their own eyes and in the eyes of their village or neighborhood. Honor (τιμή) can refer to the value of an object, namely, its price or worth, as well as to the public role and status which individuals enjoy (Schneider 1972:168–80). Honor basically has to do with evaluation and social perception: What do people think of this person? How is he evaluated, positively or negatively? Hence, it also means reputation, renown, and fame, which might just as well be rendered by a synonym such as a person's "glory" or "good name." Consider what Iago said to Othello:

> Good name in man and woman, dear my lord,
> Is the immediate jewel of their souls.
> Who steals my purse steals trash; 'tis something,
>   nothing;
> 'Twas mine, 'tis his, and has been slave to thousands;
> But he that filches from me my good name
> Robs me of that which not enriches him,
> And makes me poor indeed.
>   (*Othello* 3.3.155–161)

It would not be an understatement to say that concern for "honor" as reputation and "good name" was endemic to the ancient world; hence, we hear classicists and anthropologists calling it a "pivotal value" of the Mediterranean world, both ancient and modern.

Let us turn for a moment to Aristotle, an important native informant for the ancient world. In his description of the "great-souled man" he tells us much about honor:

> If then the great-souled man claims and is worthy of great things and most of all the greatest things, Greatness of Soul must be concerned with some one object especially. "Worthy" is a term of relation: it denotes having a claim to goods external to oneself. Now the greatest external good we should assume to be the thing which we offer as a tribute to the gods, and which is most coveted by men of high station, and is the prize awarded for the noblest deeds; and such a thing is honour, for *honour is clearly the greatest of external goods*. Therefore the great-souled man is he who has the right disposition in relation to honours and disgraces . . . since it is honour above all else which great men claim and deserve. (*Nicomachean Ethics* 4.3.9–12, italics added)

Aristotle does not define what "honor" is, but rather states its paramount importance as the object of a virtuous person. A great-souled person both claims and is worthy of "the greatest things," which is honor. Twice Aristotle calls honor "the greatest external good" that a person could acquire, which would seem to rank it at the top of the value scale in his reckoning of Greek social life. Honor, moreover, is what mortals give to the gods, not sacrifice or any material thing, but respect and reverence; it is what "great" men claim and deserve. One cannot help but notice the language which surrounds the identification of honor: "greatest," "worthy," and "noblest." At the very least, Aristotle identifies for us a phenomenon of singular worth and importance for his culture.

This brief description, however, cannot begin to tell us about the rich but complex world of honor and shame. We do not know yet how people get honor, how honor is claimed or earned, how it is displayed, and how it might be symboled. Nor do we begin to understand that values such as honor and shame imply a set of behaviors and social structures in which they are embodied and played out. The first part of this book, then, will be dedicated to a description of honor and shame.

5.0 Sources of Information about Honor and Shame

We have two excellent sources of information about this pivotal set of values, both modern cultural anthropology and ancient rhetorical theory. When we turn to the anthropological study of honor and shame, we have access to something which no number of native informants can provide us with, namely, a full, nuanced, and coherent model of honor and shame in terms of social institutions and social psychology. Indeed we are particularly blessed with remarkable cross-cultural studies of honor and shame relating to the social life of the countries which border the Mediterranean. We enjoy informed and sensitive descriptions of the importance of honor and its mechanics in the societies of Turkey (Delaney 1987), Greece (DuBoulay 1974; Dubish 1986), Cyprus (Campbell 1960; Péristiany 1966), Spain (Pitt-Rivers 1966; 1971; 1977), Andalusia (Gilmore 1987), North Africa (Bourdieu 1966), Egypt (Zeid 1966), and Morocco (Marcus 1987). It is not accidental that all of these studies have analyzed diverse cultures around the Mediterranean basin. They differ, of course, in language, history, and geography, but they all reflect typical understandings of honor and shame and indicate many common behavioral practices related to these values. Their significance for us lies in the rich, nuanced, complex model of honor and shame which they compositely offer. For they do not simply rehearse remarks in which the terms "honor" and "shame" appear, but indicate their relationship to institutions such as the family, their dynamics in terms of agonistic behavior, their expression in terms of specific virtues such as courage and endurance, and most of all their embodiment of a conventional gender division of society. A native Greek, Arab, or Spaniard raised in an honor-shame culture already knows the system which is expressed by these values, even if intuitively and unreflectively. Use of cross-cultural models based on detailed ethnographic studies is a required and invaluable tool for us non-natives. We simply have no other way into this cultural world without such formal guides.

Yet modern biblical scholarship tends to be uneasy about the use of formal anthropological models. This unease often results from training in "historical" methodology, which many think commits scholars to objectivity and inductive data gathering of precisely dated materials. Even though much contemporary biblical scholarship has learned to ask "social questions" about the scriptures in addition to historical ones, scholars remain uneasy with materials and methods of investigation employed in the social sciences (see Burke 1980:13–30; Elliott 1993:107–9). Suspicion remains about procedures and questions that are not a standard part of the task of historical reconstruction or are not related to social history and social description (Smith 1975). Thus there is a current tendency to dismiss anthropological models as the unwarranted imposition of alien frameworks on the ancient documents (see Elliott 1993:36–59, 107–9). These problems cannot be solved now, but they are addressed in the argument of this book. Great care has been taken to recover and articulate ancient rhetorical theory and forms of composition which were current at the time of Matthew. These materials indicate that honor and shame were pivotal values for authors such as Aristotle, Cicero, and Quintilian; and the content and formal shape of praise in the ancient world can be clearly identified in the formal rules for an encomium. Nevertheless, even this rhetorical material, we argue, needs to be understood in some larger framework, namely, the model of honor and shame articulated by contemporary anthropology.

A second source of information about honor and shame in antiquity comes from the ancient rhetoric of praise and blame. As we noted above, in order for Matthew to write the kind of Greek that he did, he must have had formal schooling. And invariably such schooling would have entailed mastery of the exercises in the rhetorical handbooks known as the *progymnasmata*. Although we cannot know the particular school in which Matthew studied, his teachers, or the rhetorical books from which he was taught, we are confident that the educational resources of antiquity were rigorously conventional. All rhetorical theory depended in some way on Aristotle, the first person to codify Greek practice. Directly or indirectly Aristotle's model of rhetoric appeared in Roman times in the versions of rhetoric by Cicero, Quintilian, and the author of the *Rhetoric to Herennius*. The extant works of these authors reflect the unbroken tradition of rhetoric that continued with little change over centuries of appropriation by Hellenistic and Roman elites. Furthermore, students learning to write worked from highly standardized rhetorical handbooks, the *progymnasmata*, examples of which we have from Aelius Theon, Menander, and Hermogenes. We consider these authors to be our native informants about the art of praise and blame in the ancient world. They can give exacting historical precision to the meanings of praise and honor as well as to the forms of praise, its criteria, and its public expression.

Yet one might ask whether there is any difference between the two sources or whether one is preferable to the other? Obviously the use of ancient native informants offers many advantages over models of honor and shame from contemporary cultural anthropology. Not the least is its historical primacy as a collection of voices from the very time and culture of Matthew's Gospel. And, as all historical documents do, the writings of these ancient informants describe the cultural scene with the kind of particularity which is necessarily absent from synthetic models that generalize on the basis of diverse ethnographic studies but do not include that wealth of detail in their presentation. Our ancient rhetorical informants, moreover, will be able to sharpen our focus on certain aspects of honor and shame, highlighting these values as significant items in the natives' scheme of things.

Yet the body of information provided by our native informants is radically limited. Ancient rhetoric pertains to the public life of males whose face and actions are turned toward politics. Their forums were the law courts and the assemblies, and their focus was on the public behavior of elites. The anthropological discussion of honor and shame, on the other hand, is based on a broader sample of ethnographic studies which look at peasant and village life, the world of non-elite males. It considers carefully the other major institution, namely, the family and other quasi-kinship groups. Moreover, anthropology provides a tested model of honor and shame that articulates the relationship and coherence of diverse items under consideration. It takes a systemic view of statuses, institutions, modal personality, behaviors, and values, which simply is not the case with the historical studies of the ancient rhetoric of praise and blame. If one relied only on native ancient informants, we would not know the full scope of honor and shame; they simply are not able to give us the big picture. It is necessary to employ both sources. Both must be used, and with due appreciation for the limits of each.

6.0 The Nagging Historical Question: "Mediterranean"

The use of ancient rhetoric will help to solve a theoretical problem. The original generation of anthropologists who talked about honor and shame as a "Mediterranean" value focused on Iraq, Turkey, Greece, Spain, and Morocco. In time, historically minded anthropologists took issue with this generalization—in particular Michael Herzfeld—and called for more nuanced studies of individual areas, criticizing the use of the label "Mediterranean." Historically minded biblical scholars often react similarly to our description of honor and shame as pivotal values in the ancient Mediterranean world. Everyone knows that Homeric Greece differs from classical Greece, which differs from the Greece within the Roman empire. And Greece was not Egypt, nor Egypt, Rome. And so it would seem that we should be on shaky theoretical ground talking about honor and shame and "ancient society" and the "Mediterranean" world.

One of the important contributions of this study is our eagerness to address this type of criticism. Rhetoric, it must be admitted, became a constant and conventional element in education not only in Greece, but in Egypt, Africa, Rome, and the Byzantine empire. Not that everyone was educated in rhetoric, but those who became proficient in composing Greek typically went through a formal educational process that included mastery both of the exercises in the handbooks known as the progymnasmata and of the art of rhetoric. From the time of Alexander, the rest of the Mediterranean basin was in the process of being "Hellenized" (on geocentrism in antiquity, see Malina and Neyrey 1996:xiii, 117–25). This entailed learning not simply the Greek language, but also Greek literature, institutions, and cultural values. One thinks immediately of the Hellenization of Palestine and Judea before the Maccabean revolt. Furthermore, ancient education in reading and writing was a highly conservative process, in which students learned to read and memorize important pieces of Greek literature such as Homer, Euripides, Thucydides, Xenophon, and the like (Yaghjian 1996:207–21). Education placed little emphasis on creativity, but rather on the mastery of the best writings of the past. But students did not simply memorize Greek; through it they also learned a system of values, nothing less than the code of excellence expected of public males which embodied the system of honor and shame. Composition in Greek, moreover, was hardly left to chance, but was based on imitation of prominent models and examples. The path to the kind of Greek composition represented by the Gospel of Matthew indisputably lay through the rhetorical handbooks, the *progymnasmata*, which taught composition of various genres such as the chreia and the encomium, which is the precise genre of praise.

Both secondary education by means of the rhetorical handbooks and advanced rhetorical training were stylized exercises in conventional forms and arguments. Students in this process were basically reading the same literature and practicing the same rhetorical exercises. This means that students learning to write Greek, whether in Greece, Asia Minor, Syria, Palestine, Egypt, Cyrene, Carthage, Rome, Gaul, or Britain, were being socialized in both the standard forms of praise and the value code of honor and shame which the rhetorical genres embodied. Students, moreover, whether in the Athens of Demosthenes, the Alexandria of the Ptolemies, or the Antioch of the Roman empire, learned basically the same conventional forms with which to express the common values of praise and blame. Such was the nature of rhetorical education, in which conventionality ruled the day. Thus it is appropriate to speak of a rhetoric of praise and blame which is truly "Mediterranean" and which spans centuries, not simply from classical Greece to the Roman empire, but into the Byzantine period as well. The rhetoric of praise and blame did not change. And so there truly was a "Mediterranean" culture that dominated that geographical area.

7.0 The General Code: The Rhetoric of Praise and Blame

Two things need to be emphasized: both the widespread nature of the culture of praise and its utter conventionality. In regard to the former, those who learned to read and write Greek were schooled in the literature which embodied the general code of praise and blame. Given the oral nature of ancient society, we must allow for acquaintance with Greek rhetorical culture by the general public through public recitations or readings of literature embodying the rhetoric of praise. The central parts of cities and towns, moreover, were decorated both with inscriptions in praise of benefactors (Danker 1982; Forbis 1990) and with statues and busts of ancestors, heroes, and benefactors. Even nonreaders could see the face of honor. Temples honored the gods, and even rustics could observe what majesty looked like and appreciate the gifts with which honorable people adorned the temples—all part of the larger nonverbal language of honor. The claims to honor and their display and manifestations were not restricted to elites alone, as non-elites continually sought to impress their neighbors with wit, wealth, power, and the like. Marriage feasts were excellent times to put all one's material tokens of honor on display. Aristotle lists a number of public events where honor might be visible and audible:

> The components of honor are sacrifices [made to the benefactor after death], memorial inscriptions in verse or prose, receipt of special awards, grants of land, front seats at festivals, burial at public expense, statues, free food in the state dining room, among barbarians such things as *proskynesis* and rights of precedence, and gifts that are held in honor in each society. (*Rhet.* 1.5.9)

Thus, we maintain, the "language" of honor may be uniquely articulated in the writings of Greek rhetoric that became the standard of education; but it was also known and spoken with considerable fluency at all levels of the social pyramid.

In regard to our second point, this "language" of praise and blame was utterly conventional. The contents of benefaction inscriptions do not seem to vary significantly from Gaul to Rome to Greece to Asia Minor; grave inscriptions tend to commemorate people in quite conventional terms. Hymns of praise to the gods tend to follow regular formulae. Coins and statuary all depend on the easy recognition of postures and gestures that convey status, power, and rank. The "morphology" of the language of praise and blame, then, was widespread and conventional. In addition to Aristotle's list of the conventional components of honor, the forms and genres of literature that embody the values of honor and shame were themselves formal and fixed, such that students were not so much encouraged to creative composition as to excellence in the traditional forms in which they received training. Moreover, within the particular literary discussions of praise (i.e., epideictic rhetoric) and the handbook exercises which instructed students in how to praise (i.e., the encomium of the *progymnasmata*) the meaning of honor and praise was precisely and conventionally defined. The value of these rhetorical sources lies in the way they serve both to propagate the language of praise and to establish rules and norms for what is praiseworthy. They are themselves the best evidence of its utter conventionality. Thus as Greek language, culture, and rhetoric spread throughout the Mediterranean world in antiquity, these expressed a very conventional understanding of praise and blame, from the time of Aristotle into the Byzantine period.

This leads us to claim the existence of a "general code" or a conventional "language" of honor and shame, which was widely known throughout the Mediterranean basin for centuries. Elites and non-elites, urban and rural all knew in some fashion this "general code"; all understood and spoke this "language" in their speech, clothing, self-presentation, social intercourse, and the like. That "language," then, need not be Greek.

8.0 Plan of This Book

This book proposes to read Matthew's Gospel in terms of the "general code" of honor and shame and in light of the widespread, conventional rhetoric of praise and blame. To this end, the first part will be devoted to the exposition of an anthropological study of honor and shame. We turn first to anthropologists such as Campbell (1964:263–320), Pitt-Rivers (1968a:503–11 and 1977:1–17), and Gilmore (1987:2–17), who have provided excellent studies of the values of honor and shame. Their analyses have been digested and adapted for New Testament study by Bruce Malina (1993:28–62). He in turn influenced other scholars to begin reading various New Testament documents in light of this pivotal value; among them we note Malina and Neyrey (1991:25–65), Moxnes (1988a, 1988b, 1993, 1995), Neyrey (1993d, 1995), Elliott (1995), and Hanson (1996). Likewise commentators on the Hebrew scriptures have begun successfully to read those documents in terms of honor and shame. Although Pedersen's seminal remarks on these values have been largely ignored (1991:212–44), other scholars have recently begun to return profitably to the topic, such as Stansell (1991, 1996) and Matthews and Benjamin (1991). Students of the classical world were quick to pick up on the relevance of cultural anthropology for a more sensitive and accurate reading of Greek and Latin culture. Among the many important studies on honor and shame in Greek literature, we single out those of Adkins (1960b, 1971, 1972a), Dover (1974), Fisher (1979b), and Qviller (1981), along with the significant discussions of honor in antiquity in the works of Cairns (1993), Cohen (1991, 1995), and Walcot (1970, 1978). The model we present, then, has been in constant conversation with both theorists and interpreters of literature from the ancient world; in short, it has been customized and appropriately adapted.

In addition to exposing a cultural model of honor and shame suitable to the world of the Christian scriptures, we will turn to a host of native informants from the ancient world for their reports on honor and shame. Anthropologists depend on just such native informants to provide invaluable clues and explanations of their particular world, which would otherwise be inaccessible to a stranger from another culture. So with us, we primarily consult rhetoricians such as Aristotle and Quintilian, as well as authors of rhetorical handbooks such as Aelius Theon, Menander Rhetor, and Hermogenes. These authors are of more significance to us than the general run of orators, historians, poets, and the like because they formally reflect on the nature of honor, its component parts, its expression, and the conventional literary manner of praising and blaming. Representing as they do the consensus of the "general code," they have as their task the instruction of their peers in the formal language of praise. They can tell us how to praise, what conventions to follow, and what elements constitute praise—all the while representing the common and constant voice of their culture.

In light of the ancient rhetoric of praise and blame, we will read Matthew in terms of the rules for an encomium, as articulated in the rhetorical handbooks, or *progymnasmata*. These rules indicate that one draws praise for a person by considering the various stages of his life. Hence authors should follow the conventional "general code" of honor and excellence in presenting what is praiseworthy about the subject's life: (1) origin and birth, (2) nurture and education, and (3) deeds of body, life, and fortune, and (4) noble death. Inasmuch as Matthew begins with Jesus' birth and concludes with his death and vindication, he is telling the story of Jesus' life, which is the framework of the encomium. Although we do not wish to reduce the genre of gospel to a mere "life" or encomium, it will become clear how Matthew both perfectly embodies the structural elements of the encomium and follows its aims and function as well.

Because of the inherent shameful nature of Jesus' death, we will undertake a special reading of Matthew's Passion narrative in accordance with the rhetorical rules for describing a "noble death." It is indubitable that anyone in antiquity who heard of a crucified person would immediately associate that death with "shame" (1 Cor. 1:23; Heb. 12:2). Given the cultural equation of crucifixion with shame, we will examine the rhetorical resources for describing a noble death and use that material as an appropriate horizon for assessing how Matthew's narrative turns shame into praise.

In the final part, we will devote attention to a proper cultural reading of Jesus' Sermon on the Mount. All of the parts of the sermon, especially the list of makarisms (5:3–12), the Antitheses (5:21–48), and the Instructions on Piety (6:1–18), can and should be read in the light of honor and shame. Jesus is by no means repudiating these values for his disciples, but rather redefines what is honorable and prescribes new rules for the game of gaining honor. He honors what others have shamed (5:3–12), repudiating the conventional link between honor, family, and its wealth. He proscribes the traditional ways of achieving honor (i.e., violence, sexual aggression, verbal display, and vengeance), and thus denies his disciples these avenues for gaining honor. Finally, he requires his disciples to vacate the playing field in town and village, by commanding his male disciples to forswear the public world—where deeds of piety were performed and observed—for the private world of the household, where only kin and family could know of one's duty to God.

We argue that modern readers will greatly benefit in understanding Matthew's Gospel in terms of its most basic cultural context by familiarity with the ancient rhetoric of praise and blame and with the synthetic model of honor and shame described by modern anthropologists. In particular we invite readers to consider closely the very genre of praise, the encomium, both in terms of its formal structure and in regard to what value or worth was attached by the ancients to this or that point. With this set of special cultural lenses we then wish to examine Matthew's story of the most honorable man, Jesus, glorified by God and praised by mortals.

Part One

Matthew: In Other Words

1

Honor and Shame in Cultural Perspective

1.0 Introduction: Topic and Hypothesis

Jesus remarked that "a prophet is not without honor except in his own country" (Matt. 13:57). Paul promised that those "who seek for glory and honor . . . will receive glory and honor" (Rom. 2:7, 10). What is this "honor"? Why was it so important to Jesus and Paul? This chapter will begin to present the cultural meaning of honor and shame, which was so important to the characters of the Christian scriptures. Fortunately, we are not the first to investigate this topic; in recent years the concepts of honor and shame have served as valuable lenses through which we are beginning to read the Bible (Malina 1993:28–62; Matthews and Benjamin 1996). Yet these cultural concepts may not be familiar to many readers and may not seem appropriate to the ancient world. And so this first chapter will explain what honor means and describe the system of values, norms, and behaviors that embodies it.

Ideally we might proceed inductively with data from the ancient world, yet we think it both necessary and convenient to begin with an anthropological model of honor and shame which alone can help us understand the many references to it in both biblical and classical literature. The model we present will be as comprehensive as possible to alert readers to the depth and complexity of the phenomenon of honor, while organizing that information in a way that shows honor's systematic quality. Models by their nature serve to reduce complex sets of data into manageable blocks and to suggest the relationship of those pieces. Our model, like all models, will be a general and abstract overview of the material. Readers unfamiliar with the material might consider this chapter as a set of reader-friendly instructions to guide them in understanding the Gospel of Matthew in terms of its native culture.

Readers be cautioned! At first, this material may seem abstract and foreign, but we ask for patience and openness as we introduce the cultural model of honor and shame. Even while presenting the complex model of honor, we will labor to give it historical precision and descriptive specificity by reference to literatures of the Greco-Roman world and the Bible.

When anthropologists present the cultural concept of honor, they include the following items: (1) definition of honor, (2) sources of honor, (3) conflict and honor, (4) symbols of honor, (5) display and recognition of honor, (6) collective honor, and (7) gender and honor. Thus, we plan to explain and illustrate each of these elements of a model of honor and shame.

2.0 Cultural Tour of Honor and Shame

2.1 Defining Honor and Shame.   Honor is the general, abstract word for the worth, value, prestige, and reputation which an individual claims and which is acknowledged by others (Malina 1993:30–33). According to its Greek root, "honor" (τιμή) refers to the price or value of something (Schneider 1972:169), such as the "price" paid as compensation or satisfaction for an injury or insult (see Josephus, *J.W.* 2.285). It refers also to the esteem in which someone is held (John 5:23; Josephus, *Ant.* 20.205), or the public recognition given them (Matt. 13:57), or the honors and awards bestowed on them (Rom. 2:10; Philo, *On Abraham* 185). Honor, then, has to do with public value and worth. Hence, "worthies" are they who wear white garments and walk in the company of the Lord (Rev. 3:4). He, who is himself truly "worthy" (Rev. 5:2, 9–10), acknowledges the worth of the others (see Luke 7:4 and Matt. 6:26). But honor exists only in the eyes of a public who expects certain things and evaluates individuals accordingly. It is, then, what is called a social construct, an idea created by humans which they fill with meaning.

In defining honor, Pitt-Rivers notes its complex structure: honor is a sentiment of worth felt by an individual, which is *claimed* before others and subsequently *acknowledged* by them.

> Honour is the value of a person in his own eyes, but also in the eyes of his society. It is his estimation of his own worth, his *claim* to pride, but it is also the acknowledgement of that claim, his excellence recognized by society, his *right* to pride. (Pitt-Rivers 1977:1)

The critical item is the public nature of respect and reputation. Sentiments of worth and claims to pride must be made before some public and acknowledged by it. The claims generally rest on conduct which the village or neighborhood observes and evaluates according to a local code of what is honorable or excellent (Dupont 1989:10–12). When this evaluation is favorable, the claim is then acknowledged in public and results in fame, reputation, and respect. Thus "honor" describes a process, the culmination of which is the public award of reputation, worth, and respect.

2.2 Sources of Honor.   How do individuals acquire worth and esteem? Anthropologists identify two general sources: worth and value are either *ascribed* to individuals by others or *achieved* by them. *Ascribed* honor refers to the granting of respect and given to a person from members of the two basic institutions of antiquity, namely: family/kinship or state/politics. Generally, *ascribed* honor comes simply from being born into a certain family. Families themselves have certain ratings in the eyes of their neighbors; some are noble (i.e., aristocrats), but even among village families there will always be some ranking of families in terms of their reputation, wealth, and standing. Thus, children born into these families automatically acquire the public evaluation of that family. Of course an individual's position in the birth order of the family may increase his worth in the eyes of all. For example, male children have more value than female children in the eyes of parents and neighbors; and the firstborn male, who is presumably the heir, has more status than his younger siblings. Thus the *ascribed* honor of a child is itself relative to the family's standing in the village, the gender of the child, and his or her birth order. We should include here adopted children, generally sons, who gain in social worth with their entrance into the new family or clan. *Ascribed* honor, moreover, can come as well from the political institutions of ancient society. Pilate was appointed by Caesar, just as kings and leaders designated others as their ambassadors or legates. The Psalms contain many examples of ascribed honor, such as the oath that establishes the priesthood of Melchizedek: "The Lord has sworn . . . 'Thou art a priest forever'" (Ps. 110:4//Heb. 7:21), or the adoption of the king: "He said to me, 'You are my son, today have I begotten you'" (Ps. 2:7).

Achieved honor refers to the reputation and fame an individual earns by his own merits. The traditional avenues for *achieving* honor in antiquity included civic benefaction, military exploits, athletic games, aesthetic competitions in drama and poetry, and the like. These represent the conduct that ancient elites expected of freeborn and noble males and consequently rewarded. Were we discussing the epics, drama, or poetry of antiquity, we would stop to examine what such success looked like to the ancients and the importance they gave to it (see Drees 1968:101–8). But we are studying non-elite literature, such as the Gospels, and so we ask about the ways in which typical artisans and peasants who made up 90 percent of the population *achieved* honor. They, as well as the elites, engaged in a social competition for incremental increases in reputation and prestige through the interminable game of push-and-shove called challenge and riposte. Let us examine this notion more closely.

2.3 *Achieved Honor: Competition, Aggression, and Envy.*   Although honor can be achieved in nonaggressive and noncompetitive ways (Péristiany and Pitt-Rivers 1992), we focus on the ubiquitous phenomenon of competition and aggression because of its importance in Matthew's narrative about Jesus. Aggressive public challenges were put to him throughout his career, and his death was plotted out of envy of him (Mark 15:10). Some scholars of the ancient world describe it as an "agonistic society," by which they point to its intensely competitive nature and the common envy shown successful persons (Cohen 1995:61–142; Vernant 1988:29–56; Walcot 1978:52–76; Gouldner 1965:41–77). At a high level of abstraction, most forms of agonistic behavior in antiquity might be described as challenges to reputation which demand a defensive riposte. To understand better the nature of what is meant by an "agonistic society," we borrow clues from the anthropologists about the ubiquitous game of challenge and riposte to learn why the ancients were so competitive and envious. Four things must be considered: (1) the love of honor ($\phi\iota\lambda\sigma\tau\iota\mu\acute{\iota}\alpha$) which pervaded Greece, Rome, and Judea, (2) the perception that all goods, including honor, exist in limited supply, (3) the phenomenon of envy resulting from the success of others, and (4) the general competitive nature of ancient society.

2.3.1 Love of Honor. From Xenophon to Augustine, Greco-Roman historians supply ample evidence that their world was characterized by a "love of honor"
(φιλοτιμία). Xenophon describes the Athenians as passionate for praise: "Athenians excel all others not so much in singing or in stature or in strength, as in love
of honour (φιλοτιμία), which is the strongest incentive to deeds of honour and
renown" (*Memorabilia* 3.3.13). Later, Augustine in his review of the history of
Rome likewise comments on how the Romans were utterly obsessed with the love
of praise and renown: "For the glory that the Romans burned to possess, be it
noted, is the favourable judgment of men who think well of other men" (*City of
God* 5.12). For love of praise and honor, the Romans overcame vices common to
other Mediterranean peoples: "He [God] granted supremacy to men who for the
sake of honour, praise and glory served the country in which they were seeking
their own glory, and did not hesitate to prefer her safety to their own. Thus for one
vice, that is, love of praise, they overcame the love of money and many other
vices" (5.13). Hence, in both East and West, the ancients name love of honor and
praise as their premier value.

At its best, love of honor was thought to be the very quality which distinguished humans from animals. Our native informant, Xenophon, remarked: "In
this man differs from other animals—I mean, in this craving for honour. In meat
and drink and sleep and sex all creatures alike seem to take pleasure; but love of
honor (φιλοτιμία) is rooted neither in the brute beasts nor in every human being. But they in whom is implanted a passion for honour and praise, these are
they who differ most from the beasts of the field, these are accounted men and
not mere human beings" (*Hiero* 7.3). It was for love of honor that Athenian citizens equipped war ships, funded processions and festivals, and acted as patrons
for games and other events; indeed it became an expected part of the status of
wealthy elite to spend their personal fortunes on public "liturgies" in pursuit of
honor. Demosthenes boasts how "love of honor" motivated him in this way: "I
was in a position to provide a chorus, to pay for a war-galley, and to be assessed
a property-tax. I renounced no honourable ambition (φιλοτιμία) either in public or in private life: and rendered good service both to the commonwealth and
to my own friends" (*On the Crown* 18.257). "Love of honor," then, spurred men
to excellence and ambition. But at its worst, the ancients thought it a baneful
vice utterly disruptive of civic harmony, which led to endless feuding and fighting (see Dio Chrysostom *Fourth Discourse on Kingship* 84). Plutarch describes
some students acting out of φιλοτιμία, but in ways which are utterly disruptive:
"Others led by an unreasonable ambition (φιλοτιμία) and insane rivalry
(ἅμιλλα) with their fellow students to show off their acuteness and their ability
to learn easily, avow that they have the meaning before they have grasped it" (*On
Listening to Lectures* 47D; see Phil. 1:17; 2:3).

2.3.2 Image of Limited Good. George Foster has described how certain people perceive all of the world's goods (i.e., wealth, land, happiness, honor, and the
like) as absolutely limited in supply. This perception he calls "the image of limited
good":

> By "Image of Limited Good" I mean that broad areas of peasant behavior
> are patterned in such a fashion as to suggest that peasants view their so-
> cial, economic, and natural universes—their total environment—as one in
> which all of the desired things in life such as land, wealth, health, friend-
> ship and love, manliness and honor, respect and status, power and influ-
> ence, security and safety, *exist in finite quantity and are always in short
> supply*, as far as the peasant is concerned. Not only do these and all other
> "good things" exist in finite and limited quantities, but in *addition there is
> no way directly within peasant power to increase the available quantities.*
> (Foster 1996:296; italics in original)

This perception views the things of this world in terms of a zero-sum game: the pie
will never get larger; when divided, it will be either in one's favor or against one's
interests. Foster spells out the implications of this, noting that "any advantage
achieved by one individual or family is seen as a loss to others, and the person who
makes what the Western world lauds as 'progress' is viewed as a threat to the sta-
bility of the entire community" (1972:169). If someone increases, then others must
necessarily decrease (see John 3:30). Several things are likely to happen when
people perceive reality in this way: first, they "are reluctant to advance beyond
their peers because of the sanctions they know will be levelled against them"; and
second, the person "who is seen or known to acquire more becomes much more
vulnerable to the envy of his neighbors" (1972:169). Hence, if anyone in the village acquires wealth, fame, or any other thing valued by the group, then the rest of
the village or neighborhood will perceive themselves as correspondingly losing
worth and value. Their response will likely be one of envy (see Matt. 13:54–57).

Euro-Americans, of course, do not think this way. We are socialized to expect
an ever expanding economy built on limitless resources and producing for all an
increasing standard of living. Since we may have difficulty in understanding
Foster's "image of limited good," we ask our ancient informants to tell us about it.
The clearest sample of this point of view is the saying: "People do not find it pleasant to give honor (τιμίαν) to someone else, for they suppose that they themselves
are being deprived of something" (*Anonymus Iamblici*, cited in Winkler
1990:178). For biblical scholars, the classical instance of this is the exchange between John the Baptizer and his disciples, who complain about Jesus' increasing
fame. They perceive that the Baptizer's worth and that of his disciples diminishes
with Jesus' success. While agreeing with their perception, John confesses that in
this instance Jesus' increase is right and proper: "He must increase, I must decrease" (John 3:30; see Judg. 7:2)—a most unusual concession. Similarly, Plutarch
described how some of those listening to an outstanding lecturer perceive that the
speaker's success means their own loss of honor, hence they express envy at his accomplishments: "As though commendation were money, he feels that he is rob-
bing himself of every bit that he bestows on another" (*On Listening to Lectures*
44B; see *Old Men in Public Affairs* 787D). Thus this common cultural perception
of the limited nature of all goods—honor included—serves to explain the envy
which arises at the success of another: their success means our loss.

2.3.3 Envy of Success.

Although trivial and mean to us moderns, envy was a much discussed topic and a very important element in the social dynamics of the ancient world (Foster 1972; Elliott 1992). Matthew reports that Pilate observed "that it was out of envy that they handed Jesus over" (27:18), an excellent motive in that culture for killing Jesus. Being envied brought as much honor to Jesus as it did shame to his adversaries. It was out of envy, we are told, that the devil brought death into God's perfect world (*Wisd.* 2:23–24). As our premier native informant from antiquity defines it, envy is " . . . a certain kind of distress at apparent success on the part of one's peers in attaining the good things that have been mentioned, not that a person may get anything for himself but because of those who have it" (Aristotle, *Rhet.* 2.10.1). Aristotle distinguishes envy from emulation: while envy is pain at seeing another succeed with an accompanying desire to harm the other and level his advance in prestige, emulation is likewise pain at the success of another which spurs the onlooker to equal the success observed. Envy attacks, emulation equals.

The ancients were fond of commenting that success breeds envy, just as lightning strikes the tallest trees and highest mountains. Josephus, for example, regularly comments on the relationship of his "success" and the "envy" it occasioned. Concerning his envious rival, he notes: "John, believing that my success (εὐπραγίαν) involved his ruin, gave way to immoderate envy (φθόνον)" (*Life* 122; see also *J.W.* 1.67; *Ant.* 2.10, 254).

Aristotle informs us that envy is distress at the success "of one's peers" (περὶ τοὺς ὁμοίους) (*Rhet.* 2.10.1). Cicero later echoed this: "People are especially envious of their equals, or of those once beneath them, when they feel themselves left behind and fret at the other's upward flight" (*On the Orator* 2.52.209). Generally, neighbor envies neighbor; but often we find brother envying brother, as in the case of sibling rivalry, of which the Bible is full: Cain and Abel, Ishmael and Isaac, Esau and Jacob, and Joseph and his brothers. Similarly Saul envied David who slew his tens of thousands to Saul's mere thousands (1 Sam. 18:7–9). Thus envy describes the eruption of hostile feelings at the success of others, which generally issues in some aggressive action to harm the other and diminish his prestige. In the light of the "image of limited good," therefore, any success on the part of a peer is perceived to come at another's expense, who assuredly will act to insure no further loss and to restore the previous status quo.

2.3.4 The Competitive and Combative Nature of Ancient Society.

In a world driven by love of honor (φιλοτιμία) and understood in terms of limited good, the success of others tends to be interpreted as loss by the perceiver. Envy and conflict are sure to follow. We look now more closely at the levels of competition and combat which pervaded the ancient world. Conflict, competition, and combat were pervasive elements in the social dynamics of antiquity (Dover 1974:229–34). We most readily recognize this in the reports from antiquity about interminable military combat and the rise and fall of empires and kingdoms. We find it also in the places and times when citizens were allowed to govern themselves; for in classical Athens as well as Republican Rome, we read of competition to gain an office and struggle to maintain it. Similarly, ancient Greece was famous for its competitive sports and games, either funeral games (*Iliad* 23.256–897) or the Olympic, Isthmian, Nemean, and Pythian competitions (Robinson 1981; Sweet 1987). Competitions were also held for drama and poetry (Plutarch, *Table Talk* 5.2 674D–675D). Yet such competitions are only the more formal aspects of combat and conflict. Even the Athenian law courts have been shown to be an arena where rivalry and envy were ritually played out (Cohen 1995:70–75, 90–101, 128). Plutarch identifies various forums of a male's life which were occasion for conflict and competition: "The sensible man will guard against the hatred and anger which in the market-place is imposed by rivalry (φιλονιϰία), in the gymnasia and the palaestrae by ambition (φιλοτιμία), in politics and public munificence by eagerness for glory (φιλοδοξία), at dinner and in drinking by frivolity" (*Table Talk* 1.4 622B). In summary, in his study of ancient curses and spells, Faraone identified four "agonistic contexts": "commercial curses, curses against athletes and public performers, amatory curses and judicial curses" (1991:10–17). Thus, everything good could become the object of competitiveness and envy: lovers, houses, children, clothing, beauty, reputation, and respect.

2.4 Challenge and Riposte. When we appreciate "love of honor," the agonistic nature of ancient society, the perception of limited good, and the resultant envy, we gain the proper social background for examining the most common means of achieving honor, namely, the ubiquitous game of challenge and riposte, or push-and-shove. Since honor is never genuine until acknowledged by others, the game of challenge and riposte expresses the refusal by some to acknowledge any such claims to the worth and precedence by another. Generally, the game consists of four steps: (1) claim of worth and value, (2) challenge to that claim or refusal to acknowledge the claim, (3) riposte or defense of the claim, and (4) public verdict of success awarded either to claimant or challenger. On the basis of some achieved honor (prowess in war, athletics games, and the like), a person presents himself to his peers as deserving of their respect. But his claim may well be interpreted as loss by others, some of whom will challenge that claim, either by cutting the claimant down to size and restoring the status quo or by advancing one's own worth by besting the claimant. If the challenge is such that it cannot be ignored and must be answered, a riposte must be given.

All of this takes place in public; after all, the ancient world was a face-to-face society. A man claiming honor states his claim before the public, who may either acknowledge it or reject it. If the claim is challenged, there will surely be an "affront" to the claimant; that is, it takes place *in front* of him and before the public, so that it is formally recognized as an unavoidable challenge. The public that views the interchange subsequently awards success and praise to the one they judge as the winner (see Malina-Neyrey 1991a:29–32, 49–52).

Yet who may play this game? And how is it played? Pierre Bourdieu provides a very generalized sketch of the protocols of the challenge-riposte exchange (1966:197–202; for an adaptation for the biblical world, see Malina 1993:35–37). Only equals may play. Non-elites such as peasants or slaves simply do not have the honor capital to challenge aristocrats; nor will the elites take the affront as an honor challenge, but simply punish insurrection and insubordination. Moreover, our limited evidence suggests that only males tend to play this game. Since it falls to males in antiquity both to increase and to defend the family's honor, they are the family risk-takers, who live most of the day in the public and who endlessly observe others playing this game and indulge in it themselves.

This peer game of push-and-shove can be played in any of the typical forums of social life: marketplace, gymnasium, synagogue, banquet with one's male companions, and the like. From our reading of the Gospels, it seems to have occurred whenever Jesus stepped into public space. The very pervasiveness of this challenge-riposte game indicates that Jesus was both claiming prestige and worth (as God's agent) and achieving a splendid reputation as prophet, teacher, and healer. Hence, the fact that Jesus was so regularly challenged indicates, at least on the narrative level, that he was a very honorable person who was worthy of allegiance and loyalty. It is to his credit that he was both envied (Matt. 27:18) and challenged.

2.5 Symbols of Honor: Blood and Name.   Even we moderns tend to ascribe to children born into honorable families the worth and value of that family (e.g., the Kennedys or Rockefellers). Unlike achieved honor, which is earned through prowess but susceptible to challenge, worth ascribed by birth lasted a lifetime, unless the family suffered a reversal of fortune. We recall, too, that the most important institution in antiquity was the family, which conveyed to its members their personal identity and social standing. Thus family "blood" symbolizes the ascribed honor of its members (Di Bella 1992:151–65; Malina 1993:38–39). Yet blood also symbolizes an individual's courage and conflict, other ways in which honor is gained and maintained. Thus blood can symbolize both achieved as well as ascribed honor, as J. F. Campbell notes:

> The honour of the family, and its solidarity, are symbolized in the idea of blood. In marriage a man and woman mix their different blood to produce "one blood" which is the blood of their children. Relationships in the family are a participation in this common blood . . . blood is intimately related to courage. And it is a matter of common observation that as a man loses blood, he loses strength. Since courage and physical strength are particularly the qualities that men require in order to defend the reputation of their families, it is entirely consistent that for the Sarakatsani the honour of the family is literally the honour of its blood. (Campbell 1966:144; see also 1964:185–86, 268–69)

All families enjoy some worth or value relative to their peers. This is most evident when marriage alliances are made, since they are generally contracted between social equals. People in villages and neighborhoods strive to estimate accurately the worth of a family and its reputation, so as to calculate its social standing. A family's reputation, moreover, is also based on the degree to which its members are perceived as living according to the code of expected social behavior of village and neighborhood. Thus all the members of the family share in its reputation: all rejoice in its honor and all share in its shame. Honor, then, is symbolized by family blood.

The Bible readily illustrates this in the way persons are typically introduced. We initially come to know them not as unique individuals, but primarily in terms of their family, that is, their blood and name. Ideally we would be told an individual's full range of kinship relations: immediate family, clan, and tribe. Although the scene is one of discovering a wrongdoer, the book of Joshua describes quite accurately how individuals take their identity and their worth from their extended kinship relations:

> Joshua rose early in the morning and brought Israel near tribe by tribe, and the tribe of Judah was taken; and he brought near the families of Judah, and the family of the Zerahites was taken; and he brought near the family of the Zerahites man by man and Zabdi was taken; and he brought near his household man by man, and Achan the son of Carmi, son of Zabdi, son of Zerah, of the tribe of Judah was taken. (Josh. 7:16–18)

Achan, it should be noted, is known in terms of his male line: he is "son of Carmi, son of Zabdi, son of Zerah." Whatever reputation or worth the tribe, clan, and family enjoyed constitutes the ascribed honor of Achan. The same would be true of New Testament characters as well, who are introduced in terms of their fathers or ancestors: Simon is son of John (Matt. 16:17); James and John are sons of Zebedee (Matt. 4:21; 20:20); Joseph, son of David (Matt. 1:20); and Jesus, son of David (Matt. 9:27; 20:30–31). Although individual children have their own names (James, Joses, Judas, and Simon), their worth is symbolized by their family name, that is, the name of their father and his ancestors.

Individuals inherited not just their father's name and reputation, but also his trade and status. Josephus reflects quite accurately how worth and status are family affairs and become the legacy of children born into those families. Speaking of the Hasmoneans, he remarked: "Theirs [the Hasmoneans'] was a splendid and renowned house because of both their lineage and their priestly office, as well as the things which its founders achieved on behalf of the nation" (*Ant.* 14.490; see 11.309). Thus Hasmonean children by virtue of their "blood and name" inherited royal status and even special offices, such as the priesthood. Moreover, they inherited as well the family credit rating, which was earned through "the things achieved on behalf of the nation." What was true of elite families proved true also for non-elites. Sons of carpenters became carpenters, inheriting whatever standing and respect the paternal family enjoyed.

2.6 Display and Recognition of Honor. We cannot overemphasize the importance of a viewing "public" for understanding honor (Dupont 1989:10–12). Not only did males constantly appear in public and subject themselves to the evaluation of their peers, they took great pains to conform to the code of social behavior expected by their group. They worried about what others thought of them. As we saw, claims must be displayed to the public in various ways; what is not displayed cannot be acknowledged. Now we will examine two of those, the display of honor either in one's body and physical presence, or through one's relative wealth, especially through one's clothing and table fare.

Wealth, a relative word, applies to the estates of the elites as well as a peasant's modest holdings (see Aristotle, *Rhet.* 1.5.7). Unlike our modern urban world, the bulk of the ancient population lived in villages, not cities, which were the strongholds and granaries of the elites. Historians of the ancient economy remind our industrial world that the former was an agrarian society in which "wealth" basically resided in land. About the economic significance of land, Carney writes: " . . . basically land, not capital, was of critical importance in antiquity. The vast bulk of production was agricultural. Technology was simple, and apart from slaves (used mainly in conjunction with land), inexpensive. So power and wealth went with possession of land" (1975:181). A remark of Cicero's illustrates the typical elitist evaluation of the worth of land:

> Trade, if it is on a small scale, is to be considered vulgar; but if wholesale and on a large scale, importing large quantities from all parts of the world and distributing them without misrepresentation, it is not to be greatly disparaged. Nay, it even seems to deserve highest respect, if those who are engaged in it, satiated, or rather, I should say, satisfied with the fortune they have made, *make their way from port to a country estate*, as they have often made it from the sea into port. But of all the occupations by which gain is secured, none is better than *agriculture*, none more profitable, none more delightful, none more becoming to a freeman. (*On Duty* 1.42.151; emphasis added)

Ideally, honorable elites have great estates which provide them with goods for display and consumption, such as choice wines and foods. These elites, of course, do not themselves labor, but own slaves and employ sharecroppers who work their land. Wealth, moreover, resides in large estates which are generally a safe source of income, unlike trade which was subject to storms, pirates, and other disasters.

In describing the mentality of wealthy people, Aristotle takes us one step further in appreciating how wealth displays honor and embodies claims to status and worth.

> [T]hey are ostentatious and pretentious, ostentatious because of luxury and display of their prosperity, pretentious and vulgar because all are used to spending their time doing whatever they like and admire and because they think everyone else has the same values they do. . . . This is the reason for what Simonides said about the wise and rich to the wife of Hieron when she asked whether it was better to be rich or wise: "To be rich"; for he said one sees the wise waiting at the doors of the rich. (*Rhet.* 2.16.1–3)

Hence, those who display wealth claim honor because they are "ostentatious and pretentious." They contribute to the formation of the local honor code and embody it; as pacesetters, "they think everyone else has the same values they do." Wealth, moreover, easily translates into power; for as Aristotle further commented: "Another result of wealth is that the rich think they deserve to rule; for they think they have that which makes one worthy to rule [i.e., money]" (*Rhet.* 2.16.3). Wealth, then, symbolizes one's status to friends and neighbors; it claims for its possessors respect and worth as powerful persons who act as patrons to others and who deserve to rule. But wealth is not wealth and cannot symbolize one's worth and honor unless it is displayed.

A man's physical body served as the constant stage on which honor was displayed and claimed. The most important part of a person's physical presence is the front, namely, head, face, and eyes. For example, on occasion courtiers crawled toward sovereigns with faces bowed to the ground and retreated the same way: the worth of the monarch was thus symbolized by the fact that lesser people did not see the monarch's face, much less look him in the eye. Honorable heads were anointed and crowned as marks of respect. Yet the eyes may be the most important bodily organ in the way in which honor is claimed and acknowledged; for it is one's standing "in the eyes of" others which constitutes worth and reputation. As noted above, "affronts" must occur in the front, that is, before the very eye of the insulted person, for them to constitute genuine challenges; and, of course, they must occur in public, that is, in the eyes of others. In terms of the Bible, one might "find favor in the eyes" of others (Gen. 6:8; 1 Sam. 26:21), which translates as acknowledgment of worth and value in their sight. This can lead to favorable marriage alliances (Gen. 34:11), singular benefaction (Gen. 50:4), and food to sustain life (Ruth 2:10). Conversely, when people look at others with contempt, they have clearly withdrawn respect (Gen. 16:4–5); a wife can be divorced by her husband "if she finds no favor in his eyes because he has found some indecency in her" (Deut. 24:1). Thus worth and value are signaled by the favorable glance of others. Conversely, insults are only honor challenges when done in the sight (or hearing) of the person attacked and in the view of some public evaluating the conflict. Absalom utterly shamed his father David by publicly taking possession of his father's harem of wives. Although predicted by Nathan as God's riposte for the slaying of Uriah the Hittite (2 Sam. 12:11), it did not become shame until David himself saw the insult and the people of Jerusalem judged it shameful (2 Sam. 16:22).

Other body parts likewise symbolized worth and value. The right arm and hand were generally honored, probably because they wielded weapons of war, a sure way to reputation. The penis and testicles, which are the signs of a male's fertility and his power to extend himself in time, were also honorable parts. The feet were generally not considered honorable, unless they belonged to a person of such status that others fell to the ground at them, washed, or anointed them (Luke 7:38) or unless these feet trampled on the necks and backs of enemies. Hence, God assured the enthroned king of Israel of great status by putting his enemies under his feet: "I make your enemies your footstool" (Ps. 110:1).

The loins, in particular the buttocks, are called by Paul "less honorable" parts which simply are not "presentable" in public (1 Cor. 12:23–24; see Martin 1995:94–96). Yet an insult might be given to another by deliberate exposure of either penis or buttocks. Josephus reports how a Roman soldier in the fortress Antonia lifted up his tunic and bared his buttocks to those worshiping in the temple, accompanying this display with a blast of flatus (*J.W.* 2.224); a riot ensued over this insult. Moreover, some rabbinic texts instruct a man on the proper disrobing in the privy, which expresses the challenging nature of exposing one's penis or buttocks to another: "Let no man stand naked facing the chamber of the Holy of Holies. If one enters a privy, let him turn his face neither to the east nor to the west, but sideways. Nor should he uncover himself standing up, but sitting down" (*ARN* 40; cited in Goldin 1955:168; see *b. Berakot* 62a and Josephus, *J.W.* 2.148–49). It was thought to be insulting to God if a man undressed on an east-west axis, which is the orientation of the temple; for this person would thus be exposing either his penis or his buttocks to God, giving an insult.

Yet if deliberate exposure of the loins is insulting, the involuntary stripping of clothing from another is humiliating and shaming to them. One of the most shameful aspects of defeat in war was the involuntary, enforced nudity of captives led in procession: " [S]o shall the king of Assyria lead away the Egyptian captives and the Ethiopian exiles, both the young and the old, naked and barefoot, with buttocks uncovered to the shame of Egypt" (Isa. 20:4). David's servants were most shamefully treated by Hanun, king of the Ammonites, who "shaved off half the beard of each, and cut their garments in the middle, at their hips" (2 Sam. 10:4; 1 Chron. 19:4). Thus they marched bare-bottomed back to David as a sign of Hanun's rejection of David's offer of assistance (Neyrey 1993b:120–22).

Then as now, people took pains to craft their appearance in public for maximum social effect. Even the ancients agreed that clothes made the man; for they signaled honorable role and status, while their absence implied shame. How honorable it was for both Mordecai and Joseph to be clothed in the king's own robes and displayed thus in the city (Philo, *On Joseph* 120; Josephus, *Ant.* 11.254). King Agrippa, Josephus relates, intentionally dazzled the crowds in the theater at Caesarea when he entered clothed in a garment "woven completely of silver so that its texture was indeed wondrous." As the sun rose, the king's robe "was wondrously radiant and by its glitter inspired fear and awe on those who gazed intently upon it" (*Ant.* 19.344; see also Acts 12:21). Similarly, the Essenes at Qumran signaled their pursuit of radical purity by wearing the "white robe" (Josephus, *J.W.* 2.129). Jerusalem's high priest displayed his role and status by special clothing (*m. Yoma* 7:5), consisting of a blue linen tunic worn over the ordinary one and a sash of blue, purple, and scarlet hues. Over this he wore an ephod (waistcoat), in the center of which was a breast pouch to hold the Urim and Thummim. The breast pouch was studded with twelve precious stones. The ordinary priest's cap was covered with blue embroidery and encircled with a tiered crown of gold (Ex. 28; Josephus, *Ant.* 3.151–158). In short, clothing signals to observers the precise role and status of its wearer and so displays and replicates a public claim to worth (Neyrey 1993a: 20–25).

Continuing our inventory of the display of honor, we recall that the ancients practiced their own version of "conspicuous consumption" by which they displayed their wealth and worth (Kautsky 1982:187–94). Wealth, of course, is a relative thing. Obviously monarchs have more at their disposal than peasants. But both elites and non-elites put their best faces forward on special occasions, for example, wedding feasts (John 2:1–10) or birthday celebrations (Matt. 14:6–7). Take, for example, the description of Plutarch concerning the "theatre" of the fancy meal:

> With no one to look on, wealth becomes sightless indeed and bereft of radiance. For when the rich man dines with his wife or intimates he lets his tables of citrus-wood and golden beakers rest in peace and uses common furnishings, and his wife attends it without her gold and purple and dressed in plain attire. But when a banquet—*that is, a spectacle and a show*—is got up and the drama of wealth brought on, "out of the ships he fetches the urns and tripods" [*Iliad* 23.259], the repositories of the lamps are given no rest, the cups are changed, the cup-bearers are made to put on new attire, nothing is left undisturbed, gold, silver, or jeweled plate, the owners thus confessing that their wealth is for others. (*On Love of Wealth* 528B; emphasis added)

When Plutarch calls a banquet "a spectacle and a show," he is only echoing the commonplace aptly stated by Aristotle, "wealth consists more in use than in possession" (*Rhet.* 1.5.7).

As we have noted, all claims to worth and excellence need to be acknowledged. This public recognition, which is essential to reputation and fame, may take many forms. In the highly competitive world of Greek social life, various games and contests produced winners who were recognized for their excellence with public acclaim. One thinks of athletes crowned with laurels at the various games (Drees 1968:85–86, 101–8; Finley and Pleket 1976:20–24, 110–11), or dramatists winning the annual prize (Pickard-Cambridge 1988:40–42, 79–84, 97–99), or poets lauded for their excellence in odes (Plutarch, *Table Talk* 5.1 674D–675D). How famous Alcibiades became for winning three of the top four places in one championship horse race (Thucydides 6.16.2–3), a victory so famous that it continued to be celebrated and remembered (Isocrates, *Team of Horses* 16.32–34; Plutarch, *Alcibiades* 11.1–2). In a warrior society, victorious soldiers received not only a share of the spoils as recognition for their success, but public acclaim as well; in Roman times, great generals were honored with a triumph through the capital city (Versnel 1970).

Recognition of worth could be made at public expense. Aristotle, for example, catalogues the sorts of things whereby a city recognized and celebrated someone's excellence:

> The components of honor are sacrifices [made to the benefactor after death], memorial inscriptions in verse or prose, receipt of special awards, grants of land, front seats at festivals, burial at public expense, statues, free food in the state dining room, among barbarians such things as *proskynesis* and rights of precedence, and gifts that are held in honor in each society. (*Rhet.* 1.5.9)

Indeed an outstanding warrior, athlete, benefactor, etc. would rightly feel slighted if his excellence was not thus publicly recognized and memorialized. All of these "components of honor," moreover, are public acknowledgments of worth which all in the city can observe.

Moving from the grand scale of a Greek polis, we are immediately reminded of Jesus' criticism of the scribes and Pharisees in Matthew. He claimed that their public behavior was calculated to display claims to honor for which they sought public recognition. "They do all their deeds to be seen by men; for they make their phylacteries broad and their fringes long, and they love the place of honor at feasts and the best seats in the synagogues, and salutations in the market place and being called rabbi" (23:5–7). In short, Jesus challenges them for doing what Aristotle describes as the component parts of honor: calculating their behavior to elicit public recognition of their worth. In view is their clothing, their seating locations at public events, public greetings, and special names—all claims to worth, which we saw above as public acknowledgments of their claims to precedence. By refusing his acknowledgment of their worth, Jesus challenges the scribes and Pharisees who were but acting fully within the code of Judean honor in claiming precedence by typical replications of honor, clothing, feasting, public respect, and special names.

2.7 Collective Honor. Throughout this exposition, we have alluded to the way persons in an honor-shame society tend to differ from our urban, industrial one. If we are a "face-to-space" society (i.e., individualism and separation from others), they were a "face-to-face" one (i.e., strong regard for the opinions of others). We best can describe them as collectivist or group-oriented persons, who take their basic identity from their group (especially their family and kinship network), internalize the expectations of that group, and consider life successful when they fulfill them. Although modern Westerners tend to consider this a defective personality (i.e., codependent or underdeveloped), even today it adequately describes at least 50 percent of the world's population and is a particularly apt description of ancient persons (Triandis 1990:48; see Villareal 1989; Hui and Triandis 1986). Fuller description of this type of person in relationship to biblical evidence may be found in Malina 1993:63–89; Malina and Neyrey 1991b:67–96 and 1996:154–76.

What was a group-oriented person like? Josephus provides an apt portrait when he describes the ideal Judean worshiper of God: "Our sacrifices are not occasions for drunken self-indulgence—such practices are abhorrent to God—but for sobriety. At these sacrifices prayers for the welfare of the community must take precedence of those for ourselves; for we are born for fellowship, and he who sets its claims above his private interests is specially acceptable to God" (*Against Apion* 2.195–96). He singles out a group value, temperance, which indicates bodily control. This control is more a part of his society's values than a personal decision to practice asceticism, for it represents what is expected of honorable ancient persons (see 1 Thess. 5:5–7). The group-oriented person, moreover, puts the interests of his primary social groups (family and nation) above personal wishes; he does this because he has internalized the principle that he is "born for fellowship," which means that the group comes before the individual. Plutarch offers another aspect of this when he describes the repetitive embeddedness of individuals in some sort of "natural" hierarchy: "The nurse rules the infant, the teacher the boy, the gymnasiarch the youth, his admirer the young man who, when he comes of age, is ruled by law and his commanding general. No one is his own master, no one is unrestricted" (*Dialogue on Love* 754D). Individuals, then, learn what is expected of them by others: either nurse, teacher, gymnasiarch, or general. They are always accountable to this other person and so they are "not their own master" and are never "unrestricted." Success for them derives from living up to the expectations of others. The nurse, teacher, gymnasiarch, and general are always face-to-face with members of the society and reflect approval or disapproval of individuals in terms of their success in living up to the code of expectations communicated.

These observations on group-oriented persons are a necessary part of the background for understanding what honor meant in the ancient world. For honor came largely by living up to the values and social expectations into which individuals were socialized. When they themselves acknowledge this code, they are in turn acknowledged by their peers with approval for respecting the local code. Honor, then, comes from the nurse, teacher, gymnasiarch, and general who praise the infant, boy, youth, and young man for living up to the code of proper thinking and acting that characterizes the values of that group. Thus honor is "collective" by nature: it pertains to individuals who value the opinions of others.

Honor, moreover, can also come from belonging to such-and-such a collective. As Plutarch indicated above, throughout their lives individuals in antiquity were embedded in some collective or group—either the family, which was the dominant institution of that social world, or peer groups at the gymnasium, symposium, army, synagogue, or assembly of citizens in the polis. Each of these groupings not only gave identity and direction to individual members, but conveyed worth and respect to its members by virtue of association. Anthropologists distinguish "natural" groupings from "elective" ones (Malina 1993:45–48; Malina and Neyrey 1991a:38–41). By "natural grouping" we mean the networks into which one is born and over which one has no control, such as family, clan, and ethnos. We saw above how blood and name (i.e., "natural grouping") replicate honor inasmuch as individuals in the ancient world were known in terms of their fathers and male ancestors. Ezekiel stated it most clearly: "Like mother, like daughter" (16:44), for which there is the correlative "like father, like son." This can refer not only to honorable traits, such as courage and loyalty, but to shameful ones and vices as well (Deut. 23:2; 2 Kings 9:22; Isa. 57:3; Luke 6:23).

Furthermore, people in antiquity were commonly known in terms of the stereotypical reputation of their residence. Hence, when Nathanael learns that Jesus is from Nazareth, a village of no significance, he discounts Jesus who was raised there: "Can anything good come out of Nazareth?" (John 1:46). In contrast, Paul claims honor by being born in one of the noble cities of his time; his birthplace constitutes an important piece of information about him as a worthy person and contributes to his claim to respect: "I am a Jew from Tarsus in Cilicia, a citizen of no low-status city" (Acts 21:39; Neyrey 1996a:268–71; see also Titus 1:12).

The other type of grouping, "elective" or "voluntary," depends on an individual's "choices and contracts" (Malina 1993:47). Members of the retainer class in ancient society formed associations such as the Pharisees; similarly artisans joined collegia or associations which provided burial services. It might also happen that a person in need of special favors or assistance became the client of some patron. In all these cases, individuals take on a special identity as members of a group and share alike in its reputation. We see this quite clearly in the Gospels, where readers are constantly encountering "a Pharisee" or "a scribe" or "a Sadducee." We do not know these characters by name or in terms of their individuality; all we know and need to know is their party or group affiliation. The man born blind in John 9:28 is dishonored in the eyes of some because he belongs to the wrong group; his critics, on the other hand, belong to the right group: "You are his disciple, but we are disciples of Moses" (John 9:28). Honor, thus, comes from group association.

2.8 Gender and Honor. It is generally agreed that the ancient world was fundamentally gender divided. This means that as part of the way males and females in antiquity understood their specific gender, they perceived that human beings were truly two different species of human (Malina and Neyrey 1996:104–5, 111–13). We are quick to comment that this point of view is a social construction: it represents an artificial and culturally defined way of considering gender. While the ancients-may say that such a point of view is rooted in nature and ordained by God, this too is part of their construction of a gender stereotype. Our ancient informant Aristotle reflects the gender stereotype of his cultural world when he compares males with rulers and females with slaves as though they were two entirely different species of human being. This citation comes from his discussion of the origin of the political institution in antiquity, which is based on simpler forms of social organization, especially the family.

> In the first place there must be a union of those who cannot exist without each other; namely, of male and female, that the race may continue . . . and of natural ruler and subject, that both may be preserved. For that which can foresee by the exercise of mind [i.e., male] is by nature intended to be lord and master, and that which can with its body give effect to such foresight [i.e., female] is a subject, and by nature a slave; hence master and slave have the same interest. (Aristotle, *Politics* 1.2)

Since male and female are two different species of human, and inasmuch as the ancients perceived everything in their world in terms of binary opposites (Lloyd 1966:15–171), maleness and femaleness should be completely distinct. As such, males were thought to belong to the public world and females to the private world. This meant that most things in the world could be conceptualized as either male or female, that is, as appropriate to the gender stereotype of maleness and femaleness, such as space, roles, tasks, and objects. Furthermore, the two genders should be separate and not mix or overlap. Hence, to be a male meant *not* being a female, *not* keeping to female space (private or household world), *not* assuming female roles such as mother or sexual partner, *not* performing female tasks (clothing production, food preparation, and child rearing), and *not* using female tools (spindle, pots).

In general, the ancient stereotype of a gender-divided world operated out of the pervasive cultural distinction between public and private (see Neyrey 1994a:79–82). Crudely understood, this meant that male roles, statuses, and tasks took them into the "public world" outside the household, either to the fields (if peasants), the marketplaces (if artisans), or the civic centers (if citizens). Female roles and tasks, in contrast, oriented them to the "private" world of the household and to places where household tasks were performed. Societal definitions of maleness expected men to show bravery and courage, to demonstrate loyalty to one's family and its alliances, to practice self-control, and generally to strive to maintain and increase the family's worth and standing in the village. Females, on the contrary, were expected to show obedience and submission; their worth was nearly equated with sexual exclusivity, which they must guard along with the other valuables of the family. If public males risk to gain for their families, private females stand defensively on guard over the family's fortunes.

These social constructions of gender comprise part of the code of behavior expected of males and females, and so became part of the set of social controls developed by the ancients to enforce the code. This gender code became part of the package of group values and ideas into which individual males and females were socialized from birth. Finally, it became part of the evidence used by the various publics to evaluate individuals: is this male acting like a man or a woman (with the presumption that the social group possesses a clear idea of what befits a male)? And so, individuals were assessed by neighbors and peers as to whether they knew and appropriated the code of gender expectations. The public in turn either declared them worthy if they respected these expectations or withheld a grant of good repute if they failed.

2.9 Shame and Shamelessness. So much for honor. What about shame? The simplest definition of shame is to say that it is the reverse of honor, that is, the loss of respect, regard, worth, and value in the eyes of others. But this would be to ignore a very rich understanding of the term "shame" in antiquity. Let us, then, examine a number of meanings which this word has (see Cairns 1993:14–47; Williams 1993:75–102). First of all, "shame" clearly has a positive meaning when seen in the context of a shame-regarding person. It can mean the basic awareness of the opinion of others and the fear of their censure. In this sense, "shame" would be a virtue in a world where honor (respect, reputation, worth) is a pivotal value. For if persons have "shame," they would then be full participants in the fundamental social dynamic of the ancient cultural world: they would value what others think and say of them. Such persons would respect the "court of public opinion." Thus "shame" functions as a social sanction which ensures a certain level of performance in accord with a group's norms; it serves as an element of social control (Bechtel 1991). In contrast, "shameless" persons do not care what others think of them; they flaunt convention and disregard the code of expected behavior. Shamelessness, then, means that one does not participate in the great game of reputation, and shameless people are always held in contempt by the ancients.

Second, "shame" has a decidedly negative meaning when it refers to the loss of respect and regard by some public (Daube 1973:301–24). Synonyms of shame in this sense would be loss of face, disgrace, and dishonor; a person who is shamed would be held in contempt, made little of, be dismissed, and the like. About this meaning of shame, our reliable ancient informant, Aristotle, has much to say. In treating the emotions which can be aroused, he defines both "shame" and "shamelessness": "Let *shame* (αἰσχύνη) be [defined as] a sort of pain and agitation concerning the class of evils . . . that seems to bring a person into disrespect and *shamelessness* (ἀναισχυντία) a belittling and indifference about these same things" (*Rhet.* 2.6.2; emphasis added). Shame essentially pertains to an unfavorable public reputation: "People feel shame when they suffer such things as contribute to dishonor and censures" (2.6.13) and "shame is imagination about a loss of reputation" (2.6.14). Of what sort of things should one be ashamed? Although Aristotle lists "vices," we must remember how lists of both virtues and vices in antiquity reflect the broader social code of behavior and expectations. It is shameful, he remarks, to fail in demonstrating the four cardinal virtues, such as: (1) to fail in courage by "throwing away a shield or fleeing in battle" (2.6.3), (2) to lack justice by "refusing to pay back a deposit" (2.6.3), and (3) to be deficient in temperance by "having sexual relations with those with whom one should not or where one should not or when one should not" (2.6.4). Aristotle's list of things which are shameful is very important, for it contributes to a sense of a clear public code of expectations. If various excellences are honorable, his catalogue of shameful things indicates what he and others in his cultural world considered to be violations or deficiencies of the code: flattery, stinginess, profiteering, softness, smallness of mind, boastfulness, submission, cowardice, and the like.

Finally, Aristotle describes the utterly public nature of both honor and shame. People do not feel shame before babies and small beasts or before people that they look down upon (2.6.23). Rather one feels shame "toward those whose opinion he takes account of" (2.6.14). This point is of such importance that we cite Aristotle in detail here:

> He takes account of those who admire him and whom he admires and by whom he wishes to be admired and those to whose rank he aspires and those whose opinion he does not despise. . . . And they feel more shame at things done before these people's eyes and in the open; hence, too the proverb, "Shame is in the eyes." For this reason people feel more shame before those who are going to be with them and those watching them, because in both cases they are "in" their eyes. (*Rhet.* 2.6.15, 18)

If someone violates the great code but is not found out, no shame results, for there is no loss of public regard; the deed has *not* been done "in" the eyes of others. How shamefully the son acted toward his father when he publicly refused to obey him and work in the family vineyard (Matt. 21:28–32); better the son who said "yes" publicly and did not work than the one who said "no" before others to his father's great shame. But how terrible it would be if one's secret and shameful deeds were revealed, say, at the judgment tribunal of the High God. Then, in the eyes of the Deity and the heavenly court of angels and saints, the guilty would be disgraced and dishonored. Matthew contains many parables in which people are publicly shamed in the eyes of God and the heavenly court, such as the man without the wedding garment (22:11–15), the wicked servant (24:51), the unprepared maidens (25:12), the unprofitable retainer (25:26), and the "goats" who did not show justice to the needy (25:41, 46). It is not so much a matter that they performed the shameful deed in public, but that their secret shameful deeds were eventually exposed in public to their shame.

A third meaning of shame should be noted, which pertains to the gender stereotype we described above. Anthropologists note the following association: honor : males :: shame : females. We recall, moreover, how males may be shame-regarding and how they may experience shame. But here we call attention to the broad social expectation that males will compete for honor in the public arena in contrast to females, who are expected primarily to be defensive of the family honor by virtue of their chastity. In this sense, females are by extension "defensive" on behalf of the household, its stores as well as its reputation. They are expected to display shyness, not concern for prestige; deference, not concern for precedence; submission, not aggressiveness; timidity, not daring; and restraint, not boldness (Malina and Neyrey 1991:42). "Shame" in this third sense, then, sums up the broad social expectations about females in antiquity. Thus it has a positive meaning, namely, that females have "honor" when they have this kind of "shame." That is, they are judged positively in the court of reputation when they live up to the social expectations encoded in the gender stereotype.

3.0 Summary, Conclusions, and Further Tasks

In this first chapter we have presented a general, abstract model of honor and shame drawn from many cross-cultural studies. This anthropological model, while based on modern villages and regions of the Mediterranean world, is shown to be quite suitable to reflect the particular historical and cultural features of the ancient world. Through a process scientists call "abduction," we shuttled back and forth between our data base of classical literature and inscriptions and our explanatory model (Malina 1991a, 1991b). In this way, we are not totally innocent as we read and interpret individual pieces of information, nor are we insensitive to the historical particularity of our anecdotes. We simply cannot expect to have "immaculate perceptions" of data without some explanatory framework, nor a valid interpretative model without adequate and appropriate illustrations. We hope that at this point we have presented an adequate model of honor and shame, which must necessarily be somewhat abstract and general since it represents the typical and standard understanding of an abstract value. This model will be tested, illustrated, and confirmed as we proceed with the rest of this study. The model should help us interpret Matthew's Gospel, which will in turn, when properly viewed, illustrate and confirm the accuracy and utility of the general model.

In summary, then, we define honor as the reputation, worth, and value which individuals enjoy in the eyes of the public. Honor means their positive evaluation in the typical face-to-face world of ancient cities, towns, and villages. The key to all of this is appreciation of the role of the public in evaluating and then granting or withholding approval and respect. Everything pertaining to honor must be seen in the light of some public. This public, moreover, evaluates on the basis of an implicit and/or explicit code of norms and values; individuals are measured according to a known and accepted measure. This code might be formally described in the rhetoric of praise and blame or implied in the cultural patterns embodied in literature. Yet all cultures socialize their members to perceive, value, and act according to some group norms, whether these are articulated in literature or lore. Thus all ancients, elites and non-elites alike, were subject to some socialization as to the expected code of proper behavior and values of their group, according to which they are then measured and evaluated.

In regard to a shared appreciation of what honor and shame meant in the ancient world, we argue for the existence and importance of a "general code" of honor and shame that is formally expressed in Greco-Roman rhetoric, which in turn reflects longstanding and widespread cultural values. This "general code" admits local variation, for the warrior code of Homer simply is not the operative code of Athens, with its celebration of "co-operative excellences" (Adkins 1960:37–38, 61–85), nor does the Greek system of public benefaction reflect the same social world as the Roman system of patrons and clients. Yet, we maintain, at a certain level of abstraction, both Romans and Greeks are "lovers of honor" (φιλοτιμία) and equally ambitious and competitive for glory and praise. However, within the great code of honor and praise we must allow for and expect local variations. In fact, part of the hypothesis of this book is that Matthew portrays Jesus as presenting a distinctive local variation of the general code for his followers.

Hence, we must move beyond anecdotal evidence about honor and begin to read and interpret a document in the light of a system of honor and shame. The model presented in this chapter has the distinct benefit of informing us about just such a widespread system of values and structures, that is, an integrated view of the component parts of a world where positive public evaluation is a supreme good. We have examined the sources of honor (ascribed, achieved), the competitive nature of ancient society ("love of honor," limited good, and envy), the particular form of aggressive behavior called "challenge and riposte," the symbols of worth and value (blood and name), the collective nature of honor (based on kinship), and the replication of this value in terms of gender stereotypes. Thus we have an explanatory model of what honor is, how one gets it, in what type of culture it is important, why its acquisition, retention, and loss take the shape they do, and why it is rooted in the basic institutions of antiquity, kinship, and politics. Anecdotal materials can provide illustration of various pieces of this model, but never the system as a whole and the cultural logic of its individual pieces. (For discussion of models and biblical interpretation, see Malina 1983:231; Elliott 1993:40–47; Carney 1975:1–43.)

In subsequent chapters, we will be returning to native informants for more and more anecdotal information. In chapter 3, for example, we will mine the rhetoric of praise and blame for whatever specific details this body of literature can provide about the shape of the "general code" it reflects. And in other chapters we will be examining Matthew's Gospel formally in the light of this emic or native information about the cultural world of praise and blame. Yet we will always be returning to the full, systemic model of honor and shame developed here as the appropriate and necessary interpretative framework for making sense of the information provided both by our native informants (i.e., the rhetoricians) and illustrated by the evangelist Matthew in his Gospel.

Finally, we maintain that the model of honor and shame developed in this chapter can profitably and accurately be used to interpret other New Testament documents in their proper cultural context. Whether we turn to Paul's letters and examine his self-presentation, his conflict with rival teachers and preachers, his praise of certain behavior or blame of other, or his articulation of the status and role of Jesus—all of this needs to be assessed in light of the pivotal value of his world, namely, honor and shame. Similarly, other documents directly speak about honor and shame, either the "shame of the cross" (Heb. 12:1–2), or the honor of being a chosen stone (1 Peter 2:4–8), or the glory of being the only person in the cosmos worthy of opening a scroll (Rev. 5:9–10). Conflict of all sorts is profitably examined in the light of honor and shame, whether it be between Jesus and Pharisees, Paul and Elymas, Peter and Paul, or Babylon and the church. And, of course, God too should be viewed in terms of thanksgiving rendered to a patron, glory and praise for the Deity's excellence, or vindication of the Deity's role as lawmaker and sovereign. With appropriate nuancing, the model of honor and shame articulated here can serve as an accurate and useful tool to continue reading the Christian scriptures in their appropriate cultural light.

2

Reading Matthew in Cultural Perspective

1.0 Introduction: Plan of Reading

The anthropological model exposed in the last chapter is based on innumerable field studies and represents a composite of what researchers have actually observed. It represents, then, a model based on a wealth of particular data which has been synthesized in accord with tested interpretation. We now take that model and use it as the template to read Matthew's account of Jesus, for it can safely and profitably show us the presence and importance of the value of honor in the way Jesus is presented.

1.1 Jesus' Reputation. As Pitt-Rivers noted, honor consists both in claims to worth and acknowledgment of those claims (1977:1). One's reputation, moreover, consists precisely in the acknowledgment of claims to worth, for reputation is by definition the public respect shown someone. It is striking, then, that Matthew narrates a remarkable record of Jesus' growing fame, reputation, and worth:

> Public fame at his birth: "King Herod was troubled, and all Jerusalem with him" (2:1–4).
>
> Public announcement of his worth by a prophet: "[H]e who is coming after me is mightier than I, whose sandals I am not worthy to carry" (3:11–13).
>
> Public declaration of his status by God: "This is my beloved Son, with whom I am well pleased" (3:17).
>
> "His fame (ἀκοή αὐτοῦ) spread throughout all Syria . . . [G]reat crowds followed him from Galilee and the Decapolis and Jerusalem and Judea and from beyond the Jordan" (4:24–25).
>
> Because of his reputation, crowds gathered around to hear him (5:1); "the crowds were astonished at his teaching" (7:28).
>
> "Great crowds followed him" (8:1).
>
> "They brought to him a paralytic" (9:1), obviously because of Jesus' reputation as a healing benefactor. In this regard, all requests for healing presume the spread of his reputation.

Because of his reputation, diverse peoples gather around him: "[M]any tax collectors and sinners came and sat down with Jesus" (9:10).

"And the report (φήμη) of this went through all the district" (9:26).

"They [the healed blind men] went away and spread the news (διεφήμισαν) through all the district" (9:31).

On the occasion of a healing, "the crowds marveled, saying, 'Never was anything like this seen in Israel'" (9:33).

As evidence of his widespread reputation, "John heard in prison about the deeds of the Christ" (11:2).

On the occasion of a public healing, "all the people were amazed and said, 'Can this be the Son of David?'" (12:23).

"Great crowds gathered about him" to hear him (13:2).

"Herod the tetrarch heard about the fame (ἀκοήν) of Jesus" (14:1).

"The crowd . . . followed him on foot from the towns" (14:13).

"And when the men of the place recognized him, they sent round to all that region and brought to him all that were sick" (14:34).

"Great crowds came to him . . . " (15:30); "when they saw the dumb speaking, the maimed whole, the lame walking, and the blind seeing, they glorified the God of Israel" (15:31).

Jesus tested his reputation by asking: "Who do men say that I am?" (16:13) and "Who do you say that I am?" (16:15).

Another heavenly acknowledgment of his worth: "This is my beloved son . . . " (17:5).

"He entered the region of Judea beyond the Jordan and large crowds followed him" (19:1).

"As they went out of Jericho, a great crowd followed him" (20:29).

"The crowds that went before him and that followed him shouted, 'Hosanna to the Son of David . . . ,' and when he entered Jerusalem, all the city was stirred, saying, 'Who is this?' And the crowds said, 'This is the prophet Jesus from Nazareth in Galilee'" (21:9–11).

" . . . the people held him to be a prophet" (21:46).

"And when the crowd heard it, they were astonished at his teaching" (22:33).

This important literary aspect of the Gospel touches on the rhetorical strategy of presenting Jesus as a most honorable and honored person. Moreover, it illustrates very clearly the significance of honor as fame, reputation, and public evaluation. Everyone in Galilee, Tyre, Sidon, Syria, the Decapolis, Judea beyond the Jordan, and Jerusalem has heard about Jesus. Furthermore, he enjoyed a very positive evaluation, as crowds constantly flocked to him and even served as a buffer between him and his envious enemies. Jesus may not enjoy a good reputation at Nazareth (13:57), but he does everywhere else.

2.0 Ascribed and Achieved Honor

We recall that honor comes to an individual either by ascription or achievement. People of rank and status (parents, priests, kings, etc.) may bestow honor on someone, either by birth or acceptance into the birth family (Luke 2:21), adoption (Gal. 4:4–7), blessing and consecration (Luke 2:25–35; Heb. 5:5–6) or appointment (John 19:12). Honor then flows from a person or group who already enjoys respect and worth and can demand that others respect their gift of honor to another. Alternately, individuals can earn praise through prowess at military, athletic, and literary games, by benefactions to others, or by defense of their reputation in the day-to-day challenge-riposte games of the village.

2.1 Jesus' Ascribed Honor. It was common for the ancients to praise a person in terms of both generation and geography. People derive status and worth from generation into a worthy family (parents, ancestors, genealogy) and geography, that is, by being born in a reputable locale (city, nation, country). Matthew claims for Jesus of Nazareth that he enjoys exalted ascribed honor by being born into the clan of Judah and the house of David, as well as actual birth in the royal village of Bethlehem, the birthplace of some of Israel's kings: "And you, O Bethlehem, in the land of Judah, are by no means least among the rulers of Judah; for from you shall come a ruler who will govern my people Israel" (Matt. 2:6//Micah 5:2). Moreover, by Joseph's "calling his name Jesus" (1:25), he acknowledged him to be his son, thus ascribing to him the honor of belonging to the house of David with the same status that Joseph himself enjoyed (1:20). Thus Jesus possesses exalted worth and prestige by both his generation and geography. He belongs to the kingly clan as the (adopted) descendant of a son of David; he was born in the royal city of Bethlehem, in the royal lands of Judah, this fact being attested to by the ruling elites of his day. These claims, moreover, are acknowledged by all: King Herod, the chief priests, the scribes, and Magi. Herod may seek to kill Jesus, but this only confirms that he understands Jesus' claims to worth and fears them.

In addition to the notice of royal honor ascribed to Jesus through his generation, we attend as well to the pattern in Matthew whereby God in various ways ascribes a special role and status to him, with accompanying honor and worth. God's theophanies at Jesus' baptism and transfiguration function primarily to bestow and confirm divine honor on Jesus. At the inauguration of his career, God declares of Jesus: "This is my beloved Son, with whom I am well pleased" (3:17). We do not wish to get entangled in debates of later centuries over the "adoption" of Jesus, but the baptismal theophany proclaims to the world that God regards Jesus as "beloved" and "Son," and publicly states that he enjoys God's "favor" or patronage. At the very minimum, God accepts Jesus into a most favored relationship and so ascribes to him the kinship label "beloved Son." According to the code of patronage, it belongs to the patron to show exceptional favoritism to select individuals (Malina 1988:5–6), which is surely the case here as God singles Jesus out as the person who enjoys the Diety's unique approval. We know, moreover, that patrons and clients often masked the sharpness of that relationship in the language of "friendship"; father-son relationships may also be considered as examples of patron-client ones. Thus God declares Jesus both "beloved" and "Son," informing the world that he enjoys unique honor, status, and even role ascribed by God. Scholars still labor to determine just what role "son of God" implies (Delling 1977; Hengel 1976; Charlesworth 1992:3–35). But when a theophany is the occasion for its public declaration, it denotes exceptionally high status (see Kingsbury 1986:48–54).

Turning to the phrase "I am well pleased with him," we frequently read in the scriptures that so and so finds favor in the eyes of the king or some other elite (Schrenk 1964:738). The verb εὐδοκέω has many shades of meaning, such as "to consider good," "to be pleased with," "to take delight in," or "to bow the head toward" (Gen. 24:26, 48 LXX). Moreover, it encodes patron and client relationships. For example, David sang the praises of his patron in 2 Samuel 22, returning praise to God for special divine favor: "He brought me forth into a broad place; he delivered me, because he delighted (ηὐδόκησεν) in me" (2 Sam. 22:20; see 1 Chron. 29:23; 2 Chron. 10:7–11). The terms patron and client do not appear, but only a person unfamiliar with the culture would fail to recognize the singular favoritism that David enjoys with God. Thus, when it is said that God is "well pleased with him," this declares for all to hear that God has elected Jesus, shown him special favor, and entered into a unique patron-client relationship with him.

The inaugural position of this grant of status and honor at the beginning of Jesus' career functions as a rhetorical demand by Matthew that all of Jesus' words and deeds recorded in chaps. 4–16 be considered authorized by God. Similarly, when Jesus' career takes a new turn with his journey to Jerusalem, this too implies an additional role and status for Jesus, namely, that of the Son of man who "must go to Jerusalem . . . suffer many things . . . be killed . . . and be raised" (Matt. 16:24). On the occasion of this shift in role and status, the evangelist records another theophany which confirms the favored status of Jesus in a special patron-client relationship, even as it ascribes to him a new role. The Patron who bestowed the first grant of honor now points Jesus in another direction: "The Son of man *must . . . ,*" which expresses the Patron's will that Jesus go to Jerusalem. Thus Jesus' heavenly Patron ascribes a new role and status to his client: "the Son of man" will suffer and be killed. Eventually the favored client will experience divine vindication from the Patron, that is, "be raised." Needless to say, the disciples find this change of role and status incredible and so reject it. Accordingly another narrative episode of ascribed honor is required. On the holy mountain (Hanson 1995), God-Patron says of Jesus, his client: "This is my beloved Son, with whom I am well pleased; *listen to him*" (17:5). Inasmuch as the words of God here are identical with those at Jesus' baptismal theophany, the narrator would seem to be repeating or confirming a grant of status and honor to Jesus, particularly in light of the new direction of Jesus' career. God, then, confirms Jesus' status ("beloved Son" . . . "well pleased"), even as he confirms that the new direction of Jesus' career is his will (see 16:23). Thus, at several strategic turns in the narrative, Matthew credits Jesus with God's ascription of unique favor and status, especially that of client to a most honorable patron.

God's grant of honor, however, is hardly confined to the two theophanies. God ascribes honor to Jesus through angels who appear in dreams. One angel confirms the honor of the hero's mother, indicating that her pregnancy has resulted from unique divine favor (Matt. 1:20–21a). The mother's honor, of course, contributes to that of her son. This angel goes on to give Jesus a special name, which denotes his unique role: "He will save his people from their sins" (1:21b). True to the pattern of honor claims and acknowledgments, Joseph also acknowledges these claims made on Jesus' behalf, first by taking the pregnant Mary into his house and then by accepting the son as "Jesus." Another angel commanded Joseph to take the mother and son to safety in Egypt (2:13). While no particular role or status is ascribed to Jesus in the angelic message, it nevertheless indicates unique favor from a heavenly Patron (see also Matt. 2:19, 22). Yet it becomes the occasion from which the evangelist deduces a further ascription of honor to Jesus: the dream, when realized, will "fulfill what the Lord had spoken by the prophet, 'Out of Egypt have I called *my son*'" (2:15). We note that "the Lord had spoken" this word of honor on Jesus' behalf long ago, so the Patron's favor for his client is a venerable and ancient relationship. Although no angel appeared to Pilate's wife, she had a dream, which is always sent by a heavenly person (Oepke 1967:221–25, 228–34). In it she learned something about the status of Jesus, "that righteous man" (27:19), again confirming for the reader God's ascription of honor to Jesus.

God's scriptures serve as an additional source of ascribed honor for Jesus, inasmuch as Matthew points out how Jesus fulfilled what was said by this or that biblical writer. The highlighting of a particular passage from the Bible in reference to Jesus seems to be the work of the evangelist (Stendahl 1968; Gundry 1967: 89–104) and perhaps even his sources (Brown 1993:96–104). Yet the evangelist expects his choice to be taken as God's choice. Hence, if Isaiah predicted that a virgin would conceive and bear a son whose name is Emmanuel (Matt. 1:23//Isa. 7:14), it is God speaking through the prophet who gives to the child a unique name ("Emmanuel") and an appropriate royal status and role. Similarly, in the lengthy citation from Isa. 42:1–4 which legitimates Jesus' actions, Matthew is at pains to cite much more of Isaiah than is immediately needed in the controversy. He makes sure that readers know the role and status of Jesus that God has ascribed, namely, that he is: "My servant whom I have chosen, my beloved with whom my soul is well pleased" (12:18). "Servant" need not be read as slave, for kings, patriarchs, and prophets were all named "servant" (Neyrey 1993d:44), and the role of this servant is to bring about justice, which in the context refers to the benefaction of healing. Thus in terms of the native pattern of patron-broker-client relationships, Jesus is officially designated as the broker of God's kingdom, no mean role or status. Despite criticisms by the Pharisees that Jesus is the servant of Beelzebul

(12:24), the evangelist reaffirms God's claim that Jesus is the chosen servant, who is beloved and pleasing in God's eyes.

In addition Matthew narrates that Jesus himself cites a scripture describing the unique favor he enjoys from God. Jesus had just told a parable of how certain tenants refused to acknowledge the ascribed status and honor of both the vineyard owner and his son. According to the narrative, Jesus intends the parable to shame his own enemies, who likewise reject his honor and authority (Matt. 21:14–16, 23–27). Although Jesus' role and status are rejected by some, they are nevertheless confirmed by God. In conclusion, Jesus proclaims: "The very stone which the builders rejected has become the head of the corner; this was the Lord's doing, and it is marvelous in our eyes" (21:42//Ps. 118:22–23). The chosen stone, although shamed and rejected, will be ascribed even more honor by the very God of Israel; it will become the "head of the corner." God ascribes this honor: "It is the Lord's doing," an honor claim which is subsequently acknowledged by others inasmuch as "it is marvelous in our eyes."

Similarly, in the last of Jesus' controversies in Jerusalem, he declares that Ps. 110:1 applies to himself (Matt. 22:41–45). Again the context indicates an honor challenge, as various elites press him with hard questions. Since turnabout is fair play, he then asks them a question about the ascribed role and status of the Christ: "Whose son is he?" (22:41). If he is "the son of David," as they acknowledge, then how is it that David calls him "Lord"? What status, then, does the Christ enjoy: inferior son? or superior lord? Who ascribes him this status? Matthew and the early church acknowledge that Jesus should be acclaimed as "Lord" in virtue of Ps. 110:1, which states: "The Lord [God] said to my Lord [the Christ]: Sit at my right hand, till I put your enemies under your feet" [22:44]. Hence, the Lord God of Israel declares him to be "Lord" and sits him in the most powerful and honorable position in the cosmos, "at my right hand." The early church interpreted this psalm with reference to Jesus' resurrection, that is, his vindication and enthronement by God (see Matt. 26:64; Acts 2:34–36). It represents, then, God's continued ascription of great honor and status to Jesus, as well as his legitimate assumption of the title and role of "Lord."

Therefore, Matthew's narrative expands on the traditional forms of praise by indicating that Jesus enjoyed an exalted role and status, one which was not simply attached to his birth into the tribe of Judah and the house of David through his father Joseph. Ascribed worth and honor repeatedly accrue to Jesus through the various communications of God, either theophanies by God himself or other forms of heavenly communication such as angelic messengers, dreams, and oracles. Thus the most exalted figure in the cosmos takes Jesus as Son-client, finds favor in him, and ascribes to him the roles of Savior, Christ, Son of David, Son of God, and Lord.

The narrative, moreover, contains many other people singing Jesus' praises and acclaiming him. In terms of the formal model of honor and shame, we do not consider these actions by others as "ascriptions" of honor but rather the proper and right acknowledgment of claims made on Jesus' behalf. For this reason, we will defer discussion of this material until later in this section, when it is more properly assessed in terms of the dynamic of claim and acknowledgment of honor.

2.2 Jesus' Achieved Honor in Matthew.   Besides worth ascribed to an individual by another, honor may be acquired the old-fashioned way by personal effort and achievement. The ancient Greek world was truly preoccupied with "virtue" (ἀρέτη), by which it most basically meant some form of excellence (Bauernfeind 1964:457–61; McDonald 1987:39–43). This excellence was generally demonstrated in various types of prowess: military, athletic, aesthetic, and the like. Elites also recognized as achieved honor the system of "liturgies" whereby wealthy citizens built warships for the polis, staged choruses for festivals, adorned temples with elegant gifts, and so forth (Lewis 1983; Llewelyn 1994:93–111; Whitehead 1985:55–74). In time, the system of benefaction became a clear path to honor, as is witnessed by the rich tradition of inscriptions honoring civic benefactors (Danker 1982).These native categories suggest how we might investigate the Gospel of Matthew for evidence that claims respect and praise for Jesus on the basis of both prowess and benefaction.

In terms of military prowess, John the Baptizer announced that the great person who replaced him would be "mightier than I" (3:11). This could refer to either athletic or military strength, but when Jesus echoes the remark in the context of explaining his exorcisms, we see that "might" has to do with military combat and success. As Robinson noted long ago, the exorcisms of Jesus are best understood in their native or emic context as "combat" scenes (1957:33–42). Some in Jesus' world claimed that he acted as chief warrior for the forces of the devil (12:24). The evangelist, however, records Jesus' defense of his success in terms of a military metaphor (see Paul's boast of military prowess in 2 Cor. 10:3–6). According to the logic of the argument, allies do not wage war against each other lest they foolishly destroy each other. Hence, if Jesus wages war against Satan, the two must be enemies, not allies. Jesus then compares himself to a warrior on a raiding party who "binds the strong man" because he is "mightier" than he (12:29). Jesus then plunders his house and takes a warrior's booty. The imagery, then, describes military prowess, which portrays Jesus in his exorcisms as waging war against Satan, defeating him in single combat and despoiling his kingdom—all honorable actions according to the ancient code of warfare. This military explanation, moreover, would apply to all of the combat scenes between Jesus and demons or unclean spirits: Matt. 4:25; 8:16, 29–32; 10:1; 12:22; and 15:22. The same would apply to Jesus' actions in calming a storm: he masters an evil spirit that causes such natural disasters (8:23–27; see Kee 1968:242–56). Thus, according to native perceptions of spirits attacking mortals, Jesus' success in expelling them should be appreciated as a demonstration of military might. The reactions of the crowds portray the awe, fear, and admiration which naturally follow demonstration of such prowess. One group fears his power so much they ask him to leave the area (8:34). But typically crowds generally acknowledge Jesus' power with an award of praise and worth: "The crowds marveled, saying, 'Never was anything like this seen in Israel'" (Matt. 9:33).

The Gospels say nothing about Jesus' athletic ability; he was not renowned for running, wrestling, boxing, or any of the typical sports of antiquity whereby athletic prowess could be demonstrated. In terms of Jesus' aesthetic prowess, we turn to the record of his powerful speech. Matthew, of course, stands out among the Synoptic Gospels for his extended discourses of Jesus, both in public and private. On only one occasion does the evangelist record the acknowledgment of the crowd; after the Sermon on the Mount, we are told that "the crowds were astonished at his teaching, for he taught them as one who had authority, and not as their scribes" (7:28–29). As we shall shortly see, almost all of the public exchanges between Jesus and his critics are composed in the form of the chreia. For the moment, we need only note that all of these celebrate Jesus' public speech.

Perhaps the most readily recognized form of prowess in the Gospels is the great benefaction which Jesus bestows on people. According to one anthropological analysis of "goods" which people can exchange, there are four general types: power, influence, wealth, and commitment (Parsons 1969:352–472; Turner 1969:121–34; Malina 1986:74–87). We mention this because it helps us to classify the kinds of benefactions which Jesus bestows. In regard to *power*, we refer back to his successful combat with demons and evil spirits, including "the moon" (4:24 and 17:15 speak of people as "moonstruck": σεληνιαζόμενος). In regard to *influence*, Jesus himself has unique access to and receives privileged information from God (11:27); moreover, he knows the most important information that can be known in his world, namely, Whom to go to for assistance, help, and aid. In regard to *wealth*, although Jesus himself does not have a royal treasury, he can provide superabundant food to feed thousands of people (14:13–21; 15:32–38). Such benefaction earns one fame and honor.

As Matthew and others know, God alone is the Benefactor and Source of all good things. Jesus, on the other hand, acts as broker or mediator of this divine benefaction (Oakman 1986:194–97; Malina 1988:16–18), which indicates his unique status as one with access to the supreme Benefactor. Matthew twice records incredible claims made by Jesus that he has access to God's treasure of blessings: "All things have been given to me by my Father" (11:27) and "All authority in heaven and earth have been given to me" (28:18). Figure 2.1 begins to identify many of the benefactions that Jesus distributes in his public life.

From a social science perspective it is not an indecent question to ask what Jesus receives in return for this generous benefaction. Even Matthew records the exchange between the disciples of the Baptizer and Jesus over the significance of his healings. John had "heard about the deeds of the Christ" (11:2), presumably referring to the way that Jesus' signs and wonders serve as his credentials (see John 2:11; 7:31; 9:31–33; 20:30–31). When his disciples ask Jesus, "Are you he who is to come, or shall we look for another?" (Matt. 11:3), Jesus elaborates on his benefaction of healing, the record of which should be sufficient answer to the question: "Go and tell John what you hear and see. . . ." (11:4–6). The healings function as credentials for "the Christ," in the Matthean sense that Jesus displays a royal sense of benefaction. Thus his benefactions earn him the title of "the Christ."

In terms of an honor perspective, Jesus' benefaction illustrates a claim to a particular role and status. But all claims need to be acknowledged. The notice that crowds "from Galilee and the Decapolis and Jerusalem and Judea and from beyond the Jordan" (Matt. 4:25) follow Jesus attests that many acknowledged in

1. Wisdom and Teaching: Matt. 4:23; 5:1–7:28; 10:7; 11:1; 13:1–9
2. Healing:

   "He went about all Galilee . . . healing every disease and every infirmity. . . . [T]hey brought him all the sick, those afflicted with various diseases and pains, demoniacs, epileptics, and paralytics, and he healed them." (4:23–24)

   leprosy (8:1–4)

   paralysis (8:5–13; 9:1–8)

   fever (8:14–17)

   hemorrhage (9:20–22)

   death (9:18–19, 23–26)

   blindness (9:27–31; 20:29–34; 21:14)

   dumbness (9:32–33)

   withered hand (12:9–13)

   lameness (21:14)

   summaries of healings (14:35–36; 15:30–31)

3. Feedings: 14:13–21; 15:32–38
4. Rescues: 14:30–32
5. Exorcisms: 4:24; 8:16, 28; 9:32; 12:22; 15:22
6. Forgiveness of Sins and Mercy: 1:21; 9:2, 12–13

Figure 2.1 Jesus' Benefactions

some way his role as God's agent and dispenser of God's treasury of blessings. This summary statement at the beginning of the narrative of Jesus' success as broker of God's benefaction receives subsequent specification. For example, after healing a paralytic, the onlookers "glorified God, who had given such authority to men" (9:8), which surely is acknowledgment of Jesus' distinctive role as agent of God's power. Similarly, after raising the synagogue ruler's daughter from death, "the report of this went through all the district" (9:26), surely to Jesus' credit. On the occasion of another healing, the crowds "marveled, saying, 'Never was anything like this seen in Israel'" (9:33). And in what looks to be a special summary report of Jesus' healing benefaction, Matthew tells how the crowds brought to Jesus "the lame, the maimed, the blind, the dumb, and many others . . . and he healed them"; the appropriate response follows: "When they saw the dumb speaking, the maimed whole, the lame walking, and the blind seeing, they glorified the God of Israel" (15:31). Matthew implies correctly that Jesus was acknowledged as enjoying a special role and status with the God of Israel by dispensing the widest range of divine benefactions. Quite simply, Jesus receives fame, respect, and loyalty (i.e., "faith") as a result of his benefactions. Such was the nature of the ancient system of benefaction in the cultural context of honor and shame.

Jesus is often acclaimed as "Son of David" and always in the context of some request for benefaction (9:27; 15:22 and 20:30–31). In regard to this title, the studies
of Dennis Duling illustrate the connection between benefaction and the association
of Jesus with the royal family of ancient Israel (1975; 1978; 1992). As 1 Sam. 8:10–
18 states, kings were not always acclaimed for their royal benefactions; on the contrary, they tended to extract the good things of the land for their private pleasures,
defrauding their people of manpower, wealth, and the like. Although he enjoys royal
status and an elite role (1:1) with the prestige that accompanies them (21:9), when
Jesus is addressed as "Son of David," it is always in the context of a petition for
royal benefaction, which is generously bestowed. Duling interprets this to mean that
Jesus is no mere client-king, such as the Herods. Although it belongs to kings to extract taxes (17:25–26), Jesus does not act this way; on the contrary, he associates not
with the ruling class but with those ruled. He is servant of others, that is, benefactor, not served by them (20:28). Thus he is a legitimate, if ideal, ruler whose hallmark is to be benefactor to God's people (1992:111–12). And by brokering God's
benefactions to the people, Jesus has earned their respect and achieved great honor.

3.0 Challenge and Riposte

Here we consider the typical way in which elites and non-elites acquire honor,
namely, the ongoing game of push-and-shove. We accept the remarks of the ancients that they lived in an agonistic world in which individuals, cities, and peoples
were constantly battling. Our interest lies in the typical pattern of this ongoing, agonistic contest for the light it can shed on Jesus' controversies and conflicts in
Matthew, where his honor is constantly challenged. Our investigation of these conflict scenes can be conducted along two lines: (1) the anthropological model of
"challenge and riposte" and (2) the rhetorical form of the "responsive *chreia*." As
we examine Jesus' controversies, we hope to make clear that the anthropological
model and the rhetorical form contain basically the same formal elements. In keeping with the argument of this book we will begin with the anthropological model of
typical games of push-and-shove, that is, the model of "challenge and riposte."

3.1 Challenge and Riposte: A Generalized View of Conflict. In regard
to anthropological analysis of such hostile exchanges, Pierre Bourdieu's work concerning the politics of honor and shame offers a very sensitive and comprehensive
description of the phenomenon (1966:191–241). Bourdieu's insights have been
systematically organized by Bruce Malina, first in his *New Testament World: Insights from Cultural Anthropology* (1993:34–37, 42–44), and then with Jerome
Neyrey in *The Social World of Luke-Acts* (1991a:36–38, 49–51). Malina identifies
four typical steps in a challenge-riposte exchange: (1) claim to honor, (2) challenge to that claim, (3) riposte to the challenge, and (4) public verdict by onlookers. Narratives may not always record all four stages of the exchange, for often the
claim to worth is presumed on behalf of the person challenged. And although a
viewing public may not be explicitly mentioned, we must remember that in the
world of Jesus and Matthew all significant social intercourse takes place in some
form of public arena, whether a marketplace, a synagogue, a roadside, or a banquet

hall. The challenge and the response, however, are always clearly in view, and the formal function of narrating these exchanges is to burnish the honor of the person who successfully defends his honor.

3.2 Honor Challenges to Jesus. We claim that every time Jesus appears in public, that is, outside of his own kinship circle, people engage him in honor challenges. Challenges, however, can be of two kinds: positive and negative (Malina 1993:36; Malina and Neyrey 1991:49–52). A *positive challenge* might be a compliment, gift, request, or volunteering, whereas *negative challenges*, on the other hand, are quite hostile, such as insults, physical affronts, threats, or slander (Malina 1993:35–37). Positive challenges put the recipient on the spot, but are by no means as ugly and lethal as negative challenges. Yet both seek to take something from the person challenged. Negative challenges explicitly seek to humiliate and shame the person challenged; but even positive challenges, such as a gift given or a compliment made, put the recipient's stature and reputation on the line.

By way of illustration, we note that Matthew records many positive challenges put to Jesus. Some people volunteer to be his disciples, those whom Jesus may or may not wish to have in his network. He is put on the spot by their offer of discipleship, but in turn puts them off: "Foxes have holes . . . but the Son of man has nowhere to lay his head" (8:20) and "Leave the dead to bury their own dead" (8:22). Matthew does not say whether these volunteers actually joined Jesus' circle of disciples, but the narrative implies that those who could not follow Jesus' demands were not "worthy" to be disciples. Although the Gospels do not record gifts being offered to Jesus, on one occasion a rich young man pays Jesus a compliment, which is promptly refused. In the Markan version, the man said: "Good Teacher, what must I do to inherit eternal life?" (Mark 10:17), to which Jesus replied with a rejection of the compliment: "Why do you call me good? No one is good but God alone" (10:18). Matthew's version seems to have clumsily edited this, so that the compliment is not formally stated; Jesus is addressed only as "Teacher," not "Good Teacher" (Matt. 19:16). The challenge to Jesus rests in the sense that, if complimented, Jesus would in turn be obligated in some way to reciprocate. In regard to requests, on one occasion a man pleaded with Jesus' disciples to cure his son, but they were unable (17:16). By approaching Jesus with a complaint about his disciples' lack of power, the master is himself now challenged, to which he responds with the offputting remark: "O faithless and perverse generation, how long am I to bear with you?" (17:17). Although Jesus may eventually heal the sick boy, he is presented as resenting the challenge to his and his disciples' power. Finally, the mother of the sons of Zebedee requests favored status for James and John (20:20–22), which is ultimately denied (20:23). These are all positive honor challenges, which the honorable Jesus must resist because either they attempt to take something from Jesus that he may not wish to give, or they obligate him to reciprocate in some way. It is important to note that Jesus rejects volunteers, compliments, and untoward requests. Those knowledgeable about the culture understand that in doing so Jesus defends his honor.

In regard to negative honor challenges, Matthew's narrative bristles with them from Jesus' birth to his death. According to the chronology of the narrative, we observe the following examples: (1) attempts on Jesus' life (2:16–19);

(2) temptations by the devil (4:1–11; see Rohrbaugh 1995); (3) criticisms and questions in Galilee (9:1–8, 10–13, 14–17; 12:1–8, 9–14, 24–32; 13:53–58; 15:1–20; 16:1–4, 22–23; 19:3–9); and (4) dangerous questions in Jerusalem (21:14–17, 23–27; 22:15–22, 23–33, 34–40, 41–46). Let us examine a representative sample of these challenges to Jesus in light of the choreography of "challenge and riposte," which illustrates how the game of honor and shame is played out in the ordinary social intercourse of the agonistic world of antiquity.

At the outset we should realize that not every report in Matthew of a negative challenge will contain all four steps in the choreography of a "challenge and riposte" exchange. This should not be surprising, for students of literary forms in the Bible know that a full form is not always found in each usage of it. For example, not every narrative of a negative challenge to Jesus begins with a crisp claim on his part. Inasmuch as Matthew made clear from the very beginning God's ascription of a most honorable role and status to Jesus, readers know what is being challenged. The author surely implies that Jesus' opponents in the narrative operate out of some sense of Jesus' claim to role and status precisely because they challenge him about it when they criticize him and ask him hard questions which would prove his claims to be false. Furthermore, in every instance that Jesus is in public, his readers would surely understand that males in that world were rarely home with their families, but spent the day in public with other males. Hence, Matthew presumes that Jesus acts in public before an acutely observing audience, whose business it is to evaluate the performances of Jesus and his challengers so as to acclaim the winners and losers in the honor challenge. The following typical examples of negative challenges can serve as a representative sample of how the many instances of challenge should be interpreted.

After Jesus crosses the lake and comes to his own city (Matt. 9:1), some people, presumably relatives of the sick person, bring him a paralytic. Their behavior is motivated by the previous account of Jesus' healings (8:1–34). On the narrative level, their actions illustrate in detail what was stated in summary fashion at the very beginning of Jesus' public life, how he cured all sickness, disease, and infirmity of Jew and Gentile alike (4:23–25). All of these healings, moreover, function as Jesus' credentials or claims, as the exchange between the disciples of the Baptizer and Jesus makes clear (11:2–5). Thus the narrator would have us understand Jesus' healings as a legitimate *claim* to the role and status of Christ or Son of David. The *claim* becomes actualized here when Jesus tells the paralytic, "Take heart, my son, your sins are forgiven" (9:2), which implies that Jesus legitimately possesses and exercises a unique power (see Matt. 1:21). Yet scribes immediately *challenge* his claim by condemning Jesus' behavior: "This man is blaspheming" (9:3). By this, they accuse Jesus of dishonoring God by claiming authority that belongs uniquely to the Deity, a remark made explicit in Mark's account: "Who can forgive sins but God alone?" (Mark 2:9). Faced with this serious challenge, Jesus delivers a *riposte*. Inasmuch as the challenge contained two elements: (1) Jesus' "speech" which (2) claimed power to forgive sins, the riposte matches both exactly. In regard to "speech," as we say, "talk is cheap." Following the tradition of asking questions either to challenge or counterchallenge, Jesus asks a question of his own critics about speech: "Which is easier, to say, 'Your sins are forgiven,' or to say, 'Rise and walk'?" (9:5). Obviously it is easier to say "Your sins are forgiven," because there will be no empirical proof that the words are effective; but to say "Rise and walk," proof must be immediately evident. Jesus then does the harder thing by commanding the paralyzed man to rise and walk. The reasoning behind this statement suggests that if Jesus can do the harder thing, he can do the easier thing as well. Since the challenge contested Jesus' speech, he uses the "hard word" of the physical cure precisely as proof of extraordinary power: " 'But that you may know that the Son of man has authority on earth to forgive sins'—he then said to the paralytic—'Rise, take up your bed and go home'" (9:6). In fact, the man rose and went home (9:7). This *riposte* not only turns back the immediate *challenge* to Jesus' role and status, but also confirms the *claims* with which the episode began. The episode appropriately ends with a *public verdict* in which the onlookers "glorified God, who had given such authority to men" (9:8). Jesus' role and his reputation are thus vindicated.

This instance of challenge and riposte took place in public and before a crowd which observed the intricacies of the game. According to the narrative, they clearly consider Jesus to be the winner, for he successfully defended his claims before his enemies and critics. Moreover, he gained greater honor precisely from the defeat of the scribes who were put to shame: he increased as they decreased. Furthermore, when Matthew says that "they glorified God," this means several things in the context of the story: (1) God also is honored when his claims on Jesus' behalf are respected, and (2) God is properly thanked for being a generous Benefactor-Patron to the people through the healing and saving powers exercised by Jesus. Far from competing with God for glory, Jesus is acclaimed as God's servant, client, and son by virtue of his benefactions. There is no rivalry between God and Jesus, unlike the honor competition between the scribes and Jesus.

Another example may be helpful, namely, the challenge to Jesus by the Sadducees about "the resurrection" (Matt. 22:23–33). If we follow the interpretation of Daube (1973:158–69; see Malina and Neyrey 1988:73–74), Matthew presents in 22:15–46 a series of questions asked of Jesus whose literary shape resembles the pattern of questioning described in the Talmud: "Our Rabbis taught: Twelve questions did the Alexandrians address to R. Joshua b. Hananiah: Three were of a scientific nature, three were matters of *aggada*, three were nonsense and three were matters of conduct" (*b. Niddah* 69b–70a). These four types of questions can be more adequately distinguished as: (1) questions of a "scientific nature": halachic questions about the application of laws to specific situations; (2) questions of *aggada*: supposed contradictions in the non-halachic parts of scripture; (3) "nonsense" questions: attempts to ridicule a scholar and his interpretations of the scriptures; and (4) questions about "matters of conduct": questions that deal with theoretical principles in the Torah, that is, issues larger than questions of a "scientific nature." These four types of questions, which provide an adequate test of a rabbi's acumen, are all hostile challenges which seek to "entangle him in his talk" (22:15); they are hardly neutral requests for information. When the schema of four types of questions is applied to Matt. 22:15–46, we see the following fit between literary form and narrative: (1) Pharisees ask a "scientific" question of Jesus: "Is it lawful to pay taxes to Caesar or not?" (22:15–22); (2) Sadducees ask a "nonsense" question about levirate marriage and the resurrection (22:23–33); (3) a lawyer asks about "principles of behavior": "Which is the great commandment in the law?" (22:34–40); and (4) finally Jesus asks the Pharisees the "aggadic" question: "What do you think of the Christ? Whose son is he?" (22:41–46). Thus in the course of his final week in Jerusalem, the elites of Jerusalem each challenge Jesus with hard questions according to a recognized form for testing the wisdom of a rabbi. The narrative context of 22:23–33, then, is itself one of extended hostile questioning which we interpret in terms of challenge and riposte.

Sadducees, who say that there is no resurrection, approach Jesus to challenge him about his teaching. Where is the *claim* here? The *claim*, we suggest, is implied in the address to Jesus, that is, "Teacher." The narrator would have us understand that Jesus *claims* this teaching; for whenever he predicts his shameful death, Jesus always adds, " . . . and on the third day be raised" (16:21; 20:19; see also 17:9). Furthermore, according to Matthew, Jesus has just told a parable to the Jerusalem elite about wicked tenants murdering the son of the vineyard owner (21:38–39). When the owner destroyed the wicked tenants (21:41), he was avenging his slighted honor and delivering a riposte to their insulting challenge. Jesus confirms this sense of avenging insults with restoration of honor by quoting Psalm 118 to the effect that "the very stone rejected by the builders has become the head of the corner; this is the Lord's doing" (21:42). In context this refers to some sort of posthumous vindication of the slain son, who is likened to the "rejected stone."

Matthew portrays Jesus as stepping apart from the parable to make a claim that he, too, like the slain son, will be avenged and that God will do this. Commentators on this parable constantly argue that the key figures in the parable (owner, "beloved son," and wicked tenants) and the chief elements of the story (sending of the son, his murder, his avenging) apply to the figures in the narrative controversy (God, Jesus, and the Jerusalem elite) and the events of this part of the Gospel (Jesus' mission, his death, and his resurrection). Matthew makes this identification as clear as possible by reporting Jesus' counterchallenge: "I tell you, the kingdom of God will be taken away from you" (21:43) and the reception of his insult, "[T]hey perceived that he was speaking about them" (21:44).

The point we are making is that the snatch of Psalm 118 that Jesus cites about a rejected stone which is exalted allegorically refers to his own eventual death and vindication. Jesus is the "rejected stone" which the Lord has made the "head of the corner." God trumps the play of the shameful "builders" who reject the stone by elevating it to an even higher status, that is, "head of the corner." Thus challenge (murder of the son/rejection of the stone) is met by riposte (vengeance on the murderers/exaltation of the stone). The posthumous avenging of the son (21:41) and the post-rejection exaltation of the rejected stone (21:42) are the work of God. Since Jesus proclaims this message, obviously he is credited with believing that God raises the dead, which in this case is God's riposte to the challenge to his servants and son. Jesus, therefore, can be said to *claim* certain ideas about God.

Returning to the controversy between Jesus and the Sadducees, in regard to the *challenge*, Jesus' adversaries address him as "Teacher." The literary form and the context indicate that this address is a sarcastic insult (see 22:16). In addition, a trick question is asked, which according to Daube's analysis is one of nonsense or ridicule (*boruth*, see Daube 1973:159–60); its function is to stump Jesus and make him look ridiculous. In addition to the rhetorical fact that questions tend to be aggressive challenges, this in particular makes mockery of the doctrine of the resurrection and all who hold it, in this case, Jesus (22:24–28). Whose wife will the woman be in the resurrection, for she has had seven brothers as husbands? Thus we see several *challenges*: (1) Jesus, of course, is challenged by the sarcastic insult ("Teacher") and the ridiculing question asked him; (2) God, too, is challenged, in that the Sadducees, by claiming that there is no resurrection, deny God's legitimate power. Hence, the *challenges* here indicate that the honor of both Jesus and God are put to the test.

Jesus delivers a stinging *riposte*: "You are wrong!" Wrong for two reasons: "You know neither the scriptures nor the power of God" (22:29). Returning insult for insult, Jesus defends his own honor as a worthy teacher by a clever appeal to the scriptures. But he also defends the honor of his Patron by proving that God indeed raises the dead: "Have you not read what was said to you by God, 'I am the God of Abraham, and the God of Isaac, and the God of Jacob?'" (22:32//Ex. 3:6). We note that in his *riposte* Jesus answers a question with a question, "Have you not read?" Challenge is met with counterchallenge, question with question. Jesus' response contains a serious affront, which implies that the religious elite do not read their own scriptures and thus are not worthy of their role and status. The scripture which Jesus cites, moreover, indicates that God is Patron of living persons, either current living persons or past ones: "He is not God of the dead, but of the living" (22:32). Therefore Jesus' *riposte* defends both his own honor against insults and the fullness of God's power to raise the dead against its deniers.

Inasmuch as Matthew portrays Jesus publicly discoursing in the temple, all of the events in chapters 21–22 take place in public (see 21:23). Hence, crowds observe every scene in this section. Moreover, honor challenges make no sense whatever when done in private, even if such a thing were conceivable in the cultural world of antiquity. Challenges occur in public so that onlookers and observers can savor the challenge given, evaluate the various moves in the contest, and bestow honor to the winners. After Jesus' clever *riposte*, Matthew comments: "The crowds were astonished at his teaching" (22:33), which means that their *public verdict* is a grant of honor to Jesus. In an honor-shame culture, Jesus not only maintains his honor but gains more by virtue of the loss of honor by his challengers. He is still the champion, untied and undefeated.

The anthropological model of "challenge and riposte," which describes how honor is typically acquired, may seem quite abstract at first. One may wonder if it applies to Matthew's world. But its essential dynamics are clearly replicated in the literary pattern in which most of Jesus' controversies are cast. We turn now to examine a common literary form used by the ancients to describe the typical manner in which a wise man or sage defended his honor, namely, the rhetorical form called the chreia. As we hope to show, the anthropological model of "challenge and riposte" is identical with the pattern of "provocation and response" found in the rhetorical form of a typical chreia.

Ancient rhetorical handbooks used for educating students at an intermediate level of training were called the *progymnasmata*. Among the ten or so exercises in them which students learned was the chreia, a term which refers to a reminiscence about a famous person—what we might call a vignette or episode which celebrates his wisdom. Although the ancients distinguished three types (action chreia, sayings chreia, and mixed action-sayings chreia), we focus on the sayings chreia, and in particular the variety called the "responsive chreia." In formal terms, it typically begins with a verbal *provocation* of some sort, such as a question or criticism, which prompts the sage to *respond* in a defensive manner that demonstrates his wit and wisdom (Hock and O'Neil 1986:28–32). For example, "Anacharsis, when reproached by someone because he was a Scythian, said: 'I am by birth, but not in manner of living'" (Hock and O'Neil 1986:30–31). A wise man, Anacharsis, is insulted by someone who calls attention to the fact that he came from a country with a dishonorable reputation, to which reproach he defends himself with a clever response. Thus his true reputation, which is owed him for his wisdom, is maintained, and he is granted honor. Thus we note the following replication: challenge : provocation :: riposte : clever response. Both rhetorical form and anthropological model describe in an identical manner the essential elements of the honor game of push-and-shove.

When we compare the typical form of a responsive chreia with the anthropologists' description of a challenge-riposte exchange, we note a homology (see fig. 2.2).

Responsive Chreia	Anthropological Challenge-Riposte
1. Claim (of wit or wisdom by famous person, i.e., reputation)	1. Claim (of wit, strength, achievement, or success by someone)
2. Challenge: either (a) a question or (b) praise, reproach, rebuke	2. Challenge: verbal or physical
3. Riposte: verbal response	3. Riposte: verbal or physical
4. Verdict (the very remembrance records an honor verdict by those who immortalize the event)	4. Verdict: onlookers award honor and shame respectively to winners and losers

Figure 2.2 Comparison of Responsive Chreia with Challenge-Riposte

The value of examining both the rhetorical form of a responsive chreia and a challenge-riposte exchange helps us to focus on the central value which is always contested, namely, the prestige of some notable person.

3.3 Responsive Chreiai in Matthew.   The following list enumerates most of the responsive chreiai in Matthew. We distinguish those which are overtly hostile to Jesus from those which put him on the spot, but without attempts to test or criticize him. In terms of rhetorical form, the rhetoricians did not distinguish these two but considered them both responsive chreiai. For reasons which we will shortly offer, a clear distinction should be made between them. The bulk of the controversies of Jesus contain a hostile question asked him or a carping criticism made about him or his disciples which serves as the provocation prompting Jesus to speak, as fig. 2.3 illustrates. Questions can be very aggressive weapons, such as the one

	Provocation	**Response**
9:1–8	"This man is blaspheming."	"Why do you think evil in your hearts? For which is easier to say . . . ?"
9:10–13	"Why does your teacher eat with tax collectors and sinners?"	"Those who are well have no need of a physician, but those who are sick . . . "
9:14–17	"Why do we and the Pharisees fast, but your disciples do not fast?"	"Can the wedding guests mourn as long as the bridegroom is with them . . . ?"
11:2–6	"Are you he who is to come . . . ?"	"Go and tell John what you see and hear . . . "
12:9–14	"Is it lawful to heal on the sabbath?"	"What man of you, if he has one sheep and it falls into a pit . . . ?"
12:22–32	"It is by Beelzebul . . . that this man casts out demons."	"Every kingdom divided against itself is laid waste . . . "
15:1–20	"Why do your disciples transgress the tradition of the elders?"	"And why do you transgress the commandment of God?"
16:1–4	To test him they asked him to show them a sign from heaven.	"When it is evening, you say, 'It will be fair weather; for the sky is red . . . "
17:24–27	"Does not your teacher pay the tax?"	"From whom do the kings of earth take toll or tribute . . . ?"
18:1–4	"Who is the greatest in the kingdom of heaven?"	"Unless you turn and become like children . . . "
18:21–22	"Lord, how often shall my brother sin against me, and I forgive him?"	"I do not say to you seven times, but seventy times seven."
19:1–9	"Is it lawful to divorce one's wife for any cause?"	"Have you not read that he who made them from the beginning . . . ?"
19:16–22	"Teacher, what good deed must I do, to have eternal life?"	"Why do you ask me about what is good . . . ?"
19:27–30	"We have left everything and followed you. What then shall we have?"	"[Y]ou who have followed me will also sit on twelve thrones, judging the twelve tribes of Israel . . . "
21:14–17	They were indignant, and said to him, "Do you hear what these are saying?"	"Have you never read, 'Out of the mouths of babes and sucklings . . . '?"
22:15–22	"Is it lawful to pay taxes to Caesar, or not?"	"Whose likeness and inscription is this . . . ?"
22:23–33	"[I]n the resurrection, to which of the seven will she be wife? For they all had her."	"You are wrong, because you know neither the scriptures nor the power of God . . . "
22:34–40	"Teacher, which is the great commandment in the law?"	"You shall love the Lord your God with all your heart . . . "

Figure 2.3 Responsive Chreiai in Matthew

asked by the Pharisees: "The Pharisees took counsel how to entangle him in his talk. . . . 'Is it lawful to pay taxes to Caesar, or not?'" (22:15, 17). Criticisms provide a comparable provocation; for example, when the Pharisees observed the disciples plucking grain and eating it on the sabbath, they commented: "Look, your disciples are doing what is not lawful to do on the sabbath" (12:2). Other incidents seem less hostile, but require a response just as well; for example, when children were brought to Jesus for a blessing, the disciples rebuked them, which prompted Jesus to respond, "[T]o such belongs the kingdom of heaven" (19:13–14).

In a different vein certain things are said to Jesus which, while not hostile and aggressive like questions and criticism, nevertheless put him on the spot and likewise occasion a response. Such challenges might be (1) compliments, which put the person who receives them in debt to the one who praises, (2) requests, which encroach on the resources of the person asked, (3) volunteering, which puts the person offered in an awkward position, and (4) gifts, which always expect a return gift. On one occasion people volunteer to become disciples, to which offer Jesus delivers a sharp reply (8:18–22). More commonly in Matthew people ask favors of Jesus (8:1–4, 5–13, 23–27; 9:18–26, 27–31; 12:38–42; 15:21–28; 16:1–4; 17:14–22; 20:20–28, 29–34). Requests for a "sign" (12:38–42; 16:1–4) are clearly more hostile than requests for a healing (17:14–22), yet both put Jesus on the spot and prompt a sharp response. Some requests are for healings (8:1–4), but these too seek something from Jesus without giving him anything in return, which in that culture is judged to be potentially shameful. Other requests are simply brazen (20:20–28) and so are rejected.

Thus, when we interpret the stories about Jesus in the light of their typical rhetorical form, we clearly see that they are "responsive chreiai." All such episodes begin with some sort of provocation, which may be hostile and aggressive (i.e., questions and criticisms) or challenging in a lesser way (i.e., requests, compliments, and volunteering). Nevertheless, we observe how Jesus is challenged and must offer a suitable defensive reply.

4.0 Replications of Honor

When we examine the way honor is replicated by blood and name, we are in fact looking more closely at the notion of ascribed honor. Inasmuch as kinship and family constituted for most people the dominant institution in antiquity, we wish to see how honor comes to individuals in terms of generation, that is, as members of tribe, clan, and family (i.e., blood) or in virtue of parents and ancestors (i.e., name).

4.1 Honor and Blood. In the first place, native informants tell us that the first source of praise resides in a person's "origins (εὐγένεια) and birth (γένεσις)," a topic we will develop in the next section of this study (see Aristotle, *Rhet.* 1.5.5, 2.15.1–3). Modern studies of honor and shame advise us to broaden this in two ways: (1) to include further consideration of family and kinship in virtue of adoption of grown males into another family (i.e., ascribed honor); and (2) to consider blood in terms of courage and conflict (i.e., achieved honor).

Matthew's Gospel treats at length the replication of honor in blood and kinship, which we now consider.

One expects family members to stick together and advance the common good of their kinship group. For example, we read that the mother of Zebedee's sons promoted the honor of James and John, as one would expect of kin (20:20–21). Mothers should plead for the health of their daughters (15:22), kinsmen for a paralyzed relative (9:2), and fathers for their daughters (9:18). Family blood requires concerted cooperative action. All of these relatives who press for the advantage of family members are simply doing their duty to the kinship group, which is an honorable thing. Hence solidarity and loyalty among family members go without saying. Blood replicates the honor of the family.

Yet on many occasions conflicts arise within families, where individual members stand apart from and outside the sanctions of honor expected of them in terms of blood relationships. One should be able to trust blood relatives, but not always. On such occasions, the honor of the family is at risk (see Malina 1993:38). Yet in the Gospel narrative, all is not well with Jesus' own blood relatives. When they appear for their first and only time in the narrative, the situation does not indicate good will and unfailing support of kin. Family honor is at risk. Let us examine this passage in greater detail, since it would seem that kin actually challenge Jesus' honor.

The arrival of Jesus' mother and brothers occurs within a context of conflict and rejection in Matthew 12. Previously Jesus was engaged in bitter controversy with the Pharisees, who challenged him and attacked his honor (12:1–8, 9–14, 24). Immediately after this, Jesus speaks a series of parables which seem opaque even to his disciples. When these disciples draw him aside and ask why his speech is so parabolic, Jesus distinguishes between insiders and outsiders. To the insiders, who are designated as fictive kin (Pitt-Rivers 1968:408–13), it is given to know the secrets of the kingdom; but outsiders are not given to know the secrets of the kingdom of heaven (13:10–12). The context of Jesus' meeting with his blood relatives occurs between conflict and challenge by enemies (12:1–45) and contrast between insiders and outsiders (13:10–17). Thus, when his mother and brothers arrived, they "stood outside" (12:46), a small comment which suggests that they are not "insiders" and disciples who hear his words. This family, then, appears to lack typical family solidarity and unity; its honor and reputation are questionable.

As the episode unfolds, we learn that Jesus' family is not only "outside" but asking to speak to him. Nothing in the story suggests that there is an illness for which they are petitioning a cure or a crisis for which they are requesting assistance, as is the case in John 2:3. Moreover, the literary shape of the story focuses on the disciples, who are always gathered around Jesus and who listen to his teaching. In contrast, the blood relatives are obviously *not* gathered around him, but "outside"; they are here not to listen, but to speak, which is the more powerful and honorable role. Hence, the narrator would have us understand them as *not* part of the group of disciples who follow Jesus (Brown 1978:98–99). And so the evangelist's presentation of them in 12:46 should not be taken as "an ordinary event, the desire of his family to speak with him" (Hagner 1993:359). Although Malina suggested that honor is presumed to exist among blood relations, such may not be the case in this extraordinary episode.

In terms of its form, students of rhetoric label Matt. 12:46–50 as a responsive chreia (see Robbins 1989:171–77; 1992:35–37). The arrival of "his mother and brothers" who stand outside and ask to speak to Jesus (12:46) provides the provocation for Jesus' response. Thus we understand these relatives in some negative manner, perhaps simply as "outsiders," but maybe even as critics of what Jesus is doing (see Mark 3:21). His response to their provocative request begins with a question, which frequently functions in chreiai as an aggressive weapon: "Who is my mother, and who are my brothers?" The question reveals a crisis within Jesus' kin group. In such a situation, families tend to paper over their internal problems and thus keep up appearances before others. But here Jesus exacerbates the problem between himself and his family, which threatens their public reputation. Resorting to a comparison, he establishes a non-kinship criterion for family membership: "Whoever does the will of my Father in heaven is my brother, and sister, and mother" (12:50). He identifies with a "family," but not with the empirical group standing outside; he has a "Father" to whom he is duty bound to show loyalty, the kind of loyalty that is the stuff of later parables (21:28–31, 37). According to this new index of honor, he turns away from the blood relatives standing outside and toward the disciples inside: "And stretching out his hand toward his disciples, he said, 'Here are my mother and my brothers!'" (12:49). Thus, in terms of the form of a responsive chreia, Jesus is provoked by a demand from his blood relatives. Their request that he come out to them puts them in a challenging position which endangers Jesus' sense of duty to God.

The public exposure of strained family relationships challenges Jesus' honorable standing, since all sons should honor mother and father (15:4; 19:19). By declaring his duty to his Father in heaven, not his earthly kin, he thus compares and contrasts his blood relatives with his fictive kin. His clever speech fully satisfies the demand for answering an honor challenge. In fact, he has gained more respect by demonstrating that duty to his Father always motivates him. And if he seems to lose public respect because of strained family relationships, he gains that back and more by acquiring new fictive kin who benefit from private or insider access to his wisdom and teaching. Thus honor replicated in blood, which normally expresses itself in family solidarity and the performance of kinship duties, is manifested in this case through new kinship solidarity and loyalty to a Father in heaven. Nevertheless, even in its tortured way, the story attests to Jesus' honor by blood.

Several recent studies have examined the consistent polemic against kinship throughout all four Gospels (Barton 1994:1–22) and in particular against blood relationship to Jesus as a mark of honor (see John 1:11–13; 7:5). Barton's study of the conflict between kinship and discipleship surfaces many places in the narrative where family or blood ties are either strained or rejected: Matt. 4:18–22; 8:18–22; 10:16–23, 34–36, 37–38; 12:46–50; 13:53–58; 19:10–12, 27–30 (Barton 1994: 125–28). In the case of Jesus himself, Bauckham pointed out that early Christian sources reflect a conflict concerning role and status in the early church based on kinship to Jesus (Bauckham 1990:45–133). In the former case, a disciple appears to lose honor in the eyes of his neighbors by loyalty to Jesus, whereas in the latter instance people claim honor by virtue of blood ties to Jesus. In our examination of Matt. 12:46–50 we identify still a third case, where Jesus himself risks honor by estrangement from his family. These three types of conflict over kinship all attest that much is at stake either in losing kinship ties (Neyrey 1995:144–53) or in emphasizing them. Matthew's narrative argues that honor lost because of estranged kinship relationships is replaced and even augmented by new ties to Jesus. Even Jesus, who appears to suffer in public opinion for estrangement from "mother and brothers," gains more honor by demonstrating unique loyalty to his "Father in heaven." But whether the family is constituted of blood relations or fictive ones, honor is replicated by "blood" as kinship.

4.2 Honor and Name. In his study of the Middle East, Dale Eickelman describes four aspects of the names of individuals and what such names indicate about the persons holding them: (1) personal names, (2) nicknames, (3) names derived from occupation, origin, and affiliation, and (4) patrifiliative names or names embodying one's parents and clan (1989:181–87). His observations, which are based on contemporary Arab practices, provide a useful analytical scheme for studying and classifying names in the ancient world. In general, his analysis indicates that names generally link one to family and kinship group (i.e., ascribed honor) or reflect an individual's prowess or lack thereof (i.e., achieved honor).

1. Personal or "first" names can be drawn from a range of religious and secular sources. The personal name of the son of Zechariah and Elizabeth seemed unusual to their kinsfolk (Luke 1:59–63); the culture expected the child to be named after his father (Josephus, *Life* 1.4; *Ant.* 14.10; 20.197) or grandfather (Josephus, *Life* 1.4–5; 1 Macc. 2:1–2; *Jub.* 11:15).

2. People acquire nicknames for any number of reasons, such as distinctive physical characteristics. Josephus mentions the nickname of his grandfather Matthias as "Curtus," which means "humpback" (*Life* 1.4; see references to "Tiny" in Ezra 8:12 and "Baldy" in 2 Kings 25:23). Among Jesus' disciples, James and John are known as "Boanerges" or "Sons of thunder" (Mark 3:17) and Simon as "Rock Man" (Matt. 16:16–17); Jesus dined at the house of Simon "the Leper" (Matt. 26:6). Moreover, this type of naming was very common in the culture which produced the Hebrew scriptures (Abba 1962:504–5). Nicknames that convey neutral or positive images might be used when actually addressing a person face-to-face, whereas nicknames that label a person negatively tend to be used behind a person's back as attacks to their honor and status (see Malina and Neyrey 1988:35–54).

3. Names deriving from occupation, origin, and affiliation indicate that individuals draw their role and status from the local, popular evaluation of these. Paul claims significant social status by birth as a Roman citizen in Tarsus, "no low-status city" (Acts 21:39; 22:3), and his public career lets him reside in many of the truly honorable cities of the ancient world: Antioch, Ephesus, Athens, and Rome (see Neyrey 1996a:268–76). We do not know the precise value to ascribe to the place from which Simon of Cyrene comes (Matt. 27:32), much less the honor rating of Ethiopia, the home of the eunuch mentioned in Acts 8:27, or the various

worths of the places from which the Pentecost crowd came (Acts 2:9–11). Proper honor evaluation would depend upon the ancient stereotype of these places, which can be recovered in ancient rhetorical and physiognomic literature (Malina and Neyrey 1996:24–26, 113–24).

In regard to other aspects of names, Joseph and Jesus are both known in terms of their occupation name, "carpenter" (Matt. 13:55; Mark 6:3). John, son of Zechariah, becomes identified in terms of his social role, namely, "the Baptizer" (Matt. 3:1; 11:11–12; 14:2, 8). Among Jesus' disciples, Matthew is presented as "the Toll Collector" (Matt. 10:3). In terms of affiliation, Paul tells us that he was a "Pharisee," indeed, a Pharisee's Pharisee (Phil. 3:5–6). Some people have no personal identity except the name of the party to which they belong, such as Epicureans and Stoics (Acts 17:18). Whatever honor is ascribed from this type of name depends on the local evaluation of place, occupation, and affiliation.

4. Finally, patrifilial names stand out as most important for us because they directly indicate the ascribed honor which an individual enjoys relative to some family, clan, and tribe. After all, kinship was the most basic institution in antiquity (see 1 Sam. 9:1). For example, James and John are "sons of Zebedee" (Matt. 4:20) and Simon is "son of John" (Matt. 16:17). The personal name of Salome is much less important to history than her identification as Herod's wife's daughter; her legitimacy and status were called into question by John. All we need to know is told us when Matthew narrates that "the daughter of Herodias danced . . ." (Matt. 14:6).

When applied to Jesus, this material on names yields important results. In regard to personal names, God ascribed him his personal name, "Jesus" (Matt. 1:21). Although this name does not formally link him with his kinship group, such that he would automatically enjoy honor from that association, yet it describes in a general way his honorable role and status, which is to be "savior of his people." Many personal names in ancient Israel were theophoric names, that is, names in which some relationship to the Deity was claimed. For example, Zechariah means "Yahweh has remembered" and Gamaliel, "Recompense of God" (Pike 1992: 1018–19). "Jesus," which was not an uncommon name in the first century, simply meant "the salvation of the Lord," without any particular reference to the individual's actual social status. But in a useful discussion of just this name, Philo commented on the change of names of the great Joshua and noted that this figure, who was once called Hoshea ("he is saved"), received a change of names to Jesus (Ἰησοῦς), which in fact implied a new role and status, namely, "salvation from the Lord" (σωτηρία κυρίου, On the Change of Names 121). Thus Joshua's personal name, "Jesus," describes the role that he will play in mediating God's benefaction to his people. (On "Jesus" as a theophoric name, see Meier 1991:205–8.) Returning to Matthew, we appreciate that great honor is ascribed to the offspring of Joseph and Mary by virtue of his personal name; for in the context of the Gospel his name not only indicates favor from God, but also the significant role and status ascribed to him by God, namely, Savior.

We do not know of any nickname for Jesus, although his enemies attempted to stigmatize him with many negative labels. In terms of origin, occupation, and affiliation, Jesus "of Nazareth" who is the son of the carpenter carried negative honor status with some (see John 1:46; 7:52). Elites did not work, which immediately set them apart from the 90 percent of the population that labored for its daily bread. Working for wages rather than being master of one's own farm, however modest in size, indicated a still lower status (see Cicero, *On Duty* 1.42.150–51). Inasmuch as carpenters worked with their hands for wages, they would not enjoy a recognized status as artists. We would need more native informants among the ancient classes of artisans to tell us the relative status of carpenters, potters, weavers, tentmakers, and the like (on Paul as artisan, see Hock 1980:50–65). Needless to say, people would hardly credit a carpenter from a small village like Nazareth with much, if any, worth or status in virtue of his occupation or geographical origin.

The excavations at Sepphoris have reopened speculation on Jesus as a carpenter. Long ago, Case suggested that an underemployed artisan such as Jesus might well have been attracted to seek work in the construction of the great city of Sepphoris, which was but a few miles from Nazareth (Case 1927:199–212). This suggestion has been revised as a popular hypothesis to make Jesus more urbane and to expose him to the elite cultural life of Sepphoris (Buchanan 1964; Batey 1984a, 1984b). Yet a better social reconstruction of Jesus' status has been provided by Oakman. He examined all of the possibilities and noted that a "carpenter" might build more than yokes and plows and that Nazareth might be a village specializing in carpentry (1986:175–82). Oakman argues that given what we know of the economic plight of artisans and peasants in this period, it is likely that Jesus was an underemployed carpenter. Oakman, moreover, reminds us by way of a citation from Xenophon of this likelihood: "In small towns the same man makes couches, doors, ploughs, and tables, and often he even builds houses, and still he is thankful if only he can find enough work to support himself" (*Cyropaedia* 8.2.5, cited by Oakman 1986:178). If underemployed, then Jesus' migration in search of work would be quite plausible. But Oakman cautions us from crediting much status or the opportunity to move up in status to such a marginal figure.

When, however, we consider Jesus in terms of patrifilial names, Matthew records great worth and respect owed him. We cannot help but be awed by a composite list of all the predications of "son" ascribed to Jesus (Kingsbury 1975:40–83; 1977:34–54): (1) *Son of God* (Matt. 2:15; 3:17; 4:3, 6; 8:29; 11:27; 14:33; 16:16; 17:5; 27:40, 43, 54); (2) *Son of Abraham* (1:1); (3) *Son of David* (1:1; 9:27; 12:23; 15:22; 20:30, 31; 21:9, 15); and (4) *Son of Joseph* (13:55). Fully in accord with his culture, Matthew deems it essential for the proper honoring of Jesus that his readers know his "blood," that is, his rootedness in certain ancestral families. If these are noble and honorable, so will the latest offspring be. And who can top the family of Abraham and David, much less that of God?

Yet many other names are ascribed to Jesus in the course of the Gospel, which deserve consideration in terms of the honor they claim for Jesus: Christ, King of the Jews, Prophet, Teacher, and Lord. The piling on of names seems perfectly normal in regard to people of high status. For example, in a recent article on the monarch of Thailand, his formal titles were listed: "Great King of Siam, the Chief Protector, Great Strength of the Land, Incomparable Power, the Most Renowned of the Mahidol Family and Refuge of the People" (*New York Times*, Nov. 9, 1996, A4). A detailed commentary on Jesus' many names is not warranted. But what needs interpreting, however, is the extraordinary claims made about Jesus through them. Names such as "Son of God," "Son of David," and "Christ" would claim for him exceptional status and elite roles applicable to no one else in Israel. Not all labels or titles carry the same grant of honor; in fact, some are ascribed to Jesus sarcastically ("Teacher," 22:16). The name "Lord" (κύριος) varies in value; it might simply be the equivalent of "sir" or imply a much higher status. On occasion, other names become the subject of controversy, such as "Christ, Son of the Blessed" (26:63; 27:17, 22) and "King of the Jews" (27:11). But this controversy points to a debate whether Jesus deserves the honor, role, and status implied in them. The names are thus confirmed as exalted labels signifying extraordinarily high status. For Matthew and his audience, Jesus truly deserves to be called by these names, which is the point that this book has been arguing all along, namely, that the Gospel both in terms of genre and rhetorical function claims and acknowledges Jesus' great honor. We can never underestimate the significance that names play in the ascription and acknowledgment of honor, especially patrifilial or occupation-based names. Yet this examination of personal names hardly exhausts the way names suggest worth and status, and so we continue our study.

Agency, and thus special status and role, might be expressed by commanding "in the name of" so-and-so, a pattern clearly noted in Acts where Jesus' disciples cure in his name: "In the name of Jesus of Nazareth, walk" (Acts 3:6; see 4:30; 16:18). This expression encodes power, namely, that demons who cause illness and disease will be forced to surrender their conquest to a superior person represented by a name. Power, moreover, always expresses honor in the ancient world. Thus people boast of a special relationship to Jesus because they have shared his name and power: "Did we not prophesy in your name, and cast out demons in your name, and do many mighty works in your name?" (Matt. 7:22). The use of another's name in such a situation may be unauthorized, and thus constitute a challenge to the holder of the name. For example, Jesus predicts that "Many will come in my name, saying 'I am the Christ'" (24:5). In the world of limited good, the prestige and honor of the name holder would be diminished insofar as unauthorized persons take advantage of the other's name and power (see Acts 19:13–17). When disciples report to Jesus that an unauthorized person was "casting out demons in your name, and we forbade him, because he was not following us" (Mark 9:38//Luke 9:49–50), Jesus does not view this as an encroachment on his honor; rather, he interprets this as further broadcasting his name and thus adding to his reputation (9:39). But "coming in the name of" and "acting in the name of" both claim that honor resides in the person whose name is thus used.

The phenomenon of "being called by the name of so-and-so" deserves our attention. This might signal kinship, patronage, or even ownership, as in the case of Joab's urging of David to conquer Jerusalem lest it be named by the name of the general who captures it (2 Sam. 12:28; see Isa. 4:1). Matthew and Luke's usage of the phrase "baptized in the name of . . . " indicates membership in the circle of Jesus, which was thought of in terms of kinship or fictive family (Matt. 28:19; see

Acts 8:16; 10:48; 19:5). Disciples indeed bear the name of "Christian," and thus take honor from this association (Acts 11:26). It follows, then, that if the name of Jesus is held in great esteem, those who bear it will share in that honor; conversely, if disciples are "hated because of my name" (Matt. 10:22; 24:9), then the public dishonors both Jesus and his disciples, who bear his name. If worth comes from being named with an honorable name, shame derives from having one's name blotted out (2 Kings 14:27; Deut. 9:14; 29:20; Ps. 109:13), especially from the roll book where citizens' names are recorded (Rev. 3:5).

Finally, we mention how names might be treated, either in honor or shame. For instance, loyal clients of Israel's God learn to "sing praise to the name of the Lord" (Pss. 7:17; 9:2; 18:49), proclaim the name "majestic" (Ps. 8:1), "tell of thy name to my brethren" (Ps. 22:22), and the like (see Pss. 29:2; 34:3; 44:8). If confessing, praising, and magnifying God's "name" mean giving honor and glory to God himself, how shameful it is to forget the name of the Lord (Ps. 44:20). This helps us grasp what Jesus meant when he instructed his disciples in their prayer to say: "Hallowed be thy name" (Matt. 6:9). Whether we interpret this as asking God to vindicate his name or to cause mortals to honor his name (Betz 1995:389–90), the result will be that God receives what is God's due, namely, reverence, glory, praise, and honor.

5.0 Display of Honor

Inasmuch as honor consists of both claim to and acknowledgment of worth, "claims" often consist of public display of something worthy in accord with local expectations. We recall from the last chapter the anecdote from Plutarch which described a banquet as a "theatre and show" in which to display one's wealth and thus claim honor (*On Love of Wealth*, 528B). Furthermore, in the ancient world certain things were thought displayable and so evocative of praise, such as "wealth" and clothing. Moreover, one's physical body was on display, especially certain bodily parts. Let us now survey some of the local ways in which honor was displayed.

5.1 Honor and Wealth. Wealth is a relative term that applies both to the estates of the elites as well as to a peasant's modest holdings. In regard to Jesus, Matthew describes him as an artisan without land or wealth, but also as one who disparages wealth as a replication of honor. Contrary to conventional codes of honor, Jesus' own honor is not tied to wealth as a display of worthiness. Again contrary to conventional honor codes, Jesus declares honorable those who have forsworn wealth (19:27–29) or those who have lost wealth because of loyalty to him (5:3; Neyrey 1995:139–58). Thus Matthew records an ironic subversion of the code whereby honor is attached to *lack of wealth*, not its possession, use, and display. Let us look more closely at the narrative which contains references to wealth.

Matthew narrates that wise men brought "treasure" to Jesus, namely, "gold, frankincense, and myrrh" (2:11). Yet let us attend carefully to the social meaning of these gifts, for Matthew does not indicate that Jesus became rich as a result of these gifts. Modern scholars inform us that this treasure evokes Isa. 60:6 and

72:10–11 (Brown 1993:187–88), whereas patristic writers labored to find a sym-bolic meaning for each gift. But rarely is any attention paid to the social and cul-tural significance of these gifts. Davies and Allison, however, are pointing us in the right direction with their argument that all three gifts are uniquely associated with Solomon (1988:250–51). Inasmuch as the claim is made that Jesus is born "King of the Jews," we should understand the gifts of "gold, frankincense, and myrrh" as public acknowledgment by non-Judeans of his royal claims. Because only God could send a star to guide the wise men, it is God who makes the claim for Jesus. Since these gifts function to acknowledge the royal role and status of the baby Je-sus, honor comes to Jesus both by the acquisition of "wealth" itself and especially by the ritual acknowledgment of his worth that such wealth signifies: "They fell down and worshiped him" (2:11). However, this acknowledgment of Jesus' as-cribed honor is balanced in the narrative with rejection of the claim by Herod and the Jerusalem elite who were "troubled" at the announcement of his birth (2:3). Herod's plot to murder Jesus clearly demonstrates the depth of his rejection of Je-sus' ascribed honor and status as "King of the Jews" (2:2). Thus the narrative em-phasis does not intend us to honor Jesus for his wealth so much as to see the gifts of gold, frankincense, and myrrh as acknowledgment of Jesus' claims. Honor is at stake, but not honor replicated in wealth.

This one notice of Jesus receiving rich gifts stands in bold contrast to the re-mainder of Matthew's narrative where he and his disciples move in a world of ex-treme scarcity, hardly the stuff of honor claims. Yet the narrator records Jesus discoursing about royal wealth in his parables and maxims, indicating that he knows the local code. Jesus knows that "clothes make the man," and that those in "soft clothes" live in royal palaces (11:8; see Luke 7:25; Acts 12:21). Moreover, kings displayed their wealth at banquets, such as birthday celebrations. Despite Matthew's lack of detail about Herod's birthday celebration, readers know that on such occasions large numbers of high-status courtiers were fed rich foods as they reclined on fancy coverlets and were entertained by music and dancing (14:6). Jesus knows that weddings in particular become the occasion for families to parade their wealth for all to see: festive clothing, coverlets, eating utensils, music, food, and so on (Matt. 22:1–5, 11–12; 25:1–10); insufficiency of wine (John 2:1–11) or oil (Matt. 25:1–13) would bring shame upon the family. Jesus' parable of a king's wedding banquet for his son provides just such information about such feasts: the king invited only the elites of his realm to the wedding feast; some of his numer-ous slaves provided a feast of "oxen and fat calves" and others went to summon the guests (22:4). It appears that he also supplied "wedding garments" for the guests (22:11–12). All of this wealth stands on display to impress the royal guests and so to elicit acknowledgment of the monarch's excellence, worth, and honor. This is simply part of the landscape of Matthew's narrative; it is the knowledge of the general code that serves as a foil for Jesus' lack of wealth.

If we take literally Jesus' statement that the "Son of man has nowhere to lay his head" (8:20), then Matthew presents him as totally lacking in wealth. Jesus, a land-less artisan, does not live in the family house in Nazareth. His one return visit to his native village demonstrates his rejection by his own (13:53–58), confirming that he no longer had land, family home, or any possessions left there. Even by peasant standards, he has no wealth, much less a claim to honor in virtue of this separation from the family house. His disciples likewise lack wealth, having left "everything," that is, "houses . . . lands for my name's sake" (19:27, 29). Although they lose worth and status in the eyes of their families and neighbors, Jesus promises them vast wealth ("a hundredfold,"19:29), and great prestige ("twelve thrones, judging the twelve tribes," 19:28). Whatever loss of worth befalls a disciple because of Jesus, it will be reversed in God's new calculus, where "many that are first will be last, and the last first" (19:30). Thus two codes of the social meaning of wealth appear in Matthew: the general code of ancient society, which equated wealth with honor, and Jesus' variation on that code, which awarded honor to those who renounced wealth for Jesus' sake (yet see Schmidt 1987:121–34).

Matthew juxtaposes these two codes of wealth when he narrates a story in which disciples are contrasted with a rich man. Although all of the characters talk about wealth, the topic is honor, that is, respect in the eyes of others or of Jesus. A rich, young man asks Jesus, "What good deed must I do, to have eternal life?" (19:16). In his response, Jesus tells him that "perfection" or excellence lies in "selling what you possess and giving it to the poor . . . and following me" (19:21). Here we find our first clue that the story really pertains to honor. "Perfection" (τέλειος), while it reflects Judean purity concerns and so is often translated as "blameless" (Neyrey 1991a:284–85), also connotes what is excellent in the sense of something which is full-grown, authoritative, and perfect in its kind (LSJ 1769). Yarnold's suggestion that Jesus invites the "young" man to act as an adult male is not as unsubstantial a suggestion as he feared (1968:272–73). For by assuming adult responsibility to make important decisions for his family vis-à-vis the public world, this man would be most aware of the evaluation of his behavior by a public in accord with a code of honor. Jesus invites him to play the man in an unusual way and to assume a status higher than he currently enjoys: in being "perfect" he will be totally fulfilling Jesus' code of honor. Whether he receives praise or blame, then, depends on what he does with his wealth and whose code he follows. In whose eyes does he seek praise and respect?

The narrative describes him as rich, for "he had many possessions" (19:22). Such a "young" man could only have this wealth because of a recent inheritance; and his "possessions" most assuredly consist of the family lands. As Carney observed, "[B]asically land, not capital, was of critical importance in antiquity. The vast bulk of production was agricultural. . . . So power and wealth went with possession of land" (1975:181). From both Greek and Christian traditions we know of people selling the family lands and giving the money to the new group they had joined (Acts 4:36–37; 5:1), an action praised by some as a virtue (Sterling 1994). Yet the social implications of dispensing with one's patrimony was open to criticism, if not proscribed outright by Judean law (Lev. 25:23; 1 Kings 21:3; Henery 1954; Andersen 1966). The honor and well-being of the family was thereby endangered, because the sale of patrimonial land would mean that a man disposed of the material basis for the survival not only of his family but of its reputation among its neighbors. A husband and father who did this courted shame for not being a defender of his wife, children, and extended family. According to the local code, then, it would be shameful to sell the family land.

Furthermore, Jesus tells this rich young man to give the family wealth "to the poor" (Matt. 19:21). A man might play the patron to clients who would then support him in return (Luke 16:1–8); or a man might distribute wealth to kin who would then be obligated in honor to respond with comparable gifts (see Moxnes 1988:139–43). But to give the family wealth to strangers who can extend no reciprocal gifts to the giver makes no sense in the honor culture of antiquity; after all, "charity begins at home," because family honor is at stake. When others gain precisely because one's family loses, such dispossession would stretch the code of honor beyond recognition. Who would be so foolish as to choose shame for oneself and one's family? Yet that is what Jesus' remarks imply.

In this episode, then, Matthew presents Jesus reforming the general code of honor by offering his own reassessment of what gives a person worth and respect. Jesus labels as "perfection" the loss of wealth on his behalf which is then distributed to the poor outside of a patron-client or benefactor contract. The rich young man, then, is presented with two codes of honor: (1) the conventional code, in which honor is attached to wealth, and (2) the reformed code of Jesus, in which honor comes from voluntary loss of wealth. Both are "codes of honor," that is, sets of public expectations whereby significant others evaluate behavior and bestow respect or censure. What will the Joneses think? my family? my neighbors? Jesus? The choice of the rich young heir, then, makes cultural sense within the context of some code of honor—that of his society—but not that of Jesus. Matthew narrates that he chose the code of his village and family, thus forfeiting the respect and praise of Jesus.

In summary, Jesus himself does not claim honor and worth by virtue of wealth. The treasure given him by the Magi means their acknowledgment of the claims of his royal birth; but Jesus does not thereby become a rich peasant. In regard to the social location of Jesus, we reckon him as a landless artisan who worked for wages, who worked only when work could be found. As an artisan, he and his family apparently had no land, the basic constituent of wealth in antiquity. The fact that Jesus turns out to be so mobile in his part of Galilee further attests that he is landless; as he said, the Son of man truly has no place to lay his head. Thus no honor is claimed for Jesus by the evangelist in virtue of wealth. Moreover, in regard to Jesus' teaching, we clearly see how wealth signals social worth and status. Those who left wealth voluntarily or who were dispossessed of it for Jesus' sake suffer a terrible shame, not simply because they are poor as most people were in antiquity (Malina 1986c:148–59 and 1987:354–67), but in virtue of the social meaning of wealth, which is intimately tied to family status. Yet disciples who leave all for Jesus or who forfeit the pursuit of gaining the whole world are nevertheless "rich" in Jesus' sight by virtue of the grant of honor that he himself gives them.

5.2 Honor and Clothing.   Clothing is more than mere body covering to shelter it from heat or cold (Bonfante 1989:544). It serves as a display of worth and honor by signaling claims to a certain role and status. For example, observant

Jews wore tassels on their garments, as prescribed by Num. 15:37–41. As Milgrom notes, tassels merely accentuate the hem of a garment; "the more important the individual, the more elaborate and the more ornate was the embroidery on the hem of his or her outer robe. The tassel must be understood as an extension of such a hem" (1983:61). Hence, when Jesus criticizes the Pharisees for making their "fringes long" (23:5), he challenges their honor claim to special status by display of wide borders on their garments and additional tassels (Nestle 1908). Jesus himself wears a garment with tassels (9:20), which people sought to touch for the sake of healing (14:36); but presumably its border and tassels were within the social expectations of a person with his penurious status. Israelites likewise were instructed in the Law to wear phylacteries to signal their public observance of Torah and thus their adherence to the local code of walking in the way of the Lord (Deut. 6:8; 11:18; Ex. 13:9, 16). Again, Jesus criticizes excess in the size of phylacteries, which he interprets as a claim to undeserved honor and respect (23:5). Yet fringe, tassels, and phylacteries all signal to the public claims to status and worth (Tigay 1979; on phylacteries as amulets against evil spirits, see Bowman 1959). Conversely, prophets like John the Baptizer identify their roles on the margins of society by wearing garments of skin, not cloth woven in households and thus appropriately tithed (Mark 1:6; see Heb. 11:37–38). Inasmuch as his garment is identified with that of classical prophets (Zech. 13:4), it signals a social role as well. Those who preached repentance might dress in sackcloth (Rev. 11:3), as well as those who sought repentance (Matt. 11:21), whereas wedding guests are identified as those wearing "a wedding garment" (Matt. 22:11–12).

With this important background, let us turn to Matthew and assess what honor is displayed and claimed for Jesus by his clothing. From his baptism to his arrest, we find only three mentions of Jesus' clothing. In two instances, Matthew merely says that people who touched the hem or fringe of his garment were healed (9:20; 14:36), which appears to be the ordinary and typical clothing of an artisan. Yet at the theophany on the mountain (17:1–8), Jesus' clothing was metamorphosed and became "white as light" (17:2). The emphasis rests not on the cut or quality of the clothing, but on its color. Evidence of elite clothing from carvings as well as literary sources suggests that impressive clothing was multicolored, especially purple (Reinhold 1970:7–61; Danker 1992:557–60). The priestly robes of the Judean temple were dyed in hues of blue, purple, and scarlet. Given the evidence we have for the ostentation and luxury signaled by multicolored Oriental fabrics and designs, a "white" robe appears to be very unusual, inviting us to consider a different set of symbols and claims operative here. With a few exceptions, the Hebrew scriptures are not particularly helpful. Fine (white?) linen clothing was worn by singers in Solomon's temple (2 Chron. 5:12), and festive garments might well be white (Qoh. 9:8); but "white" garments seem to signal the heavenly world of complete purity. The ancient of days is seated on his throne in "raiment white as snow" (Dan. 7:9). Angelic messengers from the sky world are generally clad in "white" garments (Matt. 28:3; Mark 16:5; John 20:12; Acts 1:10). The elders seated round the throne of God (Rev. 4:4), the martyrs raised to heaven (Rev. 6:11; 7:9, 13), as well as the heavenly army (Rev. 19:14), are all clothed in white. In one place where earthly riches are condemned, the heavenly Jesus tells the church of Laodicea to buy from him "white garments" (Rev. 3:18), apparently in contrast to the multicolored garments so popular with ostentatious elites. Similarly, white garments are "pure," not soiled, and thus reflect righteousness (Rev. 3:4–5). This material suggests that Jesus' white garments associate him with the heavenly, not earthly world. Moreover, the "whiteness" of his clothing is a benefaction from God, thus signaling divine acknowledgment of Jesus' achievement or virtuous behavior. His white clothing, then, should not be seen in terms of the typical ostentation of dazzling clothing expected of honor-seeking elites. Rather, it signals divine favor and public acknowledgment of Jesus' extraordinary loyalty and righteousness, and thus divine honoring of this "beloved son." By virtue of his "white clothing," Jesus should rightly be associated with the heavenly world of angels, elders, faithful martyrs, and God.

As well as Matthew reflects the conventional association of honor with special clothing, he similarly links shame with poor clothing and nudity. Jesus states the obvious when he remarks that "those who wear soft raiment live in kings' houses" (11:8; see Acts 12:21). The disciples of Jesus who travel about as his agents go dressed in ordinary clothing. Apart from any association of Jesus' travel instructions with the Cynics, a person with but one tunic (10:10) will clearly not be an elite nor be treated as one. These disciples do not present themselves as artisans or any of the social class of people who work for pay, including "philosophers" (Hock 1980:52–59): "You received without paying, give without pay" (10:8). They are what they appear to be: radical non-elites, a status signaled by ordinary peasant clothing as well as lack of supplies and resources. Other disciples are told that should they be robbed of "coat," they should surrender "cloak" as well (5:40). The clothing here seems quite ordinary; but the thrust of the remark rests on the shame which results both from not defending oneself against the challenge of a thief and from the subsequent nudity that will result from the loss of all clothing. Finally, in the parable of the sheep and the goats, Jesus describes how people either did or did not clothe the naked (25:36, 38, 43–44). The casual mention that people go about naked seems striking, for it would indicate widespread loss of subsistence, which constituted the basis of any worth and honor for peasants. The association of the naked with the sick, the hungry and thirsty, the stranger, and the prisoner eloquently describes the bottom of the social ladder in antiquity, namely, the expendables and untouchables who live outside cities and towns and beg (Rohrbaugh 1993a:114–27; 1993b:380–95). Their lack of clothing signals their total lack of social worth.

Finally, Matthew will present Jesus both clothed and naked in the Passion narrative. Because we will examine this material in detail in our treatment of the shame of Jesus' death, we simply mention the following points. The victims of scourging were probably nude (27:26), and this involuntary loss of clothing would be experienced and interpreted as deeply shameful. The scarlet robe put on Jesus belongs to the category of shame, for it is part of a mock investiture of him as a powerless king (27:28–31), as the soldiers mock his claims to the role and status of King of the Jews. At his crucifixion, we are told that his executioners "divided his garments" (27:36), suggesting that he was crucified nude, which only added to the shame.

Thus in terms of clothing, as was the case with wealth, the evangelist makes no particular claim to worth and respect on behalf of Jesus. Everything said about Jesus describes him as an artisan of very modest means. Jesus, moreover, appears to know about the honor claims that elites make by means of their ostentatious clothing, but neither he nor his disciples participate in that game. On the contrary, more is said about the shame of loss of clothing and involuntary nudity than about honor.

5.3 Honor and Physical Body. Bruce Malina described the physical body as a "social road map [which is] most often condensed and expressed in somewhat compact symbolic form in one's physical person" (1993:39). By this he expresses how all peoples understand the body as a social construct, that is, how they impose meaning and significance on various parts of the human body in accord with their values and their social systems. In general, people with a strong sense of honor and shame tend to give special symbolic value to certain parts of the male body: (1) head and face, (2) arm and hand, and (3) penis and testicles. Thus we will consider what sort of evaluation is given to particular bodily parts and what sorts of treatment of those indicate either respect or disrespect to the person whose body is so treated.

In terms of honor and bodily parts, Malina provided a special description of the head and face as it replicates social honor: "The head and front of the head (face) play prominent roles" (1993:40). "Heads" are ranked first, as in the "head of the table" or the "head of an organization," a generalization easily illustrated by Philo's celebration of the head of the body (*Special Laws* 3.184). Schlier's study of "head" surfaced four meanings that embody a sense of honor: "head" may mean (1) beginning or end, which are the prominent positions in any enumeration system; (2) prominent, outstanding, or determinative; (3) the part that stands for the whole, its public representative; and (4) the head of society (1965:673–77). Schlier himself did not evaluate his data in terms of the ancient value of honor, but his article provides us with numerous illustrations of it. Honor, then, resides in the head by virtue of its "high position" and its role and status as ruler (see Grudem 1985; Fitzmyer 1989). "Honor and shame," Malina observes, "are displayed when the head is crowned, anointed, touched, covered, uncovered, made bare by shaving, cut off, struck, or slapped" (1993:40). Likewise, the "face" is the locus of awareness, and so insults must be performed before the eyes of and in the hearing of those challenged, thus giving an "affront."

The honor of the head, moreover, can be more closely specified with the face and especially the eyes. In the previous chapter, we stressed that the ancients were most careful of their public behavior, for honor claims and challenges must take place in a face-to-face environment. Eyes serve as critical lights turned on the behavior of others; thus the all-seeing God knows the recesses of the human heart and nothing escapes the divine sovereignty. Cohen (1991:54–60) describes this as the "court of reputation," which evaluates an individual's behavior. But one's eyes can be forced to see shameful things, such as the torture and death of one's children and wife. Moreover, no insult or challenge need be taken note of unless it occurs before one's very eyes.

Male honor was also thought to be symbolized by the male sexual organs, the penis and testicles. According to popular notions of biology at the time, all potency or life-giving material was provided by the male. Hence, by insemination a male had the power to produce life and to extend his person in time and space. Not for nothing are the testicles called the family "jewels" in popular lore. Ezekiel was told a story about two women who proved "shameless"; one of them had paramours whose "members were like those of asses, and whose issue was like that of horses" (23:20); euphemism glossed over the literal description of the penises of these paramours, which states that they were "hung like an Egyptian horse" (Ullendorf 1979:439). Oaths, moreover, were often taken by "grasping [the] testicles and penis" (Malul 1985, 1987), thus the oath was all the more important as it was sworn on something sacred.

With this summary grammar of body as symbol of honor, we turn to Matthew's narrative. The presentation of Jesus' body is invariably honorable until the start of his passion. Until then, the bodily posture of others in relation to Jesus indicates his worth and honor. For example, John the Baptizer declares him honorable by saying that he is "not worthy to carry his sandals" (3:11), indicating that even Jesus' feet are most honorable. People frequently "fall at his feet" and give him homage (προσκυνέω): the Magi (2:11), lepers (8:2), officials (9:18), and other suppliants (15:25; 20:20). Even if they only "bend the knee" before Jesus (γονυπετέω, 17:14), their bodily posture honors Jesus. He remains standing, while they lower themselves before him, thus acknowledging his honorable role and status.

Jesus' own bodily parts are presented as honorable. His hands, for example, contain power and thus symbolize his worth. He merely "touches" and conveys the benefaction of healing (Matt. 8:3; 9:29; 20:34); at other times he "lays his hands on" those who are ill and they recover (9:18) or are blessed (19:13, 15). Suppliants ask to sit at his right hand, the place of power, resources, and status (20:21), while he himself will sit at the right hand of God (see 22:44; 26:64). Moving still higher up his anatomy, his face once shone like the sun (17:2) because of God's blessing, which thus signaled his special relationship to the Deity and so great honor. Finally, a devotee pours costly oil on his head (26:7), a universal mark of respect.

His body, however, was also shamed. His enemies seize him, "laying their hands on him" and thus restricting his power (26:50). Roman soldiers flog his body, and it is only our piety that does not allow us to imagine that they flogged his legs, thighs, and buttocks as well as his back. Humiliation and shame in this situation hurt worse than the physical pain. As regards his most honorable members, some enemies spit in his face, struck it, and slapped it (26:67), thus giving an "affront" to him. Roman soldiers repeat the same insult (27:30) to his face and head, as they mock him by putting on his head a play crown and making sarcastic gestures of obedience to him (27:29). Thus the evangelist indicates how dishonorably Jesus was treated by many people. It remains to be seen how the evangelist treated these shaming actions.

Matthew records many statements by Jesus which have to do with honor and shame and the physical body. Most significantly, Jesus tells those who are insulted by being "slapped on the right cheek" to turn the other as well (5:39). (We will have much more to say about this in a later chapter, where we examine Jesus' reform of the local honor code.) On two other occasions Matthew records Jesus telling disciples to cut off a significant member of the body to save the whole. "If your right eye causes you to sin . . ." (5:29); as we saw above, the head and face are the repository of a person's honor; yet the honorable thing to do in certain cases is to dishonor one's body, especially its favored parts. "If your right hand causes you to sin . . ." (5:30), and the right hand is deemed honorable both because it is the "right," not the left hand, and because it is the weapon- or power-wielding arm. These remarks come in the midst of Jesus' demand that disciples refrain not only from actual adultery but lust of the eye as well (5:27–28) and from divorce and remarriage (5:31–32). Is it too much of a stretch of imagination that the truly significant bodily member to be cut off is the penis, which engages in this seductive, but honor-gaining behavior?

In another situation, Jesus comments about those who have lost honor because of their eunuch status (19:10–12). After Jesus proscribes all divorce, some male disciples lament, saying, "It is not expedient to marry" (19:10), that is, no honor can be claimed by enjoying the exclusive sexual rights to a female and the offspring that marriage brings. Jesus says that there are three classes of eunuchs, those born without male honor, those who have been deprived of this honor by others, and those who voluntarily do this to themselves (19:12). It has been argued by some that in regard to the third category Jesus refers to those who do not marry again after divorce; and so, these "eunuchs" probably refer to the few disciples who take to heart Jesus' prohibition of divorce. Thus to the public, such a man has become a eunuch, with consequent loss of honor (Malina and Rohrbaugh 1992:122). And so there exists a strain in Jesus' remarks that requires disciples to experience dishonor in their physical bodies and through bodily gestures and behaviors that all observers would appreciate as shameful according to the local code: slapped cheek, plucked right eye, severed right hand, severed penis, and castration. Finally, although neither Jesus nor Matthew comments on the death of John the Baptizer, decapitation must surely rank as an extraordinary dishonor; moreover, it was instigated by the wiles of a woman (see Mark 6:25–28).

6.0 Summary and Conclusions

If successful, this chapter has done two complementary things. The cultural model of honor and shame has allowed us to surface a wide assortment of data which take on fresh and culturally correct meaning when understood in the light of this pivotal value of the ancient world. In turn, the presence of these data and their proper interpretation serve to confirm the accuracy and utility of the cultural model. As Bruce Malina has pointed out, this is the typical reasoning process used by most people, which is not simply inductive or deductive, but "abductive" (1991a). From the application of the cultural model of honor and shame, we advance the argument that Matthew indeed presents Jesus as a most honorable person. He enjoys great ascribed and achieved honor. He acts fully within the general code in both claiming his rightful place in society and defending himself when challenged. We will have ample opportunity in the next section of this book to investigate in great detail the grounds for praise and respect which were articulated in the rhetoric of praise and blame. But here we simply note that if Jesus indeed is a most prominent and honorable man, this warrants praise from his disciples. And, we add, the praise of Jesus of Nazareth is one of the rhetorical aims of the Gospel of Matthew.

Many of Jesus' remarks reflect the prevailing appreciation of honor displayed and manifested. But once we are attuned to this cultural value system, it is significant to begin to note when and how Jesus honors those whom his culture dishonors. Only with a proper understanding of the cultural value given to objects and behaviors can we fully appreciate how radical Jesus appears in challenging the prevailing code of worth and value. Yet, for all his reform and challenge of the general code, he does not appear to be overthrowing the system itself, but rather to be articulating a new set of value expectations, on the basis of which he awards praise. Nevertheless, conformity to some set of public expectations remains the chief source of respect and praise for his disciples.

Part Two

Matthew and the Rhetoric of Praise

3

The Rhetoric of
Praise and Blame

1.0 Introduction

In the first part of this book we presented a model of honor and shame which consists of a composite of elements drawn from various contemporary studies of honor. That model is a modern, scientific synthesis of honor based on field studies by anthropologists; in the jargon of the social sciences, it is an "etic" model, that is, a scientific interpretation by a trained anthropologist of data gathered directly from villages and towns (Harris 1976; Elliott 1993:38–40). Etic models such as honor and shame are based on detailed field work gleaned from both the meanings given to the scientist by local informants and the anthropologist's own scientific study. We turn now to an "emic" model of honor and shame, that is, the analysis and interpretation of this value by the very inhabitants of the ancient world. In the long tradition of classical rhetoric which goes back to Aristotle and beyond we find a species of rhetoric labeled "epideictic" or the rhetoric of "praise and blame." As we shall see, the rhetoric of "praise and blame" is the native, or emic, description of the etic phenomenon called "honor and shame." In epideictic rhetoric, then, we expect to find definitions of honor and shame, criteria for awarding them, and indices of the display or acknowledgment of them. We turn now to a select group of native informants from the ancient world who can tell us about the rhetoric of praise and blame.

In the ancient world we encounter many types of native informants about "praise and blame." Some merely repeat anecdotal materials about "praise and blame" in their native reports of events. Others, however, provide a more elaborate interpretation of the material because they formally discuss "praise and blame" in terms of the values, institutions, and behaviors of their culture. We favor these latter informants now, because not only do they provide information about this or that aspect of "praise and blame," but they take the next step of delivering some sort of systematic explanation of the material. Thus we focus on the ancient rhetoricians who discussed the rhetoric of "praise and blame." We will examine two groups of them, rhetorical theorists such as Aristotle and Quintilian, and educational instructors of young students who wrote learning handbooks called the *progymnasmata*. Aristotle and Quintilian both formally discourse on epideictic rhetoric, and represent the common tradition of the topic from 350 B.C.E. Greece and 100 C.E. Rome.

The educational authors of the *progymnasmata*, on the other hand, instruct young would-be orators how to write encomia, which are speeches that praise someone. These handbooks both synthesize the criteria for honor from common usage and instruct orators on the conventional ways of praising their subjects. Space does not allow us to survey other authors on rhetoric, such as the author of *Rhetoric to Herennius* and Cicero; but those writers would only confirm the clear understanding of epideictic rhetoric found both in Aristotle and Quintilian and the educational handbooks called the *progymnasmata*.

When we speak of the rhetoric of praise and blame, we refer to the way Greeks and Romans continually expressed value judgments on certain persons and their actions by use of the correlative pair of words, "praise and blame" (either καλός/αἰσχρός, ἔπαινος/ψόγος-ψεκτός, ἔπαινος/αἴτιος or *laus/vituperatio*). The ancient rhetoricians codified the popular understandings of praise and blame. They both gave clear descriptive definitions of these values and listed rules for apportioning them. In short, the rhetoricians articulated for their world the general code of honor which was learned by students and practiced by all. Hence, they make excellent native informants on the topic. Modern discussions of the rhetoric of praise and blame include Burgess 1902; Lausberg 1973:55–56, 129–38; Martin 1974:177–210; and Lee 1986:82–99, 178–203.

We are studying the rhetoric of praise and blame for several reasons. First, the ancient authors of rhetorical treatises can serve as excellent native informants on the topic and provide us with an emic understanding of the material. This in turn will allow us to discover the validity of the etic, or anthropological, model of honor and shame, either confirming it or causing us to adjust it to the world of antiquity. More importantly, the rules for an encomium will then serve as the emic, or native, lens for reading Matthew's Gospel and his praise of Jesus of Nazareth. The hypothesis for the next four chapters is simply this: we argue that Matthew tells the story of Jesus both in praise of him and fully in accord with the formal criteria of praise found in typical encomia. Ancient rhetoric of praise and blame, then, becomes the immediate lens for reading Matthew.

2.0 Epideictic Rhetoric: The Rhetoric of "Praise and Blame"

Epideictic rhetoric provides the most important rhetorical resource for learning about "praise and blame" in antiquity. The rhetoric of praise and blame, moreover, expresses fully what we mean by "honor and shame." Fortunately we have many reliable native informants from antiquity: Aristotle, Cicero, Quintilian, and the author of *Rhetoric to Herennius* reflect for us the current, but consistent, conventions of ancient society on the topic. Because of the conventionality of the topic, it is not necessary to examine all of these authors; so we will look closely at Aristotle and Quintilian as our best examples.

Epideictic rhetoric or the rhetoric of praise and blame is one of the three species of public discourse in antiquity. The ancients distinguished three types of rhetoric in terms of their audience and purpose: judicial (δικανικόν) rhetoric dealt with the law court; deliberative (συμβουλευτικόν) rhetoric treated laws to be enacted or rejected; and epideictic (ἐπιδεικτικόν) rhetoric focused on the praise or censure of someone. Figure 3.1 schematizes Aristotle's classification of the three types (*Rhet.* 1.3.3).

Species	Time Reference	Goal	Approaches
Deliberative	future	advantageous harmful	exhortation (προτροπή) dissuasion (ἀποτροπή)
Judicial	past	just unjust	accusation (κατηγορία) defense (ἀπολογία)
Epideictic	present	honorable shameful	praise (ἔπαινος) blame (ψόγος)

Figure 3.1 The Three Types of Rhetoric (Aristotle)

Many centuries later, Cicero distinguished these three species in such a traditional way that we can see how conventional rhetoric had become, that is, how consistent and unchanging the tradition was: "There are three kinds of speeches on special subjects: the judicial, the deliberative, and the encomiastic. . . . The end of the judicial speech is justice, from which it also derives its name. . . . The end of deliberative speech is advantage. . . . The end of an encomiastic speech is honour" (*Topica* 24.91; see Quintilian, *Inst. Orat.* 3.4.9). Our interest lies in epideictic rhetoric, the rhetoric of praise and blame.

2.1 Aristotle, On Rhetoric. Aristotle provided the first systematization of rhetorical theory in antiquity. His reporting on what was commonly practiced in Greece and his exacting classification of the elements of rhetoric in turn became the tradition that carried on for centuries. Thus it is worth our while to examine his analysis of the rhetoric of praise and blame. Aristotle distinguished two kinds of proofs. One type of proof consists of data drawn from documents, witnesses, and so forth, which can be brought into court, whereas the other type of proof must be "invented" by the cleverness of the speaker (*Rhet.* 1.2.2). Arguments in the rhetoric of praise and blame are of the latter sort, that is, evaluations of persons which are the product of the descriptive art of the orator. Later Aristotle's treatment of praise and blame begins with mention of "virtue and vice and honorable and shameful" (1.9.1). And so, the rhetoric of praise and blame tends to focus on four areas: (1) character, (2) general notions of "virtue" (or excellence), (3) manifestations and signs of virtue, and (4) audience-specific criteria for virtue. The task of the speaker is to present someone as a "worthy" character in the public's eyes. We will now examine each of these four areas to see what Aristotle has to say about them in regard to praise and blame.

2.1.1 Praise and Character. Most speeches draw persuasive arguments from character (ἦθος), line of reasoning (λόγος), or emotion raised in the audience (πάθος). But the rhetoric of praise focuses on *character*, which is shown to be either virtuous and thus honorable, or vicious and thus shameful. Aristotle says it well: "We shall also make clear those things from which we [as speakers] shall be regarded as persons of a *certain quality in character* . . . from the same sources we shall be able to make both ourselves and any other person worthy of credence in regard to *virtue* (*Rhet.* 1.9.1; emphasis added).

2.1.2 Praise and Virtue. What makes a person "worthy" and deserving of praise is what the ancients considered "honorable" or "noble" (καλός). Someone is honorable or noble who can be shown to be "good" (*Rhet.* 1.9.3), and goodness resides in actions which reflect "virtue" or "excellence" (1.9.4). Recall that according to the cultural model of honor one *achieved* worth by prowess, that is, by actions which display superiority or uniqueness or excellence. What the ancients called "virtuous" might be confusing, since we think immediately of moral qualities, whereas for them "virtue" (ἀρετή) meant something different.

What, then, did "virtue" mean? The Greek term "virtue" (ἀρετή) generally meant "eminence" or "excellence" and referred to outstanding achievements in military, political, athletic, and artistic fields (Bauernfeind 1964:458). Enormous wealth and extensive, fertile lands could make a man "outstanding"; and generous benefaction to the city could manifest a sort of "excellence" or virtue (Adkins 1960b:30–37). The Greek term for "virtue" (ἀρετή) derives from the same root from which come words such as ἄριστος, that is, "the best," and hence "aristocrats," the best people (Benveniste 1969:304). We might simply define it as "success" in the social games valued and played by Greek heroes. Thus a speaker will "invent" praise for someone primarily from the actions which the culture designates as "virtuous," that is, excellent and outstanding according to its native code (*Rhet.* 1.9.30). On occasion the ancients evaluated certain characteristics as "outstanding" that truly skirt the edges of morality as we define it in regard to deviousness, lying, and cleverness. One thinks of Odysseus (Malherbe 1983:153; Stanford 1964:72–80, 98–101). In Quintilian's celebrated description of the "good man," he allows for this excellent and praiseworthy paragon of worth to conceal the truth from a judge and to tell lies (*Inst. Orat.* 12.1.36, 38; see Gilsenan 1976). "Virtue," then, is not synonymous with morality. According to Adkins, it is often linked with competitive display in an agonistic context: "[ἀρετή] denotes and commends the qualities which a man or a god needs to defend his *moira* and *time*, and if possible, acquire more. *Arete* is very competitive, and draws a god or a man anywhere on the scale of *arete* and *time* to rise higher" (1985:49).

2.1.3 Praise and Manifestations of Virtue. What is included under the term "virtue"? Aristotle lists the parts of virtue or "excellence," some of which we are familiar with, for instance, the four cardinal virtues (justice, courage, self-control, wisdom). Others less recognized are magnificence, magnanimity, liberality, gentleness, and prudence (*Rhet.* 1.9.5). Under the category of "virtue" Aristotle lists the general ways in which men achieved excellence in the eyes of their peers, and so his list of "virtues" serves as a valuable index of what was praiseworthy in his time. In regard to these "virtues," Adkins observes that Greek notions of "virtue" developed from the warrior excellences found in Homer to the cooperative excellences needed in a democratic city-state (1960b:37, 156–63, 176–79). It is precisely in Aristotle's list of excellences that we begin to learn the native content of what was praiseworthy.

Let us allow Aristotle to tell us what he means by these excellences (see fig. 3.2).

> *Liberality* [ἐλευθεριότης], for the liberal make contributions freely and do not quarrel about the money, which others care most about.
>
> *Justice* [δικαιοσύνη] is the excellence by which all, individually, have what is due to them and not as the law requires; and injustice [is a vice] by which they have what belongs to others and not as the law requires.
>
> *Manly courage* [ἀνδρεία] [is an excellence] by which people perform fine actions in times of danger and as the law orders and obedience to the law, and cowardice is the opposite.
>
> *Self-control* [σωφροσύνη] is the excellence through which people behave as the law orders in regard to the pleasures of the body, and lack of control [is] the opposite.
>
> *Magnanimity* [μεγαλοψυχία] is an excellence productive of great benefits [for others].
>
> *Magnificence* [μεγαλοπρέπεια] is an excellence in expenditures, productive of something great, while little-mindedness [μικροψυχία] and stinginess [μικροπρέπεια] are the opposites.
>
> *Prudence* [φρόνησις] is an excellence of intelligence whereby people are able to plan for happiness in regard to the good and bad things mentioned earlier (*Rhet.* 1.9.5–13).

Figure 3.2 Aristotle's List of Excellences

We know that we are in a different cultural world with Aristotle's list of excellences. Virtues such as liberality and magnificence are generally considered as marks of vulgar ostentation in our world. But in Aristotle's world of honor and shame, it was eminently praiseworthy to act the part of benefactor and to engage in conspicuous consumption (see Kautsky 1982:187–95). Public display was part of being "outstanding." Moreover, we should not be too quick to apply the moral assumptions of our culture to virtues such as courage, justice, and self-control.

Aristotle's generic notion of "excellence" becomes more specific when he talks about the "works" and "signs" of excellence and the things which are popularly recognized as honorable. Here we find a precise list of criteria according to which an action was popularly evaluated as virtuous and thus awarded honor. At this point we are truly touching the specific and historical marks of what the ancients considered honorable. He considers an action excellent or "virtuous" if: (1) it occasioned rewards of respect rather than of money; (2) it was done voluntarily, but not in a self-serving manner; (3) it benefited one's country, while overlooking one's self-interest; (4) it was done for its own sake, not for any personal advantage; and

(5) it was done on behalf of others (*Rhet.* 1.9.16–19). In short, actions are virtuous and praiseworthy which are voluntary and not coerced (i.e., acts of free persons, not slaves), and which benefit others, but not oneself. Here are the specific marks of excellence that constitute the basis for praise in classical Greek thought.

Aristotle refines his criteria for "virtue" later in his *Rhetoric*. One can argue more persuasively that a person is worthy of praise if: (1) he is the only one, or the first one, or one of few, or the one who has most done some deed; (2) his actions surpass expectations; (3) his actions did not result from chance; (4) because of him rewards and honors were established; (5) he was the first one to receive an encomium; and (6) statues of him are set up in the marketplace (*Rhet.* 1.9.38). Thus we see that the qualities of "excellence" as the ancient Greeks understood them refer to being unique or "outstanding": "the only one, or first one, or one of few" to do a public action. "Excellence" entails being publicly acknowledged as outstanding by "public honors," "statues," and the like. It means stepping apart from the crowd by "surpassing expectations." Thus excellence or virtue is a social convention which identifies what a particular group considers noble and praiseworthy.

2.1.4 Praise and Audience-Specific Materials. Aristotle is aware that praise must also be audience-specific and audience-sensitive. What is deemed valuable and praiseworthy differs from nation to nation and place to place: "One should speak of whatever is honored among each people as actually existing [in the subject praised], for example, among the Scythians or Laconians or philosophers" (1.9.30). Even the ancients recognized differences between lands and customs. Since specific peoples and the regions in which they live have distinctive characteristics which can be the subject of praise, it behooves a speaker to know appropriate ethnic and geographic stereotypes (see Malina and Neyrey 1996:113–23).

2.2 Quintilian. Aristotle's explanation of epideictic rhetoric was constrained by political circumstances. Athenian courts and assemblies were vigorous institutions requiring judicial and deliberative rhetorical speeches, respectively. As long as such institutions remained vital, they determined which forms of rhetoric were most valuable and so most discussed and most developed. With the rise of Rome's empire, political decision making moved from the local assemblies to Caesar's palace. A decline in the need for deliberative rhetoric followed. In the changed political circumstances, it was politically safer to speak in praise of others, with the result that the rhetoric of praise and blame rapidly developed in the field of oratory and rhetoric. Political and social events, then, influenced the maturation of the rhetoric of praise and blame. And so we turn to the first-century rhetorician Quintilian, a product of this development, for a supplementary look at epideictic rhetoric in a time period roughly contemporary with Matthew, the author of the Gospel.

Quintilian's *Institutio Oratoria* follows Aristotle's assertion that the objects of praise are persons, either "gods" or "men" (3.7.6). In praising the gods, he instructs us to laud them on three points. First, one expresses in general terms veneration "for the majesty of their nature." Then in specific ways one praises their unique powers and benefactions to the human race (3.7.7). One might praise

Jupiter's power of governance of all things, Mars's power in war, Neptune's power over the sea. As regards benefits to humanity, one might extol Minerva's discovery of the arts, Mercury's patronage of letters, Apollo and medicine, and Ceres and the fruits of the earth (3.7.8). Third, one celebrates their exploits. Quintilian indicates that "exploits" may refer to their birth or their actions. "Even the gods may derive honor from their descent" (3.7.8). One praises the sons of Jupiter for being the offspring of the high god; or the children of Chaos, for their great antiquity; or Latona, for the noble children, Apollo and Diana, whom she sired. In regard to actions, while some gods were born immortal, others won immortality by their virtue (3.7.9). Thus orators "invented" praise from nature, power, benefaction, heroic deeds, as well as from antiquity and family. Quintilian's criteria for praise, moreover, hardly differ from those found in Aristotle.

Concerning praise of men, Quintilian organizes his remarks chronologically according to the time before birth, during life, and after death. "Time before birth" refers to one's parents and ancestors. Aristotle had noted that we draw praise from "good birth and education; for it is probable that good children are born from good parents and that a person who is well brought up has a certain character" (*Rhet.* 1.9.33). Quintilian, while he admits that great variety is required in praise of men (3.7.10), follows rather traditional commonplaces in enumerating topics for praise. For example, in regard to things preceding a man's birth, he identifies "country, parents and ancestors" (3.7.10) as topics under the heading of "time before birth." It will be praiseworthy if a man has not fallen short of the noble fame of his country and ancestors or if he ennobled his humble origins with glorious achievements. Omens and prophecies foretelling future greatness were also sources of praise (3.7.11; see Talbert 1980).

Under the heading of "during life," individuals derive praise from their own lives. One's "character, physical endowments and external advantages" (3.7.12) were fitting subjects for praise. For example, in regard to the physical body, one extols "beauty and strength in honorific terms" (3.7.12). Concerning "fortune," kings and princes are fortunate for the opportunity to display their prowess. About "external and accidental circumstances," one should notice "wealth, power and influence" (3.7.14). Quintilian presumes, moreover, a commonly shared understanding of these items, namely, a stereotype of what his culture expects.

Praise of individuals according to their character may be developed in two ways, one strictly chronological and the other thematic. Chronological arrangement consists in tracing "a man's life and deeds in due chronological order, praising his natural gifts as a child, then his progress at school, and finally the whole course of his life including words and deeds" (3.7.15). Thematically, one might divide praise into the categories of the four cardinal virtues, "fortitude, justice, self-control and the rest of them," and "assign to each virtue the deeds performed under its influence" (3.7.15).

Third, it may be possible to praise a man for what happens "after his death." Among the grounds for praise would be "the award of divine honors, posthumous votes of thanks, or statues erected at the public expense" (3.7.17). Public recognition itself offers further grounds for praise, suggesting how praise is linked to reputation, respect, and public regard. Posthumous praise may be given persons in light of the effects of their lives: "Children reflect glory on their parents, cities on their founders, laws on those who made them, arts on their inventors and institutions on those that first introduced them" (3.7.18). Thus heads of clans and families, founders of cities, inventors, and in general those who benefited their posterity are all worthy of praise.

Finally Quintilian raises a critical issue. Like Aristotle, he is quite conscious that praise must be "audience specific." He notes that "much depends on the character of the audience and the generally received opinion" of the virtues praised. Hence an orator must know, not merely the mood of the audience, but their likes and dislikes; in short, he must know specific stereotypes of nations and countries to which he can safely appeal. For example, "literature will win less praise at Sparta than at Athens, endurance and courage more" (3.7.24). Sparta is stereotyped as a place of physical accomplishments, such as military and athletic achievements, whereas Athens is the home of the arts. Quintilian goes on to list other examples of ethnic stereotypes: "Among some races the life of a freebooter is accounted honourable, while others regard it a duty to respect the laws. Frugality might perhaps be unpopular with the Sybarites, whilst luxury was regarded as a crime by the ancient Romans" (3.7.24). Praise must be "audience specific" as well as "time specific": for example, he does not imagine that Romans of his day censure luxury as did their ancestors. Thus as we learn the general code of the rhetoric of praise and blame, we should allow for local specification of values and local variations of behaviors, which indicates that we will probably find in diverse authors a "local code" of honor and shame.

In summary, Aristotle's contribution to our understanding of the rhetoric of "praise and blame" consists in formally exposing the basic aim, focus, and techniques of praising and blaming. (1) He focused on the character of a person as the ground for praise, (2) which is recognized in terms of commonly accepted "excellences," such as the four cardinal virtues. (3) Each "excellence," moreover, was understood in stereotypical fashion according to a larger cultural code of the ancient world. (4) He provided several lists of criteria accepted in his cultural world as marks of excellence. In particular, those deeds are praiseworthy which were voluntary, beneficial to others, unique, distinctive, and outstanding. (5) He makes clear that praise and respect are social constructions whereby people agree that specific actions in accord with public expectations are praiseworthy. Therefore, he links praise intimately with public opinion, both what it expects and how it evaluates. Aristotle's contribution to this study will be valuable when we shortly assess the character of Jesus and discern what was unique or outstanding about his actions. His lists of criteria for virtuous or honorable actions will be particularly significant in our interpretation of Jesus' death.

Quintilian provides a more practical summary of the criteria for praise. Whether praising gods or mortals, he indicates how one "invents" praise by employing an existing native model of what was culturally deemed praiseworthy. (1) Praise is generally drawn from the character of a person, (2) which is sketched in terms of three periods of an individual's career (before birth, life, and after death).

(3) Each period contains its own stereotyped sources of praise: in regard to a person's birth, one praised his country, parents, and ancestors; in regard to his life, one acclaimed his bodily attributes (beauty, strength), external circumstances (wealth, power, influence), but especially deeds; in regard to his death, one highlighted the notoriety achieved posthumously (honors, thanks, statues). (4) Praise for a person's deeds may be drawn from either the chronology of a person's life (prodigies as a child, youthful education, mature life decisions) or the thematic overlay of a model of virtue upon a person's life, indicating how he illustrated each of the four cardinal virtues by specific, but culturally expected, deeds. Finally, (5) praise is audience specific in that it takes cognizance of ethnic and geographic stereotypes.

Students of rhetoric find scant originality in Quintilian's treatment. On the contrary, his importance lies in the fact that he reflects timeless and conventional opinions on praise and blame in terms of the categories he uses and the criteria he lists. Quintilian's utter conventionality strongly supports a claim for continuity and consistency among the ancients in regard to a general culture of honor and shame. There existed a recognized general code, not simply of rhetorical practice but of the criteria for honor and shame. Everyone knew what was praiseworthy or blameable and honorable or shameful.

3.0 The Rhetorical Handbooks (*Progymnasmata*) and Rhetoric of Praise

A second group of native informants from antiquity are particularly valuable as we continue to read Matthew once more in the key of honor and shame. Instructors who taught second-level students how to write and develop speeches generally used conventional rhetorical handbooks (Russell 1980:883; Hock and O'Neil 1986:9–22; Bonner 1977:250–76; Marrou 1956:267–81). These handbooks, known as the *progymnasmata* or "preparatory exercises," come from rhetoricians contemporary with the early church such as Quintilian (1st century), Aelius Theon and Hermogenes (both 2d century), and Aphthonius (3d century). Although only a few examples of the *progymnasmata* have survived, we are struck by their utter conventionality and the way in which they contain long-standing traditions concerning the elements useful and necessary for the three types of rhetoric (Hock-O'Neil 1986:16–17). For example, in regard to forensic rhetoric, one practiced *thesis*, in which one spoke for or against something; and for deliberative rhetoric, one learned to write a *nomos*, an exercise for or against a law. In regard to the rhetoric of praise and blame, however, one learned the conventions of the *enkōmion* for praise and the *psogos* for blame. These were "preliminary exercises . . . elementary stages of instruction in schools of rhetoric" (Russell 1980:883), and they represent the enduring, common tradition of certain literary forms and the conventional rules for the three types of rhetoric. We focus now on the exercise of praise and blame called the "encomium" to learn the stereotypical categories whereby a person was praised (on the encomium, see Lyons 1985; Neyrey 1994b; Malina and Neyrey 1996:19–63).

3.1 The Encomium: Rules for Praise.   Students taught to write encomia employed the conventional topics which were observed in Quintilian's discussion of the rhetoric of praise. Like Quintilian, students considered not only the stages of life of someone, but what would make those stages "excellent." Figure 3.3 indicates the chronological approach to praise, which identified not only the stages of a person's life but the conventional headings according to which someone deserved praise:

> I. Origin and Birth
>> A. Origin: race, country, ancestors, parents
>> B. Birth: phenomena at birth (stars, visions, etc.), family
> II. Nurture and Training
>> A. Education: teachers, arts, skills, laws
> III. Accomplishments and Deeds
>> A. Deeds of the Body: beauty, strength, agility, might, health
>> B. Deeds of the Soul: justice, wisdom, temperance, courage, piety
>> C. Deeds of Fortune: power, wealth, friends, children: number and beauty of, fame, fortune, length of life, happy death
> IV. Comparison

Figure 3.3 Chronological Approach to Praise

When ancient authors illustrated these abstract categories of birth/origin, nurture/ education, and deeds of body, soul, and fortune, they supplied particular ethnographic information about their meaning and the grounds for worthiness in their society. Since this material lies at the heart of our study, we must delay over these encomiastic categories to grasp what the ancients considered honorable or praiseworthy in a person.

3.2 Praise from Origin and Birth.   Praise of a person begins with a consideration of "origin and birth" which calls attention both to excellence of breeding and background and to whatever was "outstanding" about the birth. Recall that honor was generally *ascribed* to individuals by birth, a sort of "honorable gene" inherited simply by being born into an honorable family. Hence the ancients noted that a person's blood lines were pure and worthy of praise. The rhetorical handbooks tell us very little about what was expected, since they are only summary outlines, which contain very little detail or illustration. Commenting on "good breeding," Aelius Theon lists headings, but not cultural meaning: "The good breeding of city, race and good government, and the good breeding of parents and other relatives" (9.15–17; Butts 1986:469). But given the conventionality of the categories, we turn to Aristotle for a native's understanding of what was presumed by the rhetorical instructors who developed the topic of a good or honorable birth. Aristotle's explanation, which is itself reflective of cultural conventions, is applicable to the later rhetorical handbooks:

> *Good birth*, in the case of a nation or city, is to be autochthonous or ancient and for its first inhabitants to have been leaders and their descendants

> distinguished in estimable qualities. For an individual, good birth . . .
> includes legitimacy on both lines, and, as in the case of a city, [implies
> that] the earliest ancestors were known for virtue or wealth or another
> of the things that are honored and [that] there have been many outstand-
> ing men and women in the family, both among the young and the older.
> (*Rhet.* 1.5.5; see also Ps.-Aristotle, *Rhetoric to Alexander* 35; Cicero, *On
> Invention* 1.24.34–35; and Quintilian, *Inst. Orat.* 3.7.10–11; 5.10.24–25;
> Pelling 1990:213–44)

Honor was automatically conferred to individuals whose ancestors founded the
city or colonized the land; they were the aristocrats and oligarchs of antiquity.
Birth as a "free citizen" was a prerequisite for social worth in a world where one
in four persons spent some part of their lives in slavery or debt bondage. The distinguished ancestors derived nobility from being "outstanding" in wealth or some
singular achievement or culturally accepted deed. Children of a distinguished line
were treated as "chips off the old block," thus praiseworthy just by being born into
a noble line (see Dungan and Cartlidge 1974:7–40; Schuler 1982:53–55, 92–94;
Lee 1986:113–16, 190–91, 229–34; Burridge 1992:145–46, 78, 207; Neyrey
1994b:181–82; and Malina and Neyrey 1996:24–26).

3.3 Praise from Nurture and Training.   Considerable honor came from
being schooled in the customs and behaviors deemed honorable by a particular
group (i.e., *mos maiorum* or "customs of the ancestors"). Since individuals were
not expected to rise higher than their teachers, the more excellent the teacher the
more outstanding the individual. In his advice on how to portray a person, Cicero
conveys conventional wisdom when he comments on the importance of acceptable
upbringing:

> Under *manner of life* (*in victu*) should be considered with whom he was
> reared, in what tradition and under whose direction, what teachers he had
> in the liberal arts, what instructors in the art of living, with whom he as-
> sociates on terms of friendship, in what occupation, trade or profession he
> is engaged, how he manages his private fortune, and what is the character
> of his home life. (*On Invention* 1.24.35)

Individuals are praiseworthy because they trained under honorable teachers and
masters, who presumably imparted the social expectations of their social group to
the next generation (see Dungan and Cartlidge 1974:41–49; Schuler 1982:54, 80–
81; Lee 1986:191–92; Burridge 1992:146, 178–79, 207–8; Neyrey 1994b:192–93;
and Malina and Neyrey 1996:27–28).

3.4 Praise from Accomplishments and Deeds.   The public life of the individual was next presented in terms of what was excellent and outstanding. Individuals were deemed honorable in terms of their "accomplishments"
(ἐπιτήδευμα) and "deeds" (πράξεις). Even here, we note the conventional nature
of what is considered honorable. The typical encomium divided this part into three
classes of deeds: those of the body, the soul, and fortune. As noted above, each
consisted of its own stereotypical categories of what is honorable and praiseworthy. Cicero provides us with a succinct compendium of this material:

[T]hese may be divided into mind, body and external circumstances. The virtue of the mind is that whose parts we discussed only recently. The virtues of the body are health, beauty, strength, speed. Extraneous virtues are public office, money, connexions by marriage, high birth, friends, country, power, and all other things that are understood to belong to this class. (*On Invention* 2.59.177; see Aristotle, *Rhet.* 1.5.4; *Rhet. Her.* 3.6.10)

Let us briefly consider each of these three categories of "deeds" and "accomplishments" (see Schuler 1982:58–60; Lee 1986:116–18, 137–42, 166, 201–3, 234–37; Burridge 1992:146, 179, 208; Neyrey 1994b:183–87; and Malina and Neyrey 1996:28–33).

Concerning "deeds of the body," the *progymnasmata* provide only hints, speaking of "beauty, stature, agility, might," to which others add "swiftness and strength" (Neyrey 1994b:184–85). But Aristotle, an early witness to this topic, spells out the conventionality of this material in greater detail, and so we let this native informant instruct us:

In the case of the body, excellence is *health*, in the form of making use of the body without illness. . . . *Beauty* is different at each stage of life. In the case of a youth it is a matter of having a body fit for the race course and ordeals of strength, pleasant to look at. . . . When someone is in his prime, he should be adapted to the toils of war and be thought attractive as well as fear-inspiring. An old man should have adequate strength for necessary exertions and not be painful to look at, lacking any disfigurements of old age. *Strength* is the ability to move another person physically as he wills . . . by dragging or shoving or raising or squeezing or crushing. . . . Excellence of *stature* consists in surpassing many others in height [of the body], length [of the limbs], and breadth [of the torso]. (*Rhet.* 1.5.11–13)

Aristotle describes the public figures of his world, that is, male warriors and/or athletes who embody what is needed to catch the eye of the public or to live up to its elite expectations. Such a person is able to do "heroic" deeds, to act assertively, and to claim honor and respect. We note how much "appearances" count: youths should be attractive to look at and old men not be painful to look at and lacking any disfigurement.

In praising "deeds of the soul," we noted above the cultural focus on "virtue" or "excellence" in epideictic rhetoric. The encomium formally instructed authors to know and exemplify the presence of the virtues in the deeds of the person being praised. By the time of Cicero, it had become conventional to identify only the four cardinal virtues as the deeds of the soul and to indicate briefly the specific content of each. For purposes of this book we will leave discussion of the four cardinal virtues to a subsequent chapter.

The third category among "accomplishments and deeds" consists of "deeds of fortune." These are often called "extrinsic" qualities, that is, circumstantial aspects of the worth and value of a person in the eyes of others. Again, Aristotle supplies the contents of each aspect of this category, which is summarily listed in the *progymnasmata*: "plenty of good friends, wealth, plenty of good children, a happy old age . . . fame, honour, good luck" (*Rhet.* 1.5.4). Aristotle goes on to inform us of the particular cultural meaning each category has in the ancient world.

> *Good children* and *numerous children* . . . as applied to the community means a young generation that is numerous and good—and good in excellence of body, for example, in stature, beauty, strength, athletic prowess. . . . In the individual case, being blessed with good and numerous children means having many of one's own and of the quality described. The parts of *wealth* are abundance of cash, land, possession of implements and slaves and cattle distinguished by number and beauty; and all these things [should be] privately owned and securely held and freely employed and useful. . . . All in all, wealth consists more in use than in possession. *Good reputation* is a matter of achieving the respect of all people, or of having something of the sort that all or the general public or the good or the prudent desire. *Honor* is a sign of a reputation for doing good, and benefactions, above all, are justly honored. . . . The components of honor are sacrifices [made to the benefactor after death], memorial inscriptions in verse or prose, receipt of special awards, grants of land, front seats at festivals, burial at the public expense, statues, free food in the state dining room, among barbarians such things as *prokynesis* and rights of precedence, and gifts that are held in honor in each society. The meaning of many friendships and good friends is not unclear if *friend* is defined: a friend is one who is active in providing another with the things that he thinks are beneficial to him. . . . *Good luck* means to get and keep those good things of which chance is the cause . . . and which incur envy. (1.5.17)

Aristotle's explanation of each "deed of fortune" is remarkable for its conventionality. We note how praise is tied to blood and kinship. A father gains honor for a host of male children who (1) are able to serve in some warrior capacity in time of strife or in the civic arena in times of peace and who (2) are rich in all the culturally approved virtues, especially "temperance and courage." Wealth, also an index of honor, means the ownership of estates rather than trade. Clearly elite, aristocratic views are represented by someone who displays wealth by "conspicuous consumption" (i.e., "using things"). The honorable person enjoys a good reputation ("fame") and his status and excellence are publicly acknowledged by the traditional public indices of praise: sacrifices, commemorations, public honors (such as a civic funeral or a statue or a dedication or civic gifts), and privileges such as exemption from taxes or special seats in the public theaters (Neyrey 1994b:196–98). Honor is also reflected by a man's peer associations in the local social hierarchy; such a person gives and receives hospitality and acts as patron to numerous clients. Some people are said to be "lucky," that is, favored by the gods. In short, whatever "excites envy" indicates what is praiseworthy. Here, above all, we have particularistic ethnographic details that specify the content of praise.

Since our task has been to indicate the specific, historical content of "praise," let us digest what we have learned in this cursory study of the rules for the encomium in the *progymnasmata*. (1) We possess here formal categories explicitly articulated as the contents of "praise" (or honor). There can be no doubt about just what these ancients considered "honorable." (2) Although the extant *progymnasmata* date from the second and third centuries, yet they reflect conventional topics of praise going back at least to Aristotle and continuous for hundreds of years thereafter. Persons literate in Greek learned these rules and were socialized into the values encoded in them through progymnastic education. (3) We note a remarkable constancy in the content of the categories, from Aristotle's analysis of current practice in his time, through Cicero's Republican and Quintilian's Imperial Rome, and into the Byzantine period. Rhetorical authors agreed that the cultural indices of praise are embodied in "origin-birth, education-training, and accomplishments-deeds." (4) The contents of these three categories themselves remained basically constant and conventional. Thus, while we allow for historical variations among writers on rhetoric, constancy in terms of content and point of view seems to be the norm here. For these reasons, we argue in this study for a general Mediterranean notion of worth and value, which was known by all and which existed over centuries.

4.0 Interpreting Native Informants

The rhetoric of praise and blame and the rules for an encomium offer us a particularly rich report by native informants on the world of "praise and blame" in antiquity. Now we should interpret and analyze them. The anthropological model of honor and shame developed in chapter 1 provides a reliable and penetrating way of assessing the ancient materials on praise and blame. It allows us to classify the diverse pieces of information in order to see what is clearly there, what is implied, and what may be absent.

The anthropological model helps us organize the rhetorical data and other anecdotal information into a system where relationships can be made evident and explanations offered for certain behavioral patterns. Although at one level rhetoric might be considered a system of its own, it operates at a very low level of abstraction. Rhetorical materials only describe without offering any full or coherent social psychology. Moreover, our rhetorical data reflect the concerns that pertain to civic and political life, that is, with the institution of politics. They have little to say about non-elite concerns or about the other dominant institution, kinship and family. A comprehensive model of honor and shame can make this clearer and alert us to important material not covered by rhetoric. In the end, we must also recognize that the rhetorical materials about praise and blame we have just summarized will have an effect on the very model we have employed to describe the meaning and workings of honor and shame. Rhetorical materials provide us with historical particularity about praise and blame in antiquity, thus urging us to customize the general code of honor and shame for the specific audiences of ancient Greece, Rome, and Judea.

The scientific model of honor and shame and its abstract categories provide valuable lenses through which to read and interpret the rhetorical reports of our native informants. To this end, we remember the six categories of honor and shame from chapters 1 and 2, which serve as organizing guides for this inquiry: (1) definition of honor and praise; (2) sources of honor, ascribed and achieved; (3) challenge and riposte; (4) replications of honor in blood and name; (5) display and recognition of honor; and (6) the gender component of honor.

4.1 Honor Defined.   Pitt-Rivers defines honor as both the claim to precedence and its public acknowledgment (1977:1), and specifies both aspects. "Precedence" is what, within a given context, is meant by worth or reputation. It is not an ontological or metaphysical entity, but a social construction. To learn its specific contents, we must study what people "acknowledge" as worthy. We find the same difficulty in defining "praise" in classical rhetoric, for it is itself the act of public acknowledgment of someone's excellence. But what did the ancients mean by "excellence"?

In his *Rhetoric*, Aristotle defined "excellence" in terms of "virtue" and provided a list of criteria which identify certain actions as "excellent" or "virtuous" according to the code of Athenian public life (*Rhet.* 1.9.5–13, 16–19). In his discussion of the rhetoric of praise, he did not expound a theory of virtue but rather codified what people in his culture meant by an "outstanding" person or by "excellence" in this or that endeavor. In short, "excellence" is a social construction, that is, the consensus of what honor-seeking citizens deem worthy.

Aristotle, as readers will recall, enumerated the ways in which one is "outstanding": "good birth, numerous friendships, worthy friendships, wealth, good children, numerous children, a good old age, as well as the virtues of the body, reputation, honor, good luck, virtue" (*Rhet.* 1.5.4). Outstanding people, moreover, come from outstanding families, enjoy outstanding peer relationships, and have an abundance of what that society valued (children, wealth, reputation, honor, and good fortune). "Praise" is related to "reputation," of which Aristotle says: "Reputation is a matter of achieving the respect of all people, or of having something of the sort that all or the general public or the good or the prudent desire" (*Rhet.* 1.5.8). A person is praised, then, for fulfilling the expectations of one's culture. Aristotle thus presumes a general code of excellence and admits the importance of public evaluation and acknowledgment of worth.

Aristotle's definition of "honor" presumes more than it says: "Honor" he defines as "a sign of a reputation for doing good." For Aristotle the signs of a (good) reputation are:

> The components of honor are sacrifices [made to the benefactor after death], memorial inscriptions in verse or prose, receipt of special awards, grants of land, front seats at festivals, burial at the public expense, statues, free food in the state dining room . . . *proskynesis* and rights of precedence, and gifts that are held in honor in each society. (*Rhet.* 1.5.9)

Manifested by such tangibles as public privileges and perks, honor remains essentially a matter of positive public opinion, namely, "reputation." The reputation that brings honor is one that earns praise. We recall that certain actions are tagged by Aristotle as worthy of praise, such as (1) deeds which merit honor, not money, (2) deeds done voluntarily and by choice, not servile acts of obedience, (3) deeds which benefit others, not oneself, and (4) deeds which bring fame after death (*Rhet.* 1.9.16–19). And he highlights deeds which surpass expectations or which the actor was the first or only person to perform (1.9.38).

Therefore, the intrinsic element of Aristotle's notion of "honor" is public admiration of a virtue or excellence, that is, praise of something that conforms to acknowledged canons of value and worth. Praise and honor, then, are reputation, respect, worth, and value which persons have in the eyes of their peers. In short, "praise" and "honor" are best described according to the dynamics of social psychology, whereby people agree that certain actions or qualities conform to their code of value and worth. Thus we find near total agreement between ancient notions of praise and honor and those articulated by modern anthropologists.

4.2 Sources of Honor.   According to the cultural model of honor and shame, worth and value may be either bestowed on individuals (i.e., *ascribed honor*) or earned and merited by them (i.e., *achieved honor*). Ascribed honor comes passively and through no effort of their own. It is reflected in the first category of the rules for an encomium, namely "origins," which tell of a person's ethnos, place of origin, ancestors, and parents. Honor derives from the mere fact of being born a Greek (not a barbarian), an Athenian (not a Spartan), and from an aristocratic line and prominent parents (not from peasant or slave stock). The second category of the encomium, "nurture and training," contains another aspect of ascribed honor, that is, honor derived from the reputation of one's teachers. On balance, then, our ancient rhetoric shows a cultural assumption that ascribes honor first and foremost to birth, but then to the quality of one's teachers.

Other aspects of ascribed honor were indeed present in the ancient world, but they do not surface in the rhetoric of praise and blame. For instance, worth and value were ascribed to someone by prominent persons. Examples include slaves who, once manumitted by an aristocrat, became freedmen of their former owner and thus his clients (Bartchy 1992:71–72; Martin 1990:30–42). Or, another example might be officials sent by Caesar to various Roman provinces who were ascribed their role and status by the emperor. Pilate was Caesar's "friend" or client, and owed him loyalty (John 19:12; see Brunt 1965). Not only were Cynics "sent by God" (Vaage 1994:19–22) but so were Jesus and Paul. Jesus in turn commissioned his disciples in his own name and power, thus ascribing role and status to them (Matt. 10:6; 28:19–20; Hubbard 1974:69–99). Other "servants" could be assigned to act as messengers of kings and gods or agents of elites in various business and political transactions (Collins 1990:84, 90, 169–76, 195–216). The rhetoric of praise and blame said nothing about this sort of ascribed honor, although the rules for the encomium touched on this in its list of "deeds of fortune," that is, the external qualities of a person attributed to an individual by the favor of the gods. This material truly existed in the ancient world, but we would only recognize it by virtue of a cultural model based on more diverse cross-cultural data than ancient rhetoric provides.

Acquired honor could be competed for and earned in many ways: through prowess on the battlefield, at sports games, in contests of poetry and drama, and even in benefaction. Aristotle's qualities of "liberality, maganimity, magnificence" fit here (*Rhet.* 1.9.10–11). Aristotle's two rhetorical categories for acquired honor, "the signs and works of virtue," developed this source in detail (*Rhet.* 1.9.17–19 and 38). Moreover, under the heading of "deeds and accomplishments," the rules for the encomium elaborated on the "deeds of the soul" and the "deeds of the body," whereby persons by their actions earned respect and praise. Thus in terms of the sources of honor, ancient rhetoric of praise contains in considerable detail the same data clearly organized in the anthropological model of honor.

4.3 Challenge and Riposte.   The rhetoricians stand mute about the competitive and agonistic nature of the ancient world. Indeed they presume it, but say nothing about it. The rhetoric of praise and blame, however, tells us only that individuals were competitive, but it neither explains their social perception of limited good, which triggers aggressive actions, nor describes the choreography of honor challenges. Aristotle came close to the topic when he talked about envy and emulation among the emotions which an orator might cultivate (*Rhet.* 2.10, 11). But in no way did he relate them to the highly competitive world of honor and shame. Other authors commented on the agonistic nature of the ancient world. For example, Plutarch remarked about the conflict between public groups, such as nations and cities, and private ones, such as neighbors and families:

> The Aetolians and the Acarnanians, neighboring Greek peoples, ruined one another by their aggressiveness, and the inhabitants of Chalcedon and Byzantium were led by their innate enmity to fight a battle in the Bosporus over a quarrel about a thole. And in the case of private neighbors . . . proximity sometimes provides the occasions for many affronts. (*Commentary on Hesiod's Works and Days* 49)

We can connect this observation with "love of honor" (φιλοτιμία), which led people in antiquity to compete for victory and excellence, as was discussed in chapter 1. "Love of honor," when examined in the light of the concept of limited good, goes a long way toward explaining and illustrating the competitive nature of the ancient world. This love of honor unleashed envy and the agonistic game of challenge and riposte.

The cultural model of honor and shame aids us greatly in identifying the public pathways to success and honor in antiquity and appreciating the underlying social psychology of the competitive nature of the ancient world. It allows us to identify the sources of honor, both ascribed and achieved, more extensively than ancient rhetoric does. And it offers a reliable scenario for understanding the systemic nature of combat, competition, and envy which underlies the seemingly noble love of honor endemic to the ancient world. Thus the scientific model of honor is in basic harmony with the rhetoric of praise on the two sources of honor.

4.4 Replications of Honor: Blood and Name.   Although this may seem but a variant of *ascribed honor* (i.e., "origins"), it implies much more. "Good birth" was a topic in the rules for the encomium in the *progymnasmata* and in Aristotle's *Rhetoric* (1.5.5). Ancient rhetoric affirmed that honor is replicated in blood (i.e., kinship), but does not explain the reasons or significance of this. It acknowledged that one's genealogy and embeddedness in ethnos, city, or family were sources of honor, but offered no explanation for this. On this point, then, the rhetoric of praise presumes, but does not explain, the role of kinship in honor. Once more, ancient rhetoric is well served by an anthropological model that can both identify the replication of honor in blood and explain its significance for the culture.

Rhetoric, moreover, had little to say about name as a replication of honor. It noted that honor was ascribed by virtue of one's kinship name, but did not highlight or explain this. By name is meant an individual's social credit rating or reputation. On an emic level, praise is accorded people in terms of names and titles as indices of honor (Malina 1993:38–39). For example, one's honor derives from membership in country, clan, and family, and so one's social credit rating is marked by being known and acclaimed by clan and family name, an illustration of which is found in 1 Sam. 9:1. The etic or anthropological model attends to a wider range of data than our elitist rhetoricians and both notices and explains how worth and value are attached to names, either kinship-based names, names deriving from trade and occupation, or nicknames.

4.5 Honor Displayed and Recognized. How were praise and honor symbolized and publicly displayed? Aristotle touched on this material briefly when he discussed the excellences or virtues which are the grounds for praise. Display of wealth for the sake of winning praise and public benefaction to the city appear under the heading of "liberality, magnanimity and magnificence" (*Rhet.* 1.9.10–12). And in the rules for the encomium, we found under the category of "deeds of fortune," power, wealth, friends, household, children, and fame (Neyrey 1994b:186–87, 196–201; Malina and Neyrey 1996:31–32, 96–98). The rhetorical sources, however, while they indicate general areas where worth and value may be displayed, do not tell us why these particular things replicate honor in the ancient world. For that we need to supplement the reports of our native informants with considerations about social hierarchy and aristocratic values to appreciate the full cultural significance of the "deeds of fortune."

The rhetoric of praise, moreover, did not expressly mention the symbolic interpretation of specific body parts. A man's head is considered the locus of his honor, for heads are crowned or wreathed with laurel in virtue of military victory or athletic success. The right hand or arm is the honorable member because it wields weapons in war. Inasmuch as honor and praise are discussed in the rhetorical literature as male qualities, the male sexual organs would be assumed to be preeminent body parts symbolizing male honor, a point made explicit in nonrhetorical materials. The rhetorical materials surveyed do not attend to the replication or display of honor in terms of body parts, although our anthropological model and its illustrations from the ancient world indicate how important such a point of view was in antiquity. Thus the scientific model of honor guides us into new considerations about the replication of honor in the human body, a topic which truly existed in antiquity but was not formally discussed in the rhetoric of praise.

4.6 Gender-Based Honor: The Moral Division of Labor. Both ancient rhetoricians and modern anthropologists are in basic agreement on the phenomenon of a gender-divided world. By that they mean a world of status inequality between males and females, which is replicated in terms of gender-specified spaces, objects, times, and actions. A full exposition of this etic concept is regularly recorded in the emic literature of antiquity (Neyrey 1994a:79–82).

In ancient rhetorical works only males are in view, although Quintilian mentions praise for female gods such as Minerva and Ceres. The rhetoricians praised males for their public behavior, such as prowess in war, athletics, public speech, and civic benefaction, as well as for male virtues, such as courage, and male characteristics, such as power. Clearly revealing his gender bias, Aelius Theon discussed how males and females might be compared, but only on the topic of "courage," which is stereotypically a male attribute in antiquity. Females were likewise praised in antiquity, for instance, in Plutarch's *In Praise of Women*, but public praise was normally part of the male world and celebrated male achievements. Once more, rhetorical treatises and handbooks basically reflect this gender distinction, but do not comment on it or argue for it. Fuller discussions are easily found in other ancient literature, but not in the rhetorical materials. The anthropological model, however, suggests that in a world where honor and shame are pivotal values one would expect as well radical patterns of gender division. It sensitizes us, moreover, to the areas and topics where this is most likely the case. It provides a systematic view of the gender issue and indicates, as no native informant can, the close relationship between honor and shame and specific gender spaces, times, objects, and roles.

5.0 Conclusions and Further Investigation

In this chapter we have surveyed both the rhetoric of praise and blame and the rules for the encomium from the rhetorical handbooks known as the *progymnasmata*. We have treated this material as the reports of native informants who were both sensitive to the issues of honor and shame in their own world and quite conscious of reflecting the consensus of their society on the topic. They have provided us with both the meaning of honor and praise, the grounds for it, and techniques for marshaling public opinion in this vein.

Moreover, by interfacing the rhetoric of praise and blame and the general anthropological model, we have learned several important things. By virtue of a scientific model, it is more accurately possible to classify and systematize the rhetorical data. When framed by the scientific model of honor and other anecdotal materials, the rhetoric of praise can then provide a detailed emic description of the values of honor and shame, and can offer some hints about the social system which embodies these values. The rhetorical materials both confirm the accuracy and utility of the anthropological model and indicate how it should be specifically tailored for the world of antiquity. Thus we continue the method of inquiry called "abduction," the process whereby the social science analyses are conducted. Through a shuttling back and forth between theory and testing, data retrieval, and data analysis one searches for specific materials in light of a certain theory, the finding of which in turn influences the theory itself (Malina 1991; Malina and Neyrey 1996:ix–x). The next chapters of this book will illustrate this method of proceeding, as we take the native, emic reports about encomiastic praise and use them as the model for reading and interpreting Matthew's Gospel.

We repeat the observation that rhetoric provides a truly Mediterranean model of honor and shame in antiquity. With the conquests of Alexander, the Mediterranean world both East and West was Hellenized. Not only did Greek language and culture dominate the East from the time of Alexander the Great, but its literature and culture conquered Rome, which then continued to "civilize" the world with a Roman version of Greek rhetorical culture. The education promoted in this "civilized" world was that of Greece, especially its rhetoric. Thus the school exercises in the handbooks embodied the cultural values and practices that went back to Greece, were suitable to Romans, and continued their influence into the Byzantine empire. People preparing for civic life from Britain to Babylon all learned both their rules of praise and the values encoded in them through study of the encomium in the *progymnasmata*.

Hellenistic rhetoric of praise both codified what the Greeks and Romans meant by honor and shame, and instructed new peoples into these conventions. People who learned to write Greek at a literary level or to compose addresses for public delivery would have been trained in a conventional educational system that taught the exercises of the *progymnasmata*, including the encomium or rules for praise. In this sense we can claim the existence of a Greek or Mediterranean culture which valued what is encoded in the rhetoric of praise and blame and practiced it in public life. Rhetorical education served as a vital means of articulating a general code of worth and honor in antiquity, which remained remarkably constant from Aristotle in the Greek East through Augustine in the Latin West. Rhetorical education informed the cultural world in which Jesus appeared and for which the Gospel of Matthew was written. Matthew, who learned to read and write Greek at a very sophisticated level, would most probably have been trained in all of the exercises of the *progymnasmata*, but in particular the encomium. It remains to be seen how his Gospel reflects both the contents of the encomium and its aim of praise.

4

An Encomium for Jesus

Origins, Birth, Nurture, and Training

1.0 Introduction: Topic, Hypothesis, and Plan

In the next chapters we will employ the rules for the encomium from the rhetorical handbooks known as the *progymnasmata* as the lenses for reading Matthew's Gospel. In this, we continue to examine Matthew in terms of honor and shame, but now using the native discussions of praise and blame as our immediate model. The genre of the encomium, its rules, and the cultural values encoded in it, were fixtures in the literate Hellenistic world of Matthew's times. The *progymnasmata* themselves were rhetorical handbooks belonging specifically to Matthew's period. Moreover, anyone who learned to write Greek at the level of a document such as the Gospel of Matthew would most probably have been educated by way of the rhetorical handbooks. Since the encomium taught in these rhetorical handbooks contains the categories used by our ancient informants to praise someone, we possess here an immediate native model of honor and shame.

We argue in this part of the book that Matthew tells the story of Jesus fully in accord with the categories, structure, and values of the encomium. As a literary work, the Gospel enjoys a predictable formal structure that derives in large measure from the four areas in the encomium from which one found grounds for praise: (1) origins and birth, (2) education and nurture, (3) deeds and accomplishments, and (4) noble death. Each of these four categories is further broken down into specific units in the rules for the encomium. This material provides us with a very precise grid for reading and assessing the narrative of Matthew. But it is precisely in its rhetorical aim that we consider Matthew most influenced by the rhetorical tradition represented in the encomium; for we argue that the purpose of Matthew's narrative was the praise and honoring of Jesus of Nazareth. To argue this, we will examine in the next chapters how an encomium instructs a writer to draw praise from the four aspects of a person's life mentioned above. After examining in greater detail the native rules for encomiastic praise, we will then read Matthew in light of that rhetorical model: first, "origins and birth" (Matthew 1–2) in this chapter, then "deeds and accomplishments" (Matthew 4–25) and finally "noble death" (Matthew 26–28) in subsequent chapters.

We acknowledge the important debate over the genre of "gospel," especially the arguments of scholars who have likened the structure of the narrative to that of a "life" or biography (Talbert 1977:1–23; Shuler 1982:24–57; Aune 1987a, 1987b, and 1988; Burridge 1992:55–106). In proposing to use the structure and contents of the encomium we are obviously sympathetic to proponents of gospel-as-biography. The specific contribution made here is the examination of the formal structure of the encomium and the conventionality of its rules for ascribing praise in regard to Matthew. We have no doubt that many of the same materials appear in biography, but the encomium more clearly reflects both the literary structure and the ancient understanding of praise and blame than does biography because it consciously sets forth the cultural understanding of praise. Thus, rather than argue that Matthew is either an encomium or a biography, the prudent thing to do is to examine in greater detail the categories of the encomium and see whether they fit Matthew and clarify his rhetorical purpose.

2.0 The Encomium on Origin and Birth

We have seen how worth and value are ascribed to individuals by virtue of birth into a family or kinship group. The family was the dominant social institution in the lives of the ancients, providing the basic source of identity, nurture, economic support, religion, and education for most people. Since marriages were made between families of equal social standing, we find a high value placed on the honor rating of the respective families of groom and bride (Hanson 1989a, 1989b, 1990).

2.1 Native Reports on Origins. The rules for an encomium contain clear ancient reflection on family origins and imply even more about codes of honor respecting one's origins. In fig. 4.1, four of our authors of rules for an encomium present categories important for development of a person's "origins" or descent (γένος).

Hermogenes	Aelius Theon	Aphthonius	Quintilian
ethnic affiliation (ἔθνος)	ethnic affiliation (ἔθνος)	ethnic affiliation (ἔθνος)	ethnic affiliation (*gens, natio*)
nation/city-state (πόλις)	nation/city-state (πόλις)	home locale (πατρίς)	country (*patria*)
clan/tribe (γένος)	government (πολιτεία)	ancestors (πρόγονοι)	ancestors (*maiores*)
		fathers (πατέρες)	parents (*parentes*)

Figure 4.1 Categories Important in Relation to Origins

An individual's worth and identity were rooted in his *generation* (ethnic affiliation, clan/tribe, ancestors, and family) and *geography* (city, nation, home locale) in terms that do not correspond to modern notions of nation, home locale, or clan/tribe (Malina and Neyrey 1996:17–18). *Generation* had to do with a person's "good breeding" as the first and very important source of praise. Quintilian, commenting on this topic, says:

> "Birth," for persons are generally regarded as having some resemblance to their parents and ancestors, a resemblance which sometimes leads to their living disgracefully or honorably, as the case may be; then there is nationality, for races have their own character, and the same action is not probable in the case of a barbarian, a Roman and a Greek; country is another, for there is a like diversity in the laws, institutions and opinions of different states. (*Inst. Orat.* 5.10.23–25)

Worth and honor were ascribed on the basis of generation because of the presumption that "persons generally have some resemblance to their parents and ancestors." Like the "breeding" of animals, so the "generation" of humans: from good stock should come good offspring. Strangers were always suspect in this world of conflict and suspicion. Should we trade with them? Should we marry them? Should we ally with them? To learn as much as possible about a person, first-century people examined the roots and history of a family to estimate its worth. Four centuries earlier, Aristotle considered the birth of an individual to be good if "its members are indigenous or ancient," if its earliest members were "distinguished and from them sprang many who were distinguished for qualities that we admire," and if they were "free citizens . . . founders of a line notable for virtue or wealth" (*Rhet.* 1.5.5). A noble and excellent genealogy argues well for the worth and value of the current generation.

Emphasis put on *geography* (city, nation, home locale) is rooted in similar sorts of expectations. The importance of geography rests on a theory of bodily elements (Malina and Neyrey 1996:113–25). Persons were thought to be composed of wet and dry and hot and cold elements. The ideal person enjoyed a balance of these four, and geography determined the balance of each element. The four elements also indicated character: a person with excessive heat would be such-and-such a type person, whereas people with more coldness would be another type of person. This theory of the relationship of geography and character was expressed regularly in treatises on physiognomics, such as Hippocrates' *Air, Water, and Places* (24.1–40). Ideal locations were of course either Greece or Rome, which were considered the navels of the universe where people enjoyed the perfect balance of heat and cold and wet and dry, and where the best characteristics and qualities in people could be found.

Menander Rhetor, an important author of a *progymnasmata* in the third century C.E., instructed authors of encomia to draw praise from geography, that is, from the subjects of home locale or native place (πατρίς), city (πόλις), and place of ethnic affiliation (ἔθνος):

> You will come to the topic of his native country (πατρίς). Here you must ask yourself whether it is a distinguished country or not [and whether he comes from a celebrated and splendid place or not]. If his native country is famous, you should place your account of it first, and mention it before his family. . . . This encomium is not peculiar to the emperor, but applies generally to the inhabitants of the city (πόλις). If the city (πόλις) has no distinction, you must inquire whether his nation (ἔθνος) as a whole is considered brave and valiant, or is devoted to literature or the possession

of virtues, like the Greek race, or again is distinguished for law, like the Italian, or is courageous, like the Gauls or Paeonians. You must then take a few features from the nation (ἔθνος), instead of from the native city (πατρίς), associating the emperor's praise with this also, and arguing that it is inevitable that a man from such a [city or] nation should have such characteristics, and that he stands out among all his praiseworthy compatriots, since he alone was thought worthy of the throne. (2.369.18–370.5)

Several features are clear here: certain places characteristically breed people with specific praiseworthy traits. Greeks were experts in literature and virtue, Italians in law, and Gauls in courage. Moreover, a "distinguished" locale will breed distinguished citizens. The presupposition behind this lies in the belief that "it is *inevitable* that a man from such a city or nation should have such characteristics." Why "inevitable"? Presumably Menander shares the common understanding of the relationship of elements such as hot/cold and wet/dry on character. Needless to say, knowing the geography of a person's origins tells the ancients about the person's worth and value (see Neyrey 1996a:268–74).

2.2 Native Reports on Birth.

2.2 Native Reports on Birth. Notice of the events surrounding the actual conception and birth of someone appear in the rules for an encomium. Not much is said about this particular topic, but all of the authors of *progymnasmata* include it. In referring to Achilles, Quintilian offers an example of how to draw praise from oracles announcing the hero's birth: "Other topics to be drawn from the period preceding their birth will have reference to omens or prophecies foretelling their future greatness, such as the oracle which is said to have foretold that the son of Thetis would be greater than his father" (*Inst. Orat.* 3.7.11). On the very birth itself (περὶ τῆς γενέσεως) Menander instructs an orator:

> After country and family, then, let the third heading, as we have just said,
> be "birth," and if any divine sign occurred at the time of his birth, either
> on land or in the heavens or on the sea, compare the circumstances with
> those of Romulus, Cyrus, and similar stories, since in these cases also
> there were miraculous happenings connected with their birth—the dream
> of Cyrus' mother, the suckling of Romulus by the she-wolf. (2.371.4–10)

Hermogenes comments on the praiseworthy significance of dreams which accompany a birth: "You will say what marvelous things befell at the birth, as dreams or signs or the like" (from Baldwin 1928:31).

To fill out the bare bones of rhetorical instructions, we turn to a famous and relevant example in regard to the birth of Caesar Augustus by Suetonius (69–120 C.E.). His rehearsal of the signs and wonders that accompanied the birth of Augustus is a virtual compendium of all that could be said on this topic. He begins by alerting us to "the omens which occurred before Augustus was born, on the very day of his birth and afterwards from which it was possible to anticipate and perceive his future greatness and uninterrupted good fortune" (*Lives of the Caesars* 2.94.1). An old prophecy was issued "in ancient days" when part of the wall of the city of Velitrae was struck by lightning; on that occasion "the prediction was made that a citizen of that town would one day rule the world." Suetonius tells us that this prediction of future greatness was fulfilled: "At last long afterward the event proved that the omen had foretold the rule of Augustus" (2.94.2; see Talbert 1980). Some time before the conception of Augustus, a "portent" was observed at Rome "warning that nature was pregnant with a king for the Roman people" (2.94.3). Drawing ever closer in time, Suetonius then tells how Atia, the mother of Augustus, fell asleep during a nighttime service in the temple of Apollo, during which sleep "a serpent glided up to her and shortly went away." Upon washing, "at once there appeared on her body a mark in colours like a serpent, and she could not get rid of it" (2.94.4). Augustus was born ten months after this, and "was regarded as the son of Apollo" in virtue of the serpent dream and marks. His mother dreamed just prior to his birth "that her vitals were borne up to the stars and spread over the whole extent of land and sea, while Octavius (Augustus's father) dreamed that the sun rose from Atia's womb" (2.94.4). At the moment of Augustus's birth, a certain Publius Nigidius declared that "the ruler of the world had been born" (2.94.5). Some time after this, Octavius was on maneuvers in Thrace and dreamed a dream about Augustus: "His son appeared to him in a guise more majestic than a mortal man, with the thunderbolt, scepter, and insignia of Jupiter Optimus Maximus, wearing a crown begirt with rays and mounted upon a laurel-wreathed chariot drawn by twelve horses of surpassing whiteness" (2.94.5). And the dreams and portents continue until fourteen of them have been enumerated (see Talbert 1980:133–36).

Along with dreams and omens, it was commonly accepted that the appearance of something new or different in the heavens portended the birth on earth of someone destined for greatness (Hagner 1993:25; Brown 1993:170). This tradition seems quite widespread in antiquity, including not only Greek and Roman heroes, but Israelite ones as well (Str-B 1.77–78).

Dreams, omens, oracles, and heavenly portents all serve to indicate various aspects of the worth and excellence of some new birth. Some indicate that a deity is involved in the conception of the hero, thus giving further significance to the generation or breeding of the offspring. Others identify the child born as exceptional, outstanding, and unusual, which alone would designate the person as worthy of praise. Still others predict future greatness. In short, marvelous things that precede, accompany, and follow a birth all serve as indications of great heavenly favor, which is basically what is meant by ascribed honor.

3.0 Matthew on the Origins and Birth of Jesus

Generally, biblical scholarship on the Matthean infancy narrative (Matthew 1–2) pays no attention to cultural and rhetorical meaning and focuses instead on questions such as: (1) Matthew's sources, the historical reliability of his account (Brown 1993:105–19); (2) form-critical questions about individual pieces of the narrative—that is, genealogy, midrash, and birth stories (Muñoz Iglesias 1958); (3) the "theological interests" of the evangelist (Brown 1993:37–38); or (4) the evangelist's redaction of his sources and the relationship of the infancy story to the rest of the Gospel (Nolan 1979:98–113). This monograph focuses, by contrast, on the particular contribution to the interpretation of Matthew 1–2 which the rhetoric of praise and blame indicates about the honor of Jesus. Our questions are: (1) To what extent does Matthew conform to the rules and expectations encoded in the encomium for presenting the origins and birth of Jesus? (2) To what extent does Matthew engage the general code critically? Does he subvert it? Follow it? Adapt it? (3) To what extent does his narrative purpose resemble the rhetorical aim of the encomium, namely, praise and honor?

3.1 Origins: Geography.   Taking our clue from the notice about "city," "home locale," "country," and "nationality" in the *progymnasmata*, we see that Matthew identifies many places in chapters 1–2. Countries mentioned are Judea and Egypt. Because it was the ancestral repository of Israel's history, home of its kings and site of the temple, Judea represents the locus of leadership and power. Egypt functions only as a symbolic marker in the career of Jesus, that is, the place to which he escaped and from which God led him back to his homeland. Cities most closely related to Jesus' birth are Jerusalem and Bethlehem in Judea, and Nazareth. Because they are the places most closely associated with Jesus' birth, Jerusalem and Bethlehem in Judea have much to say about his praiseworthiness, as they represent the capital city of the land and the birthplace of kings, respectively. Nazareth in Galilee indicates where the honorable child was finally reared. But what is the local evaluation of these places? From diverse studies, we learn that most places in antiquity had some sort of honor rating. Tarsus, as we have seen, is a city of "no mean status" (Neyrey 1996:268–74; Malina and Neyrey 1996:24–25). Presumably Judean natives at the time of Matthew would have learned the local evaluation of Jerusalem and Bethlehem, but Matthew conveniently puts into his narrative clues for non-Judean natives to assess the honor of these places.

The royal city of Jerusalem was the home of the kings of Israel and the site of the nation's great temple. King Herod built both a fortress in Jerusalem (*Ant.* 15.292) and a magnificent palace (*J.W.* 5.156–83; *Ant.* 15.318). According to Matthew, Herod resides there (Matt. 2:3), and from his palace he consults the religious elite of the city, the chief priests and scribes (Matt. 2:4). Typical of ancient cities, Jerusalem was also the residence of the aristocratic elite and the locus of their palaces and temple (Rohrbaugh 1991:133–37). David Magie remarks how residents of ancient cities engaged in intense "vanity and rivalry . . . in the matter of rank and titles" (1950:1496). As such, the city was an object of pride in the general code of honor. Philo called Jerusalem a metropolis, or "mother city," which spawned colonies throughout the world, thus proclaiming its importance and honor:

> As for the holy city . . . while she is my native city, she is also the mother city (μητρόπολις) not of one country Judea but of most of the others in virtue of the colonies sent out at divers times to the neighbouring lands Egypt, Phoenicia, the part of Syria called the Hollow and the rest of the lands lying far apart, Pamphylia, Cilicia, most of Asia up to Bithynia and the corners of Pontus, similarly also into Europe, Thessaly, Boeotia,

Macedonia, Aetolia, Attica, Argos, Corinth and most of the best parts of
Peloponnese. (*On the Embassy to Gaius* 281)

Yet despite Jerusalem's honorable status according to the general code of honor as
the royal capital of the land, the new king was not born there. On the contrary, he
is born in Bethlehem of Judea (2:5).

Dominant and capital cities were ringed with satellite villages (see Matt. 15:21;
Mark 8:27; Rohrbaugh 1991:130–33; Oakman 1991:160–64). Bethlehem was one
such village dependent upon Jerusalem. Yet Bethlehem means much more than
this for Matthew, for he cites the national book, the scriptures, to inform readers
of the honorable status of Bethlehem: "And you, O Bethlehem, in the land of
Judah, are by no means least [i.e., lacking honor] among the rulers of Judah; for
from you shall come a ruler who will govern my people Israel" (2:6//Micah 5:2).
The prophecy indicates that the aristocratic top of the social pyramid will come
from Bethlehem, that is, the Davidic king, the Messiah. The great ancestor, King
David, was born and raised in Bethlehem (1 Sam. 17:12, 15), anointed king there
by Samuel (1 Sam. 16:1–13), and performed his ancestral rituals there (1 Sam.
20:6, 28). Micah the prophet indicates that other kings will be born there, securing its honor as the birthplace of Judean monarchs. Bethlehem serves as a worthy
substitute for Jerusalem, the "mother city." It enjoys a noble and praiseworthy
place in the local code of honor derived from geography.

What about his home locale? Matthew and his readers know that Jesus
was raised in Nazareth of Galilee and lived in other Galilean towns such as
Capernaum. By contrast with Jerusalem of Judea, Nazareth in Galilee in the first
century had a low or negative honor rating, as John 1:46 and 7:52 indicate.
Matthew does not mention "Nazareth" until Jesus has returned from Egypt; he
tells us that because of continuing danger from Herod's successor, Joseph took
Jesus to another region, Galilee, and to the "city" of Nazareth. At this point the
evangelist cites a prophecy that is being fulfilled here which has much to do with
Jesus drawing honor from Nazareth. Brown argues that Matthew has in mind Isa.
4:3 and Judg. 16:17 when he says "He shall be called a Nazarene" (2:23; Brown
1993:223–25). According to these "prophecies," being a *nazir* was a most honorable role and status, for it meant "a holy one of God." The point is that Matthew
himself supplies the appropriate meaning for "Nazareth" by playing with the
relationship between the village's name and the prophecy about a *nazir* or "holy
one." Thus he invests Jesus with great honor because of this bit of midrashic
geography, which will offset the rejection of Jesus by Nazareth (Matt. 13:53–58).

Jesus' "home locale" will henceforth be "Galilee," not the major cities of the region such as Sepphoris or Tiberias, but the small villages in the region. Although
nothing is said about the honorable status of Galilee in Matt. 2:22–23, Matthew
shortly instructs his readers how to think about this locale when Jesus begins his
"deeds." Once more the evangelist cites a prophecy to determine the honorable significance of a place. Isa. 8:23–9:1 predicted that Galilee would be a place where
"light" would shine: "Galilee of the Gentiles—the people who sat in darkness have
seen a great light, and for those who sat in the region and shadow of death light has
dawned" (Matt. 4:16–17). Jesus evidently was that "light" which brought incredible

benefaction to a region not even considered a part of the holy land ("Galilee of the Gentiles"). Eventually Galilee gains great honor as the place where Jesus performed his great works. And so, as the rules of the encomium indicate, an individual deserves praise because of *geography*: in the case of Nazareth and Galilee, for rising above the handicap of residence in a dishonorable place. The point is made that Jesus surpassed the expectations concerning a person raised in a cultural backwater or lowly village, and so all the more he deserves our respect and honor.

In regard to the rules in an encomium on "origins" and *geography*, Matthew seems to follow convention by indicating that Jesus reversed the process and drew honor from birth in an insignificant village and from residence in a backwater town. Bethlehem ostensibly was *not* praiseworthy ("Bethlehem . . . least among rulers"); Nazareth was an insignificant village, and Galilee was a land "of Gentiles." But all three places take on great and honorable proportions when shown to be the fulfillment of prophecies that have to do with Jesus' identity and greatness. Is it too much to see here the Gospel's principle of inversion at work? Last is first and least is greatest. Appearances, then, are deceiving: kings should be born in palaces, not villages. In reversal of the status articulated by Micah 5:1–3 in Matt. 2:6, we find a hint of the way Jesus throughout his career will challenge and upset the prevailing local code of honor. Thus Jesus has ascribed honor by means of divine oracles about the geography of his "origins" and surpasses popular expectations about what can spring from those places.

3.2 Origins: Generation. Under the heading of "generation" in the rules for an encomium, we examine what was said about Jesus' ancestors, tribe/clan, and parents.

3.2.1 Ancestors. As regards his ancestors, Matthew includes a genealogy of Jesus, that is, a list of his noble ancestors. Critical scholarship has renewed its interest in genealogies (Wilson 1975, 1977; Johnson 1969), especially those in Matthew and Luke, by examining the historical connections among various ancestors, the social functions of genealogies, the females in the list, and the relationship of infancy narrative to the rest of the document (Nolan 1979:98–113; Brown 1993: 583–96). Our questions are, What is the place and function of a genealogy in the rules for an encomium? How does the list of Jesus' ancestors in 1:1–17 contribute to his honor?

The first three ancestors in the genealogy were founding fathers of Israel, the ancient patriarchs Abraham, Isaac, and Jacob (1:2). By highlighting the three most ancient patriarchs, Matthew claims for Jesus descent from the most ancient founders of his country, full membership in their clan, and inheritance of their distinguished qualities. Through them, Matthew implies a direct connection for Jesus with the covenant of promise made to the patriarchs' descendants and with their own virtues, such as Abraham's faith (Genesis 15) and obedience (Genesis 22). Recall that Aristotle praised persons whose ancestors were "indigenous or ancient." "[I]ts earliest leaders were distinguished men, and from them have sprung many who were distinguished for qualities that we admire" (*Rhet.* 1.1.5). Thus Matthew ascribes great honor to Jesus by placing him in a direct line with Israel's virtuous founding ancestors.

3.2.2 Tribe/Clan. In regard to Jesus' tribe/clan, Matthew links Jesus directly with Judah and the royal tribe from which David and Israel's kings are descended. Thus, in addition to descent from the great patriarchs, Jesus belongs to the most noble of the twelve tribes of Israel—Judah—from which finally arises a royal dynasty. He inherits, then, their exalted status and role as ruler of Israel. After David, Jesus' ancestors are all kings of Judah (Matt. 1:6–11), honorable precisely because of that royal status. Normally the virtue of the founding father or head of the clan was considered the inheritance of all its members; thus David's favor in God's eyes would be inherited by his descendants. Even if they fail to live up to the ideal of their ancestor as did such figures as Abijah (1 Kings 15:1–8), Joram (2 Kings 8:16–24), Uzziah (2 Kings 8:25–9:29), Ahaz (2 Kings 16), and Manasseh (2 Kings 21:1–18), they do not cancel out the characteristic ideal or inheritance. Once upon a time, the line was noble. Jesus, then, is associated with sinners among his ancestors. But if "Jesus" is to be savior of his people (1:21), he will not be out of character, so to speak, if he eats with tax collectors and sinners and forgives sins; for he is likewise born into a royal family greatly in need of this reform. On just this point, recall Quintilian's advice on mentioning a person's ancestors. The object of our praise may be shown not to have fallen short of the fame of his clan (David), but then he might be praised for having ennobled his ignoble or humble origins (Abijah, Joram, Uzziah, Ahaz, and Manasseh) by his own achievements (*Inst. Orat.* 3.7.10). Hence, Jesus by his own actions (see on "deeds" in chapter 5) can be said to have lived up to and surpassed his noble ancestors, and to have overcome the shame of others in his line by his own nobility. Matthew's inclusion of both honorable and shameful kings of Israel in the genealogy falls well within the rules of praise in the encomium.

The third section of the genealogy begins with the continuation of the royal family in Jechoniah (1:12). According to 1 Chron. 3:17–19, Jechoniah is the last king of Israel, and so Shealtiel and Zerubbabel belong to the royal family, even if they are not the reigning monarchs. As Davies and Allison point out (1988:180), Zerubbabel was viewed by prophets as the Lord's "signet ring" and "chosen one" (Hag. 2:23); Zechariah considered him as the hope for a restored Davidic monarchy (4:6–10). As commentators have noted, the clarity of the genealogy breaks down with Abiud (Matt. 1:13). But it would seem that the point of the genealogy has been to establish the most noble roots possible for Jesus: his descent from the most praiseworthy patriarchs, inclusion in the most honorable clan in Israel, and membership in the most prominent family in that clan. In short, Jesus was born a king, a person of exalted status and honor.

A problem in Jesus' ancestral line arises in the four figures who do not at first glance support the honor of Jesus. Four females—Rahab, Tamar, Ruth, and the wife of Uriah—have been discussed in terms of the scriptural traditions about them, which present them as deficient in the most important honorable quality for females, that is, sexual exclusivity. But midrashic and postbiblical traditions about them present them in a more positive light. On this point, Freed summarizes their thematic presence as indicative that "God intervened, not only in the relationships with the men in their lives, but also to transform their lives from those of questionable, if not sinful, natures to states of innocence and virtue" (1987:15). This continues the focus on Jesus, who is descended both from sinners and saints. Recent feminist scholars argue that the presence of these women in the genealogy gives evidence of a value system that constitutes an alternate to the dominant patriarchal focus of the narrative (Wainwright 1991:61–69, 155–71; Schaberg 1987:20–34; Brown 1993:71–74). The stress given in this study on the rules for an encomium turns our focus on the presence of the women in terms of what they say about the role and status of Jesus, not what they signify in terms of membership and status within the Jesus movement.

From a rhetorical point of view, two possible reasons may account for the females' place in Jesus' genealogy. The four women, whose status seems less than honorable, might be compared to the dishonorable kings in Jesus' genealogy. Jesus ennobled his ancestors, male and female, by his own excellence. From this point of view, the females may benefit from the noble role encoded in Jesus' very name as the one who would "save his people from their sins," past as well as present. The second possibility comes from the popular interpretation of the stories of the four females; it exemplifies how great was the divine favor that rescued them from shame, so that they testify to the divine patronage of Jesus' line, itself a mark of worth. Everyone in this line has always experienced divine favor from God. The rules for the encomium cannot settle the particular exegetical issue of whether the females are shameless or honorable; but in either case, the same rules indicate that praise can be drawn from either interpretation to attest to the worth of Jesus, client-king of the heavenly Patron.

3.2.3 Parents. As regards parents, Matthew informs us that Jesus' putative father, Joseph, is himself a "son of David" (1:20), thus reiterating Jesus' descent from the national kingly family. Besides his royal blood, Joseph is also a "just man," who according to Brown (1993:127) was blameless in keeping the law (see Luke 1:6). He is, moreover, obedient to heavenly commands, and so virtuous according to the canons of "justice" in the Greco-Roman world; he fulfilled his duties to God (1:24). At first the mother of Jesus does not appear to be praiseworthy at all because she is found to be with child, but not of her espoused husband. Yet she proves to be virtuous according to the standard of female worth, namely, sexual exclusivity; she is not an adulteress, and her conception of a child is totally God's doing (1:18–21), not any man's, even Joseph's (1:25; for a bizarre reading of this material, see Schaberg 1987:20–77). Thus Jesus is born of honorable and praiseworthy parents: his virtuous father belongs to the royal family of David, and his mother is evidently beloved of God to be given a son in a miraculous way.

3.3 Birth: Dreams, Signs, and Portents. We noticed earlier that according to the rules for an encomium "marvelous things" which accompany a birth should be noted as indications of the worth of the person born. Here Matthew appears to have followed this general code by including phenomena such as dreams, stars, and prophecies about the child.

3.3.1 Dreams. The evangelist recounts four dreams, one to the Magi that pertains to their divine protection, and three to Joseph concerning providential care of the child Jesus. In Joseph's first dream, Jesus' honor is rescued by the vindication of the sexual purity of his mother (1:20–21); as we saw above, the worth of females in antiquity lay in their sexual exclusivity. Her pregnancy, not by Joseph, puts her and her child in a shameful position. But the heavenly dream tells Joseph that her pregnancy comes about because of special divine favor: "What is conceived in her is of the Holy Spirit" (1:20). A prophecy predicting this (Isa. 7:14) confirms the fact: "A virgin shall conceive and bear a son" (Matt. 1:23). Her honor and that of her son are divinely restored. In this first of Joseph's dreams, the heavenly messenger also names the child, calling him "Jesus" (Heb. *Yeshua'*, from *Yehoshua'*). The name is significant; it is no family name, but a descriptive or functional name whereby the child to be born is ascribed from birth the noble role of a benefactor, one who "saves his people from their sins" (1:21). Thus in the first dream, the mother's honor is not merely secured, but she is elevated in status by special divine favor. And the child conceived is ascribed the honor of being named the nation's benefactor, for he will be "savior" of his people. This first dream, then, fulfills the traditional expectation that dreams herald a hero's birth and claim great worth and status for the child to be born.

Concerning divine favor shown to both Jesus and his mother, Menander Rhetor discusses in his rules for an encomium how a person should be praised according to the classical four virtues. His discourse on "piety" identifies one aspect of piety as "being god-loved (θεοφιλής) and god-loving (φιλοθεότης)": "[T]he former means being loved by the gods and receiving many blessings from them, the latter consists of loving the gods and having a relationship of friendship with them" (1.361.21–25; see Philo, *On Abraham* 50). The rhetor must "show that the greatest number or best of the gods have honoured the city with the greatest or the first or the most numerous honours" (1.361.31–362.7). Illustrating what he means by "god-loved," he explains: "Of the Athenians, how Athena and Poseidon competed for their land; of the Rhodians, that Zeus rained gold on them." Thus according to the rules for an encomium, Jesus should be honored precisely because he is "god-loved" even in regard to his birth.

The other three dreams in Matthew also illustrate that their recipients are "god-loved" and enjoy the patronage of the Deity. For example, the dream of the Magi in 2:12 indicates that the divine benefaction, which first favored them with a star to guide them to God's chosen king, now rescues them from harm. God's favor both leads them to the Christ and sees them safely home. The dreams to Joseph commanding him to escape to Egypt and return from there also illustrate divine favor, either in rescuing Jesus from Herod's imminent slaughter or in returning the heir to his rightful land when it was safe again. Matthew thereby shows Jesus to be particularly "god-loved," and thus honorable. Jesus enjoys the patronage of the most exalted person in the cosmos even from his birth. This favor was also manifested at his baptism, transfiguration, and death. From birth, through life, and in death, Jesus was truly "beloved by God."

3.3.2 Celestial Phenomena. Celestial phenomena were expected in antiquity in both history and encomia. For example, Josephus relates that a star in the shape of a sword stood over Jerusalem for about a year, presaging the destruction of the city (*J.W.* 6.289; Brown 1993:170). Josephus explains such celestial phenomena as an indication of divine benefaction: "Reflecting on these things one will find that

God has a care for men, and by all kinds of premonitory signs shows His people the way of salvation" (*J.W.* 6.310). The Deity shows favor by means of a celestial sign which instructs people either to draw near in safety or to withdraw from harm. The star in Matt. 2:2, 7, 9–10 marks an important birth, not the destruction of a city. Such a sign both heralds the worth of the person born and functions as direct benefaction to those who are "god-loved." It serves as a cosmic marker of Jesus' role and status as the newly born "King of the Jews," an identity ascribed to him by Israel's God. The marvelous event in the macrocosm signals a corresponding event in the microcosm. The star, moreover, constitutes another piece of evidence that the Magi, who are non-Jews and so strangers to God's promises and covenant, were welcomed to share special favors of Israel. For purposes of this argument, it does not matter if the celestial phenomenon was a "star" or a marvelous convergence of planets (Rosenberg 1972), since in either case Matthew and his audience would appreciate its significance as a marker of special status. Therefore, what is said about the star that marked Jesus' birth is fully in accord with the rule in the encomium to draw honor from celestial phenomena that accompany a birth.

3.3.3 Prophecies of Greatness. "Marvelous things" at the birth of an honorable person include also "prophecies" of future greatness. Matthew frequently cites prophecies from prophetic books which are prefaced with the formula: "This took place to fulfill . . . " (1:22) or " . . . so that what was spoken by the prophets might be fulfilled" (2:23; see Brown 1993:96–104). We noticed one example in the announcement of Jesus' conception in Matt. 1:23 where the evangelist himself recalls Isa. 7:14 and links the prophecy and its fulfillment (see also Matt. 2:18 and 23). The evangelist also recounts that Jerusalem's elite, the chief priests and scribes, searched for the appropriate prophecy to learn the birthplace of their king (2:6//Micah 5:2). Matthew's prophecies differ from those noted in lives and encomia. They look to the past, not the future, and so reflect a different pattern from Quintilian's notice of an oracle composed on the spot that prophesies future greatness for someone (see Luke 2:25–38; Talbert 1980). But they function in the same way, namely, as heavenly oracles that publicly acclaim the greatness of the person born. They ascribe great honor to Jesus through the events of his birth.

In summary, this examination of Matthew's infancy narrative of Jesus reveals that stereotypical categories listed in the encomium concerning "origins and birth" are fully reflected in the Matthean narrative. Whether we consider Jesus' origins in terms of *geography* or *generation*, nothing indicated in the encomia on this topic is absent from Matthew. Moreover, only by knowing the conventions of the encomium can a reader appreciate the cultural significance of what Matthew says about Jesus. Since the function of the encomium is the praise of some worthy person, we have seen how Matthew claims for Jesus the extraordinary worth both of being born from the most illustrious patriarchs and kings and of being acclaimed from his very conception as "god-loved." All of the phenomena which accompanied Jesus' birth herald him as a noble person, whether they be dreams, stars, or prophecies. In light of the rhetoric of praise, then, Matthew claims for Jesus the highest of statuses and most honorable of roles.

4.0 Nurture and Training

In the rules of the encomium, after birth, the nurture and training of a person are subjects for praise. The rhetoricians themselves inform us of this topic (see fig. 4.2).

Aphthonius	**Hermogenes**	**Menander Rhetor**
[T]hen you will take up education (παιδεία), which you will divide into inclination to study (ἐπιτηδεύματα), talent (τέχνη), and rules (νόμους).	Next, nurture (τροφή), as in [the] case of Achilles, that he was reared on lion's marrow and by Chiron. Then training (ἀγωνή), how he was trained (ἤχθη) and how educated (ἐπαιδεύθη).	Next comes "nurture" (ἀνατροφή). Was he reared in [a] palace? Were his swaddling-clothes of purple? Was he brought up in [the] lap of royalty? . . . discuss his education (παιδεία), observing here: "I wish to describe [the] quality of his mind." Then you must speak of his love of learning, his quickness, his enthusiasm for study, his easy grasp of what is taught him. If he excels in literature, philosophy, knowledge of letters, you must praise him.

Figure 4.2 Nurture and Training as Subjects for Praise

A person's education and training offer an encomiast an occasion to praise an individual both for ascribed and achieved honor. We noted earlier that ascribed honor can come from one's teacher as well as one's parents, both indications of social location in Hellenistic society. At stake is the expectation that an individual has been properly socialized into the values and behaviors of his culture. Hence the better the teacher, the surer the tradition handed on. Thus education and nurture by an outstanding teacher ascribe honor to an individual precisely because of excellence of the teacher. In terms of achieved honor, Josephus offers an apt example. After claiming great honor because of his birth into a noble family, he presents himself as honorable also by virtue of his education and training:

> I made great progress in my education, gaining a reputation for an excellent memory and understanding. While still a mere boy . . . I won universal applause for my love of letters; insomuch that the chief priests and the leading men of the city used constantly to come to me for precise information on some particular in our ordinances. At the age of sixteen I determined to gain personal experience of the several sects into which our nation is divided. These are three in number—the first that of the Pharisees, the second that of the Sadducees, and the third that of the Essenes. . . . I submitted myself to hard training and laborious exercises and passed through the three courses. Not content, however, with the experience thus gained, on hearing of one named Bannus, who dwelt in the wilderness,

wearing only such clothing as trees provided, feeding on such things as grew of themselves, and using frequent ablutions of cold water, by day and night, for purity's sake, I became his devoted disciple. With him I lived for three years and, having accomplished my purpose, returned to the city. (*Life* 8–12; see Neyrey 1994b:191)

Josephus mentions formidable endowments of memory and understanding, as well as achievements through "hard training and laborious exercises." Presumably he had teachers and mentors in each of the three sects to which he apprenticed himself, and he finally attached himself to Bannus. Thus we learn that Josephus was renowned for his quick learning and memory, that he was educated to know the particular ways of the leading sects of his day, and was schooled in the knowledge and values of his culture. Not only did Josephus enjoy tutoring of outstanding teachers (i.e., ascribed honor), he claims exceptional intelligence as a natural endowment (i.e., achieved honor). (For illustration of this topic in ancient lives, see Cohen 1979:105.)

Matthew totally ignores Jesus' nurture and training. But then, not all composers of encomia prescribed that this be included. Luke, by contrast, did include accounts of Jesus' childhood and the honor he achieved in that period of his life. According to Luke, Jesus was a precocious child, who at the age of twelve sat among the most learned men of his country "listening to them and asking them questions" (Luke 2:46). He was acknowledged as highly intelligent: "All who heard him were amazed at his understanding and his answers" (2:47). But Jesus had no teachers (see John 7:15) nor did he sit at the feet of a celebrated mentor, as did Paul (Acts 22:3). Hence he is all the more to be praised for his outstanding intelligence. A further point is implied in Luke's Gospel: Jesus' learning was focused on the Jewish scriptures and Torah, not the liberal arts of the Greco-Roman world. From this we infer that Jesus was suitably socialized into the local code of expectations of his Judean world, a matter in which he acquired honor.

Furthermore, Luke presents Jesus as fully initiated into the traditions of his people. He was appropriately circumcised on the eighth day (Luke 2:21); his mother underwent the customary purification ritual forty days after his birth (2:22), at which time Jesus himself was dedicated to God as a firstborn son (2:23). Luke narrates that Jesus' family made an annual pilgrimage to Jerusalem for the feast of Passover (2:41), a custom which Luke would have us believe continued after the dramatic visit narrated in 2:41–51. Luke indicates that Jesus continued pious practices learned in his youth when he narrates that at the beginning of his preaching Jesus entered the synagogue on the Sabbath, "as was his custom" (4:16). Thus Jesus deserves honor and respect for following the expectations of the local code of worthy behavior.

Concerning Jesus' craft or trade, Matthew's infancy narrative is silent. But later in the Gospel, Matthew informs us that Jesus is "the carpenter's son" (Matt. 13:55); it is presumed that Jesus took up the trade of his father, which was the custom of most other peoples in the ancient world. Although in the Greco-Roman world those who worked with their hands for wages belonged to the non-elite majority of society (Neyrey 1995:139–40), this evaluation of Jesus' trade does not stand out in Matthew, possibly because of the Jewish tradition of rabbis who worked with their hands (Hock 1980:22–23).

We find nothing in the childhood of Jesus in regard to encomiastic consideration of his education and training. However, being alert to this element of an encomium, we note the story of Jesus' presence with John the Baptizer. Matthew's narrative states that the Baptizer had "disciples" (11:2) and implies that Jesus was one of them at some point in his life. What kind of student was he? It is hardly accidental that the topic of John's and Jesus' respective preachings was the same:

> John: Repent, the kingdom is at hand. (3:2)
>
> Jesus: Repent, for the kingdom of heaven is at hand. (4:17)

Jesus turns out to be the exceptional student who surpasses his mentor. Matthew records that when Jesus came to the Baptizer for his purification ritual, the mentor commented: "I need to be baptized by you, and do you come to me?" (3:14). It would seem that Jesus achieves honor by surpassing his teacher and mentor. But what kind of teacher did he have? Josephus indicates that it was considered part of the education for a younger man to attach himself to a wilderness-dwelling figure, who was strangely clothed, dined differently from customary society, and practiced washing rites (*Life* 11–12). This example supports the suggestion that Jesus' association with the Baptizer, however long or brief, should be read in light of the rules in the encomium that cover nurture and training. As a result, Jesus can be said to have enjoyed an excellent training under the prophet John and to have acquired honor according to the local code of Judea. He truly learned the ways of holiness expected of reformed Judeans and practiced purificatory rites as was expected of Israel's holiest people, thereby acquiring honor as well.

5.0 Summary and Conclusions

In exposing the rules for the encomium in rhetorical handbooks, we have advanced the conversation on Matthew's infancy narrative in several ways. The encomium offers a clear rhetorical model known to people who learned to write Greek. It precisely mandates a fixed complex of items deemed pertinent to narrating the birth of a significant person in terms of *geography* and *generation*. Moreover, the encomium asks speakers and writers to search for "marvelous" phenomena accompanying a birth, such as dreams, stars, and prophecies. The rules for the encomium instruct writers on precisely what to say in terms of origin and birth. In providing formal categories for praising someone in terms of an honorable birth, the encomium offers both a unified presentation and a central rhetorical stance, namely, praise and honor. Matthew's account of Jesus' origins and birth follow in exact detail the conventions for narrating grounds for praise mandated in the rule for an encomium. We conclude, then, that it is both accurate and necessary to read Matthew in light of the encomium, which includes the function of this form, namely, the praise of Jesus as an exceptional and extraordinary hero.

What do we know if we read Matthew 1–2 according to the traditions of praise encoded in the encomium? What honor is attributed to him? First, he belongs to the line of the great and most ancient patriarchs, the most noble tribe of the nation, Judah, and the royal family of David. In terms of the local code, Jesus is ascribed the role and status of "King of the Jews." Therefore, even though his parents are peasant artisans, he nevertheless belongs to noble and virtuous stock, which also redounds to Jesus' praise. He was born, not in the capital city, but in the village famous as the source of the nation's greatest king, David, from which a new king was predicted to come. Signs and portents accompanied his birth: it was heralded by God through a star, which alerted not only magi in the East but also Israelites. God continued to show extraordinary favor toward Jesus by means of dreams which either confirmed his mother's virtue, established his royal destiny, or protected him from harm. Jesus, then, is truly "god-loved," and as such deserving of honor and praise. His role and status, moreover, were proclaimed by God even at his birth: he is "Savior," "King," and "Ruler" of the nation, all of which are grounds for praise, and so he enjoys exalted status.

In addition to framing Jesus' role and status according to the encomiastic rules applied to his ancestry, birth, and education, Matthew has apparently adapted the "general code" in accord with more "local codes," either of traditional Judaism or early Christianity. For example, Matthew's genealogy of Jesus includes both males and females who do not live up to noble standards or cultural expectations. Matthew may be legitimating Jesus' own breaking of the code later, as we shall see. This would, therefore, constitute a rhetorical strategy to offset later criticism of Jesus, by showing how God allowed sinners as well as saints to enjoy divine favor by contact with Jesus. Furthermore, Matthew appears to have adapted the "general code" with local materials drawn from Israel's scriptures and their popular interpretations to compare Jesus with the nation's greatest past heroes (Muñoz Iglesias 1958). Although Matthew's Gospel contains but one oracle that predicts future achievements of Jesus (1:21), he adapts a tradition concerning prophecies and oracles to show that events in Jesus' career have already been prophesied by God, thus securing greater and greater legitimation for Jesus. Thus Matthew can be seen to be "audience specific," a rule urged by Aristotle and Quintilian in their exposition of the rhetoric of praise and blame.

Many modern readers of Matthew's birth account and the encomia might find the emphasis on Jesus' honor and praiseworthiness banal and tedious. But to the degree that honor is truly the pivotal value of the ancient world, then Jesus is being presented for readers in that culture as a unique and exalted person. The original audience could take pride in their noble hero, and negative propaganda from Jesus' enemies could be countered through an encomiastic presentation of his virtues and worth. Thus reading Matthew 1–2 in light of rules for praise found in the encomium articulates the rhetorical strategy of the author to praise and acknowledge Jesus as worthy and honorable Savior and Lord.

5

An Encomium for Jesus

Accomplishments and Deeds

1.0 The Encomium on Accomplishments and Deeds

We have seen how Matthew draws praise for Jesus from his origin and birth. The next topics in the rules for encomia focus on a person's deeds and accomplishments. The rhetoricians who composed the handbooks known as the *progymnasmata* remain our native guides. Concerning the rhetorical treatment of deeds and accomplishments, the ancient rhetoricians have various things to say (see fig. 5.1). Aphthonius calls the rules in the encomium about deeds and accomplishments "the most important topic," which indeed it was. Here is precisely the place where speakers or writers would celebrate a man's prowess or achievements—that is, his achieved honor, the primary grounds for his praise. Most authors of rhetorical handbooks classified a person's actions and deeds in three categories: those of the body, the soul, and fortune. Because of the extent of this part of the encomium, we will divide the material. In this chapter we will examine the deeds of the soul, while in the next chapter we will take up the deeds of the body and of fortune. Recall that "deeds of the soul" refers to what we have come to call "virtues," such as the popular cardinal virtues: wisdom/prudence, justice, courage/fortitude, and temperance/self-control.

2.0 Deeds of the Soul

Two issues need to be addressed before we begin reading Matthew's account of Jesus' "deeds of the soul" in the light of the ancient conversation on virtue. First we need to examine how the material about a person's deeds was organized, and then to examine the definition of "virtue" in antiquity, which encompassed far more than moral categories.

Quintilian showed us that rhetors enjoyed the option to organize their praise of a person's life either *thematically* (according to the four virtues) or *chronologically*: "It has always proved the more effective course to trace a man's life and deeds in due chronological order, praising his natural gifts as a child, then his progress at school, and finally the whole course of his life, including words as well as deeds. At times on the other hand it is well to divide our praises, dealing separately with the various virtues, fortitude, justice, self-control and the rest of them and to assign

Aphthonius	Hermogenes	Aelius Theon	Menander Rhetor
Then, you will bring out the most important topic of the encomium, the achievements, which you will divide into the spirit, the body, and fortune—the spirit like courage or prudence, the body like beauty, swiftness, or strength, and fortune like power, wealth, and friends.	[T]he nature of soul and body will be set forth, and each under heads: for the body, beauty, stature, agility, might; for the soul, justice, self-control, wisdom, manliness. Next his pursuits, what sort of life he pursued, that of philosopher, orator, or soldier, and most properly his deeds for deeds come under the head of pursuits. For example, if he chose the life of a soldier, what in this did he achieve? Then external resources, such as kin, friends, possessions, household, fortune.	Since the good qualities are especially applauded, and . . . are connected with the soul and character, others with the body, and still others are external to us, it is obvious that these three would be the categories on the basis of which we will be able to compose an encomium. Among the external qualities, the first good quality is good breeding . . . then education, friendship, reputation, public office, wealth, the blessing of children, an easy death. Among the bodily qualities are health, strength, beauty, quick sensibility. Good qualities of the soul are the virtuous character traits and actions consistent with them; for example, that he is prudent, self-controlled, courageous, just, pious, free.	"Accomplishments" are qualities of character not in- volved with real competitive actions because they display character. For exam- ple: "He was just in his youth." Next to "accomplishments" comes the topic of "actions.". . . Always divide the actions of those you are going to praise into the virtues (there are four virtues: courage, justice, temperance, and wisdom) and see to what virtues the actions belong.

Figure 5.1 Rhetorical Understanding of Deeds and Accomplishments

to each virtue the deeds performed under its influence" (*Inst. Orat.* 3.7.15). We note that these two approaches are not mutually exclusive and can both exist in the same document.

We saw in the last chapter that a "virtue" might just as well be some form of "excellence," as a moral category. For example, Aristotle indicates in his rhetoric of praise that the parts of "excellence" (ἀρετή) are "justice, courage, self-control, magnificence, magnanimity, liberality, gentleness, prudence, and wisdom" (*Rhet.* 1.9.5), a list which includes moral virtues and civic excellences. Over time, rhetors and philosophers condensed the list to four cardinal virtues (wisdom, justice, courage, and temperance), which became a commonplace known by all (see Diogenes Laertius, *Lives* 7.92; Cicero, *Tusculan Disputations* 3.36–37; Philo, *Allegorical Interpretation* 1.65; Ferguson 1958:24–52).

3.0 Deeds of Justice as Grounds for Praise

Our procedure will be to examine the native meaning of the four traditional virtues in the rhetoricians and then to read Matthew's narrative about Jesus in the light of each virtue.

3.1 Native Informants on Justice and Its Parts.   Readers of Matthew must be on their guard, for the Greek term for "justice" (δικαιοσύνη) is translated variously as "righteousness" (RSV), "all that God requires" (NEV), and "justification" (NAB). Moreover, modern readers of Matthew are heirs to a long preaching and teaching tradition in which this term has been the subject of a controversy that has tended to narrow the discussion of it to "justification by faith," with hardly any consideration of its meaning in the ancient culture (Reumann 1982). To the ordinary Grecophone in antiquity, it simply tended to mean the virtue of "justice." An author in antiquity could presume some general acceptance of this term in accord with the standard and conventional usage of the Greek language. What did it tend to mean?

Although we can learn much from a comparative study of Greek and Roman authors on "justice," we consider the remarks of the *Rhetoric to Herennius* as representative of the tradition (see Aristotle, *On Virtues and Vices* 5.2–3, and Cicero, *On Rhetorical Invention* 2.160–61).

> We shall be using the topics of justice if we say that we ought to pity innocent persons and suppliants; if we show that it is proper to repay the well-deserving with gratitude; if we explain that we ought to punish the guilty; if we urge that faith ought zealously to be kept; if we say that the laws and customs of the state ought especially to be preserved; if we contend that alliances and friendships should scrupulously be honored; if we make it clear that the duty imposed by nature towards parents, gods, and fatherland must be religiously observed; if we maintain that ties of hospitality, clientage, kinship, and relationship by marriage must inviolably be cherished; if we show that neither reward nor favour nor peril nor animosity ought to lead us astray from the right path; if we say that in all cases a principle of dealing alike with all should be established. (*Rhet. Her.* 3.3.4)

The anonymous Roman author of this rhetorical treatise (86 B.C.E.) presents a very conventional understanding of justice, which had become a commonplace in Greek and Latin cultures. This native informant claims that justice can be observed in the public actions of a just person, who knows and lives up to the cultural norms of his society. Following tradition, he indicates that justice typically pertains to three groups: gods, parents, and fatherland, which includes ancestors. He labels a man just who: (1) rewards those worthy of reward (gratitude) and punishes those deserving of punishment, thus honoring the ancestral custom that indicates who is friend and foe of his family; (2) fulfills his duties, that is, he "keeps faith" with tradition ("preserving laws and customs of the state") and social relationships ("alliances and friendships" and "hospitality, clientage, kinship, relationships by marriage"); and (3) respects the basic social stratification of his society. In this regard, he repays hospitality with hospitality, acknowledges the reciprocal duties of patrons and clients, and recognizes his duty to kin and allies by marriage. The "just" person, then, is someone who knows and plays by the specific cultural rules of the game in his cultural context. Implied here is a "local code" of what a specific group expects in patron-client relationships, hospitality, marriage ties, and the like. Proper "nurture and education" would socialize an individual to know and value such expectations.

Menander Rhetor's rules for an encomium treat justice in the kind of code which authors such as Matthew would have learned. His discussion is particularly appropriate for us because he describes in detail a person's relationship with the Deity.

> The parts of justice (δικαιοσύνη) are piety (εὐσέβεια), fair dealing and reverence (ὁσιότης): piety toward the gods, fair dealing towards men, reverence toward the departed. Piety (εὐσέβεια) to the gods consists of two elements: being god-loved (θεοφιλότης) and god-loving (φιλοθεότης). The former means being loved by the gods and receiving many blessings from them, the latter consists of loving the gods and having a relationship of friendship (φιλία) with them. (Menander Rhetor 1.361.17–25)

Again, justice extends in three directions: to the gods, toward the departed, and to one's peers. This represents a slight variation of virtuous duties toward gods, country, and kin. Justice, moreover, is primarily understood in terms of "piety," or one's relationship with the gods. If piety means being both "beloved by God" and "loving God," then a pious or just person is one who enjoys divine favor and patronage and who reciprocates by acting as a "friend" or client of the Deity. In another place, however, Menander defines justice in terms of civic status: "Under justice (δικαιοσύνη) you should commend mildness towards subjects, humanity toward petitioners, and accessibility" (2.375.7–9). Justice is viewed in terms of a particular set of the elite social relationships of patrons and clients. A patron is just when he acts with kindness toward "subjects" and with humanity toward "petitioners." Patron-client relationships greatly occupies the attention of our native informants when they speak about justice.

3.2 Matthew's Presentation of Jesus as Just. What deeds of Jesus would Matthew label as "just" and worthy of praise in an encomiastic work? As we survey Matthew's narrative of Jesus' deeds, it is important to consider how an audience in the Greco-Roman world would likely hear this story. What would they readily understand that escapes us? We argue that Matthew's narrative contains the traditional tripartite division of justice: duties to God, parents, and the dead. When we speak of Jesus' "duties to God," we interpret the relationship of Jesus to God as one of client to patron and son to father. We need not look for formal labels expressive of this relationship. Rather our method is to examine how Matthew displays this relationship in the narrative of Jesus' deeds. How does he present Jesus' loyalty and faithfulness to his patron and how does he display Jesus' obedience to his heavenly Father in Matthew 4–25?

3.2.1 *Jesus' Justice as Faithfulness to His Heavenly Patron.* By being adopted by God in the theophany at the Jordan and commissioned as God's "beloved Son," Jesus became the client/son of God, a remarkable example of ascribed honor. Leaving the world of water for that of the desert, Jesus is immediately tempted to abandon his heavenly patron and become the client of the Tempter. The references in the temptations to "son" in Matt. 4:3, 6 and to Jesus' "obedience" are the key items in this story (Gerhardsson 1966:19–20, 25–35; Stegemann 1985:39–43). We suggest, however, that this scene is essentially about patrons and clients. God has bestowed a great benefit on Jesus, both ascribed honor ("beloved Son") and the potential for achieved honor (i.e., God's "spirit"). The rival patron first challenges Jesus to use his powers for himself and not, as an honor culture would expect, for the benefit of others (4:3, 6). Finally he offers Jesus seemingly greater benefits as his own client: "He showed him all the kingdoms of the world and the glory of them; and he said to him, 'All these I will give you'" (4:8–9). In an honor-shame perspective, the "glory" of the kingdoms of the world would be tempting indeed. Yet, in this programmatic display of Jesus' faithfulness to his true Patron, Jesus speaks traditional words which express his piety (Deut. 8:3; 6:16; 6:13; Gerhardsson 1966:36–66) and thus his loyalty to his heavenly Patron. He earns the respect of Matthew's audience as a just person, namely, as one who lives up to his duties to his God and patron (Malina and Rohrbaugh 1992:42; Rohrbaugh 1995:188–92). Matthew's inaugural story about Jesus suggests that he is both God-loved ("baptismal adoption") and God-loving (resistant of "temptation"). He deserves our praise because of his singular piety and faithfulness, which are parts of the excellence called "justice."

Another example is Matthew's description of how Jesus both teaches his disciples the proper way to address their common heavenly Father-Patron and models it. First he teaches them the prayer known as the "Our Father" (6:9–15), which fully acknowledges the basic patron-client relationship between them and God (Malina 1988:9–11). To God-Patron earthly clients render honor by acclaiming God as heavenly "Father," whose name is most praiseworthy and whose power and sovereignty should be acknowledged (6:9–10). Once they have paid their dues of honor to the Patron, clients may ask for benefaction, such as food, deliverance from debt, and protection (6:11–13). The prayer is glossed by noting the parity of our actions with those of God: forgiveness of other clients of God on earth forms a homology with God's forgiveness of his earthly clients (6:14–15). Jesus models this prayer when, as a dutiful client, he renders "thanks to thee, Father, Lord of heaven and earth," for God's benefaction toward his disciples (11:25–26). Such behavior accords well with the norms of "justice" in the general code of honor. Jesus' obedience and service as client to his Patron is further modeled according to Matthew in the scene in the Garden: "Father, if it be possible, let this cup pass from me; nevertheless, not as I will, but as thou wilt" (26:39; see also 26:42, 45).

"Justice" prescribes that one fulfill one's duties to God, and so the will and pleasure of Jesus' heavenly Patron come before Jesus' own wishes and desires.

Less obvious, at first glance, is how Jesus demonstrates loyalty or "faithfulness" to his Patron and Father. Yet a reader familiar with the ancient discussion of virtue will find many illustrations in Matthew's narrative. For example, Jesus demands that his disciples imitate their heavenly Patron and be "perfect as your heavenly Father is perfect" (5:48). Imitation, of course, acknowledges the worth or significance of what is imitated. "Perfection" in this case consists in the observance of God's Torah, which applies to both the body and spirit, externals and internals (5:21–47); it implies notions of completeness, and echoes typical notions of "purity" and "cleanness" in ancient Judean culture (see Neyrey 1991a:274–85). Similarly Jesus shows his loyalty to God by rebuking Peter, who tried to dissuade him from journeying to Jerusalem. Jesus puts God's will before Peter's notions of what is honorable: "You do not think the thoughts of God, but the thoughts of mortals" (16:23). The "ways of God-Patron" are not synonymous with the ways of the world, and God's wishes have a higher claim. These are but a few examples of Jesus' loyalty to God-Patron expressed in Jesus' teaching about seeking and keeping the "will of God," whether that refers to the Law (5:17–20) or the special ways of discipleship (16:23).

Again and again Jesus reiterates the core of Israel's ancient law, the Ten Commandments. In the antitheses in the Sermon on the Mount (5:21–48), Jesus reforms popular notions of what constitutes the observance of the Ten Words: "You shall not kill" and "You shall not commit adultery" and "You shall not swear falsely" (5:21, 27, 33). Later he criticizes members of the village who merely honor God with their lips, while their heart is far from loyalty to their Patron, for they override the commandment "Honor your mother and father" with rules favoring the enrichment of the national shrine (15:4, 8–9). When asked by a rich young man what he should do to have eternal life, Jesus reiterated the basic law of his Father-Patron: "You shall not kill, You shall not commit adultery, You shall not steal, You shall not bear false witness, Honor your father and mother" (19:18–19). And on another matter, Jesus declares loyalty to God's original plan of marriage proclaimed in Genesis when he forbade divorce allowed by Moses because of "your hardness of heart" (19:3–8). Jesus, therefore, demonstrates the virtue of "justice" by his abiding loyalty to the will and statutes of his Father-Patron, especially the Ten Commandments.

During the week before his death, Jesus demonstrated special loyalty to his Patron. First he entered the "temple of God" and chased from it moneychangers and sellers of pigeons. Although in the eyes of some this clearly indicates utter disrespect for God's holy place (21:23), Jesus justifies his actions precisely in terms of loyalty to God's interests by citing the tradition of prophets who were also zealous for the things of God: "'My house shall be called a house of prayer'; but you make it a den of robbers" (21:13//Isa. 56:7 and Jer. 7:11). As we saw, justice favors customs, laws, and traditions, but in this case Jesus displays justice of a different sort, namely, a higher loyalty or faithfulness to God his Patron in the face of custom and tradition (see Bauckham 1988). In Matthew's version, the institutional defenders of the temple then challenge him, not over the actions mentioned in 21:12–13, but over his liberal dispensation of benefaction from his Patron to "the blind and the lame" who came to him in the temple (21:14). In terms of the cultural concept of limited good, Jesus' rivals view the scene in terms of Jesus' rapidly expanding fame and reputation, and so appear to react in envy. This signals that issues of honor are paramount, not religious ideology. Jesus justifies the fame he earned from this (21:15) by appealing to a scripture passage which indicates that it is the will of God-Patron that his client be praised: "'Out of the mouth of babes and sucklings thou hast brought perfect praise'" (21:17//Ps. 8:3). Thus his loyalty to his Patron results in his own legitimate praise.

Later in that final week, opponents put a series of questions to Jesus. In one particular section of Matthew's narrative (Matthew 22), Jesus repeatedly defends the interests of his God-Patron, thus demonstrating praiseworthy loyalty and so justice. Daube (1973:158–63) pointed out a talmudic passage in which four types of questions were asked a rabbi by way of testing or challenging him: "Four Rabbis taught: Twelve questions did the Alexandrians address to R. Joshua b. Hananiah. Three were of a scientific nature, three were matters of *aggada*, three were nonsense, and three were matters of conduct" (*b. Niddah* 69b–70a). The rabbinic questions bear striking resemblance to those asked of Jesus: (1) "scientific" questions refer to halachic application of the law to specific situations, such as "Is it lawful to pay tribute to Caesar?" (22:15–22); (2) "aggadic" questions deal with contradictions in the interpretation of scripture, such as the question about David's son (22:41–45); (3) "nonsense" questions ridicule a person's teaching, such as the way levirate marriage contradicts belief in the resurrection (22:23–33); and (4) "matters of conduct" deal with theoretical principles of behavior in the Law, such as the question, "Which is the great commandment in the law?" (22:34–40). All of these questions deal with God and Jesus' defense of the honor of his heavenly Patron.

First "Pharisees and Herodians" try to trap him on a question about tribute, a question about the specific application of the Law. Their challenge begins by sarcastically crediting Jesus with "justice," that is, loyalty to God: "We know that . . . you teach the way of God truthfully" (Matt. 22:16). Having put Jesus on the spot, they then pose their difficult question: "Is it lawful to pay taxes to Caesar or not?" (22:18). Jesus' riposte demonstrates his genuine loyalty to God. He dismisses the trick question even as he calls his critics to devotion to God: "Render to Caesar the things that are Caesar's, but *to God the things that are God's*" (22:21). The clever solution to the issue of loyalty to Caesar also claims that God's rights deserve respect as well. But at this point, Jesus does not indicate what those rights are, only that he stands loyally in support of the rights of both emperor and God, which is the heart of "justice."

Second, the "Sadducees" challenge Jesus' belief in God's power when they say "There is no resurrection." Their denial is embodied in the question they ask Jesus to solve about the remarriage of one woman to many brothers according to the levirate law. "In the resurrection," whose wife will she be? This question follows immediately after "Render to God the things that are God's," and provides a succinct explanation of what we should "render to God." "Resurrection" belongs to

God; thus God's loyal client acknowledges the power of his Patron to act in this way (Neyrey 1990b:124–33). Jesus' riposte demonstrates again his loyalty to his Father-Patron: "You know neither the scriptures nor the power of God" (22:29). Loyalty and justice give credit where credit is due: God has power to raise the dead (see Cohn-Sherbok 1981).

The third challenge narrates Pharisees questioning Jesus about the principles of God's Law: "Which is the greatest commandment of the law?" (22:36). We noticed above how loyally Jesus responds on specific points of the Law. Now he answers that the foundational and greatest commandment is "love of God." "Love," in terms of Matthew's cultural world, basically meant "faith and loyalty," in this case, to God. When God shows "steadfast love" to mortals, God extends grace and favor to God's covenant people, acting as faithful Patron. Humans "love" God by expressing the attachment or loyalty expected of a client (Malina 1993b:111). "Love" of neighbor also belongs in the consideration of loyalty and justice, for it is also the "group attachment" which embodies one client's duties to fellow clients of the Patron. Thus Jesus fully displays a form of justice, expressed in loyalty and fidelity, which looks to the interests of God, country, and kin, namely, love of God and neighbor.

Thus all of Jesus' answers in Matt. 22:15–40 demonstrate "justice" in two senses: (1) loyalty and faithfulness, the traditional parts of the virtue, which (2) are directed specifically toward God and kin.

3.2.2 Jesus' Justice and Loyalty to Family.

Justice in the ancient world comprises one's duties to parents and ancestors, as well as to God. Matthew, unlike Luke, does not mention Jesus' obedience to his mother and father (Luke 2:51). Rather, expression of this aspect of loyalty comes in Jesus' discourses (see Pilch 1988:44–59). We noted above that he defended "Honor your father and mother" over local traditions about "korban" (Matt. 15:5); he thus elevated the duty of supporting one's parents over the donation of land and wealth to the temple. He repeated the commandment to honor one's parents as part of the general instruction on how to find eternal life (19:19).

Jesus called God his "Father" and instructed his disciples to do so. And so we consider this material in terms of "justice" and duties to parents. In this regard, Jesus demanded a level of virtuous public behavior that all people could see and that thus would cause them to "give glory to your Father in heaven" (5:16). Hence Jesus teaches that the heavenly Father should be treated like a typical father whose offspring act honorably in the eyes of others and so bring credit to the parent. Disciples, moreover, should imitate their Father (5:45), thus honoring him all the more. They should seek his approval and praise by acting as he wishes (6:4, 6, 17). Jesus' parable about the two sons asked by their father to work in the family fields focuses on the same issue. One son did not embarrass his father in public, but then neither did he do the father's will. The other son, who initially shamed his father by refusing to work in the vineyard, eventually did the will of the father (21:28–32). In one sense both sons fail in justice to their father. Justice requires that sons both say the right thing in public and do it in private, combining appearance with reality and words with deeds. Yet in the case where both sons lack some form of justice toward their father, at least the son who eventually "did the will of his father" receives public praise for justice, that is, fulfilling his duty to his father (21:32).

In an adaptation of the local code of expectations about justice, Matthew contains material which portrays Jesus standing against fathers and families. When James and John joined Jesus as his disciples, we are told that they "left the boat and their father and followed him" (4:22). Later we hear a question concerning the honorable status of those "who left everything and followed you" (19:27). The Gospel clearly honors this behavior, which in the eyes of the culture would seem to lack justice by failing in loyalty to one's father and family. When a disciple volunteered to join Jesus, he told him that discipleship means not burying the dead, a solemn obligation of adult children to their parents (8:21). Once Jesus commanded his followers to "call no man your father on earth" (23:9), presumably loosening the sense of duty to a parent. And he envisions discipleship dividing families, setting "a man against his father and a daughter against her mother" (10:35). In the light of Jesus' replacement of the ties of earthly kinship with a fictive kinship loyalty (12:46–50), this stream of material replaces the sense of loyalty and faithfulness owed parents with that owed God-Father. Outsiders would probably hear these remarks as indicative of Jesus' maverick status and might even conclude that Jesus does not embody traditional notions of justice; but Matthew portrays Jesus pursuing a different kind of justice, placing the interests of his heavenly Father over those of earthly parents. Far from urging lawlessness or total disregard for justice, Jesus urges that all be loyal and faithful to the heavenly Father whose interests rank higher than those of earthly ones. Jesus' own radical obedience to his Father illustrates that he is indeed just and respectful of duties to one's parent.

In summary, Matthew presents Jesus fully embodying justice in his actions and teachings. Jesus is "God-loved" and but also the "God-loving," loyal client of a noble Father and Patron. Moreover, and further enhancing his virtue and so his honor, Matthew shows us Jesus urging others to show the same loyalty to God. Jesus steadfastly defends the interests of God and always places loyalty to God who is both Father and Patron above earthly loyalties. In demonstrating that Jesus excels in justice, Matthew demands for Jesus our respect and praise.

4.0 Deeds of Courage as Grounds for Praise

Courage or fortitude is another of the cardinal virtues, whose specific cultural meaning is supplied by our native informants from antiquity.

4.1 Native Informants on Courage and Its Parts. One of Cicero's rhetorical treatises presents rhetors with a commonplace on courage and its parts:

> Courage is the quality by which one undertakes dangerous tasks and endures hardships. Its parts are highmindedness, confidence, patience, perseverance. Highmindedness consists in the contemplation and execution of great and sublime projects with a certain grandeur and magnificence of imagination. Confidence is the quality by which in important and honourable undertakings the spirit has placed great trust in itself with a resolute hope of success. Patience is a willing and sustained endurance of difficult

and arduous tasks for a noble and useful end. Perseverance is a firm and abiding persistence in a well-considered plan of action. (*On Invention* 2.163; see also Aristotle, *On Virtues and Vices* 4.4; *Rhet. Her.* 3.3.5)

Cicero is echoing here the traditional understanding of courage as the ability to face danger and hardship nobly. The great value of his definition lies in the division of courage into its major parts: "highmindedness, confidence, patience, and perseverance." To paraphrase him, the courageous man acts and is not acted upon: he contemplates and executes great projects. He acts, moreover, confident of success, the type of boldness recognized in Peter and John in Acts 4:13. Yet success rarely comes instantly; hence value is placed on patient endurance of difficult tasks and on faithful perseverance. In another place, Cicero quotes Chrysippus on bravery: "Bravery is the knowledge of enduring vicissitudes or a disposition of soul in suffering and enduring, obedient to the supreme law of our being without fear" (*Tusculan Disputations* 4.53). In other words, obedience to a higher power in patient perseverance at performing noble deeds is also a constitutive element of courage.

Menander Rhetor's rules for an encomium give us precise information about what students learning to write encomia should know about courage. Like most teachers of rhetoric, he looks to the elites of his world when he speaks of models of courage in peace and war: "Courage (ἀνδρεία) is assessed in peace and war. In peace, we see it in relation to accidents of fate—earthquakes, famines, plagues, droughts, and so on. In war, we see it in relation to [results, causes, and] actions under arms" (1.364.17–21). The defeated person bears defeat with fortitude and victory with humanity. Again, looking toward elites, he describes courage in terms of civic virtue: "Courage should be admired on the grounds of the governor's frankness (παρρησία) to the emperor, his struggles against unpleasant circumstances for his subjects' sake, and his not bowing the knee or giving way in the face of fear" (2.416.23–28). Thus Menander supplements Cicero's more traditional understanding with specific concern for public figures in the world of politics.

4.2 Matthew's Presentation of the Courageous Jesus. Matthew presents the courage of Jesus in three ways: Jesus' courageous actions, his discourse about courage, and his modeling of the virtue. We return to the account of Jesus' temptations. In addition to justice, he displays courage when "tested" by the devil. This testing (πειράζειν) should be thought of as a physical contest or battle of wits and not as a matter of conscience, as modern people are wont to understand "temptation." It is, moreover, similar to other "testings," such as the "testing" by the Pharisees who ask Jesus for a legitimating sign (Matt. 16:1), or for his opinion about divorce (19:3), or for his decision about paying taxes to Caesar (22:18; see also 22:35). These "testings" (πειράζειν) conform to the culturally recognizable form of honor challenges, which as we have seen are common in the agonistic world of antiquity. In resisting them Jesus demonstrates courage in the face of enemies to defend his own honor and the claims of his Patron. Moreover, even when the evangelist does not employ the specific language of "testing," we find instances of challenge-riposte, like those in Matthew 22, where Jesus demonstrates not only justice in his duties to God, but also courage in standing up to his opponents' plots and tricks. In all of those instances, Jesus stands firm and delivers a bold defense of his teaching and his actions. He is, then, no stranger to conflict, yet he never demonstrates either fear or flight.

As Cicero noted, courage can mean facing suffering and even death with endurance when these are understood as obedience to the will of a higher power. Thrice in Matthew Jesus tells his disciples that in obedience to God he must journey to Jerusalem where he will meet death (16:21; 17:22; 20:18). The disciples are "distressed," that is, they experience "grief," which is one of the four cardinal vices (Neyrey 1985:50–53). But Jesus steadfastly continues his way toward his enemies and the violence they will inflict on him. He demonstrates great courage in his prayer in the Garden, when, although he desires life ("let this cup pass from me"), he proclaims obedience to God and thus willingness to face his death: "Not as I will, but as thou wilt" (26:39). And when seized by his foes, he could have sought help to escape, but did not out of loyalty to God: "Do you not think that I cannot appeal to my Father, and he will at once send me more than twelve legions of angels? But how then should the scriptures be fulfilled?" (26:53–54). As a mark of courage, then, Jesus did not choose the pleasant over the difficult, nor did he flee from trials and tests. Matthew's Jesus demonstrates the virtue of courage to disciples who must "take up their cross and follow me" (16:24).

Jesus' speech directly and indirectly exhorts his disciples to courage. He twice warns his disciples of terrible crises which they will face, either as the predictable consequences of preaching Jesus' message (10:16–33) or as the events which will precede Jesus' return (24:9–14). Disciples, like sheep, live in the midst of wolves. These wolves may be either one's countrymen—who will prosecute the sheep before governors and kings, flog them before the synagogue, and deliver them up to their councils (10:16–18)—or one's kinsmen, who will rise up and put them to death (10:21). In the face of such trials Jesus exhorts them to courage: "Do not be anxious . . . " (10:19) and "Who endures to the end will be saved" (10:22). In his revelation about the trials preceding his return in glory, Jesus touches again on the same topic: one's enemies are countrymen, who will "deliver you up to tribulation, and put you to death" (24:9). In this time of hatred and betrayal all "who endure to the end will be saved" (24:13). We saw above in Cicero's description of courage that patient "endurance" is a manifestation of the virtue of courage.

In summary, Jesus personally models great courage, especially in facing his arrest, trial, and death. Because he faced conflict and neither fled nor feared, his behavior can serve as a model of courage for his disciples. His discourse, moreover, is filled with exhortations to his disciples to stand firm in the face of crisis and not to fear. He himself is supremely obedient to a higher power in accepting suffering and enduring it with patience. Therefore, in accord with the traditional notions of courage, Jesus was virtuous by the standards of rhetoric and the encomium. He deserves high praise and great honor.

5.0 Deeds of Prudence as Grounds for Praise

5.1 Native Informants on Prudence and Its Parts. To understand prudence or "wisdom" (φρόνησις), we must listen carefully to our ancient informants as they describe this unusual virtue. Aristotle's interpretation embodies the ancient tradition about prudence:

> It belongs to wisdom (φρόνησις) to take counsel, to judge the goods and evils and all the things in life that are desirable and to be avoided, to use all the available goods finely, to behave rightly in society, to observe due occasions, to employ both speech and action with sagacity, to have expert knowledge of all things that are useful. Memory and experience and acuteness are each of them either a consequence or a concomitant of wisdom. (*On Virtues and Vices* 4.1–2)

"Wisdom," Aristotle notes, refers to prudent judgment, which is both practical, in that it understands the right means to an end, and ethical, in that it can distinguish right from wrong. "Wisdom" means the proper use of this world's goods, as well as knowledge of the right or expected behavior, which refers to the social expectations to which individuals are socialized. And because the ancient world was basically a verbal or oral culture, clever and appropriate speech is highly praised as a form of "wisdom." Finally, the wise person knows and appeals to precedents and examples from the past, brings forward for imitation the best of the ancestors, and relies on tradition and the wisdom of the past. Aristotle's definition, then, places strong value on knowing the traditions of the past and showing sensitivity to the local customs of one's culture (Pilch 1991:183–89; Malina and Neyrey 1996:190–91, 197–98).

Cicero's brief description for students of rhetoric supplements the tradition represented by Aristotle. He defines wisdom as: " . . . the knowledge of what is good, what is bad and what is neither good nor bad. Its parts are memory, intelligence and foresight" (*On Invention* 2.160). Cicero describes a wise man as one who commands what is worth knowing in the traditions of his culture ("memory"), and who manifests the intelligence needed to succeed in his various enterprises, which in a competitive and combative culture have to do with gaining and maintaining honor. Finally, the wise man shows providence in planning for success, lest he be shamed for starting a project he could not complete. In all of this we are not so much envisioning a contemplative philosopher as a clever warrior, a street-smart politician, or an ingenious athlete. Odysseus might be our prime example of this.

5.2 Matthew's Presentation of the Wise and Prudent Jesus.

As we read Matthew 4–25, what might we look for as evidence of Jesus' "wisdom"? Wisdom has several faces, depending on whether the "wise" man described is a public figure or not. Greco-Roman elites were expected to be forceful public speakers, and so "wisdom" when applied to them would mean speaking ability that can compare and contrast, distinguish good from evil, and exhort or dissuade. In a culture where the past was highly venerated, a wise speaker appeals to traditional examples and precedents, and calls his audience to imitate their noble ancestors and to live up to their traditions. Yet "wise" is not the exclusive property of elites. Non-elites might also be considered "wise" for their cleverness or "street smarts"; moreover, they too demonstrate wisdom in their knowledge and respect for the local code. Matthew in particular portrays Jesus as a forceful public speaker.

Therefore we will examine Matthew 4–25 for Jesus' speaking skills and the wise content of his speaking.

Matthew portrays Jesus as an adept and forceful public speaker. There are five long speeches of Jesus in Matthew: (1) the Sermon on the Mount (Matthew 5–7), (2) the Missionary Exhortation (Matthew 10), (3) the Parables (Matthew 13), (4) the Law of Correction and Forgiveness (Matthew 18), and (5) the Visionary Exhortation (Matthew 24–25). These speeches structure the Gospel, a point commonly noted by scholars. We must bypass the interesting question of when Matthew portrays Jesus using deliberative or epideictic rhetoric. Rather we focus our attention on the mere fact that Jesus appears as an adept public speaker, a classical sign of a "wise" man according to the general code of honor of his day. Adeptness in speech is especially illustrated by Jesus' witty replies to criticisms and questions asked him.

Scholars regularly call attention to the form of Jesus' responses, correctly identifying them as "chreia." Young rhetors were taught the chreia as one of the standard exercises learned from the rhetorical handbooks we have been studying (Hock and O'Neil 1986:3–47; Mack and Robbins 1989). The chreia typically recorded a provocation addressed to a sage, to which he responds with wit and cleverness. It functioned as a showcase for the cleverness of the ancient wise men. Whether answering questions or deflecting criticisms, a wise and prudent person never lacked the right words to defend himself in conflict. Matthew regularly presents Jesus according to the literary form of the chreia. Examples abound in Matthew, such as the series of hard questions asked Jesus in Matt. 22:15–40; these can be accurately identified as chreiai in which Jesus displays his formidable wit. One other example might help, such as the story narrated in 9:9–13. After Jesus called Levi to follow him, the toll collector invited Jesus to dine with him and his associates. Opponents of Jesus criticize his eating with "tax collectors and sinners," a violation of the local code (9:11). The criticism serves as the provocation to which Jesus responds wittily in two ways. First he cites the obvious, that physicians should attend the sick and not the healthy. Supplementing this clever remark, he adds wisdom learned from his culture: "Go and learn what this means, 'I desire mercy, and not sacrifice.'" He particularly stumps his critics by citing God's word in Hos. 6:6 as superior to their appeal to purity rules; moreover, by telling these learned men to "go and learn," he shames them further. Jesus' remarks, then, portray him as responding well to a provocation in that he can summon up a simile (doctors serving the sick) and a scripture (desiring mercy). His wit, memory, and knowledge of his culture are truly admirable and thus praiseworthy.

Granted that Jesus is a "wise" speaker, what "wisdom" do we find in his words? Inasmuch as Aristotle described "right behavior in society" as an important aspect of wisdom, in Jesus' first public address he concerns himself with this code of "right behavior." Yet he does not simply repeat traditional wisdom, but propounds a new system of "right behavior" which wins the approval, not necessarily of society, but of the great Arbiter of Honor, namely, God. We will devote considerable time later in this volume to the precise ways in which Jesus reforms the code of honorable behavior in his world, but for our present purposes, let us briefly indicate the new wisdom of Jesus' articulation of "right behavior in society." In his makarisms (5:3–12), Jesus redefines what is "honorable," bestowing praise and glory on the begging poor, the hungry, the mourning, and those ostracized. In the Antitheses (5:21–48), besides demanding a higher level of observance by attention to interior attitudes as well as exterior behavior, Jesus proscribes from his male disciples the customary and familiar ways of gaining respect and honor: physical and verbal aggression, sexual aggression, verbal display, vengeance, and the like. Then in the new rules for piety (6:1–18), Jesus demands that his disciples vacate the playing field of honor, leaving the public forum where one's good deeds would be noted by all as "right behavior in society" and performing customary acts of piety in private. Thus in the first part of the great Sermon on the Mount, Jesus attends to how one acts wisely in society, but now according to a new and wiser code.

As we saw in the citation from Aristotle above, ethical wisdom has to do with the distinction between right and wrong and good and evil. Just this sort of wisdom is illustrated in the Sermon on the Mount. Jesus' rhetoric compares and contrasts what is good and therefore desirable with what is evil and to be avoided. For example, Jesus urges wise disciples to seek true wealth, not merely possessions (Matt. 6:19–21). He states with wisdom that one cannot serve two masters (6:24), exhorting his disciples to serve one master only, God, and to seek first the kingdom of heaven as their treasure (6:25–33), thus judging what is good or evil and what is desirable or to be avoided. He compares prudent disciples who hear his wisdom and practice it with those who build a house on rock that withstands storms; in contrast, people who hear his wisdom and do not practice it are likened to those who build on sand and perish in the storm (7:24–27).

The exhortation to his missionary agents contains a wide variety of practical wisdom (Matthew 10). Jesus prescribes a generous service of one's neighbor, which avoids all trace of intemperance or love of money. The disciples will "give without pay" because they have "received without pay" (10:8). Nor will they move from house to house, presumably seeking the best hospitality in recompense for their benefaction (10:11). They learn the secret of when to stay and when to leave (10:12–15), even as they receive instruction on how to withstand hostility (10:16–23). They learn by imitating their master, who was himself rejected by the crowds (10:24–25). It is a wise person who shows "foresight," as Cicero said. Hence disciples wisely anticipate hostility, both its sources (10:34–39) and its shape (10:26–33); to be forewarned is to be forearmed.

Jesus demonstrates wisdom when he anticipates the crises in his own future and predicts his passion (16:21; 17:22–23; 21:18–19). He proves by this that he is no naive peasant unaware of the likely results of his provocative actions. Courage and justice stay his course, although some, like Peter (16:22–23), think it prudent to avoid Jerusalem and its conflict. Similarly, he informs his disciples of the need for prudence to assess the future and providently prepare for it. He tells volunteers that his way includes both homelessness and loss of family ties: "Foxes have holes, and the birds of the air have nests; but the Son of man has nowhere to lay his head. . . .

Leave the dead to bury the dead" (8:20, 22). Disciples must be ready "to take up their cross and follow me" (16:24) and to "lose one's life for my sake" (16:25). For example, Matthew narrates that Jesus told a rich young man whom he loved that perfection lay in "selling all you have and giving to the poor" (19:21). Even members of Jesus' inner circle are asked if they are ready to drink his cup and be baptized with his baptism (20:22–23). Thus Jesus demands of his disciples the kind of providential prudence which he himself demonstrates.

In summary, Matthew's chreiai portray Jesus repeatedly responding to criticism and questioning with clever and witty replies. Jesus knows, moreover, the traditions of his culture and cites relevant materials in defense of his behavior. He clearly distinguishes right from wrong and good from evil, a mark of a wise man. And he manifests prudence in foreseeing crises for himself and others and devising appropriate strategies. Jesus' wit, wisdom, and prudence, therefore, deserve our praise.

6.0 Deeds of Self-Control as Grounds for Praise

6.1 Native Informants on Self-Control and Its Parts.   Temperance or self-control (σωφροσύνη), while often considered the excellence of the mind that masters bodily passions, was a much more complicated item for the ancients in the general code of honor. In one of his rhetorical treatises, Cicero presents a very traditional understanding of this virtue:

> Temperance is a firm and well-considered control exercised by reason over lust and other improper impulses of the mind. Its parts are continence, clemency, and modesty. Continence is the control of desire by the guidance of wisdom. Clemency is a kindly and gentle restraint of spirits that have been provoked to dislike of a person of inferior rank. Modesty is a sense of shame or decency which secures observance and firm authority for what is honourable. (*On Invention* 2.164)

Following tradition, Cicero defines temperance as the mind's control over passions (see Aristotle, *On Virtues and Vices* 2.5; *Rhet. Her.* 3.3.5). This means that temperate persons will know and follow the customs of their culture, thus living an orderly life according to social expectations. Cicero continues following tradition in his enumeration of the parts of temperance, "continence," "clemency," and "modesty." The wisdom which informs "continence" must surely be a culture's proverbs and maxims, such as we find in Proverbs and Sirach. "Clemency" touches on honor and shame directly as it describes the social relations of elites and non-elites; elites are temperate and clement when they do not despise those of lower honor than themselves. "Modesty" pertains to honorable temperance when persons know and behave in accord with the code of honor particular to their culture. In short, we see that temperance is not so much an individualistic virtue, but one which represents a person's honorable sense of shame. Those who know what is honorable and practice what is expected of them are temperate; they live effectively in the eyes of others.

6.2 Matthew's Presentation of the Self-Control of Jesus.

In regard to bodily appetites, let us examine how Matthew portrays Jesus in regard to three areas where temperance would be expected: food, wealth, and sex. Because esus' eating habits receive the most attention in the narrative, we focus on the way Matthew presents Jesus at table (on the anthropology of meals, see Neyrey 1996d:174–78).

Matthew has relatively little to say about the way Jesus ate except to deny the traditional slander that he was a "glutton and a drunkard" (11:19). Rather than issues of temperance and self-control, Matthew's descriptions of Jesus at table touch on two different issues: (1) fasting and (2) table fellowship. Fasting relates more to "piety," which is a part of "justice," than to temperance. For example, fasting was linked with other acts of piety, such as prayer and almsgiving, as the core of public piety (Matt. 6:1–18; Tobit 12:8; Acts 10:30–31). According to the local code of Second Temple Judean religion, fasting constituted a communal symbolic action. Individuals joined together and collectively abased themselves as they petitioned God for benefactions to their nation. Thus, in the local code, fasting points toward duties to God and nation, rather than personal moderation of inordinate desires.

In regard to Jesus' fasting, Matthew presents two conflicting stories. First, the evangelist records that Jesus began his public life as a disciple of a famous ascetic, who wore clothing of camel's hair and a leather girdle and ate locusts and wild honey (3:4). Most recognized John's behavior as symbolic of a distinctive social role as prophet and reformer, although some slandered him (11:18). We noticed earlier that Matthew claims that John was Jesus' mentor, suggesting that Jesus was schooled in an ascetic and symbolic approach to food. Matthew immediately dramatizes this by noting that after his apprenticeship with the Baptizer, Jesus himself immediately "fasted forty days and forty nights" (4:2). By refusing to change stones into bread to satisfy his hunger, Jesus proved to be both "just," or loyal to God, and self-controlled by preferring "every word which comes from the mouth of God" to mere bread (Matt. 4:4//Deut. 8:3). The location of this material at the start of Jesus' public life informs readers that Jesus is hardly a "drunkard and glutton," despite the slanders of some (see 11:19). On the contrary, Matthew presents Jesus' lengthy fast as illustrating his observance of one of the typical acts of piety in accord with the religious ethos of the time. Jesus deserves honor and praise for his fasting, but the practice represents the virtue of piety more than of self-control.

Yet later, Matthew records that Jesus refused to fast in solidarity with the disciples of the Baptizer and the Pharisees (9:14–15); the Pharisees fasted twice a week (Luke 18:12; *Didache* 8.1). Again, the issue is less one of temperance and self-control and more one of symbolic behavior in regard to God's present actions toward the nation, that is, piety. Jesus justifies his actions in terms of a special sense of timing, not as a rejection of fasting in principle. By refusing to fast at this particular time ("as long as the bridegroom is with them," 9:15), Jesus' disciples deny the need to petition God for either forgiveness of sins or needed benefactions. While Jesus, who is presumably the bridegroom, is present, God's great blessings to the Judean nation are immediately forthcoming. So in light of God's great benefaction through Jesus, the appropriate act of piety and thus the national duty becomes one of thanksgiving and celebration, not abasement and petition. Jesus' refusal to fast not only argues for a new duty toward God in light of the abundance of benefaction in Jesus, it symbolically criticizes others for failing to read the signs of the times and for demanding inappropriate behavior (see Malina 1986:185–201).

In addition to Jesus' fasting, Matthew frequently describes Jesus at table, but never in regard to temperance. For example, when Pharisees with strict purity codes object that Jesus "eats with tax collectors and sinners" (9:10–11), the criticism is not about what or how much Jesus eats, that is, temperance, but rather about the symbolic issue of Jesus' observance of purity, which belongs to the virtue of piety, or what is owed God and the nation. In Matthew and the other evangelists Jesus declares by an inclusive table strategy that God extends the benefaction of mercy and even belonging to both noncovenant members and even nonobservant ones (Crossan 1991:261–64). The complete answer to this criticism means that readers should remember divine favor shown to the Magi (2:1–10), the sending of Jesus with healing benefaction to Galilee, "land of the Gentiles" according to Isaiah's prophecy (4:13–16//Isa. 8:23–9:1), and other such actions whereby Jesus acts as "savior of his people."

Similarly, when the disciples husk grain to eat while walking through a field on the Sabbath, the symbolic issues are purity and piety—that is, what behavior honors God on that day. Perhaps included in the story is criticism of eating food not properly tithed, and thus not sanctified, which is another aspect of piety or duty to God. Matthew begins the riposte to this honor challenge to Jesus and his disciples by commenting that the disciples were "hungry" and did something similar to David's eating of the loaves when he too was "hungry" (12:1, 3). This argues that God is neither served by people's hunger nor dishonored by those who assuage it. Thus, against those who maintain a strong purity code as one's duty to God, Jesus argues for a reformed appreciation of Sabbath duty that permits assuaging hunger (12:3), healing the sick (12:10), and rescuing endangered animals (12:11–12). In short, duty extends to self and neighbor, as well as to God. Yet, like the exchange over fasting, this one too symbolizes social positions that distinguish Jesus from his rivals, the Pharisees. As such, then, they have little to say about temperance, but much about piety and purity (see Robbins 1989:107–41).

When Jesus twice feeds crowds (Matt. 14:13–21; 15:32–39), the issues in view have little to do with temperance, but rather underscore his role as broker of God's benefaction to the nation (Malina 1988:11–18). Both narratives note Jesus' "compassion" toward the crowds, first because of their illnesses (14:14) and then because of their long vigil with him in the wilderness (15:32). This suggests that Jesus responds in terms of piety to new needs among his kin and neighbors. Yet the narrative celebrates the enormity of the benefaction which Jesus can provide, so much so that the peasant crowds "ate and were satisfied" (14:19; 15:37). There is no indication of gluttony here, mere satiety of basic needs by the consumption of the most rudimentary of foods, bread and fish, whose plentifulness underscores Jesus' access to God's treasures of blessings.

As to wealth, Jesus advocates self-control in his exhortation not to be a slave of money (6:19–24; 19:24). When Jesus exhorts the rich young man to "sell what you possess, give to the poor, and you will have treasure in heaven; and come, follow me" (19:22), he indirectly describes his own way of life as one contrary to the social expectation of maintaining status. And when his disciples profess that they have left all to follow him, they are praised (19:29). In this light, the silent approval of James and John's leaving Zebedee and the family fishing trade for the sake of discipleship confirms this (4:22); likewise the demand that disciples leave the security of the family home to become disciples (8:19) belongs here. Jesus, then, was himself no lover of money and demanded the same of his disciples. Moderation in regard to wealth, moreover, signals a comparable moderation in the pursuit of honor and esteem which accompanied wealth.

As to self-control applied to Jesus' own sexual relations, Matthew remains entirely silent. He offers no information about Jesus' status as husband and father. Matthew's Gospel, in contrast to Luke, says nothing whatsoever about Jesus' own contact with prostitutes, except his statement that "tax collectors and prostitutes" by virtue of their repentance will enter the kingdom before the chief priests and elders (21:31–32).

Jesus' discourse, however, condemns both fornication and adultery (5:32; 15:19; 19:9, 18), and extends his prohibition to lust of the eye and heart (5:27–28), thus taking a stand in favor of temperance. He proscribes divorce as well, presuming that incidence of divorce was prompted by desire for other women, for either their beauty or their dowry (5:31–32; 19:8). Jesus even goes so far as to praise a eunuch, who has made himself such for the sake of the kingdom (19:10–12), which may refer to males who endure a dishonorable marriage situation (Malina and Rohrbaugh 1992:122). Needless to say, Matthew records Jesus advocating sexual temperance.

Jesus' virtue of self-control, therefore, was of little interest as such to Matthew. We surfaced nothing in regard to food and only incidental materials concerning love of money or sexual excess. Obviously Matthew did not feel any need to rebut the slander that Jesus was a "glutton and drunkard" (11:19) or to emphasize his virtue in these areas.

7.0 Deeds of Magnanimity as Grounds for Praise

In Aristotle's exposition of the rhetoric of praise, he listed other virtues besides the four that became in time the cardinal virtues (*Rhet.* 1.9.5). We consider now some of those other traditional marks of excellence which might be illustrative of Jesus' behavior.

7.1 Native Informants on Magnanimity. Magnanimity has to do with actions that benefit others, not the actor. Aristotle defined magnanimity (μεγαλοψυχία) as "a virtue productive of great benefits to others" (*Rhet.* 1.9.11). This definition became traditional as we consider Quintilian's version of it: "[magnanimity] emphasizes what was done for the sake of others, rather than what he performed on his own behalf" (*Inst. Orat.* 3.7.16; see Theon 9.30–32). Aristotle defined virtue as "an ability for doing good, the greatest virtues are necessarily those most useful to others." Those who act to benefit others, then, would be seen as illustrating the virtue of magnanimity, which is one of the traditional grounds for praise.

When we turn to the New Testament, however, the evangelists never use this precise term, which does not mean that they were ignorant of its reality. They frequently describe the deeds of Jesus as benefiting others. For example, Paul seems to allude to this virtue of magnanimity in Rom. 5:6–8 when he states that "One will hardly die for a righteous man—though perhaps for a good man one will dare even to die." But, he continues, "Christ died for the ungodly . . . ; while we were yet sinners Christ died for us" (see 2 Cor. 5:21; 8:9).

7.2 Matthew's Presentation of the Magnanimous Jesus. Again, although he does not use the term, Matthew presents Jesus as magnanimous. All of his deeds and actions were done, according to the evangelist, to benefit others, not himself. As we noticed in the last chapter, Jesus' God-given name, "Jesus," anticipates his role as the one who "will save his people from their sins" (1:21). By its position early in the Gospel, and in virtue of the importance of the naming process in antiquity, we can read Jesus' naming as a programmatic statement about the nature of Jesus' career, that is, to benefit others. Furthermore, Jesus' words and deeds correspond to his name. He was magnanimous as to healing: Matthew tells us that Jesus healed "every disease and every infirmity among all the people" (4:23). As his fame spread, the various nations brought him "all their sick, those afflicted with various diseases and pains, demoniacs, epileptics, and paralytics, and he healed them" (4:24). His healing extended to "all" people and "every disease and every infirmity." We are told that "Great crowds followed him from Galilee and the Decapolis and Jerusalem and Judea and from beyond the Jordan" (4:25). Evidently, all of Jesus' actions will be done in benefit of others, whether Judean or Gentile, rich or poor, male or female, slave or free.

Accounts of these healings (Matthew 8–9; 15:21–29) and summary statements of Jesus' healing activity occur regularly as well (8:17; 14:35–36). To these healings we should add the pair of feedings (14:13–21; 15:32–39), which obviously benefited thousands. On occasion, Matthew interprets these events for his reader, calling attention to the magnanimity of Jesus' actions: "This was to fulfil the words of the prophet Isaiah, 'He took our infirmity and bore our diseases'" (8:17//Isa. 53:4). Similarly, he describes Jesus' actions in terms evocative of magnanimity: "When he saw them, he had compassion for them, because they were harassed and helpless, like sheep without a shepherd" (9:35). Jesus frequently acts out of "compassion" (14:14; 15:32; 20:34), which actions greatly benefit the people. For this he deserves our praise, because he is an honorable person.

Matthew occasionally expresses Jesus' magnanimity in more general terms. For example, after Jesus rejects the request of the mother of James and John for seats at Jesus' right and left hand, he describes the magnanimous nature of his own role and mission. He reminds them that earthly rulers tend *not* to act with the benefit of their clients in view: "You know that the rulers of the Gentiles lord it over them, and their great men exercise authority over them" (20:25). This must not be the pattern for the disciples, who should imitate the master who benefits many: "The Son of man came not to be served but to serve, and to give his life as a ransom for many" (20:27). Thus far Jesus has acted as benefactor to the needy in actions that benefit many. But this remark goes one step further in that it indicates that Jesus will benefit "many" in the generous gesture of his dying. Later, at the final supper of the disciples, Jesus interprets the cup he distributes in terms of magnanimity: "This is my blood of the covenant, which is poured out for many for the forgiveness of sins" (26:28).

Whether "saving his people from their sins," "preaching . . . teaching . . . healing," "giving his life as ransom for many," or pouring out his blood "for the forgiveness of sins," Jesus' public actions were on behalf of others, not himself. Matthew describes him as acting out of singular magnanimity. And a man such as this must be considered honorable and worthy of praise.

8.0 Summary and Conclusions

Matthew follows a chronological pattern in presenting the deeds and actions of Jesus, from baptism, through tours of teaching and healing, traveling to Jerusalem, and dying. But his narrative of Jesus' deeds is much more than a chronological record. The various titles that Matthew periodically ascribes to Jesus and the descriptions of his actions indicate that Jesus manifested several virtues of the soul to a high degree. The rules for the encomium offer an important perspective on the rhetorical significance of Matthew's narrative of Jesus' deeds. They are told precisely as illustrations of virtue, which is the foundation of all praise, worth, and honor. This, we maintain, is also part of Matthew's narrative plan. As we review the deeds of Jesus from the perspective of our native informants, we can appreciate the extraordinary grounds for praise and honor which the narrator has provided. Jesus' actions and words, when seen in the light of the excellence known as "justice," clearly display to an eminent degree what his world highly valued by that virtue. He displayed his justice by faithfulness to his Patron-Father and by his knowledge and defense of the customs, laws, and traditions of his culture. Even when he instructs disciples to break some ties with family, this is always done with a view to a higher loyalty, namely, the will of God.

Matthew presents Jesus as courageous, especially as he faces his death. The evangelist's encomiastic intent is clear when even his executioner praises Jesus, "Truly this was the Son of God" (27:54). Jesus' wisdom and prudence appear when he regularly delivers a clever riposte to questions or criticisms, all in accordance with the rules in the *progymnasmata* for the chreia. Jesus manifests an excellent command of the scriptures, the authoritative source of wisdom in his world. His wisdom is evident in his foresight about crises to come, in his ability to distinguish good from evil, and in his wise teaching to the crowds. To a lesser degree, self-control and moderation are indicated in Matthew, as we have seen. Nevertheless, some matter for praise can be found here in Jesus' teaching and actions. Matthew portrays Jesus as magnanimous through accounts of his healings, feedings, and teachings. As he himself said, he came not to be served, but to serve others, even to the point of laying down his life for them, the most singular mark of magnanimity.

We find, as we might expect in a work of its period, that Matthew's Gospel narrates the deeds of the noble person, Jesus, in such a way as to indicate his virtues. We find in Jesus' "deeds of the soul" the virtues which the rules for an encomium and the rhetoric of praise state as the grounds for honor and praise. Clearly the rules for the encomium, thus far, have been useful markers to appreciate the rhetorical and thematic thrust of Matthew's account of Jesus.

6

An Encomium for Jesus

Deeds of the Body and Deeds of Fortune

1.0 Introduction

We focus again on Jesus' public ministry (Matthew 4–25) in terms of his "accomplishments and deeds." Whereas we considered in the last chapter the encomiastic subheading of "deeds of the soul," we focus now on the other two topics, "deeds of the body" and "deeds of fortune." "Deeds of fortune" (power, wealth, friends) reflect "external qualities," which most frequently come to an individual by fate, luck, and chance (i.e., ascribed honor). "Deeds of the body" (beauty, health, strength) are originally ascribed as honor with which a person is born. Yet one may increase and augment them by toil and labor in the city-state's *gymnasium,* thus achieving honor in this regard.

2.0 Deeds of the Body

On the topic of Jesus' "deeds of the body," Matthew is generally silent. It may be that such a category would have been more appropriate in a Greco-Roman context, rather than in Matthew's Christian-Jewish milieu. The topic would seem to be more fitting in regard to elite males who trained for war (see 2 Cor. 10:3–5) and who practiced competitive games in the local *gymnasium* (see 1 Cor. 9:24–27). Inasmuch as Jesus is said to travel constantly, especially to faraway places such as Tyre and Sidon, Caesarea Philippi, the Decapolis, and Jerusalem, we must presume that Matthew envisions Jesus as enjoying good health relative to his age. Yet neither Matthew nor any other New Testament writer tells us what Jesus looked like, whether tall, handsome, strong, agile, and so on. Apparently he had a strong voice, for he addressed large crowds. Apparently he was sufficiently strong to endure the torture that preceded his death.

Luke, however, states that Jesus was "about thirty years of age when he began his ministry" (3:23), a point which no other evangelist mentions. Two observations are in order. First, as Buchanan has shown, those who would assume leadership roles of national significance in the time of Jesus must be at least thirty years of age but not yet fifty (1995:297). Thus Luke would have us consider Jesus mature enough for an important public role. Second, "thirty years old" indicates a mature, if not older, man in the ancient world relative to both survival and life expectancy rates at the time (see Frier 1982, 1983). One social historian of antiquity offers a chilling estimate of the life expectancy in Rome, which would have been less severe than life in rural areas:

> In pre-industrial society, however, probably a third of live births were dead before they reached the age of six. By sixteen something like 60% of these live births would have died, 75% by twenty-six and 90% by forty-six. Very few—3% maybe—reached their sixties. Not for nothing do the ancients glorify youth and shrink with repulsion from ageing. A man who reached forty could well be in atrocious physical shape. (Carney 1975:88)

Hence, Jesus would belong to the 20–25 percent of the population in his age bracket and be considered a mature adult, if not an elder.

3.0 Deeds of Fortune

The authors of the textbook rules for an encomium synthesized a tradition at least as ancient as Aristotle about what brings a person happiness. Aristotle had listed the parts of "happiness" as:

> Good birth, numerous friendships, worthy friendships, wealth, good children, numerous children, a good old age, as well as the virtues of the body (such as health, beauty, strength, physical stature, athletic prowess), reputation, honor, good luck, virtue. (*Rhet.* 1.5.4)

The rules for an encomium followed the more recent tradition of dividing these into two parts: "deeds of the body" and "deeds of fortune." Although on occasion they called them "external qualities," these were, nevertheless, part of the general code of excellences that were thought of as sources of praise. We cite only the remarks of Menander Rhetor on this, while noting that all of the authors of the *progymnasmata* are identical on the topic of "deeds of fortune."

> After "actions" you should put in the topic of Fortune, saying that "favorable Fortune accompanied him in his life in every way; wealth, happiness of children, love of friends, honour from emperors, honour from cities." (2.420.27–31; see also 2.376.24–31)

All agree that reputation, friends, wealth, and power distinguish a person as having public worth. We remember that "virtue" most essentially means something which is outstanding and extraordinary, that is, something which sets an individual apart from the crowd. Such a person is therefore admired, valued, and publicly honored. For the purposes of this study, we will focus on only three of these which seem to correspond to Matthew's emphases in the narrative about Jesus: that is, reputation, friends, and power.

3.1 Reputation as Grounds for Praise. The Greeks valued reputation (φήμη) so highly that in one instance the orator Aeschines called it a deity: "[Y]ou will find both our city and forefathers dedicated an altar to Common Report (φήμη), as one of the greatest gods; and you will find that Homer again and again in the *Iliad* says, of a thing that has not yet come to pass, Common Report came to the host. . . . For all who are ambitious for honour from their fellows believe that it is from good report that fame will come to them" (*Against Timarchus* 128–29). Good reputation is precisely a grant of respect, an acknowledgment of some excellence and so a source of praise.

Chapter 2 in this study began with a list of the notices of Jesus' growing reputation, to which we call renewed attention here. According to Matthew's narrative, Jesus both enjoyed a good reputation and was acutely sensitive to what people thought of him. As he went about all Galilee teaching, preaching, and healing, "His fame (ἀκοή) spread throughout Syria. . . . [G]reat crowds followed him from Galilee and the Decapolis and Jerusalem and Judea and from beyond the Jordan" (4:24–25). Jesus enjoyed a reputation not only at home in Galilee, but in Judea and the surrounding nations as well. By attention to Jesus' fame right at the beginning of his career, Matthew serves notice of the honor of Jesus, honor which will not fail throughout his career, and which will grow beyond the confines of the narrative.

Throughout the story, Matthew notes that peoples far and near keep hearing about Jesus. John heard in prison about the deeds of the Christ (11:2) and sent disciples to confirm the news. Jesus simply tells the Baptizer's disciples to report his reputation: "Tell John what you see and hear" (11:4). Herod too "heard about the fame of Jesus" (14:1), which was based on his great deeds; he concluded that as John the Baptizer's heir, Jesus enjoys his power and "that is why these powers are at work in him" (14:2). Even Syrophoenician women learn of Jesus' reputation (15:22), as well as blind beggars (20:30). All Jerusalem heard that the famous Jesus of Galilee was coming to the city and acknowledged his worth and status by a glorious reception in which they spread garments and branches in his path and acclaimed him: "Hosanna to the Son of David" (21:9) and "the prophet Jesus from Nazareth of Galilee" (21:11). The very narrative of Matthew stands as evidence that the reputation Jesus enjoyed during his life continues.

In one particular incident, Jesus apparently demonstrates appropriate sensitivity for his reputation. At Caesarea Philippi in upper Galilee, Jesus explicitly asks his disciples about his reputation: "Who do men say that the Son of man is?" (16:13). Although much ink is spilled over the response of the disciples and the alleged secret that results, no one has bothered to ask why Jesus asks the question in the first place. From a cultural perspective, it would seem that Jesus as an honorable man is sensitive to his reputation (Malina and Rohrbaugh 1992:231). The initial answers of the disciples are true and heartening: "Some say John the Baptist, others Elijah, and others Jeremiah or one of the prophets" (16:14). Readers may judge such identifications as inadequate, which may well be part of the rhetorical strategy of the evangelist; but it is surely no mean thing to be likened to the greatest of the nation's prophets. Then Jesus asks his disciples for their own evaluation of him, that is, his reputation and fame in their eyes. By virtue of a divine revelation Peter declares that Jesus is "the Christ, the Son of the living God" (16:16). Thus at this climactic place in the narrative, Jesus enjoys the reputation as Israel's most elite person. It belongs, moreover, to honorable and praiseworthy people to be concerned about their reputation (see Demosthenes, *On the Crown* 51.15).

3.2 "Friends" as Ground for Praise. When the ancients spoke of "friends," they did not necessarily mean the interpersonal emotional relationships which moderns value so highly. Their use of the term "friend" often masked a more complicated and formal relationship between patrons and clients (Elliott 1987; Malina 1988; Moxnes 1991). For example, Luke mentions that a local centurion sent "friends" to Jesus to solicit his aid; one batch of these "friends," namely, Judean "elders," explained the formal relationship between the centurion and the synagogue: "He loves our nations, and he built us our synagogue" (7:5). "Love" here means some form of patron-client relationship with their village. As the centurion's clients, they acclaim that the centurion "is worthy to have you do this," a gesture expected by clients. "Worthy," "friend," and "love" have to do with patron-client relationships and mask by polite language the delicate negotiations being transacted (see Moxnes 1988a:54, 59; 1991:252–53). Similarly, at Jesus' trial before Pilate the crowds put Pilate on the spot with their statement: "If you release this man, you are not Caesar's friend; any one who makes himself a king sets himself against Caesar" (John 19:12b). "Friend" here refers to the object of political patronage (Bammel 1970:205–10; Brunt 1965:1–20; see Josephus, *Ant.* 12.298; Philo, *Flaccus* 40). Thus, "friends" such as Pilate owe Caesar a debt of loyalty as the patron who ascribed them the honor of being named Judea's procurator. Whatever honorable status Pilate enjoys depends on his being the faithful client of an imperial patron, namely, a "friend" of Caesar's. If we consider "friends" to be a coded expression of patron-client relationships, then does Jesus enjoy the support of a patron, and is he in turn a patron to clients? Is Jesus the "friend" of an important Patron, and does he in turn have "friends"?

When we ask about Jesus' patrons, we must consider first and foremost God. At times Matthew expresses Jesus' relationship to his Patron-God as that between a father and a son (D'Angelo 1992:623–30; Malina 1988:9–17). Like Mark and Luke, Matthew understands that at his theophany at the Jordan Jesus is a mortal person uniquely chosen for special favors by his Patron: "This is my beloved Son, with whom I am well pleased" (Matt. 3:17; see Rohrbaugh 1995:187–92). God thus sets him apart in a special role, "son," as the unique object of divine favor. This episode stands out in the narrative as the clearest statement that Jesus enjoys exceptionally high status, ascribed to him by the sole arbiter of honor in the world, who is God. And so, the appropriate social lens for appreciating Jesus' relationship to God is that of the patron-client relationship or "friendship." In light of these heavenly claims on Jesus' behalf, all peoples must acknowledge his status or face the consequence of the wrath of his Patron. Thus from the beginning of his life, Jesus enjoys God's adoption of him as "son," which was manifested to the world at the Jordan and later to select disciples on the mountain (Matt. 17:5; see 16:17).

Patronage essentially consists in the demonstration of favoritism toward select clients. The more unique the favoritism shown, the more valued the client. In regard to Jesus, Matthew tells us that Jesus' special status is that of a unique client when his heavenly Patron shows providential care to remove the infant Jesus to safety to Egypt and return from there. The event is touted as the fulfillment of what his God-Patron spoke long ago by a prophet, "Out of Egypt I have called my son" (Matt. 2:15//Hos. 11:1). Clearly, this is no ordinary child. During the course of his life, moreover, Jesus' Patron-Father bestows extraordinary benefactions on this special client, giving him (1) *esoteric knowledge* ("All things have been delivered to me by my Father; and no one knows the Son except the Father, and no one knows the Father except the Son and anyone to whom the Son chooses to reveal him," 11:27) and (2) *unique power* ("All authority in heaven and on earth has been given to me," 28:19). In addition to these formal expressions of patronage, Matthew understands Jesus' signs and wonders as special grants of power from God. Whether he heals, calms storms, or multiplies food, Jesus stands out as the unique person on earth who has ready access to limitless, but otherwise inaccessible, goods. We see Jesus, then, as a most favored client-son of an extraordinarily noble Patron. For this he deserves our admiration, praise, and honor.

Yet this same Jesus has client-friends of his own. Or perhaps a more accurate way to phrase it is to say that Jesus functions as a broker of the heavenly Patron's benefaction to God's clients (Malina 1988:11–18; Moxnes 1991:258–60; and now deSilva 1996a:94–100). Matthew repeatedly tells us that because of the disciples' association with Jesus, they are likewise blessed with divine patronage. For example, concerning the needs of these new clients, Jesus clarifies the way in which their Patron works: "Your heavenly Father knows that you need them all" (6:32). Not only that, but in virtue of special favoritism toward them, they should "seek first the kingdom of God . . . and all these things shall be yours as well" (6:34), which probably refers to sufficiency in food and clothing, the basic goods needed by ancient families. Moreover, Jesus tells these clients that they need only ask their God-Father, who will give them not only their "daily bread" (6:11), but whatever else is needed: "How much more will your Father who is in heaven give good things to those who ask him" (7:11). Even without asking, clients are assured that God-Father will providently provide what is needed (10:19–20). While not one sparrow falls to the ground except the Father wills it, so the hairs of the heads of God's clients are numbered (11:29–30). They enjoy, moreover, the special protection of angelic guardians who "behold the face of my Father always" (18:10); for it is not the will of their God-Father that "one of these little ones perish" (18:14). All of this comes to the disciples by virtue of the brokering of Jesus.

Certain disciples, because of their friendship with Jesus, enjoy a corresponding special favoritism. For example, Simon Peter's acknowledgment of Jesus as Christ and Son of God must be understood as a unique heavenly benefaction: "Flesh and blood has not revealed this to you, but my Father who is in heaven" (16:17). This same Peter experiences favoritism from Jesus four times in regard to special gifts of esoteric knowledge: (1) he saw Jesus' transfiguration and observed the subsequent theophany (17:1–8); (2) he received special instruction about the half-shekel tax and a miraculous means of finding the coins to pay it (17:24–27). Finally, he asks for special information from Jesus about (3) purity concerns (15:15) and (4) forgiveness (18:21–22). Comparably, Jesus blesses his Patron who in another context likewise shows unique favor to other of his friends: "I thank thee, Father, Lord of heaven and earth, that thou hast hidden these things from the wise and understanding and revealed them to babes; yea, Father, for such was thy gracious will" (11:25–26). These clients in turn are told how favored they are: "To you it has been given to know the secrets of the kingdom of heaven, but to them it has not been given" (13:11), and "Blessed are your eyes, for they see, and your ears, for they hear" (13:16). Jesus concludes his remarks on the favoritism shown his disciples by comparing them with former clients and favorites of God-Patron: "Truly, I say to you, many prophets and righteous men longed to see what you see, and did not see it, and to hear what you hear, and did not hear it" (13:17).

Thus, under the topic of "friends" Matthew has much to say about Jesus. He demonstrates that Jesus was himself the favorite client of the highest Patron, who is God and Father. In virtue of this Jesus should be highly evaluated as a person of worth and standing, with access to the wealth and power of so powerful a Patron. As we saw earlier in the discussion of "deeds of the soul," Jesus fulfilled the social expectations of such a client by his "deeds of justice," that is, loyalty and faithfulness to God. Furthermore, Jesus should be honored for his role as the broker of the blessings of the heavenly Patron. His disciples, who become his "friends," that is, his clients, enjoy special favoritism in access to healing, foods, wisdom, and all the other good things of this world (Matt. 8:14–15; 10:1; 19:28). Jesus' ability to provide new blessings and benefits provides convincing testimony to Jesus' unique place in the system. Finally, we saw that Jesus himself instructed his disciples in the logic of patron-client relationships. Jesus deserves, then, high praise because of his place in the network of "friends," those in heaven (i.e., God-Father) and those on earth (i.e., disciples).

3.3 Power as Grounds for Praise. In his rhetorical treatise, Cicero lists power among the "external qualities" (i.e., "deeds of fortune"): "public office, money, connexions by marriage, high birth, friends, country, power" (*On Invention* 2.59.177; see *Rhet. Her.* 3.6.10 and 3.6.14). Cicero has in mind the elites of Rome, who enjoy ascribed honor which comes from membership in a prominent family or *gens*. Earlier he defined "power" as "the possession of resources sufficient for preserving one's self and weakening another" (*On Invention* 2.56.169); thus he situates it squarely in the context of an agonistic world where challenge ("weakening another") and riposte ("preserving one's self") are the chief aims of an honorable man. Quintilian's definition stresses the beneficial results of power in patron-client relationships between the gods and mortals, an aspect of this quality which might help us understand Jesus' miracles as natives of his world would. Quintilian writes:

> [W]e proceed to praise the special power of the individual god and the discoveries whereby he has benefited the human race. For example, in the case of Jupiter, we shall extol his power as manifested in the governance of all things, with Mars we shall praise his power in war, with Neptune his power over the sea. (*Inst. Orat.* 3.7.7–8)

Power will vary from person to person, a principle which is true for gods as well as mortals (see Aristotle, *Rhet.* 2.17.1–2). Not all men will be monarchs, warriors, or athletes; many will act as patrons to benefit their clients and defend them against their enemies.

In regard to Matthew's account of Jesus, post-Enlightenment criticism generally discusses the topic of "power" under the rubric of "miracles" or "signs and wonders," with the focus on the historicity of the accounts. Recent study of Jesus' miracle stories in Matthew has focused on the collection in chapters 8–9, either comparing it with Moses' ten plagues (Grundmann 1968:245–46) or stressing its geographical distribution (Theissen 1983:209–11) or highlighting some theme, such as "mercy" (Cope 1976:65–73) or "Christology" (Held 1963:246–53). To these we bring a focus on rules for praise in the encomium, such that we aim to appreciate Jesus' miracle stories as acts of "power" and understand them in terms of the praise which they earn for Jesus. Hence, we will examine them in several ways: (1) their appropriate cultural taxonomy, (2) the honorable benefaction displayed by them, (3) their function as credentials for Jesus or grounds for his praise, and (4) the relationship of "authority" to "power." In passing we note that all of the evangelists use the term "power" (δύναμις) to describe the marvelous and miraculous actions of both Jesus (Matt. 11:20–23; 13:54, 58; 14:2) and God (22:29). The mighty deeds of Elijah and Elisha were not so labeled, although the Hebrew scriptures regularly speak of God's power (1 Chron. 29:11; Ps. 21:13; 79:11; Ex. 15:6).

3.3.1 Taxonomy of Healings: Power over Demons. Matthew narrates many types of miraculous acts of power: (1) healings, (2) multiplication of foods, (3) calming of storms and walking on water, (4) withering of a fig tree, and (5) catching of a fish with a tax coin in its mouth. By far the most important acts of power for this study are Jesus' healings, for when appreciated in their cultural background, they demonstrate extraordinary power wielded by Jesus. John Pilch, an expert on the anthropological understanding of illness and wellness in antiquity, makes the following points (1986:104–5; 1991:200–203). He identifies the appropriate taxonomy for classifying and understanding miracles in terms of spirit possession. In a prescientific world which knew nothing about germs or viruses, illness was generally thought to be caused by a superhuman agent with power to harm human beings (see Luke 13:18 and Rousseau 1993; Twelftree 1993:22–47). Matthew likewise understands illnesses such as dumbness (muteness) (9:33) and deafness (12:22–24) as caused by possessing spirits. In addition, Matthew is unique in describing how a heavenly figure, the personified moon, likewise afflicts people on earth. On two occasions he describes ill humans as "moonstruck" (σεληνιαζόμενους, 4:24; 17:15), indicating that those illnesses were caused by a celestial demon. Thus when Matthew tells us of people suffering from "disease" (νόσος) or "affliction" (βάσανος), the culturally appropriate understanding requires us to appreciate these illnesses as attacks by various evil spirits or demons, that is, acts of power that harm humans. Conversely, when Jesus heals, he too acts with power to master the possessing spirit and thus to liberate the ill person from that slavery. If we are correct in seeing how the ancients understood phenomena like storms as caused by evil spirits (see Kee 1968:242ff.; Robinson 1957:40–41), then Jesus' "rebuke" of the storm demonstrates power over the storm demon as well (Matt. 8:26). His healing miracles, then, demonstrate a superior power.

Directly related to the issue of Matthew's taxonomy of illness as spirit aggression, Matthew on two occasions uses the expulsion of illness-causing spirits to air a controversy over the source of Jesus' power. After Jesus healed a dumb man by expelling the illness-causing spirit ("When the demon had been cast out, the dumb [mute] man spoke," 9:33), the public verdict about this was both praise and blame. Some judged that Jesus' power came from God, and so gave Jesus praise; but others censured him for acting as Satan's agent (9:34). Later Matthew narrates a similar story about Jesus' power in expelling a demon that caused dumbness and deafness: "Then a blind and dumb demoniac was brought to him and he healed him, so that the dumb man spoke and saw" (12:22). Again some expressed the right verdict, and to Jesus' praise acknowledged that he enjoyed the God-given power of the Son of David (12:23; see Duling 1975, 1978); yet others censured him for acting with demonic power: "It is only by Beelzebul, the prince of demons, that this man casts out demons" (12:24). These incidents suggest several conclusions: (1) illness is caused by spirit aggression, and healing is a type of exorcism; (2) healings are acts of power which expel the afflicting demon; and (3) the source of Jesus' power is debated, resulting in either praise (i.e., he acts with God's holy spirit) or blame (i.e., he acts with the power of the prince of demons). Yet, power is always at stake. And with power, honor.

Matthew records Jesus' traditional argument to settle this controversy. Jesus' reply in 12:25–32 focuses on three points. He argues from analogy that "allies do not fight"; hence, Jesus' acts of power are not undertaken in loyalty to the prince of demons, but rather as acts of war against this enemy (12:25–26). Second, his power comes from God, and so it is "by the spirit of God" that he casts out evil spirits (12:28). Third, Jesus compares his actions to those of a victorious warrior who raids the house of a "strong man" and plunders his goods. In one sense Jesus' remarks confirm the scenario we have proposed for understanding "illness" as a form of demonic possession. Those overpowered by demons are likened to slaves and booty captured in a raid and taken to the raider's stronghold. On this point, Jesus must be "stronger than" the raiding "strong man," since he has power to "bind the strong man," enter his house, plunder his goods, and take his slaves (12:29). And so, Jesus claims power to defeat the power of demons whereby they conquer and capture. This power, moreover, comes from God, not the prince of demons, and he uses it to benefit others with "wellness" or liberation from oppression. Thus, the correct public verdict will acknowledge God as the source of Jesus' power, thus crediting Jesus with great ascribed honor that merits our praise.

Moreover, the issue of Jesus' power has been a clear and important theme of Matthew's Gospel from the beginning of Jesus' public career. John the Baptizer prophesied that Jesus would "baptize you with the Holy Spirit and with fire" (3:11), by which he meant that Jesus would have access to a great power ("Spirit") with which he would benefit God's people. This power represents a unique honor ascribed to Jesus by God: "the Spirit of God descended like a dove and alighted on him" (3:16); it led Jesus into the desert to engage a rival spirit, the devil, in combat (4:1). Later, Jesus began his career with great power in both word and deed: ". . . preaching the gospel of the kingdom and healing every disease and every infirmity" (4:23). His power was such that he could master and expel *every* sort of illness-causing demon: "They brought to him all the sick, those afflicted with various diseases and pains, demoniacs, epileptics [i.e., "moonstruck"], and paralytics, and he healed them" (4:24). For insiders, then, God is the source of Jesus' power and, when it is seen correctly as a grant of ascribed honor, warrants our praise.

3.3.2 Power as Benefaction. Power, according to Cicero, enables an honorable man to help his friends and harm his enemies (Hester 1977; Blundell 1989). Quintilian described it as the ability to benefit others. Hence let us examine how Jesus' miraculous powers demonstrate his ability to benefit friends and to bestow benefaction. In one sense, all of Jesus' healings benefited those whom he liberated from illness-causing demons. This benefaction was so highly prized that people regularly carried their ill relatives and friends to Jesus for this purpose (see 4:24; 8:16; 15:30) or came themselves to petition him for this favor (15:21–28; 17:15–18). Some people pleaded for this benefaction by asking for "mercy," which in the grammar of patron-client relationships constitutes a client's request for a special "favor" or benefaction: "Have mercy on us, Son of David" (9:27; 15:22; 17:15; 20:30; see Malina 1988:5; 1993c:83–86). Comparably, Matthew often describes Jesus in a healing context as showing "compassion" (9:36; 14:14; 15:32; 20:34), which illustrates a patron's favoritism to a client. Finally, one might look to the argument Jesus uses when he heals a man with a withered hand on the Sabbath. If it is permissible to rescue one's animals from danger on the Sabbath, all the more, claims Jesus, "it is lawful to do good on the Sabbath" (12:12); in this context "doing good" simply means benefiting another. Thus, if acts of power which benefit others constitute grounds for praise, Jesus' healings should be culturally appreciated as acts of favor, benefaction, and grace bestowed. Thus they deserve admiration and praise: "The crowds marveled, 'Never was anything like this seen in Israel'" (9:33).

3.3.3 Power as Credentials for an Honorable Role and Status. Finally, Jesus' healings and acts of power function as his credentials and thus as occasions for public acknowledgment of his honorable role and status. News of "the deeds of the Christ" prompts the imprisoned Baptizer to send agents to check on the report. When asked about his role, "Are you he who is to come, or shall we look for another?" (11:3), Jesus merely catalogues his powerful actions as the grounds for his reputation: "Go, tell John what you see and hear: the blind receive their sight, the lame walk, lepers are cleansed, the deaf hear, and the dead are raised" (11:4–5). King Herod hears of Jesus' powerful acts and concludes that Jesus enjoys a very high status and role: "This is John the Baptist, he has been raised from the dead; that is why these powers are at work in him" (14:2). Finally, when Jesus asks his disciples about his reputation, they report that the masses credit Jesus with the role of a prophet: "Some say John the Baptist, others say Elijah, and others Jeremiah or one of the prophets" (16:14; see Luke 7:16; 24:19). Although Matthew does not tell us the reasons for this identification, one plausible explanation seems to refer to his "prophetic" deeds, namely, his healings and acts of power, such as Herod heard about. Thus, Jesus' acts of power formally serve as grounds for praise, as they illustrate and confirm his high role and status, as both "prophet" and "Christ."

3.3.4 Power and Authority. Thus far we have been examining the term "power" (δύναμις), which refers to someone's ability to control the behavior of others. The power of a warrior or athlete to master others resides in bodily strength and skill; yet by virtue of age and seniority an elder of the village might also possess power to control the behavior of the village. Hence, "power" means more than brute force. In this light we examine another term in Matthew's Gospel which pertains to Jesus' ability to control the actions of other, namely, "authority" (ἐξουσία).

In a recent study, Dillon argued for a distinction between "power" and "authority," such that "power" refers to ability to act and "authority" to right or legitimacy (1995:97–99, 112–13). This distinction sorts out some differences but blurs the important similarities in the way Matthew uses the two terms. But Dillon does not bring to his study the contribution of the social sciences, which have much to say about authority and its relationship to honor and shame. For example, both "power" (δύναμις) and "authority" (ἐξουσία) refer to the "socially recognized and approved ability to control the behavior of others" (Malina 1993d:11). Two issues, then, need to be considered: (1) ability to control may be either physical (i.e., force and strength) or moral (i.e., appeal to tradition and precedent); and (2) sanctions may or may not be employed to enforce compliance. This nuancing of the abstract notion of power may help us interpret the way Matthew talks about Jesus' "authority."

In several instances, Jesus' speech and actions are intended to control the behavior of others: for example, his directives in the Sermon on the Mount (Matt. 7:28). Here the people honor Jesus for his teaching: "The crowds were astonished at this teaching, for he taught them as one who has *authority*, and not as their scribes" (7:28–29). That teaching, moreover, contains rewards for compliance and sanctions for noncompliance, which are expressed in the story of the two houses, one built on rock and the other on sand (7:24–27). Thus Jesus' teaching is invested with power to control the behavior of others, which the crowds recognize as "authority." Later, when Jesus tries to control how people behaved in the temple, the issue shifts to the legitimacy of his words and actions. Here the Gospel tradition expressly treats the issue of his ascribed role and status: "By what authority are you doing these things, and who gave you this authority?" (21:23). The public role of the chief priests invests them with power to determine what goes on in the temple and with sanctions to impose compliance. They directly challenge Jesus' role. "Authority," then, need not always refer to legitimacy, as Dillon argues; for in many instances it simply means the ability to control the behavior of others, often with sanctions to enforce compliance.

Yet Matthew often mentions Jesus' "authority" as ability to control actions and behavior. The centurion who begs a benefaction from Jesus describes his own power in terms of "authority." He himself is under the authority of a military superior who commands him: "I am a man under authority"; and as a centurion he commands others: "I say to one, 'Go,' and he goes, and to another, 'Come,' and he comes" (8:9). He wishes Jesus to speak a comparable word of "authority" to liberate his servant of the paralysis caused by an evil spirit. Although sanctions are not mentioned explicitly, they are rightly presumed in situations where relationships such as general/officer and master/slave occur: disobedience will be severely sanctioned. Hence, "authority" clearly means the ability to control others as well as the use of sanctions. When Jesus sends out his disciples in Matthew 10, he ascribes to them power, which means "authority over unclean spirits, to cast them out, and to heal every disease and every infirmity" (10:1); and sanctions are declared against audiences which do not accept the disciples' message (10:13–14). Clearly the disciples enjoy ascribed authority from Jesus, that is, delegation; and their task is one of power to control the behavior of the illness-producing demons. In both of these instances, "authority" (ἐξουσία) reflects Jesus' own power to control the behavior of demons.

Forgiveness of sins likewise comes under Jesus' "authority." After Jesus tells the paralytic "Your sins are forgiven," scribes challenge Jesus' claim and accuse him of blasphemy, which Mark explains as Jesus' presumption of a power reserved only to God (Mark 2:7). Jesus responds to the honor challenge with the powerful riposte of healing the paralytic. At stake is his word, both its power and authorization. A word which merely declares forgiveness of sins brings with it no visible proof of its effectiveness; as we say, talk is cheap. But a word intended to produce the healing of an illness must have an immediate effect. If, therefore, Jesus can say a powerful word which has a dramatic and immediate result, he must be credited with authority-as-power, in that he can cause things to happen, both in terms of overpowering the disease which afflicted the paralytic and in changing the status of the ill man. And so, by saying the harder thing, Jesus demonstrates that his speech contains power which is presumably ascribed by God: "'That you may know that the Son of man has authority on earth to forgive sins'—he then said to the paralytic—'Rise, take up your bed and go home'" (Matt. 9:6). The immediate cure of the paralytic then proves two things: (1) Jesus has power to control the actions of others—in this case, the demons who caused the illness; and (2) this power comes from God: "They glorified God, who had given such authority to men" (9:8). Thus "authority" (9:6, 8) refers both to power as the ability to control and to authorization or legitimation. One might extend the same sort of analysis to the power Jesus gives his disciples to "bind and loose" (16:18; 18:18; see Davies and Allison 1991:635–41).

Jesus, moreover, claims still more power and authority. When, seemingly powerless, he is on trial before the chief priests and the Sanhedrin, Jesus claims that shortly his status will be utterly reversed. He predicts a time in which he will be given extraordinary power and authority, when he is "seated at the right hand of the Power" (26:64). "Seated" connotes a position of power, for courtiers stand and servants bow, but rulers sit on thrones. The "right hand," moreover, means the position of power (Hertz 1960:89–113). Finally, the phrase " . . . at the right hand of the Power" is a circumlocution for God; but by the same token it tells us that the powerless Jesus will soon be given access to what the ancient world imagined as "power." Both Greeks and Hebrews alike not only associated the Deity with power but also used "Power" as one of the Deity's very names (Grundmann 1964:286–94). Thus, Jesus claims exceptional power by virtue of the benefaction of his God-Patron, who will ascribe to him all of his own divine power and authority. In fulfillment of this prediction, the risen Jesus declares to his disciples that he now enjoys that power: "All authority in heaven and earth has been given me" (28:19). Clearly such power is grounds for our praise; Jesus has been given an extraordinary benefaction which expresses a singular grant of ascribed honor.

4.0 Summary and Conclusions

The rules for an encomium offer a valuable set of native categories for interpreting various aspects of the life and career of Jesus. Of course, it is evident that Matthew's account of Jesus does not organize the deeds of Jesus according a traditional slate of virtues, as Josephus does with the Judean heroes in his *Antiquities* (see Feldman 1976, 1982, 1987, 1988, etc.). Rather he presents his portrait of Jesus in narrative terms which follow a chronological time line. Yet as we have seen, Quintilian reminds an author that both modes are acceptable for presenting the deeds of someone as warranting public praise. This chapter has tried to make us familiar with the traditional rhetorical instructions for drawing praise from a person's life, rules clearly codified in the conventional instructions in the encomium.

Equally important has been the search for the ancient meanings of certain virtues, especially the four cardinal ones. For the cultural meanings of the four virtues in antiquity are very far removed from discussions of them in our modern, individualistic culture. The traditional and conventional understanding of these virtues in the ancient world is also important to consider, for it suggests a common meaning and evaluation of them over centuries by many, many people in the culture. We hope that readers will appreciate that deeds can be presented and expected by the evangelist to have a certain rhetorical effect, even if he does not neatly label an action as this or that virtue.

The rhetorical aim of Matthew's presentation of Jesus' deeds can further be appreciated when we take into account that the evangelist is but following a long tradition in presenting Jesus as a very wise sage by virtue of the ubiquitous chreia, in which Jesus deftly deflects all challenges and both maintains his honor and grows in it as he successfully competes. Besides the scholarly acceptance of the chreia as an important form in Gospel criticism, the rules for the encomium likewise identify for us conventional appreciations of typical deeds. But most importantly, we have seen that the narration of chreiai and encomia serves the formal purpose of bringing honor, respect, and glory to someone. To the extent we agree that the deeds of Jesus are narrated as noble or worthy, then we are persuaded that the evangelist's formal aim is the honoring of the Christian Hero.

7

An Encomium for Jesus

A Noble Death

1.0 Introduction

At first glance, death offers scant grounds for praise. It means the collapse of health, the total loss of power, and the severing of status markers such as patron-client relationships. Death, moreover, ends the possibility of achieving further success and may even signal a defeat by a rival's superior power. Furthermore, Christians writing about the crucifixion of Jesus were confronted with a genuine shame and stigma. The author of Hebrews merely expressed what everyone knew by describing Jesus' crucifixion as "the shame of the cross" (αἰσχύνη, Heb. 12:2). This evaluation of crucifixion echoes what Paul said earlier, that Jews considered it a "stumbling block" and Greeks called it "folly" (1 Cor. 1:23), terms connected with shame. These Christian authors accurately reflect the cultural evaluation of a death by crucifixion in the Greco-Roman world (Hengel 1977:1–10; Neyrey 1996b:113–15). Later Christian writers had to confront the shame of the cross, acknowledging its common assessment as "a disgraceful punishment even for worthless men" (Arnobius, *Against the Nations* 1.36), suitable only for criminals (Minucius Felix, *Octavian* 9.4). Origen, for example, responded to challenges from Celsus, who charged that Jesus was "most dishonorably arrested and punished in utter disgrace" (*Against Celsus* 6.10). Jesus' death by crucifixion, then, carried with it the terrible stigma of shame.

Granted that death by crucifixion was shameful, wherein lay the shame? We ask this so that when we read Matthew's Passion narrative, we might appreciate as fully as possible the narrative task he faced. First, the ancients considered crucifixion the appropriate punishment for criminals and slaves, who utterly lacked any honor ascribed them by birth or virtuous deeds. Victors crucified "losers" such as defeated soldiers (Diodorus Siculus 14.53.4) or survivors of a defeated city (Curtius Rufus, *History of Alexander* 4.4.17) or captured rebels (Livy 22.32.2; 33.36.2). Elites rarely were crucified, a death which would utterly destroy their reputation as well as their lives. Cicero was outraged to hear that Roman citizens were so treated (*On Verres* 2.62.163; *For Rabirio* 16). Second, death by crucifixion climaxed a process of bodily degradation. It was preceded by torture and mutilation; it was occasionally accompanied by the condemned being forced to witness the brutal deaths of their wives and children (see Plato, *Gorgias* 473B–C; *Republic* 361E).

In particular, a man to be crucified might be put on the rack, be blinded by hot irons, have his hands amputated, and of course be scourged. In terms of a bodily grammar of honor and shame, his face and eyes were assaulted. He was involuntarily stripped naked, and thus shamed (Neyrey 1996b); his body was made ugly and repulsive by beatings, scourgings, and mutilations. His torture and death, moreover, occurred in public, even as entertainment for the crowds, which only magnified the victim's shame and disgrace. Philo records one such grisly "theater" of crucifixion:

> He [Flaccus] ordered the crucifixion of the living. . . . [H]e did this after maltreating them with the lash in the middle of the theatre and torturing them with fire and the sword. The show had been arranged in parts. The first spectacle lasting from dawn till the third hour consisted of Jews being scourged, hung up, bound to the wheel, brutally mauled and haled for their death march through the middle of the orchestra. (*Flaccus* 84–85)

Moreover, when the victims witnessed the execution of their children, they could not count on their heirs to carry on their name or seek vengeance, both marks of shame (Josephus, *J.W.* 13.380; Diodorus Siculus 33.15.1–2).

For these reasons, a number of authors close in time to the New Testament describe crucifixion in "superlative" terms, calling it a "most pitiable" death (οἴκτιστον, Josephus, *J.W.* 7.203), or the "ultimate punishment" (*summum supplicium*, Cicero, *On Verres* 2.5.168), or the "most cruel and disgusting" punishment (*crudelissimi taeterrimique*, Cicero, *On Verres* 2.5.165), or the "most evil" cross (*maximum malum*, Plautus, *Casina* 611; *Menaechmi* 66; 849). Celsus calls it "shameful" (αἴσχιστα, 6.10), while others call it an "insult" (Melito, *On the Passover* 96: παρύβρισται; Achilles Tatius, 2.37.3: ὑβρίζεται). These labels indicate the common cultural perception that death by crucifixion constituted the worst imaginable fate, namely, the most shameful of deaths.

Yet ancient rhetoric developed ways to consider death as grounds for praise. Orators followed accepted conventions by speaking of a "noble death." Death might be celebrated by a "funeral oration" (Burgess 1987:146–57; Ziolkowski 1981). Even the rules for the encomium indicated how a death might be grounds for praise. Hence, let us examine these rhetorical materials from our native informants in the ancient world to recover their evaluation of what makes a death praiseworthy. We will then use these data as the culturally specific lenses through which to read Matthew's account of Jesus' death. Our task remains to see how Matthew presents the crucified Jesus as a most honorable person and worthy of praise and loyalty, despite his shameful death.

2.0 The Encomium, Posthumous Honors, and Jesus' Passion Narrative

The rules for an encomium provide grounds for praise of a person's death, which resulted in posthumous honors such as "celebration of the award of divine honours, posthumous votes of thanks, or statues erected at the public expense" (Quintilian, *Inst. Orat.* 3.7.17). Hermogenes' remarks expand the range of these grounds by calling attention to: "the manner of his end, as that he died fighting for his fatherland . . . what was done after his end, whether funeral games were ordained in his honor . . . whether there was an oracle concerning his bones" (Baldwin 1928:32). Thus praise might be drawn from the manner of death or the events occurring after death, that is, divine and civic honors. The "manner of death" will be treated later in this chapter. Here we concentrate on the criterion of a praiseworthy death represented by posthumous honors. No games were held in Jesus' honor, nor was an encomium delivered at his burial. Matthew nevertheless narrates a series of events we will examine under the rubric of "posthumous honors": the phenomena accompanying Jesus' death (Matt. 27:51–54) and the appearances of the vindicated Jesus (28:1–10, 16–20).

We examined earlier the encomium's instruction to cite portents and prodigies at the birth of a praiseworthy person as grounds for praise. Similarly, in regard to certain deaths, ancient writers tell of comets appearing at the death of Julius Caesar (Suetonius, *Lives of the Caesars* 88) and heralding the deaths of Claudius and Vespasian (Dionysius of Halicarnassus, *Roman Antiquities* 60.35.2; 66.17.2). Josephus mentions seven portents that prophesied the coming desolation of Jerusalem (*J.W.* 6.289–99), which, while they do not constitute grounds for praise, indicate a popular appreciation of prodigies as status indicators. McCasland has shown that there are virtually no predecessors to such portents in Israelite literature (1932:324–33), although Str-B 1.1040–41 mentions prodigies at the deaths of certain rabbis. Yet we know that in the rhetorical world of Greece and Rome prodigies and portents regularly accompany the deaths of persons of high status and signal that the gods, or God, honorably acknowledge their demise.

2.1 Praise from the Rending of the Temple Veil. In keeping with tradition, Matthew narrates that the temple veil was rent asunder from top to bottom (27:51). Historical judgments notwithstanding, let us try to interpret the meaning of this narrative datum in the light of the ancient cultural world. Raymond Brown strongly argues that the passive voice in the phrase "was rent in two" implies that the agent of this act was God (1994:1099–1102). Moreover, he urges us to consider the cultural meaning of this report, although he himself does not use the anthropology of honor and shame in his interpretation. We suggest that God's action communicates several things: (1) a riposte to the temple personnel who instigated the death of God's client-son, which Jesus cannot himself give, and (2) confirmation of Jesus' words about the temple, for which he was accused and mocked. God is, therefore, posthumously honoring Jesus by vindicating him in the face of those who shamed him. In the light of challenge-and-riposte exchanges, let us consider the rending of the temple veil, not simply as a judgment on the institution of the temple (Sanders 1985:61–76), but as a direct response by God to the temple personnel who mocked Jesus on the cross (Bauckham 1988:86–89).

To appreciate fully the symbolic communication of God's rending of the temple veil, we must turn to the crucifixion scene and appreciate its challenge to Jesus. Matthew narrates that three sets of mockers taunted Jesus on the cross: "passers-by" (27:39–40), "chief priests, scribes, and elders" (27:41–43), and the robbers crucified with him (27:44). In terms of honor and shame, then, Jesus experiences a terrible shaming from all gathered there, a challenge to which he does not and cannot respond. The taunting itself contains several key elements, such as the mockery of his role and status as "Son of God," which both the passers-by and the temple elite reject (27:40, 43), and the ridicule of his claims to be a bene-factor or "savior" of others (27:40, 42). Moreover, the passers-by mock his claim to destroy and rebuild the temple, implying that he both insults God by this blas-phemy and vainly claims power which belongs to no mere mortal (see 26:60–61).

According to the choreography of challenge-riposte exchanges in the world of honor, the *claims* made about Jesus concerning his exalted role and status are be-ing *challenged* both by physical attack and especially by verbal mockery. Matthew's narrative describes what this hypothetical *riposte* from Jesus would look like: "If you are the Son of God, come down from the cross" (27:40) and "He is the King of Israel; let him come down now from the cross" (27:42). Yet another figure is called upon to deliver the appropriate response, namely, God: "Let God deliver him now, if he desires him; for he said, 'I am the Son of God'" (27:43). Claims and challenges, no doubt! But also a firm expectation of a riposte.

In the context of this mockery, the temple veil is rent from top to bottom. Since God alone can do this, it constitutes God's participation in the deadly game of claim, challenge, and riposte. Minimally, it communicates that what Jesus said about the temple is not offensive to God, neither the remarks in 21:12–17 and 24:1–2 nor what is charged against him at the Jewish trial in 26:60–61 and about which he is mocked on the cross (27:40). The words of Jesus concerning the na-tional shrine, then, prove true. If the high priests tore their robes in judging Jesus to be a charlatan and false prophet (26:65; see Daube 1973:23–24), God tears the temple veil in judgment of those who judged Jesus. Moreover, the tearing of the veil by God, since it occurs as a divine riposte to Jesus' adversaries, contributes to the defense of the role and status of Jesus. God responds on behalf of the one who is "Son of God" (27:40, 43) and "King of Israel" (27:42), thus vindicating the honor of Jesus. The rending of the temple veil itself does not carry the full defense of Jesus' claims, but must be seen in combination with the earthquake and the rais-ing of the dead. But, as a communication, it confirms the truth of Jesus' words, vindicates his role and status, and in part responds to the mockery, "Let God de-liver him."

The significance of the rending of the temple veil requires us to look back in the narrative to the actions and sayings of Jesus in regard to the national shrine. Tele-scoping the materials in Matthew 21–22 in the light of challenge and riposte, we discern an important pattern. *Claims*: Jesus' "demonstration" in the temple pre-sumes a claim to an ascribed role which authorizes him to act and speak as a critic of the current administration of the national shrine (21:12–13). His *claim*, more-over, contains the special Matthean comment about his healing of the "blind and lame" in the temple (21:14), which casts him in the role of mediator of God's benefaction in contrast to the temple priests. Although many in the temple ac-knowledge his *claims*, crying out, "Hosanna to the Son of David!" (21:15), those most directly affected by Jesus' increase in prestige *challenge* his claims in "in-dignation": "Do you hear what these are saying?" (21:16). Jesus immediately *responds* to their challenge by justifying the public praise accorded him by his citation of Ps. 8:2, which predicted "perfect praise" for him (21:16b).

The challenge-riposte dynamic surfaces immediately upon Jesus' next entrance into the temple. The temple personnel, whose prestige diminishes in proportion to the rise of Jesus' honor, *challenge* him by demanding to know the source of his authorization: "By what authority are you doing these things, and who gave you this authority?" (21:23). To this Jesus delivers the classic *riposte* by asking them a counterquestion about the authorization of John, who conducted rituals of purification. Matthew's audience would know that the answer to both questions is the same—namely, God, who sent John as prophet to prepare the way of Jesus and who ascribed to Jesus at his baptism the exalted role and status of "beloved son." When the temple personnel refuse to respond, Jesus has successfully defended his claims and delivered a shameful riposte to his challengers.

Challenge and riposte continue in the form of three parables Jesus then tells, all of which have the temple personnel as the object of his criticism. After the parable of the two sons, Jesus publicly shames them by exalting traditionally shameful persons over the temple personnel: "The tax collectors and the harlots go into the kingdom of God before you" (21:31). After the parable about the shaming of the messengers of the vineyard owner, Matthew narrates that the temple personnel understand that they in fact are the objects of Jesus' public reproach: "When the chief priests and the Pharisees heard his parables, they perceived that he was speaking about them" (21:45). Although publicly *challenged*, they cannot mount a *riposte*: "But when they tried to arrest him, they feared the multitudes, because they held him to be a prophet" (21:46). Thus the extended exchange between Jesus and the temple personnel may profitably and accurately be seen in the light of typical challenge-and-riposte exchanges: claims which are bitterly challenged, but which Jesus successfully defends. His repeated ripostes give him the last word in the conflict, a measure of success publicly acknowledged by various spectators in the temple (21:16, 46).

This previous conflict, then, underscores the subsequent challenges to Jesus concerning the public offense he gave to the keepers of the national shrine. Now they seem to have the last word, which is sarcastic mocking; and they appear to have mounted the ultimate challenge by working Jesus' death. Thus, by manipulating Jesus' death, his enemies call into question his *claims* to God's special authorization and patronage; and so the ultimate *challenge* has been given. But Matthew narrates that God has yet to respond, which he does by tearing the temple veil. This cannot be construed as a further discrediting or shaming of Jesus; but it admits interpretation as God's confirmation of Jesus' words concerning the shrine and God's vindication of Jesus' unique role and status as "Son" and "King." God, then, delivers the definitive *riposte*.

Our interpretation highlights the elements of honor and shame and expressly describes the events in terms of challenge and riposte. Yet this cultural reading corresponds favorably with more traditional interpretations. For example, scholars regularly see God's tearing of the temple veil as a divine confirmation of Jesus' criticism of the temple personnel (see Brown 1993:1100). Such an interpretation has literary support in *Testament of Levi* 10:3, where God unveils the shame of the wicked temple personnel by symbolically making them naked through the removal of the veil: "You shall act lawlessly in Israel . . . but the curtain of the Temple will be torn, so that it will no longer conceal your shameful behavior. You will be scattered as captives among the nations, where you will be a disgrace and a curse." This text indicates that in the Judean code of honor, one native informant interpreted the rending of the temple veil in terms of honor and shame, challenge and riposte. It represents God's response to wickedness of the temple personnel.

2.2 Praise from the Earthquake. Matthew records a second prodigy: "the earth shook" (27:51b). Brown points us in the right direction by noting biblical accounts of similar incidents as indications of divine action (1994:1121), although we differ with Brown on what kind of divine action. Were the earthquake a divine judgment against those who killed the Deity's agent and son, why were not the agents of that shameful death themselves destroyed like the wicked tenants in 21:41? While Matthew's narrative contains mention of divine vengeance for insults (21:40–41; 23:36, 38; 27:25), that is not the meaning here; for the earthquake did not harm those who shamed Jesus. Yet in a challenge-riposte context, where the patron's client-son is outraged, the earthquake—at least as a narrative phenomenon—would be quite the appropriate defense of the honor of the agent. It signals that the patron stands by the client and vindicates his honor in the face of his enemies. As such, it illustrates what Psalm 118 said, that the "stone rejected by the builders has become the head of the corner" (21:42); the earthquake functions in the vindication of Jesus. According to Matthew, Jesus' executioner correctly interpreted the earthquake and attested publicly that Jesus enjoyed great honor ascribed by God: "When the centurion and those who were with him, keeping watch over Jesus, saw the earthquake and what took place, they were filled with awe, and said, 'Truly this was the Son of God!'" (27:54). They correctly understood the significance of the earthquake precisely as a vindication of Jesus, and thus as a heavenly riposte to the earthly challenges against him. The claims of Jesus as "Son of God" are defended, not by Jesus himself, but by the Deity who ascribed this honor and status to him and who acts to secure the reputation and worth of his client. The earthquake, then, functions as a prodigy which brings "posthumous honor" to Jesus.

2.3 Praise from the Opening of Tombs. Matthew narrates a third prodigy: how, as a result of the earthquake, "the tombs were opened, and many bodies of the saints who had fallen asleep were raised" (27:52). What meaning, if any, does this have in regard to Jesus? How does it connect with his noble death or posthumous honors? This belongs in the category of divine ripostes to challenges issued to God's client-son, as the third and climactic act of divine vindication of Jesus. Like the earthquake, it does not shame those who shamed Jesus. Rather this vindicates an important aspect of Jesus' actions and teaching.

We begin by appreciating that the raising of the dead is an act proper to God alone. Like the earthquake and the rending of the temple veil, God is saying something, but what? The raising of the dead points us in several directions. As we did in the case of the temple veil, we should examine the extent to which Matt. 27:52–53 serves as vindication of Jesus' own actions and words. Closest in time to this event is the challenging question put to Jesus by the Sadducees, who say that there is no resurrection (22:23–28), that is, God does *not* raise the dead. If that were so, then those prophets, wise men, and scribes sent to Israel who were shamed, scourged, crucified, and persecuted (23:34, 37) would never have their honor restored by God. The Deity, then, would fail in loyalty to his clients, which is a shameful thing (but see Rev. 6:9–11; Matt. 23:35–36, 38–39). Jesus defends the honor of God by insulting his questioners: "You are wrong, because you know neither the scriptures nor the power of God" (Matt. 22:29). He then gives God proper glory by acknowledging that he is "not God of the dead, but of the living" (22:32). This loyal client, who has defended the power of his Patron on just this issue, deserves to be defended by the Patron in his own death. But was Jesus right? The raising of the saints in Matt. 27:52 confirms two things: (1) God indeed vindicates those who were shamed while fulfilling their assigned tasks in loyalty to God, and (2) Jesus himself was correct in defending this honorable act of God.

As he did in the case of the centurion's interpretation of the earthquake, Matthew provides narrative clues about the meaning of the raising of the saints by intertwining their raising with the resurrection of Jesus: "[C]oming out of the tombs *after his resurrection*, they went into the city" (27:53). How striking that at the very moment of Jesus' death, mention of his "resurrection" is noted (27:52)! This unique act of God will only be complete, however, when God raises Jesus; for only "after his resurrection" will it be apparent that "the bodies of the saints were raised" as they "went into the holy city and appeared to many." These are not the ghosts of the dead who linger at graves to cause disturbance until they are pacified by some rite. They represent a new act of God's power, namely, "resurrection," which Matthew intrinsically links with God's raising of Jesus himself. This prodigy, then, honors Jesus because it testifies to God's power to vindicate loyal clients.

Matthew in some way sees this as a vindication of Jesus' own words and deeds. Earlier he repeated the tradition that Jesus predicted both his death and resurrection, or in social-science terms, his shaming and honoring.

> . . . be killed and on the third day *be raised*. (16:21)
>
> . . . they will kill him and he will *be raised* on the third day. (17:23)
>
> . . . mocked, scourged, crucified, and he will *be raised* on the third day. (20:19)

Again, scholars accept the passive voice in "be raised" as indicative of God's action. Was Jesus correct in affirming that his Patron would vindicate him by raising him to life and restoring him to honor? The prodigies in 27:52–53 argue positively that Jesus' own predictions of divine vindication as well as his defense of God's power in 22:29–32 are justified. The dramatic proof, of course, is the narrative in 28:16–20, where the risen Jesus claims not merely vindication but transformation to a higher status. But 27:52–53 immediately signals that God is even then acting to confirm the ascribed role and status of Jesus as faithful and noble client. Thus, the raising of the saints at Jesus' death and their public appearances after his own resurrection confirm two things: (1) correctness of Jesus' own teaching about God's power to raise the dead and (2) the loyalty God shows in vindicating faithful clients.

2.4 Praise from the Executioner. We have shown how the three prodigies that accompany Jesus' death all admit of a cultural interpretation in the Matthean narrative as divine vindication of Jesus. Matthew, moreover, provides in the public testimony of the centurion at the cross the perfect literary device of having a narrative character correctly interpret their significance. As Jesus' executioner, the centurion served as the agent of Jesus' shame, not only confiscating his clothes (27:36), but killing him. He heard the mockery of Jesus as "Son of God" (27:40, 43), at which point he had no reason to consider Jesus other than a fool who claimed too much and was finally given his comeuppance. Yet Matthew records a transformation in the centurion. When he sees the events at Jesus' death, he correctly interprets them as singular marks of honor which cause him to re-evaluate Jesus: "When the centurion and those who were with him . . . saw the earthquake and what took place, they were filled with awe, and said, 'Truly this was the Son of God!'" (27:54). From agent of Jesus' shame, the centurion becomes the proclaimer of his honor, a cultural motif found also in some accounts of martyrs (Bammel 1970:108–12). As a result of the prodigies, he acknowledges the basic honor claim of the Gospel that Jesus is "God-favored," and is the "Son of God." According to ancient rules of evidence (Harvey 1976:18–21), he himself enjoys a position of importance, as a centurion or military official, which gives weight to his remarks. The centurion, however, does not deliver a riposte on Jesus' behalf, for God does that through the prodigies. Rather he offers a public acknowledgment of the worth and status of Jesus by his correct interpretation of the posthumous events.

2.5 Praise from the Divine Patron. Matthew concludes his narrative with an account whose primary message is God's raising of Jesus from the dead, which the ancient world would consider his vindication and apotheosis (see Nickelsburg 1972). Typical scriptural proclamations of Jesus' resurrection acknowledge it as a vindicating act of God: "You crucified him . . . but God raised him up" (Acts 2:23–24; see 3:14–15; 4:10; 5:30; Rom. 10:9–10). As we noted above, Matthew echoes this in the triple passion predictions, each of which contains a note of how God will reverse the shame suffered by Jesus. From a cultural point of view, then, let us interpret the raising of Jesus as God's honorable vindication of him.

If crucifixion meant radical shame because of loss of power, strength, and beauty, God's resurrection of Jesus undoes that shame and increases his honor. First of all, Matthew understands resurrection as a mark of divine favor to worthy persons (see 27:52–53). Moreover, as Jesus himself testifies, in his resurrection he has been ascribed supreme power and authority, which are the marks of unique worth: "All authority in heaven and on earth has been given to me"—*given* by God, of course (28:18)—that is, continued divine patronage and further ascribed honor. Thus the Gospel ends, not simply with a reversal of shame, but with divine ascription of the maximum possible honor to Jesus.

The significant element here is the claim that Jesus has been given this honor by God, his Patron in heaven. The narrative prepared us for just this claim when Jesus applied three scriptural passages to himself about his ascribed honor. According to Psalm 118, the rejected stone becomes the head of the corner because of "the Lord's doing" (Matt. 21:42//Ps. 118:22–23). Again, Jesus declared that according to Psalm 110, the Lord God will seat the Son of David at God's right hand, thus enthroning and empowering him as "Lord" (Matt. 22:44//Ps. 110:1). Finally, at his trial, Jesus cited a passage from Daniel concerning the Son of man who was rejected on earth but vindicated in heaven and given dominion, glory, and power (Matt. 26:64//Dan. 7:13–14). Thus Matthew prepares the reader for the status transformation of the crucified Jesus into the vindicated Lord by the ascription of unique power and glory by his heavenly Patron. The statement in 28:18 claims that this transformation has already happened; shame is utterly transfigured into maximum glory and honor. (On 28:16–20 as a status elevation ritual, see Malina and Neyrey 1988:113–18.)

As a final narrative consideration of divine patronage, we recall the earlier discussion how at Jesus' birth divine favor was shown him by God's providential rescue of him from Herod's death squad. At the very minimum, Matt. 2:13–23 indicates that Jesus should be honored as "God-beloved" (θεοφιλής): the heavenly Patron who ascribed to Jesus his honor, role, and status also vindicates it. We have argued elsewhere that the events in Matthew 26–28 form an inclusion with those in Matthew 2 (Malina and Neyrey 1988:115–16; see Nolan 1979:104–7), a point of considerable significance in the present inquiry. The parallels suggest that we see the same divine patronage at work on the occasion of Jesus' death as was effective at his birth (see fig. 7.1).

Infancy Narrative	Passion Narrative
1. Jesus = King of the Jews (2:2)	1. Jesus = King of the Jews (27:11, 29, 37)
2. Jesus = Son of God (2:15)	2. Jesus = Son of God (27:40, 43, 54)
3. Negative reaction: all Jerusalem was troubled along with the chief priests and scribes (2:3–4)	3. Negative reaction: chief priests (26:65) and all Jerusalem (27:25) reject him
4. God's providential care of Jesus: rescue from death (2:13–14, 20) and defense of Jesus' role and status	4. God's providential care of Jesus: rescue from death (28:6), vindication of Jesus' role and status (27:51–54), and ascription of maximum honor (28:18)
5. Prodigies at his birth (2:2, 7–9); dreams on Jesus' behalf (2:13, 19)	5. Prodigies at his death (27:51–54); dreams on Jesus' behalf (27:19)

Figure 7.1 Jesus' Divine Patronage

This diagram indicates that the actions of God at Jesus' birth are both grants of honor and defense of that honor; thus Jesus is confirmed as "King of the Jews" and "Son of God." Herod perceived himself threatened by the newborn rival king and sought his death. Yet although the child cannot give the adequate riposte, God acts on his behalf by rescuing him and thus confirming Jesus' special status as God's client-son. The same pattern occurs at the end of the narrative: the honor of Jesus as "King" and "Son of God" are again challenged. Because he dies, Jesus cannot give the riposte; but God does, both by the posthumous honors which accompany his death and by Jesus' own subsequent vindication and resurrection. All of his life, then, from birth and through death, Jesus remained honored and defended by God. It belongs to the code of ancient rhetoric to maintain that what befalls infants and children marks them for life and reveals their essential character (Malina and Neyrey 1996:25–28); blessed by God at birth, they remain all their lives blessed by God. Jesus, therefore, always enjoyed the patronage of God, especially after his noble death. The parallelism between Matthew 2 and 26–28 accords with the rhetoric of praise and rules for the encomium. Jesus' honor, then, is defended.

3.0 The Rhetoric of Praise and Blame and Jesus' Death

Previously we saw that the rhetoric of praise identified virtue as grounds for praise (see Aristotle, *Rhet.* 1.9.3–13, 14–27, 38–41), which appeared also in the rules for encomia under the rubric of "deeds of the soul." We propose to read Matthew 26–27 in the light of these criteria to see if, and to what extent, the remarks about virtue by our native informants apply to Jesus' trials and death. Just as we examined the events in Matthew 4–25 in terms of "deeds of the soul," namely, the cardinal virtues of wisdom, justice, courage, and temperance, so we extend that mode of reading to Matthew 26–27.

3.1 Praise and Virtue: Courage.   It seems likely that if Matthew portrays Jesus as dying a virtuous death, the key virtues will be courage (ἀνδρεία) and piety (εὐσέβεια). We recall the advice of Quintilian that in tracing the course of a man's life, one may organize the material thematically according to the four cardinal virtues or follow a chronological schema and praise virtue as it occurs (*Inst. Orat.* 3.7.15). We find no trace of the former organizational structure; Matthew does not gather all of Jesus' "courageous" deeds together, much less his acts of piety. But according to the canons of ancient rhetoric, is Jesus manifesting either of these two virtues in his Passion narrative by his actions and words?

Courage stands out as the premier virtue among males in a society that celebrated military and athletic prowess. Our ancient native informants can provide for us a crisp summary of what they meant by courage. Males manifest courage in various ways: (1) willingness to undertake dangerous tasks and endure hardships; (2) obedience, especially to a higher law; (3) steadfastness and perseverance; (4) actions which either gain glory or defend family and city; (5) confidence of success; and (6) an unvanquished death. Courage, thus, admits of a wide spectrum, validating a hero's active deeds as well as a Stoic's passive endurance.

A strictly linguistic search of Matthew 26–27 for the precise terms "courage," "endurance," or "confidence" will be disappointing, as these terms do not occur in the Passion narrative. We find no formal mention of Jesus' courage, patience, endurance, or confidence. Yet let us ask what words or actions of Jesus exemplify what the ancients understood by "courage." We offer three incidents for consideration:

(1) Jesus' conscious anticipation of a future time of hardships, trials, and death (26:36–46); (2) the trials he patiently endured (26:59–68); and (3) his painful but noble death (27:26–31, 35–50).

3.1.1 Courage in the Garden. Courage aptly describes Jesus' behavior in the Garden episode: Jesus clearly confronts the awesome trials awaiting him and freely chooses a noble action (on the nobility of freely choosing such a fate, see Moline 1989). Knowing what he must endure, he declares himself obedient to the one who requires that he submit to labors, trials, and death. First of all, Jesus admits that he has a choice: either to escape the awesome tribulations and maintain his life or to accept the challenge and die nobly. This kind of choice constitutes a regular part of the literature on "noble death." Praiseworthy individuals, when faced with a choice of a shameful life that flees from hardships and death, freely embrace danger and toil, even at the cost of their lives. One native informant clearly articulated the theory: "To courage it belongs to be undismayed by fears of death and confident in alarms and brave in the face of dangers, and to prefer a fine death to base security" (Aristotle, *On Virtues and Vices* 4.4), and "To cowardice it belongs to be easily excited by chance alarms, and especially by fear of death or of bodily injuries, and to think it better to save oneself by any means than to meet a fine death" (*On Virtues and Vices* 6.6). Although Matthew narrates that Jesus initially pleaded to escape from "the cup," he immediately balances this petition with a definitive choice to follow the will of his Patron-Deity: " . . . nevertheless, not as I will, but as thou wilt" (26:39). The evangelist's interest focuses squarely on Jesus' clear choice of God's fate for him, which in this case means a noble death in obedience to the will of his Patron-Father. Matthew narrates that Jesus makes this choice twice more, as he prays the same prayer three times (see 26:42, 44).

Cicero remarked that "bravery is a disposition of the soul obedient to the highest law in enduring vicissitudes" (*Tusculan Disputations* 4.53). This obedience of a free person contrasts sharply with the enforced compliance of slaves, who have no choice in their fate. In regard to this, Xenophon celebrates the obedience of ancient warriors to the command of their military leader:

> As you yourselves will expect to exercise authority over those under your command, so let us also give our obedience to those whom it is our duty to obey. And we must distinguish ourselves from slaves in this way, that, whereas slaves serve their masters against their wills, we, if indeed we claim to be free, must do of our own free will all that seems to be of the first importance. (*Cyropaedia* 8.1.4)

Thus Matthew's readers have grounds for evaluating Jesus' obedience to God's will as "courageous" in itself and his acceptance of "the cup" of hardships and death as the noble choice of a free man. Hence, Jesus freely meets his fate: "Rise, let us be going; see, my betrayer is at hand" (26:46).

3.1.2 Courage on Trial. If the Garden episode showcased the noble, free choice of Jesus to accept hardships, other parts of the narrative display him actually undergoing them. In one scene Jesus stands trial for crimes of which he is innocent. A remark by Cicero might help us to appreciate the courage displayed by freely accepting arrest, trial, and death. Cicero admits the shame of the process but also the honor to be gained if one endures it well: "How grievous a thing it is to be disgraced by a public court; how grievous to suffer a fine, how grievous to suffer banishment; and yet in the midst of any such disaster some trace of liberty is left to us. Even if we are threatened with death, we may die *as free men*" (*For Rabirio* 5.16, emphasis added). According to Matthew's account, Jesus could have pleaded with God for rescue (26:53), accepted the resistance offered by a disciple (26:51–52), or fled like the disciples (26:56). By allowing himself to be arrested (26:56), he stands trial in a spirit of courageous obedience and free acceptance. But what constitutes virtuous behavior at a trial? All that is left Jesus is speech; hence let us examine the quality of his speech while on trial.

It belongs to a free citizen to speak boldly in the appropriate public forums where men gather. The author of 1 Timothy reflects this when he encourages the man of God to "Fight the good fight of the faith; take hold of the eternal life to which you were called when you made the good confession in the presence of many witnesses" (6:12). It is honorable to act with courage by "fighting the good fight," persevering, and "making a good confession" in public, presumably against adversaries. This public speech, the author claims, models the honorable public speech of Jesus "who in his testimony before Pontius Pilate made the good confession" (6:13). Comparably in Matthew 10, Jesus describes for his disciples a situation of conflict in which they must endure trials and hardships: "I send you out as sheep in the midst of wolves. . . . [T]hey will deliver you up to councils, and flog you in their synagogues, and you will be dragged before governors and kings for my sake, to bear testimony before them and the Gentiles" (10:16–18). Courageous public speech is required: "When they deliver you up, do not be anxious how you are to speak or what you are to say; for what you are to say will be given you in that hour" (10:19). Bold public speech in a crisis situation is mandated because it constitutes a defense of honor claims made on behalf of Jesus in a challenge-riposte situation. In special social circumstances, however, silence might also be the heroic action, if honor challenges and ripostes are not an issue. Silence may connote patient endurance and stoic perseverance.

To speak or not to speak in such a forum is highly symbolic behavior. As Rohrbaugh has observed, "Honour status determined who spoke and who listened" (1995:196). Jesus at first refuses to reply to false and slanderous accusations (Matt. 26:62–63). It is possible that in such a case silence might even connote a contempt of injustice, and thus a superior posture (see John 19:8–10). But Jesus finally does speak when his honor is directly challenged: "Tell us if you are the Christ, the Son of God" (Matt. 26:63b); and his speech models the ancient virtue of "boldness" (παρρησία), the hallmark of a free citizen: "You have said so. But I tell you, hereafter you will see the Son of man seated at the right hand of Power and coming on the clouds of heaven" (26:64). For his courageous speech, Jesus suffers contempt and insults: "'He deserves death.' Then they spat in his face, and struck him, and some slapped him" (26:66–67). In narrative logic, had he not spoken with courageous "boldness," he would not have suffered such insults. But he was obligated to speak because the honor of his Patron was at stake. He must claim and defend his God-assigned role and status and thus defend God's interests. The word "courage" never appears in this episode, but Jesus acts like a free man who speaks boldly, defends the vital interests of his Patron, and endures hardships as a result (see Fitzgerald 1988:87–100).

3.1.3 Courage and a Painful Death.
Finally, Jesus demonstrates courage by resolutely enduring the hardships of scourging, crucifixion, and death. Of course the narrative does not explicitly state this, but rather it does what narratives do, portrays it. At Jesus' scourging and mocking (27:26–31), we are told nothing of his emotions and feelings, which in an honor culture are unimportant. Given the non- and even anti-psychological nature of the ancient world (Malina and Neyrey 1996:12–18), this is hardly surprising. Moreover, even if one suspects that Matthew is either sanitizing an episode to present Jesus as heroic or crafting a story of heroic endurance, the result would be the same: Jesus endures terrible hardships, both physical torture and bitter mockery, with remarkable endurance, for which courage he deserves our praise. The narrative states that Jesus does not react, either crying out in pain or cursing those who mock him. Since speech would be his only weapon of self-defense, his silence here should be taken as prima facie evidence of heroic or noble endurance and patience, which the ancients define as marks of courage.

Similarly, when Matthew narrates that Jesus was "crucified" (27:35) and mocked three times (27:38–44), these events should be interpreted as part of the dreadful hardships he endured. The narrator does not need to elaborate on them, for he can presume that his audience fully appreciates the bitterness of the shaming and the sharpness of the bodily pains endured. Yet that is precisely our point: he endured them. And inasmuch as he endured them in silence, his perseverance is all the more salient as a heroic or noble display of courage.

3.2 Praise and Virtue: Piety.
If Jesus may be said to manifest the virtue of courage both in his words and actions, what then of his piety? From our previous sketch of the ancient understanding of virtues, we recall four items. (1) The parent virtue is "justice" (δικαιοσύνη), one of the four cardinal virtues. (2) Among the parts of "justice" are "piety" (εὐσέβεια), fair dealing, and reverence: piety toward the gods, fair dealing with men, and reverence toward the departed. (3) Piety to the gods consists of two elements: "being god-loved (θεοφιλοτής) and god-loving (φιλοθεοτής). The former means being loved by the gods and receiving many blessings from them, the latter consists of loving the gods and having a relationship of friendship with them" (Menander Rhetor 1.361.22–25; Russell and Wilson 1981:62–63). (4) Finally, piety is demonstrated by loyalty and faithfulness.

Although Matthew never used the precise term "courageous" or "courage" of Jesus, the same is not true of "just" and "pious." Pilate's wife received a dream concerning Jesus, which means that she received a communication from the highest possible authority: God. As a result, she advises Jesus' judge, "Have nothing to do with that *just* (δίκαιος) man" (27:19). According to the logic of dreams, we are expected to take this as a statement about Jesus from God that indicates a favorable moral evaluation. Hence, this small item suggests two things: (1) Jesus is "God-loved," since God speaks on his behalf, and (2) Jesus is virtuous, indeed "just." In his treatment of this incident, Donald Senior confuses the reference to Jesus' "just" character in Pilate's wife's dream with "innocence" (1975:245; Brown 1994:806). He links 27:19 with the unjust shedding of "innocent blood" mentioned in 23:35. Several things should be distinguished. Martyrs whose "innocent blood" was shed did not deserve the suffering they endured; but the person acclaimed "just" is positively credited with an excellence, even a virtue, which is the grounds of praise. It is one thing for Jesus to be declared innocent (ἀθῷος) in 27:4 and for Pilate to declare his own guiltlessness in Jesus' death (27:24). But it is quite another thing for a heavenly communication in a dream to declare that Jesus is "just" (δίκαιος), that is, virtuous and worthy of praise. They simply are not the same thing. Thus on the basis of the dream in 27:19, Jesus is held worthy of praise on two counts: he is himself virtuous, that is, "just," and he is also "God-loved," since dreams of this sort were thought to come from God.

3.2.1 Piety and Prayer: Garden and Cross. Beyond the mere labeling of Jesus as "just" or "pious," the evangelist presents him twice acting and speaking in ways which demonstrate his piety. Matthew dramatizes Jesus' piety by presenting him at prayer in the Garden (26:36–46). Although some "prayers" may be manipulative (i.e., superstition), prayer is generally an honorable communication with the one who controls one's existence, who might be addressed as either Lord/Sovereign, Patron, or Father. As we saw, piety (εὐσέβεια) looks to what is due to the gods, one's country, parents, and the dead. Jesus' prayer in 26:39 focuses totally on the will and plan of his Father-Patron: " . . . nevertheless, not what I will but what you will." Daube (1959:539–45) has shown how stereotypical Jesus' words are in terms of the prayer patterns of Israel. As such, this speech displays a pattern of piety approved by the local culture, and thus it constitutes the grounds for evaluating Jesus favorably. Moreover, the evangelist tells us that Jesus prayed the same words three times, thus reinforcing his presentation of Jesus as one who is demonstrably pious toward God; he is "God-loving" (φιλοθεότης) as well as God-loved.

Matthew presents a second scene of Jesus praying when he narrates Jesus' final words on the cross. One rarely finds in the literature any consideration of Jesus' dying words as a prayer, much less a demonstration of piety. For example, Senior is typical of commentators who are content merely to label "My God, my God . . . " as "words of abandonment" (1975:298). Even though Senior suggests that these "words" embody the "theme of abandonment and dereliction" which has parallels in the Old Testament, he does not go beyond a simple background analysis. Raymond Brown seems content to argue the plausibility and appropriateness of Jesus' "feelings" at the moment (1994:1046, 1051); his exposition, moreover, criticizes those who reject the literal import of the Jesus' words (1994:1047–50). Yet Brown does call the final words a "prayer," although he does not pursue the import and significance of this in any detailed way. Nevertheless, "prayer" is the proper exegetical direction of our investigation. Let us, then, examine the dying words of Jesus as a prayer and see what this means for his presentation as a virtuous—that is, pious—man who is worthy of praise.

3.2.2 A Critical Reading of Jesus' Dying Words.   In regard to the literary context of Matt. 27:46, we note that Jesus speaks in his mother tongue, which accounts for the narrative detail that his words are misunderstood by those standing by (27:47, 49). Matthew retains very few samples of Semitic speech; while he keeps "Hosanna" (Matt. 21:9//Mark 11:9) and "Golgotha" (Matt. 27:33//Mark 15:22), he omits "Talitha koum" (Mark 5:41), "korban" (Mark 7:11), "Ephphatha" (Mark 7:34), and "Abba" (Mark 14:36). The retention of Jesus' dying words in his mother tongue, therefore, seems intentional. Second, those at the scene misunderstand his words, for they think that Jesus calls on the great prophet Elijah to rescue him. According to them, Jesus seeks an end to his trials and an escape from his fate. As understandable as it may seem to us moderns—for who would not seek to escape imminent death?—in the ancient world Jesus' request for deliverance would be unheroic and lacking in courage. It might also be judged as Jesus' failure in the loyalty which he pledged to God in the Garden prayer, saying three times " . . . not my will, but your will be done." The narrator, however, presents this interpretation as a misunderstanding of Jesus' words or as a false interpretation of what he said. Jesus neither addresses Elijah nor does he ask to be saved from his fate. Third, Jesus addresses God; he does not speak to the crowds or his executioners, although they hear his speech. They are neither the topic of his speech (escape from *these* men) nor its addressees. This leads us to a fourth item: whatever previous relationship existed between God and Jesus as patron and client would be implied here. As Brown observed, the address to "Abba, Father" in the Garden is being balanced with the question to "My God" on the cross (1994:1046).

We highlight the important narrative clue that Jesus' dying words are misunderstood by the crowds. This might be another example of the common ancient pattern which contrasts exoteric and esoteric meanings of speech. Misunderstanding is also a characteristic feature of Jesus' speech in all of the Gospels, whereby most of his public remarks to the crowds are parabolic, mysterious, and not correctly understood. Yet he explains the hidden meaning in private to his disciples (see Matt. 13:11–13; 15:1–11/12–20; 19:3–9/10–12 and 16–22/23–30). In this, Matthew exemplifies the exoteric/esoteric distinction commonly found in ancient literature, Jewish and Hellenistic (see *4 Ezra* 14:4, 44; Diodorus Siculus 3.3.5–6; Origen, *Against Celsus* 1.7; Iamblichus, *On the Pythagorean Life* 17.72). The correct interpretative step, then, is to inquire into the esoteric meaning of Jesus' dying words, which is available only to Matthew's readers.

Because we consider Jesus' dying words as a prayer addressed to God, let us conduct a form-critical assessment of them. The evangelists record different final words spoken by Jesus:

Mark 15:35	"My God, my God, why have you abandoned me?"
Matt. 27:46	"My God, my God, why have you abandoned me?"
Luke 23:46	"Father, into your hands I commit my spirit."
John 19:28	And to fulfill the scriptures perfectly, he said, "I thirst."

The choice of Jesus' final words would seem to be either Matthew's own editorial choice or at least his acceptance of the tradition he received. But in the world of intertextuality (Robbins 1994a:387–91; 1994b:179–85), these words are decidedly esoteric; they are "restricted speech" (Douglas 1982:28–33, 157–60) in the sense that their full import is restricted to an "in group" who has familiarity with the Hebrew scriptures, especially the Psalms. Their misunderstanding by the bystanders confirms this: the correct meaning of Jesus' words requires readers to appreciate his speech as a Hebrew psalm, that is, a prayer, an esoteric meaning reserved for insiders. As insiders, we are supposed to know that all three sets of dying words are citations from diverse psalms: "My God, my God . . . " = Ps. 22:1; "Into your hands . . . " = Ps. 35:1; and "I thirst" = Ps. 22:16 (see Brown 1994:2.1072–74). But what does this psalm communicate?

Not every mention of a psalm in the Gospels means that it is being prayed. On occasion, the citation of a psalm may undergird the honorable role and status of Jesus (Matt. 21:42//Ps. 118:22–23; Matt. 22:44//Ps. 110:1), or serve as a prophecy of what is being currently fulfilled (Matt. 21:16//Ps. 8:3), or heighten insight into what is occurring (Matt. 26:38//Pss. 42:5, 11; 43:5; see Gundry 1967:205–15; Brown 1993:96–104 and 1994:286–89, 647–52; Senior 1975:146–47, 152–69). But because Ps. 22:1 is speech explicitly addressed to God, we take it to be a "prayer" (Malina 1980:214).

What, then, of Matthew's choice of Ps. 22:1? To exoteric ears it hardly sounds noble or faith-filled! Culturally sensitive readers must be alert in assessing the cultural meaning of Jesus' dying words so that they do not impose on the ancient world modern notions of emotions. While in our therapeutic and individualistic world we are encouraged to treasure personal emotional display, many ancients held that "emotions" were weaknesses of the soul (Neyrey 1985:50–54); it would not be "natural" or beneficial to display them. Depending on the emotion, it might be shameful to be overcome by it. In fact, ancient understanding of what it meant to be a person encouraged a distinction between what is displayed for public consumption (and likely public criticism) and what is reserved for private sharing (e.g., Matt. 26:38). Even then, we should be aware of the highly conventional expressions of feeling and emotion, that is, emotion which is socially sanctioned and controlled (Malina 1989b:137–39). Only some emotions may be displayed (e.g., sorrow at death, compassion and pity at misfortune, etc.); others such as "fear," if displayed, indicate a lack of virtue and so merit blame, not praise. We mention this because it allows us to sidestep so much of the recent speculation on the emotional importance or personal meaning of Jesus' words (Brown 1994:1043–51), which lacks the discipline of culturally contextualizing Jesus' words.

3.2.3 If a Prayer, What Kind of Prayer?

If the dying words are formally a prayer to God, what is that prayer? To be clear about "prayer," we appeal to one of the few social-science examinations of the topic. Bruce Malina defines "prayer" as " . . . a socially meaningful symbolic act of communication, bearing directly upon persons perceived as somehow supporting, maintaining, and controlling the order of existence of the one praying, and performed for the purpose of getting results from or in the interaction of communication" (1980:215). Thus prayer is "communication" made for the purpose of "getting results," but what results? Malina lists a series of possible purposes, which range from direct requests for something to exchanges of information:

1. *Instrumental* ("I want . . . ."): prayer to obtain goods and services to satisfy individual and communal material and social needs (prayers of petition for oneself and/or others);
2. *Regulatory* ("Do as I tell you"): prayers to control the activity of God, to command God to order other people and things about on behalf of the one praying (another type of petition, but with the presumption that the one praying is superior to God, hence generally considered idolatrous and insulting to God);
3. *Interactional* ("me and you"): prayers to maintain emotional ties with God, to getting along with God, to continuing interpersonal relations (prayers of adoration, of simple presence, to examining the course of a day before and with God);
4. *Self-focused* ("Here I come; here I am"): prayers that identify the self (individual and social) to God, expressing the self to God (prayers of contrition, of humility, of boasting, of superiority over others);
5. *Heuristic* ("tell me why"): prayer that explores the world of God and God's workings within us individually and/or in our group (meditative prayer, perceptions of the spirit in prayer);
6. *Imaginative* ("let's pretend"): prayer to create an environment of one's own with God (prayer in tongues, prayers read or recited in languages unknown to the person praying or reciting them);
7. *Informative* ("I have something to tell you"): prayers that communicate new information (prayers of acknowledgment, of thanksgiving for favors received). (1980:217–18)

As we classify Jesus' prayer, we must remember that prayers may combine several of these purposes. His prayer in the Garden (Matt. 26:39) contains an instrumental or petitionary aspect ("If it is possible, let this cup pass from me") as well as informational element ("nevertheless, not as I will, but as thou wilt").

Jesus' dying words are **not** *instrumental*. Although the prayer of Jesus in Heb. 5:7 may petition for a special request, not so Jesus' prayer in Matt. 27:46. The crowd misunderstood Jesus' words when it interpreted them as a petition to Elijah to come and save him. While phrased as a question, Jesus' address does **not** seek to know theodicy or the broad theory of God's ways, which would be *heuristic*. **Nor** is the prayer *regulatory*, *imaginative*, or *informative*. It seems to be primarily *interactional* communication, inasmuch as Jesus seeks to maintain emotional ties with God. Yet, as Malina explained, interactional prayer focuses on the addressee, and implies that something is amiss with the person addressed, not with the speaker. Thus, if a prayer, what sort of *interactional* communication? The editorial choice of a psalm for Jesus' dying words already indicates that the communication lies within the context of accepted speech in biblical culture: it is permissible to address God in this manner. Thus the precise citation of Ps. 22:1 likewise is socially sanctioned. What, however, is sanctioned?

3.2.4 Psalms of Lament in Social Science Perspective.
In form-critical studies of the Psalms, scholars have analyzed the category of lament or complaint (see Westermann 1980:29–70; Balentine 1993:146–98; Miller 1994:55–134). As everyone knows, the psalm of complaint or lament generally contains five formal elements: (1) address, (2) complaint, (3) petition or request, (4) affirmation of trust, and (5) vow to praise God. Inasmuch as Matt. 27:46 presents only a piece of the psalm, we find in it only the first two items, namely, address ("My God, my God") and complaint ("Why have you forsaken me?"). Patrick Miller offers a descriptive definition of the complaint which provides an adequate summary of current thinking on it:

> The questions of complaint are varied, but all of them are a direct challenge to the way God has acted or threatened to act. . . . The present circumstances of distress seem to indicate to the ones praying a terrible inconsistency on the part of God. The Lord seems to have caused or allowed things to happen in a way inappropriate to the faithfulness and compassion that are characteristic of the Lord of Israel. The fundamental query of all these complaining questions is: Why are you doing this or allowing this to happen? They are a protest, not a request for information. (1994:71)

We note that "complaints," although they appear in the form of questions, are "protests" and not requests for information; they are *interactional* prayer, not *heuristic*. Moreover, they arise from a sense that God is not doing his part or living up to his duties in a patron-client relationship, implying that the client in distress has fulfilled his or her duty and maintains loyalty and faithfulness in the relationship.

As Miller noted, "complaints" in the psalms are phrased in terms of questions, such as the following:

Why, O Lord, do you stand far off?
Why do you hide yourself in times of trouble? (Ps. 10:1)

How long, O Lord? Will you forget me forever?
How long will you hide your face from me? (Ps. 13:1; cf. 89:46)

How long, O God, is the foe to scoff?
Is the enemy to revile your name forever?
Why do you hold back your hand;
Why do you keep your hand in your bosom? (Ps. 74:10–11)

These complaint-protests point in two directions: namely, the situation of the person praying and the seeming unresponsiveness of God. In terms of the latter point, the questions listed above, while different linguistic statements, all share a common point: the perception of God's lack of response. At a certain level of abstraction, these complaint-protest questions express the same thing: "God's inability or disinterest in helping a faithful but suffering member of the community articulate the psalmist's predicament, that he or she has trusted in the Lord but to no avail in time of trouble" (Miller 1994:74). In terms of their content and tone, they register a similar complaint, namely, that "God is hiding the face, forgetting, abandoning, being far off, rejecting and casting off " (Miller 1994:75) . Similarly, we can itemize the individual expressions of complaint and protest which reflect the predicament of the pray-er who laments being "shamed, taunted, reproached and mocked" (Miller 1994:75). On occasion, this mockery may come from God (e.g., "You are to me like a deceitful brook," Jer. 15:18), but more generally it comes from those who taunt the distressed and complaining person who prays to God out of this situation:

People say to me continually, "Where is your God?" (Ps. 42:3)

As with a deadly wound in my body, my adversaries taunt me,
while they say to me continually, "Where is your God?" (Ps. 42:10)

O Lord, how long shall the wicked,
how long shall the wicked exult? (Ps. 94:3)

The complaint, then, appeals to God in the situation where the pray-er finds himself shamed and mocked by others.

This sense of shame and reproach is occasionally developed at great length, as in the case of Psalms 44 and 69. In Psalm 44, the complaining person expresses bitter lament at the taunting of others, a point that a study of honor and shame can readily surface. We note the highlighted terms of shame and dishonor which form the basis for the lament in Psalm 44:

You have made us a *taunt* of our neighbors,
    the *derision* and *scorn* of those around us.
You have made us a *byword* among the nations,
    a *laughingstock* among the peoples.
All day long my *disgrace* is before me,
    and *shame* has covered my face
at the words of the *taunters* and *revilers*,
    at the sight of the enemy and avenger.
                    (Ps 44:13–16)

Similarly, in Psalm 69, another psalm of lament, we find a comparable catalogue of insults and shame as the basis for the complaints:

It is for your sake that I have borne *reproach*,
    that *shame* has covered my face. (v. 7)
The *insults* of those who *insult* you have fallen on me. (v. 9)
When I humbled my soul with fasting,
    they *insulted* me for doing so. (v. 10)
You know the *insults* I receive
    and my *shame* and *dishonor,*
Insults have broken my heart,
    so that I am in despair. (vv. 19–20)

Thus, we see that the psalm of lament and complaint arises precisely in an honor-shame context, where a client of God who is insulted turns to God for vindication. If the mockery is a challenge to his claim to be a client of the Deity, then the lament effectively solicits a riposte to this challenge and a restoration of honor and favor from the Patron. At the very least, this review of the psalms of lament indicates that they are prayers, that is, acts of piety toward God, and, in the cultural world of the Bible, they are socially sanctioned speech. It is acceptable to address one's heavenly Patron in this manner.

3.2.5 Piety in Prayer on the Cross.   This detour through the landscape of psalms of complaint has important relevance for our interpretation of Jesus' dying words. In the light of the foregoing investigation, we know that: (1) Jesus prayed an *interactional prayer*, (2) which prayer belongs to the socially sanctioned body of prayers known as the *psalms*. (3) The dying words express the stereotypical sentiments of the *complaint-protest psalm*; and (4) characteristic of this type of psalm, the addresser speaks out of *a context of shame and reproach* to an addressee who seems unresponsive to that shame. In regard to this last point, let us note the triple mocking of Jesus on the cross recorded by Matthew (see Donaldson 1991:7, 12–15).

> *First Mockery:* "And those who passed by *derided* him (ἐβλασφήμουν), wagging their heads and saying, 'You who would destroy the temple and build it in three days, save yourself! If you are the Son of God, come down from the cross.'" (27:39–40)

> *Second Mockery:* "So also the chief priests, with the scribes and elders, *mocked* him (ἐμπαίζοντες), saying, 'He saved others; he cannot save himself. He is the King of Israel; let him come down now from the cross, and we will believe in him. He trusts in God; let God deliver him now, if he desires him; for he said, 'I am the Son of God.'" (27:41–43)

> *Third Mockery:* "And the robbers who were crucified with him also *reviled* him (ὠνείδιζον) in the same way." (27:44)

(5) Although couched in the form of a *question*, Jesus' dying words are *a complaint-protest*, not a request for information. Like similar complaints, the protest is an *interactional* prayer which indicates that the problem lies not with the one praying, but with God, who seems unresponsive to the shame of the one praying. (6) Thus "My God, my God . . . " should not be taken as reflective of a *lack of faith* on Jesus' part or a *weakening of his faithfulness*; rather his dying prayer *protests* the apparent *lack of honor* shown to him on the part of his Patron. Therefore, Jesus in no way lacks piety (εὐσέβεια) by his prayer; rather, he proclaims his piety-faithfulness and calls on the Deity to acknowledge it as well. (7) God, then, is *put on the spot* to give a response of some sort to Jesus. God, who is both Patron and Father, must deal with the shame and reproach of Jesus, son and client, and so deliver an "answer" or response to Jesus' lament and protest. (8) As we saw above, the events in 27:51–54 function precisely as the divine *response* which addresses the reproach suffered by Jesus. God's actions, which speak louder than words, confirm the truth of Jesus' piety and his relationship as a client faithful to

his Patron. Therefore, by posthumous honors God vindicates Jesus and thus fulfills his duty as Patron. This honoring, moreover, offsets the terrible mockery and shame which formed the context for Jesus' prayer of lament. And so we should interpret Jesus' complaint-protest as honorable and socially sanctioned speech, which conforms to what is both permitted and even valued in Jesus' cultural world. It embodies Jesus' piety and loyalty, even as it laments a seeming lack of it on God's part. The very fact that God answered his complaint confirms our sense of Jesus' piety, even as it restores his honor.

According to this form-critical analysis, we are not inclined to assess Jesus' dying words simply as "sentiments of feeling forsaken" (Brown 1994:1051). We would go so far as to challenge Brown's objection that those who interpret Jesus' words as positively as we have "take them [in] almost the opposite meaning of what Jesus is portrayed as saying" (1994:1050). Brown and others who follow his line of argument should be faulted for taking the dying words too literally (as "abandonment"), too anachronistically (as appropriate or understandable "emotions"), and too far removed from the thrust of psalms of complaint-protest. Only by ignoring their meaning in the context of psalms of complaint-protest can readers take them in the negative sense that Brown urges. But by contextualizing them as a citation from a psalm of complaint-protest, we see them for what they are: claims to loyalty and piety and demands for acknowledgment of that loyalty.

Brown notes that the "most frequently offered argument for softening the dour import of the Mark/Matt. death cry is based on the general context of Ps. 22" (1994:1049). That is, many scholars have argued that Matthew has, not just the opening line of Psalm 22, but the whole psalm in view (Senior 1977). Although we can never be sure that Matthew expected his audience to know the whole of Psalm 22 and invoke the entire text of it as Jesus' lengthy prayer, he has much of it clearly in view. Scholars all agree that as well as the citation of Ps. 22:1 in Matt. 27:46, the psalm stands in the background of the crucifixion scene in terms of the division of Jesus' clothes (Matt. 27:35 = Ps. 22:18) and the mockery of the passersby (Matt. 27:39 = Ps. 22:7–8), which Matthew received from an earlier tradition. Yet Matthew adds to this one more piece of the psalm, Matt. 27:43 (see fig. 7.2).

Psalm 22:8	Matthew 27:43
He committed his cause to the Lord;	He trusts in God,
let him deliver him,	let God deliver him now,
let him rescue him,	if he desires him;
for he delights in him	for he said, "I am the Son of God"

Figure 7.2 Matthew's Use of Psalm 22:8

Granted this is mockery of Jesus, yet the shaming succeeds only if there is a basis for it, namely, some claim on Jesus' part that can be publicly ridiculed. His mockers challenge the claim that Jesus has a faithful relationship with God ("He trusts in God"). Their challenge asserts that he is a fool, for he would never have come to this point if God judged him pious and honorable. The point is, both the psalm and those who historicize it in Matt. 27:43 attack the piety or virtue of Jesus. This very piety or "trust" in his heavenly Patron forms the basis for Jesus' own complaint-protest in verse 46. The addition of Ps. 22:8 to the mockery of Jesus stands as cogent evidence that Matthew was not putting any ordinary speech on Jesus' lips as his dying words. Rather, by the addition of Ps. 22:8 as the third mockery of Jesus, Matthew has formally linked Jesus' piety with mockery, which as we saw above is the typical context for psalms of lament and protest. Thus Jesus' dying words, which are themselves drawn from a psalm of lament, express precisely the piety that has been mocked.

This suggests several things: First, the content of Jesus' words derives from psalms of lament and is only rightly interpreted in light of such protestations of piety. Second, since the social situation of those who pray such psalms consists of shame, reproach, and mockery, the psalm of complaint-protest calls for vindication, or the removing of the shame. This means a confirmation of the patron-client relationship and thus a vindication of the piety claimed by the one who prays. This is best done by the outright honoring of the one who prays: God-Patron must acknowledge the client's piety, thus confirming his status as "God-loved." Such a manifestation of the client's worth and standing will serve as a riposte to the challenges of the mockers and replace shame with honor. Thus, the use of the psalm of complaint-protest moves the spotlight from Jesus to God-Patron, who must manifest his loyalty to his loyal and faithful client and confirm his piety. Indeed God did, both by means of posthumous honors (27:51–54) and through God's resurrection of Jesus and his enthronement (28:18).

3.3 Summary: Praise to Jesus. Therefore, according to the criteria of praise from epideictic rhetoric, we see that Matthew presents Jesus' actions and words in the Passion narrative as illustrations of two key virtues of his culture. Because of his patient endurance of hardships, pain, and even death, Jesus should be seen as courageous. He voluntarily accepts his fate, and so he does not die as a slave or a victim. His obedience to God's will indicates that he dies freely and nobly.

Similarly, as we examine his prayers both in the Garden and on the cross, Jesus displays a remarkable piety, which is one of the parts of the virtue of justice. He never fails in loyalty to his Patron, even in death. The proper literary and social interpretation of his dying words indicates that Jesus died praying a traditional prayer, Psalm 22. By narrating that Jesus died praying a psalm prayer, Matthew communicates two things: (1) Jesus performed one last act of piety, that is, he prayed to the Deity; (2) the content of his prayer contains a stereotypical but socially approved mode of address to one's Patron-Deity. Thus, according to the local code of approved behavior, Jesus acted fully in accord with what his culture accepted as sanctioned behavior and speech.

Jesus' prayer, moreover, was heard by his Patron-Deity. Commentators regularly speak of his resurrection as the "vindication of Jesus as God's Son" (Senior 1975:322; see Nickelsburg 1980). The prodigies or posthumous honors which accompanied his death (27:51–54) indicate that God acted immediately to remove the shame of his death. Thus Jesus' piety and his unique relationship to his Patron-Deity is confirmed and held up as grounds for praise. If mockery of Jesus' relationship to God constitutes the true pain of the cross (27:40, 43), then confirmation of that relationship, which immediately follows his death, cancels out that shame.

4.0 Summary and Conclusions

Despite all of the excellent research on Jesus' Passion narrative, it is unfortunately the case that commentators have not begun to read it in the light of the pivotal values of Jesus' world: honor and shame. This may be due to two factors: either commentators, who are modern westerners, simply do not know or appreciate the culture of honor and shame, or they deem anthropological materials irrelevant for biblical study. We hope to have shown how erroneous that latter judgment is and how necessary and successful such a perspective can be.

Among the benefits from reading Matthew 26–28 in light of honor and shame, we list the following results of our investigation. First and foremost, we benefit by appreciating the cultural way in which people in the ancient world instinctively interpreted crucifixion as inherently shameful. It was labeled in antiquity as the cruelest and worst possible death. Although intensely painful, it was dreaded most of all because of the total deprivation of honor that accompanied it. Thus a thorough investigation of Jesus' death must take into account the ancient cultural perception and evaluation of crucifixion as "shame" or "foolishness."

Furthermore, this chapter has provided modern readers with a precise "grammar of shame" with which to appreciate the cultural meaning of Jesus' death. The anthropological model assisted us in a conscious and reflexive way of knowing precisely what was shameful and why it was so. We are able to interpret in a culturally sensitive way individual items in Matthew's narrative and appreciate them in terms of the larger system of social values and structures of the ancient world.

As a result of learning the "grammar of shame," we have been sensitized to the paramount cultural problem faced by Matthew and others who undertook to write about the death of Jesus. They surely were aware of how audiences who heard the Gospel accounts of Jesus' crucifixion would instinctively interpret it in terms of the dominant values of their cultural world. Matthew and his audience, then, share knowledge of the general code in this regard. Knowing this, we can then appreciate the delicate editorial process whereby Matthew tells the story as grounds for praise of Jesus.

We surfaced the rhetorical resources available in Matthew's world that could be brought to bear on describing a "noble death." It continues to be part of the argument of this book that Matthew's narrative follows the conventional format and guidelines for telling the life of a praiseworthy person from birth, through life and death. Thus, it has been our aim to recover what native informants considered noble about a person's death. Besides the miscellaneous references to "noble death" that embody the code of praise, we have both the rules for the encomium and the epideictic rhetoric of praise. All three sources provide a coherent, clear, and culturally appropriate description of how death could be viewed as a source of praise and honor.

According to the rhetoric of praise, Jesus' death was honorable on three accounts: (1) it was voluntary; (2) it benefited others; and (3) it was a death befitting a victor, not a slave or victim. According to the instructions for the encomia in the rhetorical handbooks, Jesus' death is honorable because of the posthumous honors awarded him. Finally, according to the epideictic rhetoric of praise, his death would be noble and praiseworthy because: (1) it produced honor, not wealth; (2) it was voluntarily accepted and freely chosen; (3) it benefited others; and (4) it was unique to him. Moreover, just as the deeds of a person's life which are excellent according to the canons of virtue serve as grounds for praise, so too Jesus can be seen displaying both courage and piety in his death. According to these reinforcing criteria, Jesus deserves great praise for the manner in which he died, despite the shame of the cross.

Who, then, is this Jesus who was crucified? According to native categories of honor, Matthew would have us acknowledge Jesus in the following manner. He was no victim, but a hero who knowingly, voluntarily, and courageously embraced his trials and death. He was never shamed by ordinarily shameful events, but endured them courageously and fittingly. In the face of every challenge or insult, he maintained his honor and dignity and was never defeated. The challenge of his death did not go unanswered; for he was posthumously honored by God (27:51–54), vindicated before all, and greatly exalted by his heavenly Patron (27:18). Moreover, he manifested great virtue in his death, both courage and piety. Jesus died in such a noble manner that he fulfilled all of the various rhetorical criteria mentioned by a host of native informants for a "noble death." Everything about his death, then, is grounds for his praise and honor. Therefore he deserves our highest praise.

Part Three

The Sermon on the Mount
in Cultural Perspective

8

Matthew 5:3–12

Honoring the Dishonored

1.0 Introduction

After the publication of Betz's commentary on the Sermon on the Mount, it would seem that nothing of significance remains to be said about it. While Betz's remarks on the Sermon indicate many affinities with the Greco-Roman world of moral exhortation and philosophy, it lacks appreciation of the cultural values reflected in the Sermon. How would the Sermon be heard in a world whose pivotal values are honor and shame? How would males socialized to love honor and fear shame understand Jesus' words? Such important interpretative work remains to be done.

1.1 Hypothesis: Reading in the Key of Honor and Shame. In the next three chapters we argue that in the Sermon on the Mount, Matthew presents Jesus reforming the fundamental value of his culture, namely, honor. His reform consists not only in refining and correcting the Torah of Israel, but in engaging the values and consequent social structures of his social world. Jesus did *not* overthrow the honor code as such, but rather redefined what constitutes honor in his eyes and how his disciples should play the game. The person who declared that last is first and least is greatest is surely redefining the criteria for worth and respect (see Matt. 23:12). Moreover, Jesus proscribed certain ways of gaining and maintaining honor and prescribed others. For example, he forbade his disciples to play the typical village honor game by forswearing honor *claims* (i.e., boasting), *challenges* (i.e., physical and sexual aggressiveness), and *ripostes* (i.e., seeking satisfaction and revenge). Moreover, he attempted to redefine whose *acknowledgment* (i.e., grant of honor) truly counts. He did this by forbidding male disciples to live up to the social expectations of their neighbors, both in challenging and defending themselves, and in forgoing public performance of the typical acts of public piety: prayer, almsgiving, and fasting, which comprise the grounds for an ordinary grant of honor in the village. On the contrary, true honor comes from living up to Jesus' new code and receiving the "reward" of praise of the heavenly Father. Jesus, then, changed the way the honor game was played and redefined the source of honor, namely, acknowledgment by God, not by neighbor. As a result, by conforming to the image of the Master, disciples are shamed in the eyes of their peers and become least and last before their neighbors. But Jesus honors them himself with a grant of reputation and respect that far surpasses what could be hoped for in the public arena of the village ("How honorable are you . . . "). Therefore, Matthew's Sermon on the Mount must be appreciated on its basic cultural level as a discourse that not only speaks the language of honor and shame but fundamentally reforms the way the typical village honor game is played. Honor, then, is neither an optional mode of investigation nor an extraneous social value in the Sermon on the Mount. Reading the Sermon without appreciation of this foundational cultural code means ignoring its basic cultural context.

1.2 Three Sections of the Sermon and Honor and Shame. For reasons of space, not all of Matthew's Sermon on the Mount can be discussed here. We focus on three distinctive units of the Sermon for appropriate cultural analysis. In the Makarisms (5:3–12), Jesus begins the Sermon by undoing the shame which disciples suffered on his behalf. Those who have lost honor by becoming Jesus' disciples receive instead his unique grant of praise and respect. Next, in the Antitheses (5:21–48), Jesus forbids the disciples to engage in the typical cultural patterns of behavior which either gain them honor or defend it in conflict. Finally, in the Instructions on Piety (6:1–8), he removes males from the very playing field by telling them to avoid male public space where almsgiving, prayer, and fasting are part of the expected public behavior. In contrast, they must quit the public arena for the private one, namely, the household, which to their neighbors is "secret." Moreover, he supplants the judges and awarders of honor and respect, claiming that the heavenly Father alone "rewards" with grants of genuine honor and praise.

The scenario we presume in the Sermon on the Mount envisions it as being addressed primarily to males in Jesus' audience. Matthew indicates that the audience is "the crowds" (5:1), which may include males and females, but surely separated into separate groups of males and females/children. Certainly females belonged to the "crowds" present at the multiplication of the loaves (14:13, 21). Our use of the cultural scenario of honor and shame, however, invites us to examine who is actually addressed in the various parts of the Sermon. We contend that in the Antitheses in particular, Jesus addresses males, because the behavior proscribed there characterizes, in antiquity, males rather than females: murder, verbal assaults, sexual aggression, false and vain speech, and feuding and vengeance. We ask female readers not to feel ignored or excluded if we suggest that the honor game, for better or worse, was a male game played by males in public.

2.0 Matthew 5:3–12: How Honorable Are Those Who Are Shamed

2.1 Not "Blessed," but "Honorable." In an article entitled "'Makarisms' and 'Reproaches': A Social Analysis," Hanson (1996) argues that *'ašrê* and *makarios* should be translated as "esteemed," and *hôy* and *ouai* as "disreputable" or "shame on." He brings to his linguistic investigation of these Hebrew and Greek terms the appropriate cultural appreciation of these labels from the prevailing cultural world of honor and shame: "The terminologies of Hebrew *'ašrê* ('esteemed') and *hôy* ('disreputable'), and their Greek counterparts *makarios* and *ouai*, are part of the word field of 'honor and shame'" (1996:87). Hanson would have us forgo attempting to translate μακάριος as "blessed" or "happy," and render it instead as "honorable." And so, Jesus declares certain people "honorable" because of their shameful experiences, not "happy" or "blessed." Hanson suggests, moreover, that when we approach Matthew's makarisms (5:3–12) from their proper cultural perspective of honor and shame, we should be alerted to several things. First, public honor is being accorded or denied certain people who fit or do not fit the categories described according to cultural expectations of that ancient world (i.e., "poor," "mourning," "ostracized"). Second, if "poor" means someone who cannot maintain his or her status and so suffers loss of honor as well as economic hardship (Malina 1986c:152–56), then the makarisms contain an oxymoron: "How honorable are those who suffer a loss of honor . . . "

Reading the makarisms in terms of honor and shame is compatible with current research on them. Commentators regularly point to parallels to the makarisms in both Jewish and Greek literature (Str-B 1.189; Hengel 1987; Dodd 1968:1–10; Davies and Allison 1988:431–34; Betz 1995: 92–105). And the pivotal value of both Greek and Hebrew culture was honor. Moreover, some allege that typical makarisms have a close relationship to morality and ethics, which means that the praise or "blessing" constitutes a public acknowledgment of the worth and value of commonly held values and expected behavior. This, of course, is the basic meaning of honor, namely, public acknowledgment of worth grounded on local expectations of value. For example, in 2 Enoch a long series of blessings are listed, all of which praise the expected code of behavior: "Honorable is the man who reverences the name of the Lord, and who serves in front of his face always, and who organizes his gifts with fear, offerings of life, and who in this life lives and dies correctly" (42:6; see Ps. 1:1–2). The man who has acted in public according to the local expectations of honoring God ("serving in front of his face" . . . "organizing gifts" . . . "lives and dies correctly") receives public acknowledgment of worth ("honorable"). Or, makarisms honor a person who is deemed to be favored by the gods, as in the case of Aseneth: "Honorable are you, Aseneth, because the ineffable mysteries of God have been revealed to you" (*Joseph and Aseneth* 16:7). And as we have regularly seen, favor from God (or the gods) is one of the main criteria for praise and honor; mortals thus acknowledge the role and status of the person to whom God ascribes this honor. Encoded in declarations of "blessedness" is the public honoring of someone for a behavior or status which the group values.

Moreover, honor is not honor until there is acknowledgment, which is generally expressed by the term μακάριος, or "How honorable!" For example, Philo pronounces a blessing and thus honors a proselyte who has converted to the true Deity:

> The proselyte exalted aloft by his happy lot will be gazed at from all sides, marvelled at and held "honorable" (μακαριζόμενος) by all for two things of highest excellence, that he came over to the camp of God and that he has won a prize best suited to his merits, a place in heaven firmly fixed, greater than words dare describe. (*On Rewards and Punishments* 152)

We note how being publicly declared "blessed" or "honorable" is linked with being "exalted aloft" and "gazed at" and "marveled at"; the grant of honor comes from the general public ("from all sides . . . by all"). Philo gives two reasons for this grant of honor: the wise decision to serve the true God (achieved worth) and the reward of a heavenly "prize" or the honoring of him by the Deity (ascribed worth). Thus the proselyte acts according to common wisdom and does the expected right thing, for which he receives a grant of honor and respect. Thus, acknowledgment of worth is typically pronounced on people who either act according to cultural expectations (achieved honor) or are recognized as favored in some way by the Deity (ascribed honor). They are honored, then, precisely in terms of what the group values.

Yet Hanson's study indicates that honor in Matt. 5:3–12 is being bestowed on people who are *not* acting according to accepted wisdom and who are *not* acknowledged as favored by their neighbors—on the contrary. That they are honored is not the issue; but honored by whom and for what reasons? Hanson's study alerts us that Jesus revalues what has been disvalued; he honors what has been shamed.

2.2 The Original Four Makarisms. Modern criticism of the Sermon holds that there were originally only four makarisms. Scholars base this observation on comparison with Luke's list, which comprises only four (see fig. 8.1).

Matthew 5:3–12	Luke 6:20–23
3 *Honored* are the poor in spirit	20 *Honored* are you poor
4 *Honored* are those who mourn	21b *Honored* are you that weep now
6 *Honored* are those who hunger and thirst for righteousness	21a *Honored* are you that hunger now
11 *Honored* are you when men revile you and drive you out and utter all kinds of evil against you falsely	22 *Honored* are you when men hate you, and when they exclude you and revile you and cast out your name as evil
on my account	on account of the Son of man

Figure 8.1 Makarisms in the Sermon

Traditional scholarship has tended to ask certain questions and adopt certain points of view in regard to these, such as questions about the history of these four makarisms. Were they always grouped together (see Kloppenborg 1986:36–44; Horsley 1991:194)? Might they individually have been spoken on different occasions? The *Gospel of Thomas*, for example, has only three of them side by side: "Blessed are you when you are hated and persecuted. . . . Blessed are those who have been persecuted. . . . Blessed are they who are hungry," nos. 68–69). Furthermore, some have maintained that the first three describe "the general human conditions of poverty and suffering," whereas the fourth "is oriented toward the specific situation of persecution of the Christian community" (Kloppenborg 1987:173; Betz 1995:114). About the first issue, it does not impinge on the present study, which focuses directly on the fact that at a certain point in the tradition, these four were gathered together and arranged into a certain sequence, as Matthew and Luke bear witness to. Concerning the second, we advance a fresh hypothesis: the makarisms speak of disciples (Matthew: "on my account"; Luke: "on account of the Son of man"), not general humanity. Moreover, they do not necessarily describe the fate of four different disciples, but the composite fate of one disciple who has suffered a dreadful shaming by his family. All four describe, not "the general human conditions of poverty and suffering," but the full extent of the specific fate of disciples who have suffered the most serious of misfortunes because of Jesus, that is, banning by the family.

3.0 The Causes of Public Shame

3.1 The Shame of Banning (Matt. 5:11–12). We begin our examination with a closer look at the climactic fourth makarism. It is generally acknowledged that Matt. 5:11–12 is "climactic" for reasons of length and position, but not content (Betz 1995:109). It enjoys the significant rhetorical position of being last (Daube 1973:196–201); it is triple the length of the others; it changes the pattern from "Honorable are *they*" to "Honorable are *you*"; and Jesus clearly addresses those who have responded to him. Although the wording of their versions differs, Matthew and Luke both describe a frightful loss of honor to someone because of discipleship with Jesus (see fig. 8.2).

Matthew 5:11	**Luke 6:22**
Honored are you when men	*Honored* are you when men
revile you	hate you
drive you out	exclude you
utter all kinds of evil	revile you
against you falsely	cast out your name as evil
on my account	on account of the Son of man

Figure 8.2 Honor in Relation to Discipleship

But we argue that it is climactic by virtue of its content, for it gives the reason why disciples become "poor," "hungry," and "mourning": they are driven out or banned from the household by their families because of loyalty to Jesus ("on my account"). In focus, then, is the cause of shame, that is, banning. Translations which render Matthew's term "drive out" (διώξωσιν) as "persecuted," are infelicitous here because they are too imprecise, and do not adequately indicate either the source of the opposition or its social and cultural results. This hostility, moreover, is not the formal or informal excommunication from the synagogue (Strecker 1988:44; Betz 1995:150), but banning or shunning by the families of disciples.

3.1.1 A Composite of Social Shame. As we examine the fourth makarism more closely, let us focus on its verbs and read them in terms of their social and cultural meanings.

1. "Revile" (ὀνειδίσωσιν): reviling and reproaching are acts of shaming another. Jesus publicly shames Chorazin and Bethsaida for denying him honor after the great benefaction of his miracles (Matt. 11:20); and Jesus is himself shamed by the thieves with whom he is crucified (27:44; see Mark 15:32; see 1 Peter 4:14). The dominant sense is "'disgrace,' 'shame,' 'scandal,' then 'abuse,' 'objurgation'" (Schneider 1972:238).
2. "Drive out" (διώξωσιν): although it can mean "persecute" (Matt. 10:23; Gal. 1:13; 1 Cor. 15:9), it also means "drive away/drive out." For example, it is synonymous with "remove" (αἴρω: 1 Cor. 5:2, 13) and "cast out" (ἀποσυνάγωγος: John 9:22; 16:2). It has the sense of "to outlaw" someone from a social group (Fitzmyer 1981:635).
3. "Speak all evil against you" (εἴπωσιν πᾶν πονηρὸν καθ ὑμῶν): a man's personal name or reputation is at stake, and the issue here is defamation and slander (Betz 1995:150). Luke speaks of slander, that is, the attack of another's public reputation in the eyes of village or town.

Taken together, the verbs of the fourth makarism describe the separation of a man from his basic social group through the control mechanism of banning or expulsion. As a result, his reputation and name are publicly attacked. He is being completely shamed in the eyes of his neighbors (Cohen 1991:72–73). We accept that the banning takes place "on my account," that is, the shaming described in Matt. 5:11 results from discipleship. Yet who is doing the shaming and why? What social and economic effects will this have?

Whence this hostility? Previous studies of the "forms of persecution" which befell the early disciples of Jesus focused on exclusion from the synagogue—not, however, the formal *niddui*, but rather "an informal ban employed by every community . . . toward individuals it despises" (Hare 1967:53; see Forkman 1972; Saldarini 1994:107–16). Although the New Testament speaks of disciples "cast out of the synagogue" (John 16:2) or simply "expelled" (John 9:34; Hauck 1968:527–28), there is another possibility for banning or exclusion, namely, family sanctions against rebellious sons. I suggest that a likely scenario for the fourth makarism is the situation of a son being disinherited by his father and shunned by his family for joining the circle of Jesus' disciples (" . . . on my account").

3.1.2 Shame and Loss of Wealth. In the case of the fourth makarism, the public shame of ostracism results in a severe loss of wealth. Matthew describes the person as "driven out" (διώξωσιν), which will result in the loss of not simply physical and social space, but also the material advantages that come from them. A man "driven out" has lost his wealth and land (if he is a farmer's heir), or market stall (if he is an artisan's son), or patronage (if he is a day laborer). Total economic ruin, as well as corresponding collapse of social standing, quickly follow.

Readers are reminded of the discussion above in chapter 1 about the way that wealth is related to honor, primarily its public display. A man who is forcibly deprived of wealth and property by being ostracized will lose all grounds for respect and worth in the eyes of his neighbors. He will be doubly shamed, first by being publicly declared a deviant and second by being denied the very grounds of worth in a peasant society, his financial equity. "Wealth," of course, is a relative term. It applies to kings gorgeously appareled and living in luxury (Luke 7:25; see 16:19). But even a peasant might have "wealth" in terms of the size of his fields and flocks. But banning and ostracism would surely disrupt both the sources of wealth and the patterns of exchange among village neighbors. The Tosefta describes the plight of someone banned: "One does not sell to them or receive from them or take from them or give to them. One does not teach their sons a trade, and does not obtain healing from them" (*t. Ḥullin* 2:20). The loss is both financial and social. If the man banned is an artisan, then public reproach will result in loss of employment and trade; if a peasant farmer, the loss of cooperation in planting and harvesting, a break in marriage contracts which are essentially reciprocal, an absence from the reciprocal feasts among villagers at weddings, and the like. Meaningful social intercourse would vanish, as the ostracized party suffers a total collapse of wealth and status. Therefore, the ostracism envisioned in the fourth makarism would have immediate and severe repercussions on the economic and social status of the person.

3.1.3 Reading the Other Makarisms in the Light of the Fourth One. We will now examine the other three makarisms in the light of the fourth one, for they can be profitably understood as specifying precisely the economic and social loss that follows the loss of honor and social standing because of ostracism (see Robbins 1985:39–44 and 51–54). Our strategy is to avoid allegorizing them into statements of the general human condition, and to imagine them as literally and realistically as possible in the economic and cultural world of peasants and artisans, which includes the values of honor and shame. In particular, we will want to consider the other original makarisms as the concrete results of the fourth makarism, which describes banning and ostracism. For, if a person is banned by his family, he will most assuredly be "poor," "hungry," and even "mourning" because of his lack of kinship.

3.2 The Shame of Begging Poverty (Matt. 5:3). What does "poor" mean here? Most peasants and artisans in antiquity possessed little material wealth; but the ancients did not automatically classify the economically deprived as "poor." If peasants had what sufficed, Plutarch did not call them "poor," a term restricted to those who lack basic necessities: "In what suffices, no one is poor" (*On the Desire for Wealth* 523F; see Seneca, *Letters* 25.4). Although most people had little wealth, they had sufficiency, and so were not classified as "poor." The commonplace, "Be content with what you have," is generally addressed to the non-elites in antiquity who have little, but are not destitute (see Luke 3:14). "Contentment" with "sufficiency," of course, made a virtue of necessity, a point found in Greco-Roman, Jewish, and Christian literatures (Attridge 1989:388). It is presumed that God provides sufficiency for all creatures (Gen. 33:11; see Matt. 5:45). Our point is: typical peasants and artisans with few of this world's goods have, nevertheless, what is deemed "sufficient"; and so they are not called "poor." Who, then, are the poor?

The Greeks distinguish two terms, both of which are translated as "poor": πένης and πτωχός. Dictionaries often translate πένης as "poor man" (e.g., BAGD 642), which misses the root meaning πένομαι, "to work hard." The word πένης refers to one who does manual labor, and so is contrasted with πλούσιος, a member of the landed class who does *not* work (Hauck 1968b:887). At stake is the social status of a "worker." Hamel writes of the πένης, or working poor:

> [H]e was forced to work to live and had to receive some form of wage and to sell; the craftsman was dependent on others' goodwill. In this respect, he was similar to servants and slaves, free but fettered by various customs. . . . This lack of time and self-sufficiency, some philosophers argued, made the craftsman unfit to be a citizen, at least an honorable one. One had to be rich to avoid the ties of dependence usually associated with work and be able to live like a true Hellene. Work, because it meant subservience and dependence, was seen as an impediment to this ideal and was therefore contemptible. . . . The *penêtes* were all those people who needed to work in shops or in the fields and were consequently without the leisure characteristic of the rich gentry, who were free to give their time to politics, education, and war. (1990:168–69; see Hands 1968:62)

In contrast, a πτωχός is reduced to begging; that is, he is someone destitute of all resources (Hauck 1968b:886–87; Hands 1968:62–63). As Luz noted, a πένης works, a πτωχός begs:

> "Poor," according to Semitic usage, means indeed not only those who are lacking in money, but, more comprehensively, the oppressed, miserable, dependent, humiliated . . . the translation by the Greek word *ptôchos*, the strongest available Greek word for social poverty, speaks in favor of this interpretation. The basic rule is: The *penês* has to work, the *ptôchos* has to beg. (Luz 1989:231)

A πένης with little wealth was still thought to have "sufficiency," and so is not called "poor." In contrast, the πτωχός lacks sufficiency and most other economic and social resources, such as social standing. Hamel remarks: "The *ptôchos* was someone who had lost many or all of his family and social ties. He often was a wanderer . . . a foreigner for others, unable to tax for any length of time the resources of a group to which he could contribute very little or nothing at all" (1990:170). Hence, the "poor" in Matt. 5:3 (πτωχοί) are not the ubiquitous peasants with little of this world's goods who labor in fields and shops. They are certainly not those who choose poverty for philosophical reasons (Betz 1995:115–17). When Matthew calls them πτωχοί, not πένητες, he identifies them as the begging or destitute poor. We will shortly argue that they are people who have suffered a recent and tragic loss of whatever goods, wealth, land, social standing, and family they had. But what happened to make them "poor"? Who did this to them?

In the first makarism (Matt. 5:3), we understand the reference to πτωχοί as a general statement concerning the social status of persons who have suffered a recent and severe loss of means (Guelich 1976:426). More specificity is given in subsequent makarisms as to the social implications of being destitute and begging. Thus we will argue that "poor" is a topic statement given specificity by "mourning" and "hunger."

3.3 The Shame of Loss of Family (Matt. 5:4).

Those who "mourn" most likely are mourning for the dead (see Gen. 50:3; 1 Macc. 12:52; 13:26). Inasmuch as they will be "consoled," they are not lamenting sins or awaiting the eschatological day. One hard fact needs to be taken into account, that is, the wretchedly short life span of ancient peoples (Carney 1975:88). Given the pervasiveness of "widows and orphans" in ancient literature, we should not spiritualize Jesus' remarks too quickly (Strecker 1988:34–35; Luz 1989:235; Betz 1995:120–23). Moreover, since we find the normal combination of "mourning" for the dead and "comfort" in ancient literature, the mourning envisioned here most probably involves the loss of family and kin. Someone lacks parents, family, and kin, with all the economic and social loss attendant upon this. But is this loss one of death, or could there be another reason for a man to have lost his family, such as banning by the family? The cultural point needs to be made that people without family or kin truly lack, not just the economic resources that come from this institution and that give worth and standing in the eyes of one's neighbors, but also marks of identity and value that derive from ascribed honor or birth into a family. Thus social as well as economic worth is envisioned; those who mourn have suffered a blow to their social standing, that is, their honor and worth. We will need to see other materials in Matthew which deal with fractured families to appreciate more fully that "mourning" probably refers to loss of family through banning.

3.4 The Shame of Hunger (Matt. 5:6).

Given the peasant nature of Jesus' audience, the literal and simple meaning of "hunger" as lacking food seems warranted. Drought and famine may cause hunger in the land (Josephus, *Ant.* 20.51–53; Acts 11:28; Garnsey 1970:219–23), as well as excessive taxation (Kloppenborg 1991:86–88). While landed peasants have resources and relationships to alleviate starvation, not so landless peasants. They have scant money with which to purchase food; even if they had, the money could hardly last for long. These "hungry" folk are promised that they will "eat their fill," but at present they are *ptôchoi* in regard to their daily bread (Hamel 1990:8–52; Oakman 1986: 22–28).

If literally hungry, then these peasant followers of Jesus lack sufficiency and thus fall in a status lower than the working poor. They are males who cannot provide for themselves or their families, and thus fail in the eyes of their neighbors to live up to the basic expectations of manly worth. Their hunger, then, brings with it a social stigma of shame.

3.5 Banning as the Source of Poverty, Mourning, and Hunger.

Throughout this discussion, we have interpreted the four original makarisms as a unit. We maintain that they are addressed to disciples, not the general mass of peasants in Jesus' audience. They describe the composite state of shame and misfortune which certain people have suffered on account of Jesus, and so are not discrete, individual descriptions of the general sad state of peasants. The key to this unity rests in appreciating the social and economic results of the situation described in the fourth, climactic makarism, which refers to banning or ostracism.

If there is any relationship among the original four makarisms, the fourth offers a plausible scenario for understanding the other three. If a son were banned or disinherited by his father, he would be "reviled" by the family, "driven out" from the family house, and forced off the family land. He would then truly be "poor" (πτωχός), that is, a person suffering a severe loss of all resources, material as well as social, so that he is destitute and reduced to begging. He would truly be said to be mourning the loss of kin and experiencing the loss of status that comes from being without family; recall that one's basic worth and value is ascribed through birth into a family and clan. If the kinship group denies this worth, total social shame follows, with severe economic results. Finally, if a son were driven away from the family land, he would immediately lose access to the grain, vegetables, fruits, milk, etc., which were the daily food of peasants. No doubt he would literally be hungry and thirsty. The ostracism described in the last makarism, therefore, describes a plausible and concrete situation which can adequately explain the other three. Thus, the four makarisms, either individually or taken together, describe a genuinely poor person, that is, someone who has suffered a loss of subsistence and so cannot maintain the social position and status into which he was born.

As a result of banning, this peasant would suffer a true and total loss of honor and status. His name would be reviled, his reputation held up to rebuke, and his character defamed. Business deals and marriage arrangements with such an outcast would be unthinkable. With loss of wealth, he would hardly be in a position to maintain his social obligations and social status. His loss of honor would be complete: loss of family, from which a man is ascribed his basic status and honor; loss of wealth, which was the public index of status; and loss of reputation, which comprises the essence of honor. A person who is "reviled, driven out" has "all kinds of evil uttered" against him. This loss of honor, I suggest, would deprive him of all standing in the village or town. He would be looked on by his neighbors as a person reaping a harvest of shame for his folly, which is "on account of me." Discipleship has brought upon him family outrage.

4.0 A Man's Foes Will Be Those of His Own Household

The scenario just described is by no means the only one possible. Some suggest war, famine, and the like as causes of poverty, mourning, and hunger. What would make it probable? Several passages in the same Q source support the probability of the scenario described above. Two describe *family crises* (Matt. 10:34–36//Luke 12:51–53 and Matt. 10:37–39//Luke 14:26–27) and two deal with *loss of wealth* (Matt. 6:25–34//Luke 12:22–32 and Matt. 6:19–21//Luke 12:33–34). Three of these passages are found in one continuous discourse in Luke 12; and if the general presumption of the originality of the Lukan sequence prevails here, then the materials on family crisis were originally linked with those about loss of wealth. The loss of family could be the probable context for loss of wealth and thus of honor.

4.1 Crisis in the Family.   In one place Jesus attacks the social debt of obedience owed by sons to their fathers and family (Matt. 10:34–36//Luke 12:51–53), as shown in fig. 8.3.

Matthew 10:34–36	Luke 12:51–53
Do not think that I have come to bring peace on earth; I have not come to bring peace, but a sword.	Do you think that I have come to give peace on earth? No, I tell you, but rather division;
	for henceforth in one house there will be five divided, three against two and two against three;
For I have come to set a man against his father, and a daughter against her mother, and a daughter-in-law against her mother-in-law;	they will be divided, father against son and son against father, mother against daughter and daughter against her mother, mother-in-law against her daughter-in-law and daughter-in-law against her mother-in-law.
and a man's foes will be those of his own household.	

Figure 8.3 Division among Family Members

In contrast to sayings supportive of the family (Mark 7:9–12; see Pilch 1988:32–59), Jesus here attacks the basic solidarity and loyalty which family members owe each other. This passage implies that the division of the family occurs precisely because of Jesus ("I have come to . . . "); it envisions some members loyal to family traditions but others joining the circle of Jesus, espousing his teachings, and thus incurring the hostility of the family. The interpretation of this passage is by no means certain. For example, Kloppenborg suggested that this passage could be understood either as an apocalyptic *topos* "used to signify the utter chaos and social disorder which will portend the eschatological intervention of God" or as a concrete reference to "the rejection and violence experienced by members of the community itself " (1987:151–52). Yet the parallels with apocalyptic literature that are supposed to legitimate the former interpretation do not truly correspond to what Matt. 10:34–36 states. In *1 Enoch* 99:5, mothers abort or kill their infants, but for no particular reason; *1 Enoch* 100:1–2 describes a family bloodbath, but as part of a general bloodletting characteristic of general lawlessness; *Jubilees* 23:16–19 describes the righteous members of a family attacking its sinful ones. Matthew 10:34–36 does not describe general and insane killing of family members; it does not envision a time of lawlessness or insanity. Family violence occurs precisely because of loyalty to Jesus, not sinfulness in general (see Milavic 1995:136–42).

Linked with this is a second passage (Matt. 10:37–38//Luke 14:25–27), one that also has to do with family loyalty. It presents a totally divided household (see Fig. 8.4).

Matthew 10:37–38	Luke 14:26–27
He who loves father or mother more than me is not worthy of me; and who loves son or daughter more than me is not worthy of me.	If anyone comes to me and does not hate his own father and mother and wife and children and brothers and sisters, yes, and even his own life, he cannot be my disciple.
And he who does not take up his cross and follow me is not worthy of me.	Whoever does not bear his own cross and come after me cannot be my disciple.

Figure 8.4 Worthiness in Whose Eyes?

Matthew's version emphasizes "love X more than me"; this connotes respect for or acceptance of the approval of another, which is the essence of honor. But who "loves X more than me" is "not worthy" of me, and "worthy" is another term for honor (see Rev. 4:11; 5:9). Who loves the family group (with its social standing, land, and wealth) cannot find affiliation, status, and respect in Jesus' group. Again the issue focuses on the source of honor; either from family or Jesus; loyalty either to family or to Jesus occasions the choice.

Both Matthew and Luke exhort disciples to "take up one's 'cross'" and become members of Jesus' fictive-kinship group. The "cross" here must surely be a metaphor for negative experiences, physical sufferings (begging, hunger) and/or social ones (loss of family, shame)—just the kinds of things mentioned in the original makarisms (5:3–12). Matthew clearly states here that these sufferings are not the result of taxation, drought, or some other calamity, but precisely the results of becoming Jesus' disciple. The "cross," moreover, was inextricably associated with "shame," as we saw in the previous chapter on the death of Jesus. But according to Matt. 10:37–38, disciples would experience shame from the family, but honor from Jesus.

It takes little imagination to see how hatred toward and from one's family would lead to a "cross." Disobedience to one's parents, a paramount virtue sanctioned by custom and law, can easily lead to social and economic ruin. A rebellious son should be banned by the family (Deut. 21:18–20). If banned, he will surely take up a "cross" to be Jesus' disciple, namely, suffering as physical (hunger) as it is social (mourning, begging, being an outcast). The crux of the crisis, however, lies in honor and loyalty—either traditional loyalty to parents and family with its concomitant honor, wealth, and status or affiliation with Jesus and corresponding loss of family status and approval. Loss and gain: loyalty to Jesus entails *loss of honor* in the family and kinship network, because the honor code between father and son is violated, but also a *gain of honor*, because Jesus honors those loyal to him and acclaims them "worthy."

Although these passages do not say that the father eventually bans the rebellious son and disinherits him or that the son quits his father's house, they offer the most immediate and plausible scenario for the ostracism described in the fourth makarism. If any form of banning or disinheriting results from a son's loyalty to

Jesus, then he will truly be "poor," as well as hungry and mourning; he will certainly suffer a total collapse of honor in the eyes of family and neighbors.

4.2 Crisis over Loss of Wealth.   Two other passages need be examined: Matt. 6:24–34//Luke 12:22–32 and Matt. 6:19–21//Luke 12:33–34. Their correct social interpretation can shed light on the economic and cultural effects of families being divided over loyalty to Jesus. In Matthew and Luke both passages are linked together, an editorial clue which we respect.

Matthew 6:25–34//Luke 12:22–32 explicitly treats loss of wealth and its relationship to honor. The passage begins with a topic statement:

> Do not be concerned about
>> what to eat
>> what to wear
>>> (Matt. 6:25//Luke 12:22)

But who is being addressed? General humanity (Betz 1995:462)? And why are they failing in subsistence in the two basic necessities of life (Guelich 1982:336)? Is this a general exhortation to all against "anxiety" or a specific address to a concrete situation? Again, we prefer to examine this material in terms of its specific meaning for peasants, rather than spiritualize it in terms of "anxiety" over the general human condition.

The scenario envisioned here reflects another aspect of the honor-shame world of antiquity, namely, the gender division of society: a male world (public tasks in public places) and a female world (private or household tasks in the household). Of all modern commentators on the Sermon, only Luz notices that sowing and harvesting are male tasks, while clothing production is female (1989:405; see Arnal 1997:77–86). This observation, however, does not influence his interpretation, which still regards the addressees as general humanity. In light of a gender-divided world, we argue, the person "concerned about what to eat" is a male, whom I call the husband. When he looks at the birds of the air, he "sees" fields, which in the gender-divided world of antiquity were male places, where males did the male task of farming. Birds, however, do not perform the tasks typically done by males, i.e., "sowing, reaping, gathering into barns or storehouses" (Matt. 6:26//Luke 12:24). Yet God gives them subsistence food. The issue is food production, the proper concern of a male peasant.

Alternately a female scenario is imagined. The female in the family concerns herself about "what to wear," i.e., "clothing," which was produced by females in the household. This female is presumably the wife of the male addressed above, so that the primary tasks of a peasant household are in view. Thus, Jesus' remarks envision a basic family unit which is typically divided into the characteristic gender-specific spaces and tasks—males = fields and food production, and females = home and clothing production. When this female looks at the fields with a gender-specific eye, she sees stuff for weaving. The lilies "neither toil nor spin," yet they are more gorgeous than the royal robes woven by Solomon's harem.

Beyond this gender-specific reading, the exhortation treats the loss of wealth, that is, insufficiency of food and clothing. Here the male and female peasants lack sufficiency in these two basic areas, such that they must be considered genuinely "poor" (πτωχοί), that is, destitute and reduced to begging. The text does not say why their situation is so desperate, but the options are limited: (1) drought, which produces famine for humans and lack of fodder for wool-bearing sheep, or (2) excessive taxation, which leads to peasant indebtedness, which when foreclosed results in lost of land (Luz 1989:402), or (3) family conflict, such that a son (and his wife) were disinherited, "driven away" from the family farm, and set adrift without land or animals. Which option seems appropriate? Since the exhortation is addressed to disciples (see Luke 12:22), loss of wealth is formally related to issues of group loyalty, and not to "the general human condition."

The passage, moreover, links wealth with honor and status. At the very beginning, Matthew announces the topic with a value statement that the "soul" is of more value (πλεῖον) than food, and the "body" of more importance than clothing. The simple comparative term "more" (πλεῖον) relates to the world of worth. Whether it has a quantitative or qualitative note, "more" ranks one thing above another in some sort of value pattern (Betz 1995:472), thus giving respect and honor to it. After the male is told to look at the birds, he is asked whether he is "of more value" than they, another term connoting honorable status. Of course a man is "more" than a bird; his honor is that of a creature made in the image of God (Gen. 1:26) and as one who was made little less than the gods (Ps. 8:4–8), with dominion over land and birds. Rhetorically this repeats the earlier value question: "Is not life more than (πλεῖον) food and the body more than clothing?" and provides an answer which explicitly bestows honor on a male who lacks food (and land). A male disciple is worth more than mere birds! Likewise with the female; after she looks at the lilies of the field, she is told that a paternal figure values her more than them, and so is promised honor and respect (on clothing and honor, see Neyrey 1993:20–22, 120–22).

What may we say about this passage? The husband and wife are peasants who are falling below the subsistence level in regard to food and clothing. Nothing in the passage explicitly states that loss of land, especially family land, is at stake. But something is missing from the horizon: there is no family, no household, and no kinship network to catch them as they fall. In fact, the addressees are told to turn to a new paternal figure ("your heavenly Father"), rather than to the obvious kinship network (Matt. 6:26, 32; Luke 12:30). Of course, the family may have all died out; but then the son should have inherited his father's land. Nevertheless, the loss of wealth by this husband and wife entails a concomitant loss of honor and social standing, for a major element in the exhortation has to do with "worth" and "value," i.e., honor. Therefore, this husband and wife are truly becoming "poor" in the eyes of the rest of the peasants, thus losing familial honor but gaining worthiness and respect in Jesus' and God's eyes.

Family banning or disinheritance of a rebellious son would adequately account for the loss of subsistence envisioned here, as well as the loss of honor attendant on such an economic and social catastrophe. This option becomes plausible and probable when we recall that this passage from the Q source represented by Luke 12 explicitly links family conflict with loss of wealth and with issues of "true treasure." We presume that Luke retains the correct sequence of the original Q source:

> do not be anxious about your life . . . (12:22–32)
>
> treasure in heaven . . . (12:33–34)
>
> a house divided . . . (12:51–53)

This Lukan collection, moreover, concerns itself with disinheritance (12:13) and covetousness (12:15), the former directly dealing with family conflict. The original source, then, saw a connection between loss of wealth, family conflict, and discipleship. It envisions a scenario that would make a person needy of food and clothing as described in 12:22–32, namely, loss of family through disinheritance or banning.

In an adjoining passage (Matt. 6:19–21//Luke 12:33–34) disciples are instructed about "treasure." Like the previous passage, it begins with a command from Jesus: "Do not lay up treasure on earth" (Matt. 6:19), or "Sell your possessions and give alms" (Luke 12:33). Since Luke regularly exhorts disciples to give alms (Luke 11:41; Acts 3:2–6; 9:36; 10:2, 4, 31) Matthew probably contains the more original wording here. The imperative in Matt. 6:19 ("Do not lay up treasure") is formally parallel in structure to the exhortatory command in Matt. 6:25//Luke 12:22 ("do not be anxious").

Jesus' remarks about "treasure" are clearly hyperbolic, for subsistence peasants simply do not have "treasure," especially in this period of ruinous taxation. Peasants could have an ox (for plowing), some sheep (for wool/clothing), some goats (for milk), and some fruit trees and vines (for food). But this is hardly "treasure." The moth threatens the few blankets and garments the peasant has (on the cost and scarcity of clothing, see Hamel 1990:64–67), and corruption (βρῶσις) rots wood (house or wooden plow) and corrodes metal (an iron plow?). Thieves (κλέπται) abound in Galilee in this period, whose prime targets would be villages unprotected by walls (on widespread banditry, see Horsley and Hanson 1985:48–87).

However meager his wealth, it is a peasant's "treasure" and the key indicator of status in the village. Jesus' remark, moreover, tells the peasant not to value what all his family and neighbors value, but rather to value something else superior to "treasure on earth." At a minimum, Jesus attacks peasant covetousness (Luke 12:15 and Delling 1968:266–70) and the honor attached to wealth. Nothing explicit is said about loss of wealth here, except that moth, corruption, and thieves cause loss. But we remember that wealth and honor reside in the family, not the individual. Hence a family's collective honor is in view. Loss of "treasure" would mean loss of honor and worth and status for all of them.

4.3 Summary and Conclusion. From this discussion, one clear theme emerges. The early tradition of Jesus' sayings contains a number of statements which attack family unity and loyalty. These statements, moreover, are often linked with remarks on loss of wealth and honor. Thus crisis within the family over loyalty to Jesus emerges as the probable cause of the shunning and banning envisioned in the fourth makarism. Such a radical action by a family against a disobedient or rebellious son would surely entail immediate, severe economic and social loss.

In conclusion, we focused on the banning or shunning described in the fourth makarism and asked about its source and consequences. As regards consequences, the person so treated would immediately become "poor," not the working poor (πένης), but the begging poor (πτωχός). These destitute poor are truly hungry and thirsty, and generally lack family to aid or support them. Thus a person who suffered the shameful experience of banning or shunning would also be "poor, hungry, and mourning." The original four makarisms, then, describe the complete fate of someone and indicate a cause or source for "poor, hungry, and mourning" in the banning and shunning of 5:11–12. This fate, moreover, specifically befalls a disciple and so should not be inflated as "the general human condition."

4.3.1 Loss of Family = Loss of Honor. But what caused the banning or shunning? We turn to other remarks in the same Q tradition which link or juxtapose division of the family and loss of wealth. In the face of the powerful control that families exerted on their members to conform and live up to their honorable expectations, Jesus proclaims that those who love family more than himself are "not worthy" of him, that is, they are dishonored by him. This statement invites sons to boldness in standing against their families, thus incurring their wrath and scorn; as a result they will surely carry a "cross," namely, loss of family, its honor, wealth, and identity.

In terms of honor, the fourth makarism indicates that Jesus' disciples will be utterly shamed ("reviled, driven out, all kinds of evil uttered against them"). If the banning were done by the village, the man could still fall back on his family for respect and sustenance, although there would surely be a loss of honor in the eyes of one's neighbors. But if the ostracization came precisely from the man's own family, the loss of honor would be immediate and complete. Since honor derives from family and is displayed in wealth and depends totally on public acknowledgment of worth, the son banned by his family would lose all these bases of honor. No acknowledgment of worth, but rather "reviling . . . uttering all kinds of evil against you." No wealth, but "poor . . . hunger." No family, but "mourning."

Yet honor remains the issue. From whom should a disciple seek honor? In the Ten Commandments a certain primacy is given to the honorable relationship of son to parents: "Honor your father and your mother" (Matt. 15:4; 19:19). A later parable (Matt. 21:28–32) indicates a tension between publicly agreeing/disobeying a father and publicly shaming/obeying him. The parable presents a genuine honor conflict: is it enough to say "yes" to one's father in public and thus let him save face but not to obey him, or is it honorable to shame the father in public by a refusal but ultimately to do his will? Honoring parents, then, is a complicated social issue in this Gospel. For Jesus asks disciples to "love" him more than father, mother, and family (10:37), which in the world of limited good means that the family elders will receive less "love" and honor. On one occasion Jesus predicted fearsome and shameless family conflict: "Brother will deliver up brother to death, and the father his child, and children will rise against parents and have them put to death" (10:21–22). The situation we are examining does not envision sons dishonoring their parents by killing them, but rather by disobeying the social controls which the parents exercise over their sons, even adult ones, to have them conform to village expectations. Thus by discipleship they shame their parents and are in turn shamed by them.

Jesus envisions some disciples paying a fearful price to join his circle, namely, the loss of their honorable reputation and status in the eyes of family and village. He acknowledges that following him may evoke public shame (banning) and result in the loss of the basic elements of honor. Yet his makarisms promise honor, that is, honor from Jesus himself and from his heavenly Father. Such a person acquires honor in a new kingdom, comfort from a new family, and satisfaction of needs and a great reputation in heaven. Thus last becomes first, and least greatest; what has been shamed becomes honored. "How *honorable* are you when you are *shamed* for my sake!" Therefore, Jesus is not attacking the system of honor as such, but redefining where true honor is to be found. At stake are two sources of worth and respect, one's father and family or Jesus and his group. The issue is: whose approval counts as "treasure" or worth? That of the father and family? Or that of Jesus and his Father? But honor, which is the public acknowledgment of worth, remains the primary concern.

4.3.2 The Makarisms and Gender Considerations.

Is there a specific gender component to the makarisms? Do they apply equally to male and female disciples? If the use of honor and shame modeling is taken seriously, then this becomes not only a legitimate, but an important issue in interpretation. In the gender-divided world of antiquity, some behavior is more probable for males in certain circumstances than for females. Females begin life under the authority of a father, and continue life under the authority of their husbands. Since marriages were arranged by families, and since voluntary virginity in antiquity, precisely as an act of rebellion against marriage, was rare, although not unknown, we find relatively little scope in the ancient world for females being summarily banned by the family and set adrift. Whatever lack of sufficiency they suffered would mean the catastrophe of either the father's family or the husband's.

On the contrary, given the inheritance laws in ancient Judea, which favored the bulk of the family resources, especially land, going to the eldest son, a different sort of scenario suggests itself. First, if the son who stood to inherit was banned by his family, his loss would be staggering. Because he stands to lose more than his noninheriting brothers, one might imagine that he would truly be confronted with a chilling dilemma: loyalty to family (which means "wealth") or loyalty to Jesus (which means penury). The noninheriting sons, who might either remain on the family land or migrate elsewhere to seek their fortune, have less to lose and so might hear the invitation of Jesus more readily. Thus, in the gender-divided world of antiquity with its clear codes of expected social behavior, it seems more probable that males are addressed in Jesus' makarisms, who along with their wives (6:25–34) would together suffer loss of wealth and honor for joining Jesus' circle of disciples.

5.0 The Other Makarisms in the Key of Honor and Shame

What about the other makarisms? What does it mean to read some of them in terms of honor and shame? Let us consider "meek," "merciful," "peacemaker," and "persecuted" in the light of this pivotal value.

5.1 How Honorable Are the Meek (Matt. 5:5).   Most commentators interpret "meekness" as an ethical concept, even a virtue (see Betz 1995:126). Some describe it as an "active attitude and deliberate acceptance of fate" (Hauck and Schulz 1968:645), thus making it an honorable action. From its use in the Greco-Roman world, it can indeed be understood as grounds for praise for refusing to be a victim. Yet as we shall see, there is compelling evidence from the ancient world to consider "meekness" in terms of shame. For example, "meekness" is never used of God in the LXX (yet see Philo, *The Worse Attacks the Better* 146), presumably because it connotes weakness or loss of power. We should, then, examine this term more closely in the light of honor and shame; for even if we metamorphose it from shame to honor, it is clear that many in the ancient world understood it as shameful.

Commentators generally define "meek" by its opposites. It is the antithesis of "rough, hard and violent . . . angry, brutal" (Hauck and Schulz 1968:645–46). Respected males were quite likely to achieve honor through actions which are rough, violent, and brutal or which arise out of anger. In contrast, "meekness" connotes being a victim or target of another's violent actions, which is never desirable. Moreover, it stands in opposition to "anger" (Aristotle, *Nicomachean Ethics* 4.3.5), which the ancients described as the passion aroused because of an injury or insult that demands revenge. Epictetus's description of "meekness" positions it in terms of agonistic behavior, which by philosophical alchemy becomes honorable, not shameful.

> Is it possible, then, to derive advantage from . . . the man who reviles me? And what good does his wrestling-companion do the athlete? The very greatest. So also my reviler becomes one who prepares me for my contest; he exercises my patience, my non-anger, and my meekness (πϱᾶον). (*Discourses* 3.20.9)

Epictetus describes an honor-shame situation where "reviling" occurs (λοιδοϱοῦντος); the conflict is likened to a wrestling match, that is, an agonistic encounter, in which the reviler trains the philosopher in unusual postures, i.e., "patience," "non-anger," and "meekness." He insists that the reviled person does *not* respond to his attacker and does not seek honorable revenge, which is sanctioned and expected by the general culture. This means that when a male is challenged, provoked, or reviled, a few ancients considered it virtuous and honorable not to give a riposte. Epictetus's reevaluation of "meekness" transforms what his culture deemed shameful; for failure to respond to challenges will entail a loss of honor for the person so reviled. Thus the general code understands "meekness" as victimhood and thus dishonorable, a value judgment contested by a few of the ancients.

The makarism in Matt. 5:5 gives few clues as to an actual situation of "meekness" envisioned. But according to the choreography of honor challenges, the "meek" person could be one who makes no honor *claims* (e.g., Matt. 21:5), or, more likely, one who does not give a *riposte* to challenges and does not respond in anger to insults. In this light, a "meek" person disengages entirely from the typical honor games of the village. This "meek" person might even be a victim of insult or injury, such as is described in 5:11–12. It is striking that the antidote for the shame of "meekness" is the honor of "inheriting the land," presumably something the person lost when banned and shamed by his family. According to 5:5, the man who lost land (the "meek") will eventually "inherit land"—honor lost will be restored.

Is this person honorable, or shameful? It depends on which code of honor he follows. The general code thinks that a "meek" person has ample reason for anger, retaliation, and satisfaction because of some wrong done him. That code expects and values revenge and vengeance. But Jesus praises a "meek" person who has been injured, yet does not take satisfaction, which the general code would view as an expression of shameful weakness or cowardice. We saw how Epictetus's unusual code evaluates "meekness" as virtuous and thus praiseworthy; but we must remember that he transforms popular notions of "meekness" as shameful into philosophical honor. Hence, this understanding only confirms the traditional claim that vengeance gains respect but "meekness" shame. Which code, then, should the disciples follow? That of the village or Jesus? What is honorable for disciples? Vengeance or meekness? Jesus honors "meekness," a strategy of nonretaliation totally at odds with his cultural world. Thus, the very form of the makarism implies both honor and shame: (1) honor from Jesus, for that is what the makarism means (μακάριος = "how honorable!") and (2) shame in the eyes of one's neighbors for failure to seek revenge. The grammar of Jesus' makarisms is such that he honors those who have been dishonored on his behalf. He creates a new code of honor by metamorphosing shame into honor.

5.2 How Honorable Are Those Who Show Mercy (Matt. 5:6).

Commentators indicate that "mercy" can have different meanings. One trajectory links "mercy" with benefaction: almsgiving (Matt. 6:2–4), succor of the needy (25:31–46), and healing for the sick (9:27; 15:22; 17:15; 20:30–31). Another cluster of meanings pertains to the pardoning of wrongs and the forgiveness of debts (18:22, 23–34; see Guelich 1982:104) or a "response to violence and enmity" (Betz 1995:133). Moreover, the correspondence between Jesus' remark and similar sayings in the literature of ancient Israel (Str-B 1.204–5), the New Testament (James 2:13), and the early church (*1 Clem.* 13:2; *2 Clem.* 4:2) indicates that "mercy" is part of some code of virtuous behavior, but not necessarily the general code. The precise meaning of "mercy," therefore, cannot be determined by appeal to parallels, but needs to be assessed in its cultural context. Hence, we will examine "mercy" in regard to (1) the form of the original makarisms, (2) their logic of honoring those who were shamed, and (3) the choreography of honor challenges.

We argue that "mercy" generally has to do with forswearing of vengeance and forgiveness of debts. The original four makarisms indicate that Jesus declares "honorable" what others have labeled "shameful," thus reversing the popular evaluation of someone or something. Davies and Allison argue that "It is almost certain that Q had the following sentence in the sermon on the plain: 'Be merciful (οἰκτίρμονες) even as your heavenly Father is merciful (οἰκτίρμων)'" (1988:454). Hence "mercy" can be said to belong to the same disvalued world as "banning," "destitution," "mourning," and "hunger"; while others see these as shameful, Jesus declares them honorable. Thus, if honoring the "merciful" belongs in this pattern of praising what others declare shameful, then it means that Jesus and others know of grounds in their cultural world for considering "mercy" as dishonorable, despite all the positive parallels to it. It belongs to the honorable man to defend himself when attacked, not to pardon the insult. Aristotle, for example, praises the honorable man who takes revenge and shows no mercy: "[Those things are honorable] to take just vengeance on enemies and not to be reconciled" (*Rhet.* 1.9.24). Thus, it is probable that those who forgo vengeance would be shamed in their culture, a shame that Jesus reverses.

According to the choreography of honor challenges, if a man does not respond to violence and hostility, he risks shame by forswearing a riposte. In doing this, he would appear to his neighbors as a weakling, a dishonorable man who does not know how to defend his honor and worth. As Aristotle indicated, the general code requires vengeance, not mercy. As a result, this merciful man would lose face in his neighbors' eyes. This can be confirmed later in the narrative when Jesus tells disciples who have been "sinned against" that they may seek some redress, either by "telling" the aggressor "his fault" or by accusing him before some assembly (18:15–17). Here a disciple has been challenged ("sinned against") and responds to those challenges, even to the point of expelling the offender from the group, which is stiff satisfaction indeed. This material is fully in accord with the general code of honor we have been studying. Here "mercy" is not a socially accepted option; honor is maintained by counterchallenge. Immediately juxtaposed to this is Jesus' requirement of "mercy" (18:21–22). The situation is the same: someone has "sinned against" (18:15, 21) a disciple, that is, they have challenged another by insult or injury. Yet now Jesus requires "forgiveness," not seven times but seventy times seven, which is tantamount to a total refusal to seek satisfaction and revenge. Challenges may *not* be responded to; injury and insult may *not* be redressed. Clearly Jesus has changed the general code of honor in 18:15–17 by declaring praiseworthy the acceptance of insults and injury without a riposte (18:21–22). But those who live according to the general code would see this as shameful behavior. Thus when we view Matt. 5:6 and 18:15–17, 21–22 in light of honor and shame, we find two contrasting approaches to challenges, one in which defense and retaliation are honorable and another which proscribes revenge and prescribes "mercy." The former was traditionally an honorable posture, which Jesus replaced with his endorsement of what others would see as shameful. How "honorable," declares Jesus, "are those who are shamed for showing 'mercy.'"

5.3 How Honorable Are the Peacemakers (Matt. 5:9). Commentators tend to see this makarism in terms of the general value of "peace" and so interpret it as a broad exhortation toward virtue (Guelich 1982:106–7; Betz 1995:137–40). In this view, "making peace" is a positive quality, which can apply even to Jesus and God. Yet one cannot avoid the association of "peace" with war, hostility, and conflict. Jesus "makes peace" by means of his blood to bring warring parties together, and so the instrument for making peace is his shameful death (Eph. 2:15; see Col. 1:20). Moreover, one method of defining "peacemaking" points out explanatory parallels within the Sermon on the Mount, such as (1) Matt. 5:23–24 —a demand for reconciliation, (2) 5:38–42, 44–48—love of one's enemies,

(3) 5:21–48—repairing relationships, (4) 6:12, 14–15—forgiveness of wrongs, and (5) 7:1–5—refusal to judge. As we shall see, the Antitheses proscribe all honor challenges and ripostes; previous challenges must be stopped and honor restored. Thus the mention of "making peace" in 5:9 may well require us to wait until further analysis of 5:21–48 to appreciate what it might mean in terms of the typical games for gaining honor.

It is often noted that Jesus denies that he came to bring peace: "Do not think that I have come to bring peace on earth. I have come not to bring peace, but a sword" (10:34). In this context, peace touches on issues of conflicts of loyalty, either to Jesus or to one's family. If the reward promised reverses the previous shame (i.e., the hungry are filled, the mourning consoled), then being "called sons of God" (5:9) implies that some earthly status has been lost by a peacemaker, which God more than restores with this honorific label. But it seems unlikely that a "peacemaker" refers to a conflict of loyalty within the family, for this would mean that a disciple reconciled loyalty to Jesus with loyalty to his family, something Matthew does not see happening. Thus Matthew contains data which indicate that "making peace" is a negative quality and grounds for shame, not honor. Since we know that "peace" is related to "conflict," what kind of conflict? Pursuit of honor at the expense of one's neighbor? Is resolving this conflict popularly thought of as honorable, or shameful?

We are drawing closer to its meaning within the agonistic culture of antiquity when we consider the synonym of "peacemaking," namely, "reconciliation." On occasion, the aggressor is told to be reconciled (διαλλάγηθι) with the person whom he has injured (Matt. 5:23–24). Or the aggrieved party is said to be reconciled to the persons who caused the injury or delivered the insult. For example, Paul describes how God did "not count their trespasses" against them, but reconciled the world to himself in Christ (2 Cor. 5:18–19). When challenged, God did not seek revenge, but strove to remedy the challenge. Third, mutual feuding parties, such as husband and wife, are urged to be reconciled (καταλλαγήτω, 1 Cor. 7:11), that is, to forswear further aggression. A "peacemaker," then, arises in a situation of hostility to call off the feud and stop the spiral of riposte and revenge.

How would this be understood in an honor-shame world? We maintain that Jesus is declaring "honorable" someone who has suffered dishonor for behavior at variance with cultural expectations. In terms of the choreography of honor-shame dynamics, we might describe a "peacemaker" in various postures in the challenge-riposte game. If he is the aggressor who must reconcile himself to the person whom he injured (5:23, 25), then "peacemaking" means undoing an honor challenge (5:23–24). Neighbors will see the aggressor as someone who cannot finish what he started, which invites mockery. If he is the aggrieved person who has been slapped or otherwise insulted (5:38–42), then "peacemaking" means forswearing a riposte to an honor challenge; no eye for an eye, which is culturally shameful behavior. If such a person is either the challenger or the challenged, then honor is very much at stake in the cessation of hostility. Thus the "peacemaker" must stop playing games for gaining and maintaining honor, a very risky proposition.

What if the "peacemaker" is a mediating third party who reconciles warring factions? For example, Betz (1995:139) noted the example of Demonax and Apollonius (Lucian, *Demonax* 9; Philostratus, *Life of Apollonius* 1.15; 6.38). Windish pointed out that some ancient rulers were honored by the epithet of "Peacemaker" (1925:240–60). Although such parallels indicate how honorable a third-party mediator might be, the bulk of the materials in the Sermon on the Mount clearly point toward one of the parties involved in conflict or feuding who acts as reconciler and peacemaker within the situation in which he is personally involved. This person is either the challenger himself, who calls off his challenge, or the one challenged, who forswears a riposte. Both of these figures stand to lose face in the eyes of their neighbors for this behavior; both are likely to experience shame for lacking courage or some other aspect of honorable male behavior. For cultural reasons, we interpret the "peacemaker" as a man shamed in the eyes of his neighbors for stepping apart from the expected behavior. Shamed by his neighbors, he is honored by Jesus.

5.4 How Honorable Are Those Who Are Persecuted (Matt. 5:10).

Most commentators see this statement as the creation of the evangelist who expanded the climactic fourth makarism in 5:11–12 (Luz 1989:242; Betz 1995:142). Moreover, they tend to be somewhat expansive in understanding "persecution" in terms of group conflict that has become political. Betz at one point allegorized "persecution" of the righteous as "part of the human predicament generally" (1995:146). In keeping with other voices in Matthean scholarship, we will argue that "persecution" is a poor translation here; as we saw earlier, the verb in question (δεδιωγμένοι) is better understood in terms of "driving out" or ostracizing, rather than political persecution. And it should be examined in terms of the cultural values of honor and shame.

Neither Jesus nor Matthew seems to be concerned about general political "persecution"; neither envisions formal judicial proceedings from Rome or Jerusalem as the background of these sayings, unlike Acts 9 and 22–26. Rather, this "driving out" is more likely the hostile reaction of families and neighbors (Saldarini 1994:84–94, 107–16; Hummel 1966:28–33). As we saw in regard to Matt. 5:11–12, the verb in question occurred in combination with reviling and slandering. It is, then, a term which denotes shame. But who is being shamed, by whom, and why?

Agents of Jesus are shamed when their message is rejected (10:14). Yet in the continuation of Jesus' remarks (10:16–39), the implied audience is broadened to include more than the Twelve whom Jesus sent forth in 10:5. The official spokesmen will face informal proceedings, before either elders or the assembled community (10:17–19); the term "sanhedrin" (συνέδριαν) may mean simply a "meeting" or council (Josephus, *Life* 368; MM 604); it need not be the Great Sanhedrin in Jerusalem. "Their synagogues" may simply mean local assemblies (Josephus, *Ant.* 20.200), in the midst of which disciples might experience the shame of flogging (see 2 Cor. 11:24–25). But especially in view is intense family conflict: "Brother will deliver up brother to death, and the father his children . . . " (Matt. 10:21), with the result that "you will be hated by all for my name's sake" (10:22).

After these remarks, the disciple is warned that just as Jesus is slandered, so they will be reviled even more (10:24). In short, "persecution" comes from one's family and neighbors, which is the face-to-face arena of honor and shame. It results in defamation of one's name, devaluation ("hate") by all, and shameful treatment ("flogging"), all of which means a tragic loss of honor with accompanying shame. In 10:16–39, Jesus does not declare these shamed disciples "honorable," as he does in the makarisms in 5:3–12. On the contrary, the discourse there continues with further indications of shame among family members (10:34–36), indications of "unworthiness" (10:37), and demands to take up the shameful cross (10:38). But for our purposes, it seems sufficient to appreciate that "persecution" of the sort described in 10:16–39 is face-to-face encounter with family and neighbors, which results in shame. This, we suggest, gives us strong parameters for understanding those "persecuted" in 5:10 as children banned and "driven out" by their parents or disciples driven away by villagers.

Furthermore, if the antidote to hunger is satiety, to mourning, comfort, and to meekness, inheritance, we should expect a possible correlation of "persecution"/ shame and antidote/honor. For the shame of "persecution" Jesus offers "the kingdom of heaven." If something was indeed lost through "persecution," then "kingdom" replaces or reverses it. Guelich offers an explanation of "kingdom" from parallel comments in Matthew's Gospel which give considerable specificity to what might seem a vague "eschatological" term (1982:78). He links "kingdom" with "vindication," thus seeing it as a reversal of present negative and shameful circumstances. The "kingdom" becomes the "inheritance" of those who showed compassion on Jesus' poor and destitute (25:34) and of those who left or lost family for Jesus' sake (19:29). It stands for the time and place where present conditions are reversed (10:39; 19:30; 20:16; 23:12), that is, where "last," "least," and "lowly" become "first," "greatest," and "exalted." These positive labels, moreover, are precisely what we mean by "honor." Conversely, on occasion the wicked are shamed by being excluded from the kingdom (13:40–43; 22:13; 24:51) or by being declared "unrecognized" (25:12). The "kingdom" of heaven, then, both reverses the experiences of faithful disciples and undoes the shame that inevitably accompanied them. It connotes God's time to honor, declare the worth of, exalt, and bestow an inheritance on those who follow Jesus precisely in the ways that bring public shame.

Does it add anything if these disciples are shamed "for the sake of righteousness"? Throughout this study we have proposed a meaning for "righteousness" (δικαιοσύνη) in keeping with popular theories of virtue and the rhetoric of praise. While it surely admits of many nuances, "righteousness" refers basically to one of the four cardinal virtues, namely, "justice." Moreover, the ancients divided this virtue into three parts: duties to God (or the gods), parents, and ancestors. Since Matthew presents Jesus as prying disciples loose from their kinship duties (10:36–39), it would seem that a new loyalty or "justice" is being proposed here, namely, loyalty to Jesus. Although it might appear shameful in the eyes of one's family and neighbors to love Jesus more than them, Jesus affirms that such loyalty is honorable, even courageous. His response to this loyalty is a grant of worth and respect.

6.0 Summary and Conclusions

The basic form of the original Makarisms consists in the honoring by Jesus and his Patron of those who have suffered misfortune and social shame on his behalf. If Hanson is correct, and we think his argument is sound, then the blessing Jesus pronounces should be interpreted as a grant of honor by Jesus: "How honorable are you . . . " Hence Jesus reforms the general code by declaring honorable what others label shameful. The values of honor and shame, then, are reformed, not abolished. The public approval of one's worth and standing by Jesus, God, and the group of disciples still counts, which is the basic meaning of honor. In one sense, the pattern of honoring what had been declared worthless or shameful reflects what is found elsewhere in the New Testament, such as in the Magnificat (Luke 1:51–53). And in the broadest terms, the form of the makarisms resembles the vindication of the suffering righteous noted in the Bible. What others value as "last," "least," and "small," Jesus declares "first," "greatest," and "significant."

This pattern of honoring what was deemed shameful applies not only to the original four makarisms ("poor," "mourning," "hungry and thirsty," "driven out"), but also to four other ones ("meek," "merciful," "peacemaker," "persecuted"). These people, as we saw, were all engaged in challenge-riposte situations. Jesus declares them honorable in his eyes for *not* delivering a riposte or seeking revenge. Honor generally demands a response to challenge and insult, such that failure to give a riposte would be shameful. Yet Jesus reverses the general code and declares honorable nonretaliation, forswearing of revenge, and pardon of insults.

We argued that in the case of the original four makarisms the disciple who is declared "honorable" by Jesus has suffered a total collapse of social worth on Jesus' behalf. As the climactic fourth makarism states, "Honorable are you when men revile you, drive you out, and utter all kinds of evil against you falsely *on my account*" (Matt. 5:11). This basic social disaster of banning by the family explains the subsequent financial and social misfortunes of "poor," "mourning," and "hungry and thirsty." The root of this total collapse of fortune and honor lies in the shaming of sons by their families for joining the circle of Jesus' disciples, as 10:34–39 indicates.

Yet the cause of the predicament of the "meek," "merciful," "peacemakers," and "persecuted" is less clear in the text because of the jejune nature of the makarisms. We insist on reading Jesus' honoring of these people in terms of the values of honor and shame, if for no other reason than that the blessing by Jesus is a formal and public grant of honor to them. We favor interpreting them according to the same pattern as the original four makarisms, that is, the honoring by Jesus of those who have been dishonored. Hence, we base our interpretation on the following factors: (1) the form of the original makarisms ("how honorable are they who are shamed"); (2) the lexical meanings of the terms "meek" and "merciful" as victims of aggression; (3) the choreography of challenge-riposte exchanges—they have suffered insult or challenge, but have not delivered a riposte or sought revenge; (4) the discussion of these very themes in the next part of the Sermon, the Antitheses (5:21–48); and (5) subsequent parallels to these materials in the rest of Gospel.

If we are correct in seeing that Jesus honors those who have been shamed for his sake, then we are invited to consider how in general Jesus and Matthew counter shame with honor. The "meek," who have presumably suffered some loss, especially family land, are made heirs of an inheritance; the "merciful," who presumably have suffered some injury or affront and who do not retaliate, are promised similar treatment by God; the "peacemakers," who in the context are those who have either challenged others (5:23–24) or been challenged in turn (5:38–42), become the honored sons of a noble household; and finally, the "persecuted," who have experienced public reproach, censure, and loss of respect and reputation, are vindicated in the kingdom of heaven, where earthly statuses are reversed. Honor from Jesus reverses the social shame which disciples have suffered.

Hence, we do not consider the makarisms as in any way addressing the "general human condition"; nor are they a celebration of popular virtues such as one would find in Greco-Roman philosophy. We do not deny that researchers can readily find celebration of virtue in the general culture, but the situation envisioned in the makarisms represents the social disgrace which disciples have suffered "on my account" (5:11).

Are the makarisms "entrance requirements" or "eschatological blessings"? When Guelich raised just this question (1976:417–19), he cited the study of E. Schweizer (1972:121–26). Schweizer carefully studied the parallels to the makarisms in Jewish wisdom traditions and argued both that the makarisms in no way set forth conditions of practical wisdom (i.e., virtue or ethical principles) and that they depend exclusively on Jesus' word of authority. While conceding Schweizer's point on most makarisms, Guelich maintains that "the additional Beatitudes (5:7, 'merciful'; 5:8, 'pure in heart'; 5:9, 'peacemakers') reflect virtuous behavior, 'types of behavior which have God's approval'" (1976:419). Thus he considers them entrance requirements as well as blessings. Since we insist that even the other makarisms be viewed in the cultural context of honor and shame, our analysis finds more agreement with Schweizer than Guelich on this point. Because they are "blessings," all of the makarisms basically bestow a grant of honor or social worth on someone, first from Jesus and then from his Patron, God. The grant is not simply future (hence, "eschatological"), but present. There may be a divine vindication ultimately for these suffering righteous disciples, but Jesus honors them now before family, village, and town. They have worth now in his eyes; their shame is now offset by his praise and evaluation of them. Schweizer's point that the makarisms depend exclusively on Jesus' word needs to be taken more seriously.

Moreover, it seems a mistake to contrast so strenuously the prophetic and the wisdom traditions, as Guelich does. In doing this, he ignores how both streams embody the values of the cultural world of honor and shame. Prophetic woes, as Hanson has noted, should be read as declarations of "How shameful. . . ." And wisdom literature, which sets out the social expectations of honorable people, praises the wise and shames the foolish, using specifically honor-shame labels (Matthews and Benjamin 1991:222–26). Moreover, in the rules for composing an encomium, students are instructed precisely to "praise" someone in terms of not only virtue, but honorable birth, honors, etc. Notions of honor and shame, then, are not the exclusive preserve of either prophetic or wisdom literatures, but stand behind both because they represent a cultural horizon for Israel, even in its ancient and earliest times (Pedersen 1991:212–44).

9

Matthew 5:21–48

Calling Off the Honor Game

1.0 Introduction

The Antitheses in 5:21–48 have been the object of intensive historical and literary investigation (Dietzfelbinger 1975; Guelich 1976; Strecker 1978, 1988; Betz 1995). Here we ask different questions which seek to understand the Antitheses in terms of the cultural values of the world of Jesus and Matthew. Betz noted that all six Antitheses deal with "broken relationships" (1995:205). The focus is on the village and its face-to-face dynamics. But instead of "broken" relationships we prefer to label them as aggressive and conflictual relationships. For some Antitheses are addressed to victims of aggressive behavior (5:22–26, 38–42) and others as would-be aggressors (5:27–32). And so we will be considering the Antitheses in the context of honor and shame, and specifically in terms of challenge and riposte.

Let us recall certain aspects of the cultural model of honor. First, as regards the sources of honor, scholars distinguish between ascribed and achieved honor. The Makarisms describe *ascribed honor*, which normally comes to a man by birth or adoption into a family or appointment to office (Matt. 27:2). The Antitheses in 5:21–48, however, reflect how *honor is achieved*, that is, how a man achieves a grant of respect by his prowess or aggressive behavior. Second, honor might be achieved by athletic success (1 Cor. 9:24–25), military prowess (2 Cor. 10:3–6), benefaction (Luke 7:4–5), or cleverness. Matt. 5:21–48 introduces us to other ways of achieving honor, namely, through aggressive behavior, such as physical or verbal abuse and sexual exploits, the typical ways in which Mediterranean males achieve and express their manhood (Gilmore 1990:9–29; see Herzfeld 1985a and 1985b). Third, understanding the choreography of an honor challenge enables us to read the Antitheses in terms of their cultural setting. It consists of four elements: (1) claim to worth or status, (2) challenge, (3) riposte, and (4) public verdict. There were specific, recognizable ways to challenge someone: physical affront (kill, strike), verbal abuse (name calling, lying), and sexual seduction of another's wife. When honor is impugned, the man challenged should seek satisfaction, either requiring an eye for an eye or seeking revenge from his challenger. As we shall see, Jesus proscribes all of these games: his disciples may not claim honor or challenge others for it or give a riposte if challenged. And if they have themselves challenged others, they must undo the challenge. In short, they may not play the game at all.

2.0 All Aggressive Behavior Prohibited to Disciples

In the first Antithesis (Matt. 5:21–26) Jesus requires his disciples to withdraw completely from certain forms of aggressive behavior. When challenged and provoked to anger, they may not respond by either physical assault (killing) or verbal abuse (name calling). Jesus begins by explaining the social situation of a disciple who has been challenged and made angry. Concerning anger, the ancients all understood it as the natural or honorable reaction to a hurt or affront from another. It presumed some sort of challenge to which the angered person responded. Let us consider "anger" in the culture of honor and shame.

2.1 Anger, Challenge and Riposte, and Revenge. Aristotle defined anger as the desire for revenge: "Let anger be [defined as] desire . . . for conspicuous retaliation because of a conspicuous slight that was directed, without justification, against oneself or those near to one" (Aristotle, *Rhet.* 2.2.1; see Seneca, *On Anger* 1.3.3 and 1.6.5; Plutarch, *On Moderating Anger* 454B–C). Anger arises because of "slights," and so it is the culturally expected reaction to a challenge, assault, or insult. Aristotle further notes that insults "bring shame (ἀτιμία) to the sufferer" (2.2.5). The "slighting" of another may take the form of "contempt, spite and insult" (2.2.3–5). Considering the origins of anger, Plutarch describes how anger arises from honor-related slights: "Even a jest, a playful word, a burst of laughter or a nod on the part of somebody, and many things of the kind, rouse many persons to anger" (*On Moderating Anger* 454D). Anger might also be the reaction of a warrior like Achilles, who was publicly insulted by Agamemnon when the king took both Achilles' booty and his slave girl (*Iliad* 1.137–39, 184–87). Similar examples of anger may be found in the reactions of Esau to the theft of his blessing (Gen. 27:43–44) and of Potiphar to the alleged advances against his wife (Gen. 39:19).

Furthermore, the ancients speak of anger and the desire for vengeance precisely in terms of honor and shame. For example, Aristotle describes "insult" in accord with the general cultural values of honor and shame:

> The person who gives insult also belittles; for insult (ὕβρις) is doing and speaking in which there is shame to the sufferer. . . . The cause of pleasure to those who give insult is that they think they themselves become more superior by ill-treating others. . . . Dishonor is a feature of insult, and one who dishonors belittles; for what is worthless has no repute, neither for good nor evil. (*Rhet.* 2.2.5–6)

The insulting person "dishonors" his victim, claims to be superior, and so acts in ways which "belittle" another, all parts of an honor challenge. The insulted or angry person, on the other hand, is the victim who has suffered "dishonor": having been rendered "worthless," he "has no repute" or reputation in the eyes of his neighbors. Finally, we note that insults might often be verbal as well as physical, such as "gossip and scurrilous talk" or "speaking ill" of someone (Plutarch, *On Moderating Anger* 454E and 457F) or "doing and speaking in which there is shame to the speaker" (Aristotle, *Rhet.* 2.2.5). As noted above, Aristotle remarks that an angered person "desires conspicuous revenge" (*Rhet.* 2.2.1). In fact, he lists revenge among the grounds for praising a man: "To take just vengeance on enemies (τιμωρεῖσθαι) and not to be reconciled; for to retaliate is just" (1.9.24).

In terms of the choreography of honor challenges, the insulting person challenges the worth of another. The person thus challenged becomes angry, which emotion publicly registers the insult and socially sanctions his desire to deliver a fitting riposte, which is revenge. Were the insulted person not to become angry or to seek revenge, he would be dismissed by the viewing public as one who has no worth; he can be shamefully dismissed as one who does not know how to defend himself. In either case, lack of anger and the absence of revenge signal to onlookers a state of shame or worthlessness.

2.2 The Shame of Not Seeking Revenge.

Returning to the first Antithesis (Matt. 5:21–22), the old law prohibited "killing," whether it was a physical challenge given to another or a retaliatory response as part of a blood feud. Honor may not be gained or maintained by "killing." But in 5:22, the man who is angered (ὀργιζόμενος) has been challenged or provoked by another. Yet he may *not* engage in any sort of revenge or riposte; otherwise he would be "liable to judgment," that is, a public verdict. The parallelism of Jesus' remarks indicates that "anger" would be manifested by a riposte of name calling, which Jesus prohibits.

Everyone who is	*angry*	with his brother	is liable to judgment
who says	*"Empty Head!"*	to his brother	is liable to the council
who says	*"Fool!"*		is liable to the hell of fire

If the parallelism is significant, then name calling ("Empty Head" and "Fool") functions here as a riposte or act of revenge to the challenge ("angry"). But Jesus proscribes all riposte or revenge, which means that disciples will be publicly shamed for failing to defend their honor and defend themselves. Should a challenged person (i.e., one who is angered) deliver a riposte to an honor challenge, he would thereby be tried by a public court ("judgment . . . council . . . hell"), which would, ironically, condemn him. Thus Jesus has made shame (i.e., nonretaliation) honorable and made shameful what the village deems honorable (i.e., revenge). Moreover, the choreography of honor challenges helps to sort out the dynamics in 5:22: (1) a *challenge* which provokes anger, (2) the expected *riposte* prohibited, and (3) a *public verdict* which would now go against the avenging person if he takes vengeance.

Contemporary studies of Matt. 5:22 virtually ignore how labels such as "Empty Head!" and "Fool!" function as insults (see Davies and Allison 1988:511–14) and fail to consider them in any cultural way (see Luz 1989:282; Strecker 1988:67; Betz 1995:220). For example, Bertram sees only a moral meaning in the term "Fool" and totally ignores its cultural valence (1967:833–44). Jeremias claimed that "Fool" was a harmless insult (1971:219). But labels such as "Raka" and "Fool" are genuine social weapons intended to cause serious injury (Malina and Neyrey 1988:35–38). Matthew 5:22 considers "Raka!" so severe an insult as to warrant condemnation by the council, which in Jeremias's opinion meant condemnation to death by the supreme court (1968:975). In an honor-shame culture, there is no such thing as a harmless insult. "Empty Head!" and "Fool!" are fighting words; and in 5:22 they function as ripostes to insults.

2.3 Calling Off an Honor Challenge. Jesus then tells his disciples a harder saying about honor challenges. A group member is ostensibly doing an honorable thing by "offering a gift at the altar." But he has apparently sought honor by challenging his brother in some way, for that brother "has something against you." The New Testament regularly understands this phrase to mean that the person who "has something against you" is the victim of a challenge and that "you" are the aggressor or challenger (Mark 11:25; 1 Cor. 6:1; Rev. 2:4; see Betz 1995:223). The man offering the gift, then, is the challenger, while the man who "has something against you" is the victim of aggression, who presumably desires revenge (Davies and Allison 1988:517).

In general, Jesus tells the disciple to stop the typical honor game. The gift-offerer must go and make honor satisfaction and so disengage from the game of seeking honor at another's expense: "Be reconciled ($\delta\iota\alpha\lambda\lambda\acute{\alpha}\gamma\eta\theta\iota$) with your brother" (v. 24). If insult was given, satisfaction is required; if theft, restitution; if dishonor, honoring. But in this case, honor will be restored, not by revenge and riposte of the person challenged, but by the very challenger himself who must find a way to withdraw his challenge and restore the injured honor of the other.

The term "reconcile" has something to do with "exchange" (LSJ 401; Büchsel 1964:253); and in its noun form, it can mean a "change" from hostility to friendship (Herodotus 1.21), in the sense that two warring nations cease hostilities. What "exchange" does a challenger make to those whom he challenged? He can offer "satisfaction," that is, a balance which redresses, such as an appropriate fine or a suitable penalty. But what does "reconciliation" look like in antiquity (Marshall 1978:118–21)? David sought to be reconciled with Saul through some propitiating action, such as bringing him the heads of his Philistine enemies (1 Sam. 29:4 LXX). At best, David hopes to find favor again in Saul's eyes by honoring the king in a socially appropriate way. Similarly Jacob sent "gifts" to Esau (Gen. 32:13–21), not to say "I'm sorry," but to "find favor in your [Esau's] sight" (33:10). When Agamemnon is reconciled with Achilles, he achieves it by gift-giving and honoring Achilles, not by words of remorse. Hence, reconciliation is not exactly what we moderns mean by declarations such as "I'm sorry" or "Pardon." Rather, some balance is restored where there was damage or loss. Jesus' remark, then, tells the challenger not just to cease challenging another's honor, but to restore the honor damaged or threatened.

2.4 Making Friends with an Accuser. Matthew 5:25–26, the final piece of this collection of material on physical and verbal aggression, envisions a disciple being brought before some judicial forum by a person he has injured, who is called his accuser ($\mathring{\alpha}\nu\tau\acute{\iota}\delta\iota\kappa o\varsigma$). The brother, then, has acted as the aggressor against someone who has a legitimate claim to redress. The remarks in 5:25–26 envision the man addressed as the unjust aggressor and the "accuser" as the victim of that aggression who is seeking satisfaction, if not revenge. Thus, we identify the man addressed as the *challenger* who has injured another person. The challenged party offers his *riposte* by means of a lawsuit, a not-uncommon means of seeking revenge in antiquity (Cohen 1995). The conflict, moreover, is public, for they are on their way to some *public forum* where elders and/or magistrates render a *public verdict* for or against someone. Jesus tells the challenger to withdraw the challenge by "making friends with" (εὐνοῶν) the man he has attacked, which will surely mean a tragic loss of face for the challenger.

"Make friends with" requires our attention. It is not the emotional term we use to express cordiality and intimacy among close associates. Most basically it refers to "being well inclined toward . . . favorable toward" (LSJ 723). How does a person either *make* this favorable gesture or *show* it? Herodotus describes how a person demonstrated that he was "well disposed toward" (εὐνοεῖ) Xerxes the Persian king by speaking well of him in public (7.237). Xenophon describes a master who created this favorable impression by benefaction of his goods (*Oeconomicus* 12.5–7). Some public gesture, either word or deed, can both demonstrate and create the public impression of being "friends with" or "well disposed toward" another. This is a grant of respect or honor.

In Matthew, the public gesture will necessarily include a restoration of the balance upset by the challenge: if theft, repayment; if slander, truth; if physical assault, adequate monetary recompense. The challenger must voluntarily make public amends, lest he be forced involuntarily to do so; and involuntary actions connote loss of power and control, and thus loss of honor. Therefore, in terms of honor and shame, the challenger must withdraw the challenge; whatever gain he achieved by his challenge must be requited and returned. This will surely mean a loss of honor to the challenger who was unable to sustain his challenge.

Shame, moreover, generally results from not being able to finish what one started, especially if it is an aggressive action. Luke records two parables on this topic. The first one tells how a rich man who could not finish building a tower was shamed: "All who saw it begin to *mock* (ἐμπαίζειν) him, saying, 'That man began to build, and was not able to finish'" (14:29–30). Luke's second parable describes a clear honor challenge, "a king going to war with another king" (14:31). Great shame comes upon the aggressor when he must "ask about the health of " his kingly opponent (Thackeray 1913:395). Yet the local code of honor of Jesus' audience would expect the challenger to "tough it out," and sustain the challenge in the face of his accuser's riposte. Having set out to gain honor from another, the challenger ought to maintain that strategy, for it is the honorable thing to do. But Jesus proscribes this and commands that the challenger withdraw his challenge and make satisfaction immediately. This will result in a certain loss of honor to the challenger.

2.5 Summary. The following conclusions can be drawn from this analysis. First, in Matt. 5:21–26 Jesus proscribes typical aggressive male behavior: no physical assault and no verbal abuse. Then, the choreography of honor clarifies the scenario imagined in the Gospel: (1) the man challenged may not give a riposte (5:21–22) and (2) the challenger must withdraw his challenge (5:23–24, 25–26). Thus, it is possible to argue that 5:22 illustrates what was referred to in the Makarisms as "meekness" and "mercy," that is, the forswearing of revenge and the acceptance of insult and injury. Similarly 5:23–26 can illustrate what "peace-maker" meant in 5:9, that is, one who calls off an honor challenge against another and makes satisfaction for his own injury and insult. Third, all of 5:21–26 envisions a public setting: verbal abuse works only when delivered where all in the village can hear it; a public sacrifice is interrupted for undoing one's affront; and "favorable" gestures are made on the way to the public judicial forum. The public, then, will see how a disciple steps apart from the honor game, which in their eyes is not an honorable thing to do. Fourth, when the aggressor undoes challenges already made, he disregards the code of honor and impugns his own worth and honor. For, if previous challenges must be rescinded, the challenger will necessarily be "mocked" for something he started but could not finish. Finally, since all challenges function as vehicles for gaining honor in the eyes of one's neighbors, Jesus' prohibition of them means that his disciples may not play the basic male games of aggression in their culture. It is not that they forswear honor, but they may not seek it in conflictual behavior which necessarily injures others. This is truly one of the "hard sayings" in the Gospel.

3.0 All Sexual Aggression Prohibited

In Matt. 5:27–32 Jesus balances the prohibition of acquiring honor by physical or verbal aggression with the proscription of acquiring honor by sexual aggression, either adultery with another man's wife or the taking of another man's (divorced) spouse as a new wife. The issue is not simply the avoidance of sexual immorality, which is best understood under the rubric of purity and pollution (Neyrey 1990:117–21; 1986:138–42; see Luz 1989:295). Here Jesus proscribes adultery, which means the seduction of another man's wife, an act which brings shame on the husband and shamelessness on the woman. In the androcentric, honor-based world of antiquity, adultery meant the violation of another's rights, that is, an honor challenge.

Concerning the cultural meaning of adultery in antiquity, David Cohen summarized the underlying principle at stake, namely, the relationship of male honor and female chastity:

> The crucial point is here that the honor of men is, in large part, defined through the chastity of the women to whom they are related. Female honor largely involves sexual purity and the behavior which social norms deem necessary to maintain it in the eyes of the watchful community. Male honor receives the active role in defending that purity. A man's honor is therefore involved with the sexual purity of his mother, sisters, wife and daughters—of him chastity is not required. (1991:140)

Thus any attack on the virtue of females in another family engages the honor of the female's father, brother, or husband. Although we will be considering adultery and seduction here, slanderous speech and gossip about females were equally shaming. For example, Demosthenes said of the mother of Aeschines: "Your mother practiced daylight nuptials in an outhouse next door to Heros the bone-setter" (*On the Crown* 18.29).

3.1 Sexual Double Standard. As is well known, the ancient cultures of Israel, Greece, and Rome demanded unconditional fidelity in marriage only of the female. Males in antiquity accepted a double standard of morality in regard to male and female sexual behavior. Whereas sexual exclusivity was prescribed for females, no such prohibition existed for males, in either polygamous Israel or monogamous Greece and Rome. Demosthenes, for example, states: "Mistresses (ἑταίρας) we keep for the sake of pleasure, concubines (παλλακάς) for the daily care of our persons, but wives (γυναῖκας) to bear us legitimate children and to be the faithful guardians of our households" (*Against Neaera* 59.122). We become aware of another aspect of the honor code of antiquity: different gender expectations in regard to sexual exclusivity.

In general, males gained honor by aggressive sexual behavior, either marriage (especially harems and polygamous unions), rape, or seduction (Stansell 1992, 1996). While adultery may be viewed as a moral fault in males, it was equally a mark of male honor or manliness as well as a very destructive weapon:

> The adulterer affirms his manliness through the seduction of the women
> of others, and affirmation of manliness is positively valued. On the other
> hand, he is the destroyer of reputations and families . . . a source of disor-
> der in the community. (Cohen 1991:67)

Yet what achieves honor for the aggressive male results in a loss of honor for the males in whose charge the seduced females were placed, either fathers, brothers, or husbands. They fail in one of their primary duties, which is to preserve the exclusiveness of their females (see Aristotle, *Politics* 5.10 1311a35–37).

3.2 Adultery and Shame. As an illustration of the link between adultery and shame, let us examine the defense Lysias composed for a husband who exposed the seduction of his wife. A man charged with murdering Eratosthenes mounts a simple, culturally acceptable defense: he caught Eratosthenes in bed with his wife. In describing his situation, the defendant links his own loss of honor with the adulterer's insults and the seduction of his wife. The central point of his defense rests on showing the judges that "Eratosthenes had an intrigue with my wife, and not only corrupted her but inflicted disgrace (ᾔσχυνε) upon my children and an outrage (ὕβρισεν) on myself by entering my house" (*Against Eratosthenes* 1.4). He first learned of his wife's adultery from an old woman in the marketplace who told him: "The man who is working both you and your wife's dishonour (ὑβρίζων) happens to be our enemy" (1.15–16). He then laid a trap for and caught the adulterer in the very act. He asked him "why he had the insolence (ὑβρίζει) to enter my house" (1.25). The defendant finally claimed that he did not murder Eratosthenes but rather took legitimate vengeance: "Whoever takes his vengeance on an adulterer caught in the act with his spouse shall not be convicted of murder" (1.30–31). Vengeance, we have seen, is honorable; murder is a criminal offense. He makes clear once more the shame that he and his family have suffered at the loins of the adulterer:

> The lawgiver considered that those who use force deserve a less penalty
> than those who use persuasion; for the latter he condemned to death,
> whereas for the former he doubled the damages, considering that those

who achieved their ends by force are hated by the persons forced; while those who used persuasion corrupted thereby their victim's souls, thus making the wives of others more closely attached to themselves than to their husbands . . . and caused uncertainty as to whose the children really were, the husband's or the adulterer's. (1.32–33; see Xenophon, *Hiero* 3.3)

Thus adultery was viewed as an insult or honor challenge to the husband; it inflicted "disgrace" on him, his children, and his house (see Philo, *On the Decalogue* 121–28; Demosthenes, *Against Aristocles* 23.53–57). So great was the insult that the law allowed vengeance with impunity (see Aeschines, *Against Timarchus* 1.91).

Furthermore, the cuckolded husband represents the most shameful male in his world: "If the community expects men to preserve their reputation through guarding the sexual integrity of their women . . . it ridicules those who fail in this endeavor" (Cohen 1991:62). Cohen supports this with reference to fieldwork which investigated the shame that befalls the cuckolded husband:

> Among Arabs the man who does not do so [guard the sexual integrity of his females] is termed "cuckold" (*dayyuth*), a term that in a religious context confers the strongest opprobrium in meaning "reviled one." In one of its popular meanings *dayyuth* refers to an animal that stands by and watches while other males make sexual connection with his mate. (Antoun 1968:680; see Sinclair 1993:43–46)

Fear of being shamefully cuckolded helps us understand the suspicion, jealousy, and feuding of which Isocrates speaks when adultery is discovered: "For since I realized that all men are most jealous for their wives and children, being above all quick to resent offenses against them, and that wantonness in these relations is responsible for the greatest evils—many have lost their lives because of it" (*Nicocles* 2.36). Moreover, husbands who discover that they have been cuckolded often fear public shame for this insult and prefer to keep silence about the insult, lest they add to their loss of honor by airing their folly in public (Aristotle, *Rhet.* 1.12.35).

3.3 Sexual Aggression in Groin and Eye. This cultural background alerts us to the aggressive behavior proscribed in Matt. 5:27–28. Just as Jesus forbade physical and verbal aggression in 5:21–26, he forbids all sexual aggression, both genital and ocular. Part of the general code of gender expectations lies hidden here: females were expected to remain within the female or "private" world of the household, which included outdoor tasks, such as fetching water from the well, cooking at common ovens, and other things pertinent to food preparation, clothing production, and child rearing. Males, however, should be in the male or "public" world of the marketplace or fields, where they attended to male tasks. Thus females will not be seen by non–kinship related males, and so no lust of the eye will occur or plots of seduction begin. But this gender separation of space represents an ideal which could not be achieved short of the construction of elite female chambers or harems in family residences. Males in villages and towns will have occasion to look at females who are out and busy about their household tasks. The occasion for adultery, then, rises up in a male's eye as well as his groin.

Typical of many in antiquity, Jesus links physical acts of sex with voyeurism (Epstein 1967:117–18). Hence he proscribes "looking at a woman with lust," just as he does adultery itself. Although the following reference comes from a later Jewish writing, it illustrates the connection between eye and loins in regard to adultery:

> You are not to say that only he is called an adulterer who uses his body in the act. We find Scripture saying that even he who visualizes himself in the act of adultery is called adulterer. And the proof? The verse *The eye also of the adulterer waiteth for the twilight, saying: "No eye shall see me"* [Job 24:15]. (*Pesiqta R.* 24; Braude 1968:506)

Blake Leyerle, who has examined the aggressive nature of the male "gaze," opens her study by defining it:

> Feminist film criticism has charted with increasing precision the mechanics and pleasures of "the gaze," a term denoting the socially ascribed and iconographically confirmed position of woman as spectacle—"body to be looked at, place of sexuality, and object of desire"—and man as "bearer of the look." (1993:159)

Applying this to the works of John Chrysostom, she illustrates the aggression of the eye. After citing the general Greek understanding of "eros . . . a pathology of the eyes" (160), she points out how sexual gazing, that of women as well as men, was likened to "blows inflicted by the eyes" (160), "eye torture" (161), and "snares, nets, chains, fetters" (168). "Gazing" is occasionally likened to stripping a virgin naked (173). Finally, she notes how Chrysostom accused men of lust-filled eyes: "You carry out the deed, if not by intercourse, then by the eyes" (*Fem. Reg.* 1.67–69; Leyerle 1993:167). Leyerle's study illustrates the aggressive power of sexual "gazing" in Greco-Roman antiquity, a fact well attested in Jewish literature as well (Str-B 1.229–300). If we are correct in appreciating "lustful looking" as aggressive behavior, then, in terms of an honor challenge, males may not challenge other males in terms of sexual aggressiveness, either by actual adultery with another's wife or by visual assault.

Jesus' comment about plucking out the offending eye or severing the right hand (5:29–30) communicates more than a sense of pollution and contamination. The head and face constitute the most honorable parts of the body. The eye, especially the right one, is the jewel of the face, whereas a male's right hand and arm wield weapons of power, and so are likewise honorable members. Hence, when Jesus prescribes that the right eye be plucked out and the right hand be cut off, he is also making an honor-shame statement. The story of Nahash the Ammonite in 1 Sam. 11:2 illustrates the shame attached to the loss of the right eye. The besieged men of Jabesh offer a truce to Nahash, who lays down a humiliating condition: "On this condition I will make a treaty with you, that I gouge out all your right eyes, and thus put disgrace upon all Israel." Yet Jesus claims that the shame of self-inflicted (i.e., foolish) disfigurement and the maiming of the most visible and honorable parts of the body are preferable to the shame of separation from the group and banishment into Gehenna. Curiously, Jesus does not mention cutting off the offending sexual member (see Gal. 5:12), although 19:12 presents the reader with an extensive discussion of eunuchs. Yet there is some evidence that the Hebrew word for "hand" (*yad*) can be understood as a euphemism for the penis (see Isa. 56:5 and 57:8; Ullendorf 1979:441). If sexual mutilation were implied in 5:29–30, it would represent a very great loss of male honor (Malina and Rohrbaugh 1991:122). Hence, the very choice of bodily parts (right eye and hand, possibly penis) must also be assessed in terms of bodily, and especially male, honor.

3.4 Sexual Aggression: Divorce (and Remarriage).   The prohibition of sexual aggression includes also the proscription of divorce in 5:31–32. Once more we must examine this in the light of cultural notions of marriage and honor and shame (Malina 1993:126–42). Two scholars have proposed a cultural scenario for reading about marriage and divorce in Matt. 19:1–12 relative to our investigation (Malina and Rohrbaugh 1992:120–22). Marriage in non-individualistic cultures is the joining of two families through the union of a son and daughter. Romantic love, i.e., individual choice of spouse for interpersonal fulfillment, played little part in ancient marriages, which were generally arranged by families for economic, political, and social reasons beneficial to both groups. Hanson, in his study of marriage and divorce among Herod and his children, makes the point even clearer:

> Marriage is a sexual, economic and (at times) political and religious relationship contracted between families (segments of the same family) for a male and a female. In pre-industrial, traditional societies, marriage is seldom (if ever) an arrangement between a man and a woman. This is particularly true of first marriages. Herod #1, for example, does not merely choose Mariamne #1 as his wife; he makes a marriage contract with the *family* of Hyrcanus ([Josephus, *J.W.*] 1.300). (Hanson 1989b:142)

Thus honor from an advantageous marriage accrues primarily to families, whose wealth, power, and reputation are presumably enhanced by the union.

Therefore, a husband's divorce of his wife entails the dissolution of these family ties, with the inevitable insult to the wife's family. On occasion divorce led to feuding, a form of honor challenge and riposte. Once more Hanson's study of Josephus's treatment of the marriages and divorces of Herod points us in the right direction: "It becomes clear that divorce is as social an arrangement as marriage: it has immediate implications for the family, and not merely the individuals. And furthermore, it is always tied to the value of honor" (1989b:148–49). In his conclusion, Hanson presents a cogent summary of his study of divorce in the Herodian family: "The divorces in the Herodian family demonstrate the competition for honor in marriage strategy. A spouse could be dropped when a better alliance became available" (1989b:150). For example, Herod divorced Doris to marry Mariamne to secure an alliance with the Hasmonean royal-priestly family; this divorce severed Herod's ties to Doris's family as well as the potential claims of their children to inheritance and access to the throne (*J.W.* 1.431–33).

In light of this cultural view of marriage, divorce, and honor, what might we say of divorce in Matthew? Twice he links "divorce" with "adultery": (1) the divorcing husband makes his divorced wife commit adultery and (2) the man who marries a divorced woman commits adultery. In regard to the first case, we must remember that Jesus proscribes all divorce. Hence the divorced wife, should she enter another marriage, would be committing adultery because the former marriage is still valid; and her divorcing husband, who is allowing her subsequent union, would then be her panderer (Betz 1995:249; see Philo, *Special Laws* 3.31). The husband who allows his divorced wife to remarry makes his wife shameless and so brings shame upon himself. After all, she is still his wife, and one of his prime duties as a male is to guard her sexual exclusivity. In the second case, where a man marries a divorced woman, according to Hanson's study, this marriage is most likely one of social climbing and seeking advantage, rather than passion or romance. Malina and Rohrbaugh provide the culturally appropriate appreciation of "adultery," which results in this second case: marriage to a divorced woman brings dishonor to her previous husband, to whom she is still married in Jesus' eyes; the new husband is thus committing adultery with another man's wife (1992:53). Males, then, are either failing in their honorable duty to preserve the sexual exclusiveness of their own wives or acting aggressively in illicit sexual conquests of the wives of other men.

In Hanson's analysis of Herod's affairs, marriage and divorce were strategies to gain honor. Then might we not presume that the husband marrying a divorced woman is himself recently divorced? Why divorced? Most likely because a more advantageous marriage became available. Thus the man marrying a divorced woman is likely to be acting aggressively, shedding one wife for a more profitable one. He would gain honor both by his ability to have more females, especially those of other men, and by the more favorable alliances that result from the new marriage. Therefore, if the husband stands to gain honor both by marriage and by divorce, who loses honor? Who is shamed by the divorce? Three people are shamed: (1) surely the wife who has been rejected, (2) but also the wife's family, especially her father and other male relatives, and (3) the wife's husband, if he is losing his wife to another man.

The exception clause ("except in the case of uncleanness," 5:32) should also be viewed in light of honor and shame. As we have seen, "adultery" means "shame" to the aggrieved husband. In both Greek and Judean traditions, the aggrieved husband must put away the guilty wife if he is to avoid being the victim of "shame" himself (*m. Soṭa* 5.1); apropos of Greek practice, Hauck remarked, "If the wounded husband is not himself to fall victim to *atimia* (i.e., 'shame') he must put away the guilty wife" (1967:732–33). In the early Christian tradition, a husband's control over a household is not only a qualification for bishops and deacons (1 Tim. 3:4, 12) but a general prerequisite for an honorable male (Verner 1983:132–34). The issue, then, involves honor and shame, inasmuch as marriage and divorce were common strategies for gaining status and wealth. Thus adultery enjoys a decidedly social and cultural meaning in terms of honor (to the adulterer) and shame (to the aggrieved husband). In the choreography of honor challenges, the adulterer challenges, while the cuckolded husband is challenged.

In conclusion, Jesus continues to proscribe a common avenue for male acquisition of honor, namely sexual conquest. Only in regard to the exception clause ("except for adultery") does Jesus support the existing honor code; elsewhere in 5:27–32 he forbids his disciples both the sin of adultery and the acquisition of honor that comes with this action. Again, he requires that his disciples cease to play the aggressive game of acquiring honor at another's expense.

4.0 All False and Vain Speech Prohibited

Jesus' prohibition of false and vain speech is structured in two parts: the old laws (Matt. 5:33), which he upholds, and his reform and expansion (5:34–37). At stake in both parts is verbal display calculated to gain honor for the speaker.

4.1 False Swearing and Performing One's Vows. Jesus upholds certain forms of verbal display: (1) "You shall not swear falsely" and (2) "You shall perform to the Lord what you have sworn" (5:33). Assessing these in terms of honor and shame, "swearing a false oath" can mean either swearing falsely/committing perjury or breaking an oath (BAGD 296). Thus the first part of 5:33 refers to false swearing, i.e. lying (Duling 1990:16), and the second part of 5:33 points to doing what one says, i.e., fulfilling vows. In both cases the author envisions situations of public speech, the arena where honor is claimed, awarded, or denied.

(False) swearing may occur in forensic situations, such as those referred to in Matt. 5:22 ("the council") or 5:25 (before "a judge"), where a man is asked for his "word of honor" and swears to tell the truth (Malina 1993a:43). Here lying, i.e., not telling the truth, is the focus (Prov. 24:28). According to a social-scientific typology of lying (Pilch 1992a), out of many reasons for lying, people are observed to lie both to get ahead (see 1 Kings 21:8–14) and to defend themselves in potentially shameful situations. In terms of challenge-riposte dynamics, lies function as both *challenges* to others by attacking their reputations, and *ripostes* for oneself to cover up one's shameful behavior. False swearing, then, functions as a means of either acquiring honor at another's expense or defending one's own honor.

"Performing vows to the Lord" refers to the honorable behavior urged and praised in the Bible (Lev. 22:21; 2 Sam. 15:7; Job 22:27; Pss. 22:25; 50:14; 116:14). But it is not uncommon to find people saying one thing and doing another (Neyrey 1993:59–63), especially in Jesus' world. Later in Matthew's Gospel, Jesus tells a parable about two sons: one said publicly that he would work in his father's vineyard but did not, and the other son publicly refused to work, but eventually did so (21:28–32). This Gospel, then, is familiar with people who say one thing and do another. Moreover, oaths and words of honor given in such public situations often serve to save face: the one who swears claims honor for truthfulness by virtue of the oath or vow. But such may be vainglorious claims, intended only to garner respect and praise, especially if the vow is never paid. By confirming these traditional verbal acts, Jesus continues to proscribe all involvement of his disciples in the game of gaining honor by whatever means.

4.2 Honor Claims: Verbal Display. In 5:34–37 Jesus extends his control of vain speech and thus the pursuit of honor. All oath taking, whether truthful or false, is forbidden his disciples: "Do not swear at all." In addition to the ethical and moral implications of this command (Betz 1995:259–62, 266–72), let us examine the phenomenon of oath taking in terms of expected male behavior in the cultural world of honor and shame. Jesus' remarks make two points: (1) no oath taking at all, and (2) no florid or verbose oaths.

4.2.1 Oaths and Popular Speech. We have considerable ancient evidence about the frequency with which males took public oaths. In enumerating four types of oaths—rash oaths, vain oaths, oaths of testimony, and deposit oaths—the Mishnah suggests how common swearing was in ancient Judea (*m. Shebu'ot* 3:7–11; 4:3; 5:1–2). Philo, moreover, states that the taking of oaths was unfortunately a common feature of daily life in his time:

> There are some who without even any gain in prospect have an evil habit of swearing incessantly and thoughtlessly about ordinary matters where there is nothing at all in dispute, filling up the gaps in their talk with oaths, forgetting that it were better to submit to have their words cut short or rather to be silenced altogether. (*On the Decalogue* 92)

His remarks indicate that verbal display, even "where there is nothing in dispute," is a common form of posturing, which forms the basis of claims to honor. Some oaths suffered from verbosity, that is, inflated rhetoric and exaggeration (Lieberman 1942:116). In Matt. 6:7, we actually hear censure of people who are fond of words (πολυλογία); yet excess of words may be honorable, as in the case of Plato's praise of Athens as "fond of talk (φιλόλογος) and full of talk (πολύλογος)" (*Laws* 641E). Philo again clarifies the social function of such verbal display:

> [S]o highly impious are they that on any chance matter the most tremendous titles are put on their lips and they do not blush to use name after name, one piled upon another, thinking that the continual repetition of a string of oaths will secure them their object. (*Special Laws* 2.8)

Thus hyperbolic, flowery, and excessive speech seems to characterize the verbal display of males in antiquity (Luz 1989:315). Jeremias savored the cultural flavor of such behavior when he described 5:34–36 as "the oaths with which the oriental constantly underlines the truthfulness of his remarks in everyday speech" (1971:220).

4.2.2 Oaths and Honor. But who swears oaths? In what contexts? And for what purposes? The narrative envisions males in public situations, possibly courts or marketplaces, where oaths may be required of legal witnesses or proffered by voluble salesmen (Malina and Rohrbaugh 1992:55). The New Testament tells us that Peter "cursed and swore" that he did not know Jesus (Mark 14:71), whereas Paul claimed respect by occasionally punctuating his letters with oaths attesting to his truthfulness (Rom. 9:1 and Gal. 1:20). Peter deflected shame by loud and verbose oaths, whereas Paul claimed honor for speaking a sincere word. Furthermore, the honor of God can become involved in human oaths. As Philo notes, "an oath is nothing else than to call God to bear witness in a disputed matter" (*Special Laws* 2.10). If the matter is frivolous or false, then the oath wastes God's honor or impugns it: " . . . but to call God to witness to a falsehood is the very height of profanity" (Philo, *Special Laws* 2.10).

Furthermore, honor pervades the very content of many oaths that invoke God: "Do not swear . . . by heaven, for it is the throne of God, or by earth, for it is his footstool, or by Jerusalem, for it is the city of the Great King" (Matt. 5:34–35). "Throne," "footstool," and "royal city" connote a person of very high role and status, the most honorable of all persons in the cosmos: God (yet see Duling 1991:297–309). Thus even the content of frivolous oaths partakes of the world of honor, as symbolized by the furniture and dwelling of a most honorable person. Thus oaths both frivolous and false, vain and verbose should be seen as honor claims. Yet all such verbal display is forbidden by Jesus, who mandates simple speech that makes no honor claim or boast: "Let what you say simply be 'Yes!' or 'No!'" (5:37; see Philo, *Special Laws* 2.4–5; see James 5:12).

4.3 Summary. By proscribing all oaths and verbal display, Jesus forbids his male disciples to participate in typical village games of seeking honor by their speech. Men may not take oaths at all, and so they may not challenge others or defend themselves with them. Nor may they claim honor and status by posturing before their neighbors and swearing in verbose and grandiloquent ways so characteristic of peoples of the Mediterranean (Patai 1983:49–59; see Matt. 6:7). Jesus' disciples simply may not play the games whereby males earned and defended their public reputations.

5.0 All Defense of Honor Prohibited

Although the literary form of "antithesis" continues, the remarks of Jesus change direction in terms of honor and shame. Whereas remarks about adultery/lust and false witness should be seen as honor challenges, the statements in Matt. 5:38–42 are best viewed as prohibiting ripostes to honor challenges. When challenged, disciples may not defend their honor.

5.1 Revenge Is Sweet! Jesus cites the *lex talionis*, the norm of satisfaction for honor assaults: "An eye for and eye . . . a tooth for a tooth" (see Ex. 21:24; Lev. 24:20; Deut. 19:21). In view here are the most honorable parts of a man's body, his head and face. If challenged by physical assault and especially an affront to the face ("eye" and "tooth"), a man is permitted and even expected by the local code to give a riposte in kind and so restore his damaged honor. Whether repayment and satisfaction occur through equivalent physical mutilation (Lev. 24:20) or by payment of money as satisfaction (Ex. 21:19, 22, 30, 32, 34; Daube 1973:255–63) the *lex talionis* should be seen in the light of compensation for injury and insult. On just this point, Daube's study of "an eye for an eye" illustrates how notions of honor and shame were intrinsic parts of such a system of retribution. On the one hand, Daube points to the provision in Roman law that compensation was due an "injured" person, not only for physical damages, but also for insult (1973:260). And he cites the rabbinic ruling on compensation, which likewise includes "insult" among the things for which a person may seek compensation:

> If a man wounded his fellow he thereby becomes liable on five counts: for injury, for pain, for healing, for loss of time, and for indignity inflicted . . . "For indignity inflicted"—all is in accordance with him that inflicts

and him that suffers the indignity. (*m. Baba Qamma* 8:1; on the compensation for "indignity," see *m. Ketubot* 3:7 and *m. 'Arakin* 3:4)

The basis of the compensation for insult/indignity is rooted in Deut. 25:11, a most revealing choice of texts: "When a wife . . . seizes him [the man attacking her husband] by the private parts, that is, by his honorable male members . . . " (Daube 1973:261–63). "Indignity," then, was equivalent to grabbing a man in public by his testicles, a remark that retains its insulting character even today. Although the Mishnah requires monetary compensation for all five reasons, we note the obvious fact that "injury" extended also to "insult," which is clearly in the arena of honor and shame." Hence, the law of retribution included in its very functioning notions of honor-shame and challenge-riposte.

The taking of revenge, moreover, was broadly approved in the ancient world. For example, we repeat the remark of Aristotle, our reliable ancient informant, on revenge as an honorable act for which a man deserves praise: "[Those things are honorable] . . . to take vengeance on enemies and not to be reconciled; for to retaliate is just, and the just is honorable, and not to be defeated is characteristic of a brave man" (*Rhet.* 1.9.24). Jewish traditions also celebrate revenge. Some writers consider it honorable for God to avenge insults to his divine honor (Ps. 99:8; Nahum 1:2; Isa. 34:8; Jer. 46:10; 50:15) and to requite those who hate him (Deut. 32:41). Honorable prophets cry to God for vengeance (Jer. 11:20; 20:12) and the righteous rejoice when they bathe their feet in the blood of those who persecute them (Ps. 58:10; see Rev. 6:10). Satisfaction occurs when insult is met with insult and assault with assault. Hence, the *lex talionis* endorses the game of honor and shame, giving legitimation to defense of one's honor and the seeking of honor satisfaction.

5.2 No Revenge, No Honor for Disciples. Jesus' remarks in 5:38–42 prohibit his disciples from playing the honorable game of seeking satisfaction and revenge and from delivering ripostes to challenges. As with verbal display, he states the general principle: "Do not stand against the evil man." We envision this "evil man" as unjustly attacking a disciple; hence, he is the challenger and the disciple the one challenged. The verb "stand against" (ἀνθίστημι) may describe an honor *challenge*, as in the case where Elymas the magician "stood against" Paul (Acts 13:8) or where Paul "stood up to" Cephas (Gal. 2:11); conversely it may refer to the *riposte* that Christians give to the assaults of the devil (James 4:8; 1 Peter 5:9). Here, however, we best understand "*not* standing against" as *not defending* one's honor. Thus in terms of the choreography of honor contests, disciples not only do *not* challenge others (Matt. 5:21–22, 27–31), but do *not* give a riposte when challenged.

5.2.1 The Right Cheek. Jesus illustrates his general principle with three examples of nondefensive behavior. First he describes an unambiguous affront, "If anyone strikes you on the right cheek" (5:39). Two points need be noted: First, the Hebrew scriptures commonly describe this insult to head and face, either the striking of a cheek (1 Kings 22:24; Job 16:10; Isa. 50:6; Micah 5:1; 1 Esdras 4:30) or the breaking of teeth (Pss. 3:7; 58:6). All would readily understand the meaning of this gesture. Second, Greco-Roman as well as Jewish culture interpreted the slap on the face as an "extreme humiliation" (Betz 1995:289), in other words, an "insult" rather than an "injury" (see Lam. 3:30). Thus was Jesus shamed during his trials when his face was struck (Mark 14:65; Luke 22:65; John 18:22).

Why the right cheek and not the left one? Commentators note that the striking of the *right* cheek may mean a slap either with the back of the hand or with the left hand (Luz 1989:325). A left-handed slap adds insult because that hand is unclean by virtue of its use for toilet purposes. A backhanded slap also adds insult, for *m. Baba Qamma* 8:6 requires a double penalty as satisfaction for it. Moreover, the mishnaic text notes an honor factor in the retribution: "This is the general rule: all is in accordance with a person's honour."

The situation here implies that the disciple is receiving a challenge in the most insulting form possible. In the face of such honor challenges, Jesus tells the disciple "turn to him the other also." Betz interprets the turning of the other cheek as "a highly provocative challenge" (1995:290). If we are reading this scene correctly in terms of the choreography of typical honor-shame dynamics, then Jesus requires his disciples to step apart completely from the honor game: they may not offer any riposte or defense of their honor when challenged. To offer a "highly provocative challenge" misses the point; disciples simply may not play the game; they are not in any way seeking to win, even by passive aggression. On this point Strecker seems more culturally attuned: "The one struck is to offer the other cheek also, as proof of unreserved compliance that seeks neither to preserve one's own honor nor to maintain one's position of power" (Strecker 1988:83–84).

5.2.2 The Shirt Off One's Back!   Next Jesus describes another unambiguous scene of honor challenge. A man is being sued, presumably before a gathering of elders at the gate, where such honor challenges were regularly settled (McKenzie 1964). The context suggests that once more the disciple is the victim of aggression. Again an "evil man" challenges a righteous disciple who is losing his shirt, as our idiom goes. By putting up no defense, the opponent would take the victim's χιτών, the tunic worn close to the body, the ordinary garment. This would leave the man naked; and to be stripped naked was a grave honor challenge (Neyrey 1993c:121). Besides the honor challenge, an economic hardship is envisioned, for we should not imagine that peasants have closets of clothes to replenish lost and dirty garments as Euro-Americans have. Loss of a peasant's sole external garment would entail loss of honor. This cloak (ἱμάτιον), the peasant's outer garment used as a blanket for sleeping and for warmth in winter weather, should be protected by Jewish law (Ex. 22:26–27; Deut. 24:12–13), and so defended by the court. Here its loss constitutes great public shame.

In terms of honor-shame exchanges, then, disciples are faced with a challenge. But Jesus again forbids them to give a riposte to this insult. Rather they should allow themselves to be challenged and shamed further by the loss of all their garments. And so the shamed disciple has no defense or riposte whatever, not his own nor that of the court of elders. Complete vulnerability and total shame are envisioned, a shame which the challenged man will not seek in the least to deflect, much less avenge.

5.2.3 Tote That Barge! Lift That Bale!   Jesus then describes a scene of corvée labor required of a peasant by either an occupying army or some aristocrat:

"If any one forces you to go one mile" (Matt. 5:41). Ancient peasants were forced to give service without pay to those more powerful than themselves who could impose their will, for example, Simon of Cyrene (Matt. 27:32; see Josephus, *Ant.* 13.52; Epictetus, *Discourses* 4.1.79; Horsley 1981:36–45). In this powerless situation, Jesus tells disciples not to resist displays of power and so not to give a riposte to the shame of them. On the contrary, disciples are to be shamed even more by "going with him two miles."

Two scholars have suggested an appropriate historical context for understanding 5:38–41. Theissen argues that these remarks reflect the situation of "wandering charismatics" among the disciples of Jesus (1992:171–49), especially in the period after the Jewish war (132–37). Milavec contests Theissen's unprovable and overly specific argument by suggesting a social situation more widespread, namely, hostility from one's family (1995:136–42). He presents parallels between Matt. 5:38–41 and *Didache* 1.4, where no war is envisioned. Of importance here is Milavec's argument that backhanded slaps, loss of clothes, and enforced labor can adequately be explained in terms of intra-family dynamics of socialization and control. Milavec, moreover, seems much more attuned to comparable examples of public dishonor that come from *not* acting according to expected cultural norms, e.g., the endurance of shame by the Cynics. On balance, Milavec's discussion points us in the direction of "cross-generational" conflict within households, where actions such as are described in 5:39–41 can occur in terms of social control of sons, especially ones who are intent on becoming disciples of Jesus. The importance of this lies in the observation that the disciples are being socialized to expect such treatment, and thus are given a new set of social expectations, the living up to which is the basis of honor.

Although the terms "honor" and "shame" are not formally mentioned in 5:38–41, a knowledge of this cultural dynamic is required to understand just what Jesus demands of disciples. First, in terms of the physical body, only the honorable parts are in view: eye, mouth/tooth, and face (5:39). If all garments are surrendered, enforced nudity results, which in such a context is always shameful (5:40). Finally, corvée labor requires bodily gestures of submission (5:41). Shame, then, will be visible to all. Second, all of the actions against the disciple are clearly aggressive ones, which are preeminently insulting rather than painful. Insults not responded to earn the victim shame in the eyes of his neighbors. Third, in terms of the choreography of honor conflicts, in each instance the disciple plays the role of the person challenged by another. But Jesus forbids the next step in the ballet, namely, the expected riposte by the one challenged. It was one thing to proscribe honor challenges to disciples (adultery, false witness) whereby they could gain more honor; but it is quite another thing to tell disciples to lose honor by yielding to insult and not making a riposte. If the former is difficult, the latter seems nigh impossible to follow. Finally, in all cases, not only does the disciple *not* give a riposte, but he becomes that much more shamed by following Jesus' words: he turns the other cheek, surrenders the rest of his clothing, and takes on extra servile labor. These exaggerated responses are certainly not ripostes in any form that ancients would recognize (see Betz 1995:291). On the contrary, they represent the utter loss of respect and face before one's neighbors. For Jesus requires males to play the role of the victim, the submissive one, the person imposed upon, but *not* the honorable man who defends his worth at all times and at any cost. Jesus' injunctions, then, strike at the heart of ancient notions of manliness, and thus honor.

5.2.4 *Charity Begins at Home.* The last of Jesus' commands at 5:42 describes a situation of giving and lending to a suppliant who may be a neighbor or a stranger. We recall from the major model of honor the distinction between negative and positive challenges (Malina 1993:34–37; Malina and Neyrey 1991:49–52). Negative challenges to a man's honor occur when someone physically or verbally attacks him, seduces his wife, or bears false witness against him. Positive honor challenges, however, are not calculated to dishonor a man, although they may diminish his honor rating. Positive challenges may take the form of gift giving, compliments, volunteering, or requesting. A request for miracles or financial assistance challenges a man because such requests seek something the man may not want or be able to give. He is being involuntarily pressured to comply with the request, and involuntary compliance is shameful. In terms of honor challenges, a request challenges a man because it seeks to take something from him involuntarily. The appropriate riposte is to reject the request. After all, "charity begins at home"; what is given from family resources to others means that there is that much less available to the donor and his family. If a man gives to all who ask him, he will be seen as failing to defend what belongs to his family or be seen as a man who is easily taken advantage of.

In regards to gifts and requests, Aristotle does not praise indiscriminate generosity. Rather, he called it virtuous for a man "to give to the right people, the right amounts, and at the right time" (*Nicomachean Ethics* 4.1 1120a 25). The virtuous person will "refrain from giving to anybody and everybody, that he may have something to give to the right people at the right time" (4.1 1120b 3–4). He does not specify exactly who are these "right" and "wrong" people. But several important considerations are embedded here: (1) economic issues: what will the giver receive in return for his benefaction? and (2) social issues: whom is it honorable to assist? Charity begins at home; limited resources are best expended on the interests of the family; resources expended to outsiders should be repaid to the family —all because of the loss of honor which comes from loss of wealth. Hence by "giving" and "*not* turning away" a man does not resist the challenge, and allows himself to be taken advantage of; he forgoes control of his assets. Gift giving may redound to his credit, if he is acclaimed as a benefactor. But it just might result in being taken for an easy mark, a naive person, with consequent loss of honor as well as diminished assets.

There are several reasons why we should read Matt. 5:38–41 in terms of an honor challenge. First, the narrative structure includes it in the sequence of other rejections of ripostes in defense of one's honor (5:39–42, 43–47). Second, our understanding of the dynamics of honor and shame indicates that such requests are positive challenges; and so, giving in to them could mean a refusal to defend one's honor. Although exhortations to benevolence were commonplaces in the Gospels (Matt. 6:1–4; Luke 11:41; 12:33) and Jewish literature (Str-B 1.346–53; Nissen

1974:267–77), Jesus' command goes beyond demands for generosity, for it puts a disciple on the spot by demanding that he *not* defend his honor when challenged.

6.0 Loving One's Enemies?

We continue our attempt to interpret this last antithesis in terms of honor and shame. Matthew 5:44 has been amply examined in terms of its relationship with comparable exhortations in Jewish, Greek, and Eastern religious traditions about dealing with enemies (Luz 1989:340–41; Betz 1995:309–11). This most celebrated of all Gospel statements has been hailed as the key element in Christianity. It is not our intention to slight the traditional discussions of 5:43–44, but certainly we need not rehearse them here. We simply wish to add one more dimension to that conversation, that is, a cultural reading of 5:43–48 in terms of the dominant value of Jesus' cultural world.

6.1 How Honorable to Hate One's Enemies! From earlier discussions, it should come as no surprise that our ancient informants overwhelmingly agree with the remark of old: "Love your neighbor and hate your enemy." As Mary Blundell has noted, "Greek popular thought is prefaced by the assumption that one should help one's friends and harm one's enemies" (1989:26). In regard to what was expected of a man in antiquity, Betz called attention to the ancient proverb: "A man's virtue consists in outdoing his friends in kindness and his enemies in mischief" (Betz 1995:305). It should be clear, then, that (1) "loving" one's group (family, clan, village) satisfies the social expectations of one's neighbors, and so is the honorable thing to do, and (2) standing by the group against its enemies likewise fulfills those same expectations and so is honorable. Both "love" and "hate," then, adequately fulfill the expected social behavior of members of a group; and living up to such expectations gives others grounds for awarding a man a grant of honor and respect (see Malina and Rohrbaugh 57–58). A person who lived up to the old rule that "You shall love your neighbors and hate your enemies" (Matt. 5:43) would be doing the culturally correct thing and so deserve the respect of all.

When Jesus tells his disciples that they must "love" an "enemy" and "offer blessing prayers" for "a persecutor" (5:44), he upsets the typical honor code and reverses what is expected of male disciples. History-of-ideas approaches to 5:44 have amply indicated that Jesus' remarks had "precedent and preparation," although they did "represent a new step at the time" (Betz 1995:311). But our question is one of culture, not history. Betz simply never asked the cultural question: How would this sound in a culture structured on honor? When we diagram the behavior according to the choreography of honor and shame, we begin to see what is happening. If one has enemies, then a feud is already occurring; that is, challenges have already been issued and defenses prepared, in a seemingly endless cycle of challenge and riposte. Jesus, however, tells those challenged that they may not give a riposte to challengers (i.e., "hate enemies"). Not only that, they are to step completely apart from the game of push-and-shove and positively benefit their challengers, namely, "pray for them." In terms of honor and shame, then, Jesus urges irrational behavior. His remarks may accord with a number of injunctions in the scriptures (Ex. 23:4–5; Prov. 24:17–18; 25:21–22), but they fail the test of plausi-bility in an agonistic society. Such a person would be a "fool" in an honor-shame world.

6.2 Imitating a Shameless God? If honor is lost by loving enemies and praying for persecutors, nevertheless honor is gained through the imitation of one's heavenly Father, which is a correct cultural path to respect. The terms of the new honor embody classic elements of an honor-shame world: sons, fathers, imi-tation, and social expectations. Sons, who are shamed by their families for disloy-alty to their social traditions, are honored by adoption into a new and better family, that is, "sons of your Father who is in heaven" (5:45). This new Father, moreover, is the most honorable person in the cosmos and He loves enemies and blesses blas-phemers: "He makes his sun rise on the evil and the good and sends rain on the just and on the unjust" (5:45b). Hence Jesus' disciples trade one set of expectations for another. Instead of living up to the honor code of their families and neighbors, they fulfill the expectations of the code of God-Father and thus become "chips off the old block." If honor is lost before one's kin and neighbors in the village, honor is gained in heaven by imitating God.

Yet if it is not honorable to be indiscriminately generous, then does Jesus por-tray God as likewise "dishonorable"? Does he imply that God is "foolish" for making no distinction between friends and enemies? Is God "shameful" for not re-quiting an insult? When put in these terms, is Jesus rejecting popular notions of theodicy or retribution (Betz 1995:313–14)? Probably so, and it is worth our while to savor the importance of honor in traditional notions of theodicy.

Since "hating" enemies probably means giving them a fitting riposte for past injury, let us examine the kinds of reasons offered by the ancients for punishing evildoers. Why do mortals (and presumably God and the gods) punish the wicked? An important ancient informant, Aulus Gellius, repeats the common wisdom on the topic as he catalogues three reasons for punishment: "It has been thought that there should be three reasons for punishing crimes" (*Attic Nights* 7.14): (1) cor-rection and reformation of the wicked, (2) defense of the honor of the lawgiver, and (3) exemplary warning to others. We call attention to the second reason listed: honor requires a lawmaker to punish, requite, and take vengeance for injury:

> That reason for punishment exists when the dignity and prestige of the
> one who is sinned against must be maintained, lest the omission of pun-
> ishment bring him into contempt and diminish the esteem in which he is
> held; and therefore they think that it was given a name derived from the
> preservation of honour. (*Attic Nights* 7.14; see Neyrey 1993:200)

A sovereign, therefore, should repay lawbreakers with punishment, because in do-ing so he defends his honor. This is what is expected of an honorable ruler, namely, to give an appropriate riposte to an honor challenge. But when Jesus says that God does good to enemies, God might be said either to ignore public opinion or to be giving sinners time to repent (see 2 Peter 3:9). But God is *not* portrayed in Matthew 5:45 as delivering a riposte to an honor challenge; God risks his honor by not retaliating.

Therefore, Jesus' remarks in 5:39–41 and 43–45 prohibit the disciple from any defense of his honor. When challenged, he gives no riposte at all. When the honor game is played by his neighbors, the disciple refuses to play, which is a shameful thing in itself in this cultural context. Jesus' exaggerated responses to honor challenges (offering the other cheek, giving one's cloak, and going another mile) will surely lead to even further loss of respect in the eyes of one's neighbors. The villagers could only interpret such actions as a total forswearing of one's honor, a thing unimaginable and unforgivable. Such a person would be perceived in this cultural context as completely valueless, totally worthless, and a person with whom one should not associate.

7.0 Conclusions: The Antitheses in Cultural Perspective

How would typical males in the cultural world of honor and shame hear Jesus' words? First, when understood in terms of the general code of honor and shame in the ancient world, each Antithesis touches upon areas which males viewed as acceptable avenues for gaining respect, worth, and honor, even if such are hemmed in by biblical restrictions. The Antitheses, therefore, should be seen not only in the light of Greek philosophy or Jewish theology, but also in terms of the cultural world of antiquity. It was an agonistic world in pursuit of honor, where males strove for a reputation through physical, verbal, and sexual aggression. Second, according to the choreography of honor-shame behavior, each Antithesis is adequately described in terms of claim, challenge, and riposte (see fig. 9.1).

Claim no honor claims:
                boasting, verbose oaths (5:34–37)

Challenge no honor challenges:
                physical aggression (5:21)
                sexual aggression (5:27–32)
                false witness against someone (5:33)
            if challenge is already issued, it must be undone:
                reconciliation (5:23–24)
                settle with opponent (5:25–26)

Riposte no retaliation or vengeance if challenged:
                no verbal retaliation (5:22)
                turn the other cheek (5:39–42)
                love one's enemies (5:43–45)

Public Verdict loss of honor and respect in the eyes of one's neighbors

Figure 9.1 The Antitheses in Cultural Perspective

Jesus' discourse sets up another set of expectations. But the issue remains the same: living up to what is expected of an honorable man brings public approval and thus honor. Disciples swap the approval of their kin and neighbors for that of Jesus and God. They do not stop their pursuit of respect and honor, but rather turn to Jesus and God for the public verdict of approval.

Third, this particular reading of the Antitheses inevitably indicates that the implied audience is male. Male behavior in public space remains the focus throughout, from physical aggressiveness to sexual aggressiveness, retaliation, and feuding. But then, it was the ancient world of males that was obsessed with love or honor. Finally, inasmuch as honor is lost, where is honor gained? Jesus, of course, claims honor by challenging existing readings of the law. More to the point, however, Jesus offers honor to loyal disciples who forswear all other honor games. As we saw in the last chapter, the Makarisms serve precisely this role, namely, to honor those who have been shamed on Jesus' behalf. The fourth, climactic makarism (Matt. 5:11–12) describes disciples who have been utterly shamed "on my account," but who are nevertheless honored by Jesus. We argued there that honor to the "meek," "merciful," and "peacemakers" refers to people who have been challenged and have lost honor by not seeking revenge or delivering. Although no honor was proclaimed in the Antitheses for those who do not retaliate and who forswear revenge, the honor was promised in the Makarisms.

In conclusion, what is the likely status of a disciple who indeed practices Jesus' Antitheses? To be a disciple of Jesus, a typical male would have to forswear the pivotal value of his cultural world. He would be prohibited from seeking honor, especially in the ways defined by eastern Mediterranean culture: by physical assault, sexual conquest of women, or lying. Should he already have challenged another or participated in a family feud with outsiders, he must call off those challenges. Nor may he defend his own honor or seek honorable satisfaction and revenge for injury and insult. This disciple, then, will be considered a weakling, a wimp, a worthless no-account who cannot defend his honor, a person of whom one takes advantage, a man to be ashamed of. This, we maintain, is the "cross" of following Jesus: the loss of honor.

10

Matthew 6:1–18

Vacating the Playing Field

1.0 Introduction

Standard readings of Matthew 6:1–18 have examined the text in terms of traditional methods of biblical criticism, such as formal structure, source and redaction, and history of religion parallels (Luz 1989:353–56; Betz 1995:330–49). We wish to add questions concerning the meaning of 6:1–18 in terms of the pivotal cultural value of honor. How would those who love honor and fear shame understand Jesus' teaching? How would males have heard it who were socialized to certain behaviors deemed essential to maleness? As we have examined both the Makarisms (5:3–12) and the Antitheses (5:21–48) in light of honor and shame, let us continue this cultural interpretation of the instructions on piety in 6:1–18.

1.1 Honor and Gender Expectations. In raising the cultural question, we recall certain elements of the cross-cultural model of honor and shame presented in chapter 1 that are relevant for this inquiry. It is generally accepted that the ancient world structured itself as a radically gender-divided society. Prevailing expectations for males (and females) entail a near total gender division of the world: certain places, times, and things are classified exclusively as appropriate to either male or female. The sexes are basically separated and divided into two equal worlds: one for males and one for females. During the day males are expected to be "out of doors," in the open spaces and in public, where they associate with other males. Males, moreover, are assigned public tasks: if a peasant farmer, then sowing, reaping, and gathering into barns; if an urban elite, then attendance at the gymnasium, participation in civic discussions, and the like. Whether peasant or elite, males should be away from the home except for eating and sleeping. Every male would be carefully socialized by other males in his family and village to know what is expected of him in this regard. For in the world of honor and shame, one's worth and standing depend on both knowing and living up to those expectations and thus maintaining one's own honor and that of one's family. An important aspect of these social expectations is a requirement for a male to be present with his male peers in the public world as much as is possible.

1.2 Native Informants on Male Public Space. It will be helpful to consider the remarks of two ancient informants who describe the gender-divided stereotype of the ancient world. Philo describes the space culturally appropriate to males and females, namely, males in public and females in private.

> Market-places and council-halls and law-courts and gatherings and meetings where a large number of people are assembled, and open-air life with full scope for discussion and action—all these are suitable to men both in war and peace. The women are best suited to the indoor life. (*Special Laws* 3.169)

In this generalized summary, Philo, an urban elite (30 B.C.E.–45 C.E.), locates males in "open-air life," namely, public places such as "market-places" and "council-halls" and places where males typically gather. In contrast, females are linked with the "house" or household world. Hierocles (117–138 C.E.) presents a summary of this gender stereotype in which he spells out the actions appropriate to males and females that correspond to public and private worlds respectively.

> Before anything else I should speak about the occupations by which a household is maintained. They should be divided in the usual manner, namely, to the husband should be assigned those which have to do with agriculture, commerce, and the affairs of the city; to the wife those which have to do with spinning and the preparation of food, in short, those of a domestic nature. (*On Duties* 4.28.21 in Malherbe 1986:98–99; see also Xenophon, *Oeconomicus* 7.1–43)

Males in public space undertake tasks appropriate to outdoor life: peasants farm, artisans trade, and urban elites discuss and administer. Comparably, females in the household or private world attend to the essential labors that maintain it: food preparation, clothing production, and child rearing. Since these are the cultural expectations of rural and urban males alike, Philo and Hierocles tell us that the honor of a man consists in living up to these general cultural norms for his gender, that is, in being out of his house, in the marketplace (*agora*) of his village or town, engaging in male activities that characteristically take place in that male space. Moreover, male presence is a matter of honor and shame. Xenophon explicitly says that it would be dishonorable for a man to be found at home in his house among females, rather than in public among other males: "[T]o the man it is shameful (αἰσχρόν) rather to stay indoors than to attend to the work outside. If a man acts contrary to the nature God has given him, possibly his defiance is detected by the gods and he is punished for neglecting his own work, or meddling with his wife's" (*Oeconomicus* 7.30–31).

According to this stereotype, Jesus would understand that male disciples should be in the "assembly" or synagogue on Sabbath or other holy days. The synagogue was probably not a building (Kee 1990) so much as a part of the *stoa* or shaded porch around the marketplace where male Judeans gathered to hear the Torah, offer prayers to God, and perform other public (and therefore male) acts of observance. Male honor maintenance required them to "assemble" and satisfy the socially expected male behavior. Isocrates indicates how necessary it was for Greeks to be seen giving public worship, the point we are arguing here as well:

"Do honour to the divine power at all times, but especially on occasions of public worship; for thus you will *have the reputation* both of sacrificing to the gods and of abiding by the laws" (*To Demonicus* 1.13; emphasis added). "Reputation" counts, which is earned precisely by public performance of expected duties. "Reputation," moreover, means honor.

Conversely, when males were banished or exiled, they suffered a greater penalty than imprisonment, because they were removed from the arena of honor. And the same could be said of banning, shunning, or excommunication on the village level. As one classicist has put it:

> In Athens . . . to be shut out of the public space where men gather, whether by force of law or by public opinion, eliminates the possibility of maintaining one's standing in the eyes of the community, and marks one with dishonor. (Cohen 1991:73)

The general code of honor, then, expects males to be seen constantly by other males as they go about performing gender-specific tasks in gender-specific places.

2.0 Jesus' Demand: Vacate the Public Space/Quit the Playing Field

Jesus issues a summary demand at the beginning of his remarks on piety which requires that males vacate the public place where the general code of honor requires them to be: "Beware of practicing your piety before men" (6:1). At first all he seems to be telling his disciples is to beware of a self-serving motive for their acts, as he adds a reason for his warning, " . . . in order to be seen by them." Shortly he will proscribe certain places ("synagogues, street corners") and prescribe others ("in secret"). Disciples, then, must vacate the playing field and so not perform expected acts of piety in public where they can be seen and evaluated by the public. At stake, then, is the impossibility of males living up to the code of gender expectations which are grounds for respect and honor. Shame cannot be far away.

2.1 Male Shame: Piety in Public. Jesus' opening remark acknowledges several items which are essential parts of the cultural world of honor and shame. It is clear that males generally perform their piety "in public," that is, in the presence of other males (ἔμπροσθεν τῶν ἀνθρώπων). Jesus' statement thus surfaces an important aspect of honor-conscious behavior, namely, living up to the gender expectations for males. Moreover, the qualifying phrase, "so as to be seen by them," touches on the widespread cultural motive for these actions, namely, the honorable desire by males to be seen fulfilling the expectations of their culture. Being seen by others is an essential element for earning a good reputation, worth, and honor. Furthermore, the crux of Jesus' remark in Matt. 6:1 centers on the ironic warning that such public performers actually risk losing honor and acquiring shame. If male disciples perform acts of piety before other males to win their approval, then they will lose the approval or "reward" of honor from their heavenly Father. Honor remains the continuing motive for behavior; but whose approval and grant of honor counts? That of one's neighbor? Or God's? Honor in the eyes of one public, however, will bring shame from another public. Therefore, the disciple who follows Jesus' words is certain to receive both honor and shame as a result of Jesus' remark.

Aristotle can clarify the cultural assumptions behind Jesus' opening statement. He declares the man "shameless" who shows contempt for the opinions of others (*Rhet.* 1.10.4). Furthermore, he explains the importance *of being seen* by citing the ancient proverb, "The eyes are the abode of shame" (Euripides, TGF frag. 457), thus indicating that shameful actions are shameful because they are observed. Conversely, honorable actions are honorable only when seen.

> They are also ashamed of things that are done before their eyes and in broad daylight; whence the proverb, The eyes are the abode of shame. That is why they feel more ashamed before those who are likely to be always with them or who keep watch upon them, because in both cases they are under the eyes of others. (*Rhet.* 2.6.18)

Thus, if love of honor motivates males in antiquity, they will make sure that they are constantly seen by other males so that their actions can be assessed as virtuous and excellent and so win them a good reputation. Conversely, evil deeds must be kept from the eyes of others, lest shame and censure follow.

Yet the advice in Matt. 6:1 seems to contradict the words of Jesus in Matt. 5:16 that his disciples *should*, in fact, let their light shine "before men" (ἔμπροσθεν τῶν ἀνθρώπων), the same phrase found in 6:1. Figure 10.1 highlights the differences between 5:16 and 6:1.

Prescribed Public Actions: Matt. 5:16	Let your light so shine	before men	that they may see your good works	and give glory to your Father in heaven
Proscribed Public Actions: Matt. 6:1	Beware of practicing your piety	before men	in order to be seen by them	you will have no reward from your Father in heaven.

Figure 10.1 Comparison of Matthew 5:16 and 6:1

Matthew 5:16 serves as the conclusion of Jesus' demand for excellence from his disciples: they must be the "salt of the earth . . . light of the world." The various elements in that remark all have to do with honor and shame. For example, "your light" refers to honorable actions that live up to the same code of honor and excellence (see Eph. 5:8; Phil. 2:15). They are unspecified actions, and we cannot be certain whether they refer to the so-called virtues endorsed in the Sermon on the Mount. "Before men" clearly means that the deeds are done in public. Actions done in public are intended to be observed and evaluated, hence these are done "so that they [observers] may see your good works." The honor which results, however, does not accrue to the disciples, but to their heavenly Patron (see John 15:8;

1 Cor. 10:31; Phil. 1:11; 1 Peter 2:9). Thus honor results from public actions, but in the case of Matt. 5:16, the glory goes to God.

In regard to 6:1, this remark is a topic statement for verses 2–18, not a conclusion, as was 5:16. Both 5:16 and 6:1, then, have different rhetorical functions in their respective contexts. As a topic statement, it informs Jesus' revision of the local code of honor in regard to "piety" (δικαιοσύνη). Elements of honor and shame likewise pervade it. For example, whereas males normally act so as to be seen (Matt. 5:16), in regard to acts of piety they should avoid public exposure: "Beware of practicing your piety before men." As noted, the issue is "piety," which is expressed in almsgiving, prayer, and fasting, very specific actions pertaining to ethnic identity and self-definition. These are not generic virtuous actions that earn one respect and praise. Moreover, because acts of piety promote group identity and solidarity, they ought to be done in public, much like the public offering of incense to the gods, which indicates support for the welfare of a city or loyalty to a monarch like Caesar. Such acts of piety, then, have a decided social function.

The motive cited by Jesus, "in order to be seen by them [male observers]," does not simply imply hypocrisy, although "hypocrites" will be shamed in subsequent verses. As Aristotle indicated, all males in the ancient cultural world should act in public precisely to be seen. Thus we take the phrase in 6:1, "in order to be seen by them," as referring to the honor principle that motivated all males. Everything they do is done in public so as to be seen. This is what the code of honor is all about. In this case, however, shame results. Their heavenly Father will not grant them the desired result, "a reward." Although Jesus does not use the explicit term "honor," we argue that "honor" is the "reward" (μισθός) of which he speaks (see Rom. 2:10). Let us not interpret "reward" in terms of anachronistic discussions of Pelagian or Reformation controversies over works versus grace; nor let us restrict our discussion to theology (Betz 1995:346–47). In light of the culture of honor and shame, "reward" here has to do with commendation and praise. As we have seen, honor that is claimed becomes "honor" only when acknowledged. Acknowledgment, then, is the "reward" or grant of honor. But actions claiming worth that are not acknowledged become a source of shame. Therefore, honor withheld, as in 6:1, means shame. Whereas in 5:16 the general public is the court of honor and shame, in 6:1 God is the only public and the sole arbiter of worth. Divine approval or disapproval, moreover, may well be at variance with aspects of the local code.

Both 5:16 and 6:1, then, reflect common elements of the system of honor and shame. Both speak of (1) deeds done in public, (2) in conformity with group expectations, (3) which normally bring approval and so a grant of honor. In both cases Jesus does not dispute that a male may legitimately seek this grant of honor. Rather he specifies where true acknowledgment and thus genuine worth reside, namely, in God's eyes, and not one's neighbors'. In regard to this, Matthew and Luke state that servants are "praised" before any tangible reward is added to that praise (Matt. 25:21, 23; Luke 16:8; see also Luke 12:37–38, 42); correspondingly, they are shamed before any punishment is allotted them (Matt. 25:26; Luke 11:40; 12:20). Praise is more valuable than gold, and blame more bitter than death.

2.2 Jesus' Remarks: Challenge and Claim.   Let us examine Jesus' remarks in terms of their cultural form, namely, the choreography of honor conflicts. In each case, Jesus himself issues an honor challenge to the prevailing practice of males performing acts of piety in public. While conceding the legitimacy of seeking honor and the value of the acts of piety, he challenges the typical cultural sources of honor, namely, living up to the expectation of one's neighbors. Let us examine the literary shape of 6:1–18, not simply with an eye to its rhetorical structure, but also in terms of what is proscribed and prescribed, that is, what is either blamed or praised (see fig. 10.2).

A. Challenge to Public Honor Claims

Proscribed Action:	do not blow a trumpet	do not be	do not look dismal
Exposure of False Honor Claims:	as the hypocrites do in the synagogues or on the streets	as the hypocrites, for they love to stand in the synagogues and on the corners of the streets	like the hypocrites, they disfigure their faces
	to be given glory by men	to be seen by them	so as to appear fasting
Shame, Not Honor:	they have lost their reward	they have lost their reward	they have lost their reward

B. Claims to True Honor

Prescribed Action:	do not let your right hand know what your left hand is doing	enter you room and shut the door	anoint your head and wash your face
True Honor, "in Private":	your alms will be "in secret"	pray to your Father "in secret"	so that you may not appear to men to fast, but to your Father "in secret"
Honor, Not Shame:	and your Father who sees "in secret" will reward you	and your Father who sees "in secret" will reward you	and your Father who sees "in secret" will reward you

Figure 10.2 Challenge and Claim in Matthew 6:1–18

As regards the cultural form, Jesus refuses honorable acknowledgment of actions which he proscribes for his disciples: "Do not blow a trumpet . . . stand on the street corner . . . disfigure [your] faces." In challenging the claims of those who do these actions, he refuses acknowledgment of them as valuable and thus pronounces shame and dishonor. This challenge, moreover, takes the form of labeling those who do these deeds as "hypocrites." The context clearly indicates the highly insulting connotation of this term, although its exact meaning is quite difficult to pin down (Malina and Neyrey 1988:16, 64–65). As Betz noted (1995:347), 6:1–18 is structured as a comparison, a common element in the rhetoric of praise and blame (see Butts 1987:495–505). "Hypocrite" originally meant an actor in the theater, which was extended to mean a dissembler, a connotation that is relevant here. In Matthew, it becomes the favorite insulting term used to challenge adversaries in general; and it tends to have the basic meaning of a "wicked person" (Wilckens 1968:563–68).

But if Jesus challenges traditional practice, he also makes claims. The very actions that bring shame when done in public earn honor when done "in secret." Jesus' claim consists essentially of his assertion that he is right and others are wrong; for he offers no reason in support nor cites an authority such as the scriptures. Because he is a prophet with ascribed authority from God, he speaks authoritatively, thus claiming for himself respect and acceptance. He claims, moreover, that his way alone leads to honor, and that those who act in accord with his directions will receive a "reward" of praise from God. Furthermore, the key issue in his claim resides in his redefinition of male space—"in secret" instead of "in public." On this point, Jesus flagrantly challenges the great code of honor. The critical issue, then, emerges as the contrast between "public" and "private," which demands consideration in terms of the cultural expectations of the gender-divided world of honor and shame in antiquity.

2.3 The Cultural Significance of "In Secret." Custom expected that males be "in public" ("streets," "synagogues," and "street corners") and act according to prescribed behaviors ("give alms," "pray," "fast"). Betz recognizes Matt. 6:1–18 as a formal set of traditional cultic instructions (1985:55–69; 1995:330–35), which means that Jesus' endorsement of almsgiving, prayer, and fasting is fully in accord with Judean local codes of expected behavior. The local code, however, expected males to perform their acts of piety in public either in local synagogues or in the temple. Fasts were *public* fasts; prayers, like the Eighteen Blessings, were public prayers (see *m. 'Abot* 1:2). Performing "in public," moreover, allowed honor-oriented males both to claim and to receive acknowledgment of honor for their behavior (see Matt. 23:5–7). In addition, many have noted the commonplace criticism of people in antiquity who performed pious acts in public so as to be seen (Luz 1989:357–58; see Downing 1992:82–86). We find, then, a code of cultural expectations for male behavior that expects participation in public rituals which beseech the Deity for benefit and protection (see 2 Macc. 6:21). Yet Jesus proscribes "public" and prescribes "private" rituals for his male disciples. Thus what does "in private" or "in secret" mean? Recalling the cultural expectations of males as expressed by Xenophon and Philo, we would expect that "public" and "private" have cultural significance. It is, then, no minor matter for Jesus to tell males to quit the "public" world for the "private" one. His remarks touch on issues of culture, that is, of expected honorable behavior for males.

First, let us examine some of the suggestions about Jesus' injunction to "secrecy." As regards almsgiving, Geza Vermes (1973:78) cites a text describing a specific place in the Jerusalem temple called "the Chamber of Secrets" into which pious people secretly deposited alms and from which poor families took in secret: "There were two chambers in the Temple: one the Chamber of Secrets and the other the Chamber of Utensils. Into the Chamber of Secrets the devout used to put their gifts in secret and the poor of good family received support therefrom in secret" (*m. Sheqalim* 5:6). While an intriguing suggestion for Matt. 6:4, it neither explains what "in secret" means in regard to prayer and fasting, nor does it address the cultural issue of male behavior in public. Alternately scholars have pointed out parallels in both Judean and Greco-Roman sources to the demand that pious males were to give alms anonymously and shun ostentatious behavior (Betz 1995:360). Yet, while a clear tradition about this exists, it too should be read in light of the pivotal value of ancient culture: honor and shame.

How, then, should we interpret "in secret"? "In secret" (ἐν τῷ κρυπτῷ) basically refers to something which is "hidden" (κρύπτειν). In general, we know that valuable things are hidden from prying eyes and hands; special information is also hidden from the masses and revealed to the elect (Matt. 11:25; 13:35; Luke 19:42). People, especially Jesus, hide themselves (John 8:59; 12:36); they might also move about "in secret" to avoid detection (John 7:10; 19:38). Even disciples are told to play the hypocrite by fasting and hiding the visible manifestations of it (Matt. 6:17–18). Yet we also find the demand that males *not* act in secret, especially if they wish to gain a reputation (John 7:4; Matt. 5:16); honorable males are public, not private creatures (John 18:20). So, there is more to Jesus' demand that his male disciples do acts of piety "in secret" than that they simply do them to avoid ostentation.

Jesus offers a radical reform of the general code of expected male behavior when he values "private" over "public." We saw just such a reversal of the code in the Sermon when Jesus declared "honorable" what others had labeled shameful. But like the strategy of Jesus displayed in the Antitheses, Jesus here refuses to let disciples play the game. Not only must they refrain from playing the typical games for gaining honor (5:21–48), the disciples must vacate the playing field, at least in regard to deeds of piety.

By proscribing "public" and prescribing "in secret," Jesus mandates that his disciples stay away from synagogues and refrain from joining other Judean males in their customary acts of piety. Moreover, he informs them that the honorable place to practice piety is the household, not the synagogue (Betz 1995:343). In proscribing the public forum where loyalty to the old forms of Judean piety were practiced, Jesus effectively challenges his disciples to break their social and ceremonial ties with their neighbors, ties that functioned to confirm their identity and give them honor. As we saw in chapter 7, Jesus honors those who have left the institution of kinship and household for his sake; in Matt. 6:1–18 he honors those who make a similar sort of break with village public institutions. Let us not underestimate the effects of Jesus' demands: (1) a rejection of gender expectations for males, the effect of which is (2) a challenge to previous social relationships, which will result in (3) shame from one's neighbors. Jesus requires of his male disciples nothing less than a radical break with the public world and an espousal of the household as the locus of piety. Thus we interpret the phrase "in secret" to mean the household, the private world of females. Jesus' demands will cost the disciples dearly in the court of public opinion for avoiding male but frequenting female space.

2.4 Apart from the Crowds. Jesus' command to shift the locus of piety from public synagogue to private house can be supported from other statements in the Gospel. First, apart from his five major speeches, Jesus is constantly portrayed as "entering a/the house" (8:14; 9:23, 28; 13:36; 17:25; 26:6) or "leaving the house" (13:1; see Malbon 1986:113–20, 131–36); the "house," then, is the preferred space of Jesus himself. Moreover, Matthew presents Jesus as often "alone" with his disciples or "apart" from the crowds (κατ᾽ ἰδίαν: 14:13; 17:1, 19; 20:17; 24:3). Hence, in terms of Jesus' own location in the narrative, "in secret" (ἐν τῷ κρύπτῳ) is not radically different from "in the house" (εἰς τὴν οἰκίαν) or "apart" (κατ᾽ ἰδίαν). Furthermore, in terms of opposed spatial locations, the narrative speaks of "their synagogues" (4:23; 9:35; 10:17; 12:9; 13:54) and "your synagogues" (23:34), expressions which have suggested to many commentators a spatial separation of Jesus' disciples from the traditional loci of Judean piety (Saldarini 1994:66–67). Moreover, according to Jesus' parables and discourses, the best and only place to be is "inside" some building: how shameful it is to be "thrown out of" a banquet or wedding feast (8:12, 31; 21:12, 39; 22:13; 25:10). Several things are clear from these data: (1) on many occasions Jesus himself is not in public, but in private; (2) his disciples draw around him, thus withdrawing from the public and leaving the crowds; and (3) disciples indeed gather, but not in traditional public places.

Moreover, when Jesus commands his disciples to perform acts of piety "in secret," we should not envision a modern house of many rooms where an individual might find personal privacy. Nor should we allow ourselves to impose our Western notions of privacy on the ancient world. Modern individualist personalities demand radical privacy, which is even protected by the penumbra of First-Amendment rights according to the U.S. Constitution. Ancient persons, however, were strongly group oriented, especially in regard to their families, and rarely did anything "alone." Hence, when Jesus says in regard to prayer that a male disciple should "go into his 'room' and shut the door," he envisions a peasant's house of only several small rooms, one of which is the family "storeroom" (ταμεῖον). The "room" of which Jesus speaks does not refer to the family living room, the den, or the man's bedroom. Rather, it is a "storeroom," the place where grain and perhaps tools were stored (Philo, *Every Good Man Is Free* 86; Krauss 1966:44). It stands to reason that this room would not front the alley, but would be as "inner" or "secret" as possible, to protect it from thieves who break through walls (6:19–20). Thus it has the connotation of a hiding place (Josephus, *Ant.* 8.410) where treasure may be securely stored (18.312). In Jesus' discourse on the Mount of Olives, he cautions his disciples to be on guard if anyone says, "Behold, he is in the inner rooms/storerooms" (ταμείοις, Matt. 24:26). Thus the extremely small size of peasant houses in antiquity, the cultural appreciation of collectivist persons generally gathered in groups, and the precise historical nature of the "storeroom" to which Jesus directs his disciples further suggest that "in secret" points us in the direction of the private world of the household. The direction is homeward and the orientation is to a social group different from that of the synagogue. Hence, Betz's remark is far off the cultural and social mark on this point: "Hidden from the crowds, even from other family members, the prayer can become what it is supposed to be, communion between the individual and the transcendent God" (1995:362). It is simply anachronistic and ethnocentric to ignore the cultural meaning of public and private in regard to a gender-divided world and to impose modern notions of individualistic personality on ancient group-oriented persons (Malina and Neyrey 1996:153–201).

2.5 Conclusions: The Cost of Vacating the Playing Field.

What, then, is Jesus telling his disciples to do? What are the probable results of this? In essence, the disciples must separate themselves from "their" synagogues; they may not join other observant Judeans in publicly practicing almsgiving, prayer, and fasting. But inasmuch as these symbolic actions create and reinforce group identity and loyalty, refusal to join one's neighbors would be interpreted as rejection of group identity, loyalty, and the code of gender expectations. The disciple's spatial and social separation flaunts public opinion (in itself a shameful act) and risks incurring hostility and shame for *not* fulfilling those expectations. As a result, he will be looked upon with suspicion and hostility; his reputation will be in jeopardy; and honor will be lost for nonparticipation (see Malina 1986:190–203). Jesus' male disciples, then, will lose face before their neighbors as well as consequent opportunities for honorable interaction such as public feasts, marriages, and the like. This is a costly teaching indeed.

In regard to the value of honor, several things should be noted. First, Jesus contrasts grants of honor from neighbors ("praised by men," Matt. 6:2) with grants from God ("your heavenly Father will reward you," 6:4, 6, 18; see John 12:43). As always, people require some acknowledgment of their worth. Second, even in his rhetoric, Jesus himself plays the honor game, challenging others and claiming honor himself. He does not attack the honor system in itself; in fact he operates out of it by challenging other versions of it and by ranking one grant of honor over another. Far from dismantling the system, he redirects how honor is bestowed and withdrawn. Third, Jesus invites disciples to join his honorable world, where the opinions of neighbors do not count for much and where their expectations do not control one's behavior. And so he replaces the cultural expectations of the local code with his own expectations. Fourth, Jesus' subversive commands would not be imaginable to disciples unless an alternate structure for worth, reputation, and respect were put in place, namely, honor from Jesus and reward from one's heavenly Father. Let us not exclude by Matthew's time the very "church" which had formed and preserved Jesus' words: it too served as a court of public opinion. Jesus, then, essentially confirms the value of honor and its social dynamics, but redefines how the basic game is to be played, namely, with grants of honor from himself and God. He does not abolish the game, but rather commands his disciples to vacate the traditional playing field. Thus his commands have genuine, severe social implications, which can be appreciated only when interpreted in terms of the dominant cultural values of his world.

3.0 Honor and the Rest of the Sermon on the Mount

Do the cultural values of honor and shame play any role in the way we read the rest of the Sermon on the Mount? Are they part of the content of Jesus' speech? Time does not allow us to treat the rest of the Sermon in the same detail as we have Matt. 5:3–12, 21–48, and 6:1–18, but we hope that the following rapid reading of other passages from the Sermon may surface aspects of honor and shame and point to their importance in the overall communication by Jesus.

3.1 Salt of the Earth and Light of the World. Immediately after Jesus honors those shamed for his sake (5:3–12), he ascribes honor to his disciples by means of several comparisons. They are "salt of the earth" and "light of the world" (5:13–15). As we shall see below in regard to 7:13–14, one of the chief means of praise is to single out someone as "the only one or the first or one of a few or one who most has done something" (Aristotle, *Rhet.* 1.9.38). Those who are salt "of the earth" and light "of the world" are singled out as unique; and since salt and light are highly valued commodities, those declared to be "salt of the earth . . . light of the world" are thus acknowledged as having great worth. Moreover, Jesus indicates that the disciple who receives this praise both accepts and lives up to Jesus' expectations, that is, "your good works," which are the basis for all honor. Alternately, he describes a situation of "shame," which is to lose one's former status and to be "thrown out" and trampled under foot. Whatever is under the feet of others is of no worth. Third, the salt is shamed because it has become "foolish" (μωρανθῇ) which is rendered in English as "lost its taste." But we recall that this is the same Greek term which constituted the great insult in 5:22, "Fool!" (Μωρέ; cf. 7:26), which now appears in the verbal form here. If someone or something becomes foolish and shameful in Jesus' eyes, then it has no place with him. The foolish is thereby ostracized by him, which, according to 5:11, represents a severe form of dishonor. Hence, Jesus is capable of awarding and denying worth and honor, just like the rest of the people in his cultural world. Finally, contrary to what he commanded about appearing in public in 6:1–18, Jesus here demands a display of some excellence and thus a public claim to honor on the part of his disciples. Their good deeds *should* be seen, because they are a claim for the honor of the Patron-God of both Jesus and his disciples. Thus God will be honored when the disciples are honored—just as when messengers are received, the one who sent them is likewise received (10:40). Notions of honor and shame, then, greatly inform our reading of 5:13–15.

3.2 Honor and One's "Treasure." In regard to the "treasure" in Matt. 6:19–21, this term refers to what is commonly held to be valuable. And so the very labeling of anything as "treasure" appeals to a group-formed conscience and thus to notions of value and honor. We must be dealing with a hyperbolic statement here, for the peasant disciples of Jesus could hardly be said to have "treasure," although they had possessions that signaled their social importance to their neighbors (e.g., dowries, lands, the wherewithal for a wedding feast). We recall that people generally signal their worth by conspicuous consumption and display. Our ancient informant, Aristotle, commented in regard to the grounds for praise that "wealth" consists in the use of possessions and not the mere having of them (*Rhet.* 1.5.7). This remark of Jesus, then, must be seen in light of the previous behavior of disciples, who forsook "treasure" to follow Jesus (Matt. 4:20, 22), and in anticipation of the failure of a rich young man to relocate "treasure" from material goods to discipleship with Jesus (19:16–22). He was promised that for spurning goods of earthly honor he would receive "treasure in heaven," which in the context must include the praise of God (19:21). Thus even the term "treasure" includes notions of honor and praise.

The rhetorical form of Jesus' remark is likewise significant. Two treasures are compared, one of which is praised and the other blamed. Comparison is both a topic within the genre of encomium and an independent genre in the rhetorical handbooks (the *progymnasmata*). Evidently Jesus values one over the other and attempts to socialize his disciples to the same code. The final comment in 6:19–21 points to the world of value: "Where your treasure is, there will your heart be also." The court of public opinion, which normally instructs the ancients in what is valuable and holds people accountable to its standards, is being replaced by another conscience, namely, the teachings of Jesus.

3.3 Evil Eye and Envy. In 6:22–23, the focus is on the eye of the disciple. John Elliott has argued that we should view the contrast between the "integral" and the "wicked" eye in terms of prevailing beliefs in antiquity about the Evil Eye (1994:65–68; see also 1992:52–65). His study cites innumerable parallel passages from Judean, Greek, and Roman literature about this phenomenon, among which one illustrates in particular the aggressive or challenging nature of the Evil Eye. He cites Pliny's report of what others have said about African peoples and their Evil Eye traits:

> [Isogonus and Nymphodorus] report that there are families in the same part of Africa that wield the Evil Eye, whose praises cause meadows to dry up, trees to wither and infants to perish. Isogonus adds that there are people of the same kind among the Triballi and the Illyrians, who also injure by the evil eye and who kill those at whom they stare for a longer time, especially with furious eyes and that their evil eye is most felt by adults. (*Natural History* 5.2.16–17, cited in Elliott 1994: 56–57)

Elliott's insistence that we interpret Matt. 6:22–23 in terms of the Evil Eye tradition has direct bearing on the value of honor. The logic goes as follows: belief in the Evil Eye is intrinsically related to envy, and envy is a form of challenge to the worth, wealth, reputation, and honor of another. Given a world where all goods, especially reputation and honor, are perceived to exist in limited supply, the increase by another person invariably means a decrease for oneself. Hence envy arises, which takes the form of the Evil Eye. It is intended to harm or diminish the success of the person thought to be increasing in value. In one sense, Evil Eye aggression can be seen as another form of honor challenge. Jesus warns that such envy, i.e., the pursuit of honor that harms another, is simply wrong, or worse, shameful.

3.4 Serving Two Masters: Shameful Behavior. In regard to the statement about two masters in Matt. 6:24, no male can have such divided loyalty and still be honorable. He will become a hypocrite and a liar to one of them, which is shameful. "Loyalty," moreover, has to do with virtue; and virtue is the grounds of praise (Aristotle, *Rhet.* 1.9.3–4); but where virtue is lacking, there cannot be praise, but only blame. Faithful service to a master generally brings the reward of honor: "Well done, good and faithful servant . . . " (25:21, 23), as well as material rewards (19:29). The ancient world, moreover, was fundamentally structured around social relationships with either one's family or friends, since a man is known by the company he keeps, whether the friends he has or the patrons or clients to whom he relates. Preferring "mammon" to God indicates a process of evaluation, that is, of giving and denying worth; honor and shame are at stake. How shameful, then, for someone to prefer "mammon" to God, a judgment that effectively disvalues and thus dishonors God. Such a person, moreover, will surely be lacking in "justice," which prescribes one's duties to God. Honor is lost all around.

3.5 Shame for Judging and Blaming. It takes little imagination to interpret "judging" in Matt. 7:1–5 as an aggressive, challenging action. Earlier in the Sermon, Jesus had proscribed all honor challenges to his disciples, either physical and verbal assault or sexual aggression. The game of judgment and public criticism of another belongs in that group of games forbidden the disciples. Jesus here condemns aggressive and challenging speech, which in the public forum of ancient social relations was inevitably an honor slight. "Not judging" seems to be quite different from the scenario of rebuking a brother in Matt. 18:15. There the person addressed is the victim of aggression ("If your brother sins against you . . . "), and the rebuke takes place between the two of them alone. No such delicacy is envisioned in 7:1–5, where "judging" has the connotation of reproach, fault finding, criticizing, and thus shaming. It is presumably done in public, the normal place for such confrontation. Curiously, Jesus describes people looking eye-to-eye to find specks or logs; and "eyes" are the locus of honor and shame, inasmuch as all worthwhile behavior was done in public for all to see and all insults must occur before the eyes of the person challenged. Finding fault in the eyes of another would seem to be the opposite of finding favor in their eyes; thus "eyes" are the locus of both praise and blame. And judging others is a very challenging action.

3.6 Elitism and Honor. Aristotle considers valuable and worthy of praise the person who is the first to do something or one of a very few who act in a certain way. Most worthy is the person who is the only one ever to have done such and such (*Rhet.* 1.9.38). We recognize this aspect of honor readily in the liturgical prayer in which Christians proclaim: "You alone are the Holy One! You alone are the Lord! You alone are the Most High, Jesus Christ!" Generally, the New Testament honors God in particular by acclaiming that God "alone" knows secrets (Matt. 24:36), or that God "alone" is wise (Rom. 16:27) or holy (Rev. 15:4), or that God "alone" is Deity (1 Tim. 1:17; John 17:3) and sovereign (1 Tim. 6:15). Honor, therefore, comes to the person who is singular in status or behavior according to what is considered excellent and honorable.

In Matt. 7:13–14, only a few disciples enter through the narrow gate, in contrast to the many who travel the easy, wide way. Just such a comparison, which we have noted as part of the rhetoric of praise, both bestows worth on what is singular and denies it to what is common. Although singularity and uniqueness count only in regard to things that all value, such as military and athletic prowess, being egregious, however, would mean deviance from common norms and behavior, and thus bring shamefulness. But it is on just this point that Jesus celebrates his "deviant" disciples for being the elite few. They are the ones who do *not* play the typical honor game of challenge and riposte; they do *not* frequent the public space to perform their acts of piety to gain the respect of their neighbors. These seemingly shameful disciples, however, become by grant of respect from Jesus the new elite, the few, the unique, the honorable ones. Shameful behavior in the eyes of their neighbors becomes honorable in Jesus' eyes.

3.7. The Shame of Crying, "Lord, Lord." In Matt. 7:21–23, the master inside the house shames a client with a terrible reproach: "I do not know you." Honor and shame function in every aspect of this story; in fact, "shame" is the rhetorical point made here. Some male has attempted to honor his patron by publicly acclaiming him "Lord, Lord!" which ought to merit the patron's respect. This man even claims to have eaten and drunk with this lord at his table, which are marks of singular respect and worth. He acted as agent for his patron, performing public actions "in your name" that should have brought praise to the patron: "Did we not prophesy in your name, and cast out demons in your name, and do many mighty works in your name?" (7:22). As we saw earlier, the "name" of someone is the public manifestation of his worth, such that "proclaiming the name of so-and-so" honors him, but "taking [his] name in vain" shames him. The lord, however, does not acknowledge these claims to honor from his client (Malina and Rohrbaugh 1992:69). Claims to honor that are intentionally *not* acknowledged become vain and foolish claims, which make the claimant liable to shame. Here the patron shames his client by saying "I do not know you!" and by dismissing him from his sight.

When the patron says "I do not know you," he does not lack accurate knowledge, but rather withholds a grant of respect. He acts in the same way the bridegroom did who shamed negligent maidservants who failed to prepare adequately for his royal wedding feast. He shut the door in their face and withheld recognition of them as persons worthy of his presence: "Amen, amen, I do not know you" (Matt. 25:12). In one of the pastoral epistles, God is said to honor certain people by "knowing" or "acknowledging" them: "The Lord knows those who are his" (2 Tim. 2:19). Long ago Bultmann argued that "knowing" not only has the sense of having information about some one or thing, but also public recognition of someone (1964:704–5; see Picirelli 1975; Neyrey 1993d:149). In this regard, one of the *Odes of Solomon* states: "I do not turn away my face from them that are mine, for I know them" (8:14). Thus God's "knowing" or "*not* knowing" someone refers to God's praise or blame of them. This honorable acknowledgment is formally identical with the later remark of Jesus whereby he would "know" those who "knew" him, but shame those who shamed him: "So everyone who acknowledges (ὁμολογήσει) me before men, I will acknowledge (ὁμολογήσω) before my Father in heaven; but whoever denies (ἀρνήσηται) me before men, I will also deny (ἀρνήσομαι) before my Father who is in heaven" (Matt. 10:32–33).

We note, moreover, the element in the story about the failure of the client to "do the will of my Father who is in heaven" (7:21). The client demonstrates verbal loyalty to his patron by acclaiming him publicly as "Lord, Lord." But he does not honor him by doing his will. In this he resembles the two sons of the father who were asked to work in the family vineyard. Both said one thing publicly, but did another privately; both equivocated on their honoring of the father. Equivocation was not uncommon in the ancient world (Neyrey 1993b:59–63), nor necessarily a shameful thing. Shame occurred when this discrepancy was made public. Hence, the patron exposes the disloyalty of his client, and compounds the embarrassment by disowning him and dismissing him from his presence. He will never again be the "apple of his eye."

3.8 Ultimate Praise, Ultimate Blame.   The conclusion to the Sermon on the Mount praises some and blames others (7:24–27). Two characters are contrasted, which reflects the rhetorical form of "comparison," part of the genre of the encomium. Moreover, the two characters resemble the typical honorable and shameful persons found in wisdom literature: the "wise" man (φρόνιμος) and the "fool" (μωρός) (see Matthews and Benjamin 1991). We have twice seen how the term "fool" is used to shame someone (5:22) or something (5:13).

The criteria for assigning praise and blame is also a stock element in the ancient world of honor and shame, namely, the hearing and acceptance of the group's code of expectations. Those who know (i.e., "listen to") and act in accordance with what they have heard are generally evaluated favorably by their peers. In this case, those who listen to the words of Jesus and put his code of behavior into practice are praised, whereas those who listen only and do not act according to the code of Jesus are shamed. They prove to be foolish, like a man who built his family's house on sand. For them there is only disaster and shame.

By saving this comparison for the very end of the Sermon, Jesus underscores the worth of his remarks. Acceptance of the speech of one "who taught them as one who had authority" brings success, which is always grounds for praise; rejection, however, leads to disaster, "and great was the fall of it." Thus Jesus provides a sanction for compliance or rejection. In this he also praises those who act by his code, but shames those who reject it.

In short, then, our survey of other parts of the Sermon indicates that honor and shame also form part of the narrative rhetoric by providing evidence of a new code of noble behavior expected of disciples. Whether the focus be on Jesus' rhetoric of praise and blame (Matt. 6:22–23; 7:13–14, 24–27), on the choreography of the honor game (6:22–23; 7:1–5, 21–23), or on the new sources of expected behavior and grants of honor and shame (6:19–21, 24; 7:13–14), the remainder of the Sermon warrants closer analysis in terms of the dominant cultural value of Jesus and Matthew.

4.0 Summary

In this part of the book, we have attempted to read the major portions of the Sermon on the Mount in the light of honor and shame. We saw that in Matt. 5:3–12, Jesus praises or honors his disciples who have been shamed for following him. Discipleship often meant cross-generational conflict within families, with the result that some disciples of Jesus were shamed by their parents, families, and neighbors (5:11–12), with consequent loss of wealth and family support, which loss meant immediate and catastrophic loss of respect in the village. "How honorable" are disciples who have been "shamed" for following Jesus. In 5:21–48, Jesus enunciates a pattern of discipleship in which male disciples would have to cease totally from the customary ways of seeing honor in their villages. They are forbidden to make any honor claims, challenge others, or defend themselves when challenged. They may not play the game. In 6:1–18, Jesus tells the disciples to vacate the very playing field. They must withdraw from "public" or male space and perform their acts of piety within the household, not in the public forum. Thus they are to seek the approval of their heavenly Parent, not that of their neighbors.

4.1 The Game of Honor: New Rules and a New Playing Field. Inasmuch as honor comes to people who live up to the social and cultural expectations of their neighbors, Jesus appears to be replacing one set of expectations with another. The ways of the village do not necessarily win an award of honor from Jesus. On the contrary, adhering to those ways may well inhibit the disciple from ever joining Jesus in the first place. By reconstituting social expectations, Jesus socializes would-be disciples to a new set of expectations about what is honorable and shameful. The functional payoff of this seems obvious, namely, loosening family and village pressures for conformity, with the possibility of finding respect and worth apart from them. The social and cultural dimensions of the Sermon on the Mount should not be ignored.

Matthew portrays Jesus, not as destroying the traditional honor game, but rather as reforming it in his own interests. Worth, respect, and praise remain the aim of disciples; and Jesus himself generously makes grants of these. But he challenges the conventional definitions of honor, the typical ways of achieving it, and the obligatory public forum for gaining it. Indeed, Jesus "honors" those who were "shamed." He insists that "reward" awaits his disciples, namely, praise from their heavenly Parent. But the conventional ways of achieving honor (physical, verbal, and sexual aggression) are forbidden them. The expected defense of one's honor when challenged is proscribed for the disciples. The public forum for seeing and being seen is denied them. New rules, new umpires, and a new playing field are envisioned for the game of honor.

4.2 The Fate of Those Who Follow Jesus. What would be the social fate of a disciple who followed Jesus? Some parts of the Sermon envision the disciple experiencing a terrible loss of honor for following him. Matthew 5:11 and supporting materials indicate that some disciples, at least, were liable to banning and shunning by their families, which would mean both complete loss of respect in the eyes of their neighbors and immediate loss of status through loss of wealth. Not all disciples faced such formidable control mechanisms as the withholding of honor by parents and kin, but those who did so suffered genuine shame with serious social consequences. Moreover, all disciples who follow Jesus may not play the typical male games of gaining and maintaining honor. It is one thing to forgo aggressive behavior to gain more honor; but it is quite a serious matter to abandon ripostes to honor challenges. The former would fix a disciple at a certain level in the eyes of his neighbors, but the latter would mean a serious loss of honor. Finally, withdrawal from public acts of piety will surely result in hostility and shame from one's neighbors. The bottom line is that Jesus' disciples, because they cannot play the honor game as usual, will lose respect, value, and worth in the eyes of kin and neighbors. They will lose what is considered vital to meaningful life among the ancients, namely, respect. We cannot emphasize enough how bitter and difficult an experience this would be. Following Jesus can lead to a wretched fate according to worldly standards.

Bibliography

Aarde, Andries G. van
1992   The *Evangelium Infantium*, the Abandonment of Children, and the In-
         fancy Narrative in Matthew 1 and 2 from a Social Scientific Perspective.
         Pp. 435–53 in *Society of Biblical Literature Seminar Papers 1992*.

Abba, Raymond
1962   Name. *IDB* 3:501–8.

Abel, E. L.
1973   The Genealogies of O XPICTOC. *NTS* 20:203–10.

Adkins, Arthur W. H.
1960a   "Honour" and "Punishment" in the Homeric Poems. *Classical Studies*
         7:23–32.

1960b   *Merit and Responsibility: A Study in Greek Values*. Chicago: University
         of Chicago Press (Midway Reprint).

1969   Threatening, Abusing and Feeling Angry in the Homeric Poems. *JHS*
         89:7–21.

1971   Homeric Values and Homeric Society. *JHS* 91:1–14.

1972a   Homeric Gods and the Values of Homeric Society. *JHS* 92:1–19.

1972b   *Moral Values and Political Behaviour in Ancient Greece from Homer to
         the End of the Fifth Century*. New York: W. W. Norton & Co.

1976   Polupragmosune and "Minding One's Own Business": A Study in
         Greek Social and Political Values. *CP* 71:301–27.

1982   Values, Goals, and Emotions in the Iliad. *CP* 77:292–326.

1985   Cosmogony and Order in Ancient Greece. Pp. 39–66 in Robin W. Lovin
         and Frank E. Reynolds, eds., *Cosmogony and Ethical Order: New Stud-
         ies in Comparative Ethics*. Chicago: University of Chicago Press.

Al-Khayyat, Sana.
1990   *Honour and Shame: Women in Modern Iraq*. London: Saqi Books, 1990.

Andersen, Francis I.
1966   The Socio-Juridical Background of the Naboth Incident. *JBL* 85:46–57.

Anderson, Janice Carol
1982   Matthew: Gender and Reading. *Semeia* 28:3–27.

Antoun, R.
1968   On the Modesty of Women in Arab Villages. *American Anthropologist* 70:671–97.

Arnal, William E.
1977   Gendered Couplets in Q and Legal Formulations: From Rhetoric to Social History. *JBL* 116:75–94.

Attridge, Harold W.
1989   *The Epistle to the Hebrews*. Philadelphia: Fortress Press.

Aune, David E.
1981   The Problem of the Genre of the Gospels: A Critique of C. H. Talbert's *What Is a Gospel?* Pp. 6–90 in T. R. France and D. Wenham, eds., *Gospel Perspectives II: Studies of History and Tradition in the Four Gospels*. Sheffield: JSOT Press.

1987a   The Gospels as Hellenistic Biography. *Mosaic* 20:1–10.

1987b   *The New Testament and Its Literary Environment*. Philadelphia: Westminster Press.

1988   *Greco-Roman Literature and the New Testament*. SBLSBS 21. Atlanta: Scholars Press.

Avery-Peck, Alan J.
1994   Rhetorical Argumentation in Early Rabbinic Pronouncement Stories. *Semeia* 64:49–71.

Balch, David L.
1982   Two Apologetic Encomia: Dionysius on Rome and Josephus on the Jews. *JSJ* 13:102–22.

1991   *Social History of the Matthean Community: Cross-Disciplinary Approaches*. Minneapolis: Fortress Press.

Baldwin, Charles S.
1924   *Ancient Rhetoric and Poetic*. New York: Macmillan Co.

1928   *Medieval Rhetoric and Poetic*. New York: Macmillan Co.

Balentine, Samuel E.
1993   *Prayer in the Hebrew Bible: The Drama of Divine-Human Dialogue*. Minneapolis: Fortress Press.

Bammel, Ernst
1970   *The Trial of Jesus*. SBT, 2d series 13. London: SCM Press.

1984   The Trial before Pilate. Pp. 415–51 in Ernst Bammel and C. F. D.
        Moule, eds., *Jesus and the Politics of His Day*. Cambridge: Cambridge
        University Press.

Barr, David L., and Judith L. Wentling
1984   The Conventions of Classical Biography and the Genre of Luke-Acts.
        Pp. 63–88 in Charles H. Talbert, ed., *Luke-Acts: New Perspectives from
        the Society of Biblical Literature Seminar*. New York: Crossroad.

Barrett, Charles K.
1972   I Am Not Ashamed of the Gospel. Pp. 116–43 in his *New Testament Es-
        says*. London: SPCK.

Bartchy, S. Scott
1992   Slavery (Greco-Roman). *ABD* 6:65–73.

Barton, Stephen C.
1994   *Discipleship and Family Ties in Mark and Matthew*. SNTSMS 80. Cam-
        bridge: Cambridge University Press.

Batey, Richard A.
1984a   Is Not This the Carpenter? *NTS* 30:249–58.

1984b   Jesus and the Theatre. *NTS* 30:563–74.

Bauckham, Richard
1988   Jesus' Demonstration in the Temple. Pp. 72–89 in Barnabas Lindars,
        ed., *Law and Religion: Essays on the Place of the Law in Israel and
        Early Christianity*. Cambridge: James Clarke & Co.

1990   *Jude and the Relatives of Jesus in the Early Church*. Edinburgh: T. & T.
        Clark.

Bauer, David R.
1990   The Literary Function of the Genealogy in Matthew's Gospel. *SBLSP*
        1990:451–68.

Bauernfeind, Otto
1964   ἀρετή. *TDNT* 1:457–61.

Bechtel, Lyn M.
1991   Shame as a Sanction of Social Control in Biblical Israel: Judicial, Po-
        litical, and Social Shaming. *JSOT* 49:47–76.

1994   The Perception of Shame within the Divine-Human Relationship in
        Biblical Israel. Pp. 79–92 in Lewis M. Hopfe, ed., *Uncovering Ancient
        Stones*. Winona Lake, Ind.: Eisenbrauns.

Belkin, Samuel
1936   Dissolution of Vows and the Problem of Anti-Social Oaths in the Gospels and Contemporary Jewish Literature. *JBL* 55:227–34.

Bellefontaine, Elizabeth
1979   Deuteronomy 21:18–21; Reviewing the Case of the Rebellious Son. *JSOT* 13:13–31.

Benveniste, Emile
1969   *Indo-European Language and Society*. Coral Gables, Fla.: University of Miami Press.

Berger, Klaus
1974   "Amen, I Say unto You" in the Sayings of Jesus and in Early Christian Literature. *HTR* 67:177–82.

Bertram, Georg
1967   μωρός. *TDNT* 4:832–47.

Betz, Hans D.
1984   *Essays on the Sermon on the Mount*. Philadelphia: Fortress Press.
1995   *The Sermon on the Mount*. Minneapolis: Fortress Press.

Black, Matthew
1990   The Doxology to the *Pater Noster* with a Note on Matthew 6:13b. Pp. 327–38 in Philip Davies and Richard White, eds., *A Tribute to Geza Vermes*. Sheffield: JSOT Press.

Blank, Josef
1959   Die Verhandlung vor Pilatus Jo 18:28–19:16 im Lichte johanneischer Theologie. *BZ* 3:60–81.

Blinzler, Josef
1959   *The Trial of Jesus*. Westminster, Md.: Newman Press.

Blok, Anton
1969   Variations in Patronage. *Sociologische Gids* 16:365–78.

1981   Rams and Billy-Goats: A Key to the Mediterranean Code of Honor. *Man* 16:427–40. Reprinted in Eric Wolf, ed., *Religion, Power and Protest in Local Communities: The Northern Shore of the Mediterranean*, pp. 51–70. Berlin: Mouton Publishers, 1984.

Bloomer, W. Martin
1992   *Valerius Maximus and the Rhetoric of the New Nobility*. Chapel Hill, N.C.: University of North Carolina Press.

Blundell, Mary
1989   *Helping Friends and Harming Enemies: A Study in Sophocles and Greek Ethics*. Cambridge: Cambridge University Press.

Boissevan, Jeremy
1974   *Friends of Friends: Networks, Manipulators and Coalitions.* New York: St. Martin's Press.

Bonfante, Larissa
1988   Clothing and Adornment. Pp. 1385–1413 in Michael Grant and Rachel Kitzinger, eds., *Civilization of the Ancient Mediterranean: Greece and Rome*, vol. 3. New York: Charles Scribner's Sons.

1989   Nudity as a Costume in Classical Art. *American Journal of Archaeology* 93:543–70.

Bonner, Stanley F.
1977   *Education in Ancient Rome: From the Elder Cato to the Younger Pliny.* Berkeley, Calif.: University of California Press.

Borg, Marcus
1984   *Conflict, Holiness and Politics in the Teaching of Jesus.* Lewiston, N.Y.: Edwin Mellen Press.

Bourdieu, Pierre
1966   The Sentiment of Honour in Kabyle Society. Pp. 191–241 in J. G. Péristiany, ed., *Honour and Shame: The Values of Mediterranean Society.* Chicago: University of Chicago Press.

1977   From the "Rules" of Honour to the Sense of Honour. Pp. 10–15 in his *Outline of a Theory of Practice.* Cambridge: Cambridge University Press.

Bowen, N. R.
1991   Damage and Healing—Shame and Honor in the Old Testament. *Koinonia* 3:29–36.

Bowman, J.
1959   Phylacteries. *SE* 1 (= TU 73): 523–38.

Bradley, D. G.
1953   The *Topos* as a Form in Pauline Paraenesis. *JBL* 72:238–46.

Brandes, Stanley
1980   *Metaphors of Masculinity: Sex and Status in Andalusian Folklore.* Philadelphia: University of Pennsylvania Press.

Brandon, S. G. E.
1968   *The Trial of Jesus of Nazareth.* London: Paladin Books.

Braude, William
1968   *Pesikta Rabbati: Discourses for Feasts, Fasts and Special Sabbaths.* New Haven, Conn.: Yale University Press.

Bridenthral, Renate, and Claudia Koonz, eds.
1977   *Becoming Visible: Women in European History*. Boston: Houghton Mifflin Co.

Brown, Raymond E.
1978   *Mary in the New Testament*. Philadelphia: Fortress Press.

1993   *The Birth of the Messiah*. Rev. ed. New York: Doubleday & Co.

1994   *The Death of the Messiah*. New York: Doubleday & Co.

Brunt, P. A.
1965   "Amicitia" in the Late Roman Republic. *Proceedings of the Cambridge Philological Society* 191:1–20.

Buchanan, George W.
1964   Jesus and the Upper Class. *NovT* 7:195–209.

1995   The Age of Jesus. *NTS* 41:297.

Büchsel, Friedrich
1964   ἀλλάσσω. *TDNT* 1:251–59.

Bultmann, Rudolf
1964   γινώσκω. *TDNT* 1:689–714.

Burgess, Theodore C.
1902   Epideictic Rhetoric. *Studies in Classical Philology* 3:89–261.

Burke, Peter
1980   *Sociology and History*. London: George Allen & Unwin.

1993   *History and Social Theory*. Ithaca, N.Y.: Cornell University Press.

Burridge, Richard A.
1992   *What Are the Gospels? A Comparison with Graeco-Roman Biography*. SNTSMS 70. Cambridge: Cambridge University Press.

Burton, Laurel Arthur
1988   Original Sin or Original Shame. *QR* 8:31–41.

Butts, James R.
1986   The Progymnasmata of Theon: A New Text with Translation and Commentary. Dissertation, Claremont Graduate School.

Cadbury, H. J.
1937   Rebuttal: A Submerged Motif in the Gospels. Pp. 99–108 in R. P. Casey and Silva Lake, eds., *Quantulacumque*. London: Christophers.

Cairns, Douglas L.
1993   *Aidôs: The Psychology and Ethics of Honour and Shame in Ancient Greek Literature*. Oxford: Clarendon Press.

Cameron, Averil, and Amélie Kuhrt
1983   *Images of Women in Antiquity*. Detroit: Wayne State University Press.

Camery-Hoggatt, Jerry
1992   *Irony in Mark's Gospel: Text and Subtext*. Cambridge: Cambridge University Press.

Campbell, J. K.
1964   *Honour, Family and Patronage: A Study of Institutions and Moral Values in a Greek Mountain Community*. Oxford: Oxford University Press.

1966   Honour and the Devil. Pp. 139–70 in J. G. Péristiany, ed., *Honour and Shame: The Values of Mediterranean Society*. Chicago: University of Chicago Press.

Carney, Thomas F.
1975   *The Shape of the Past: Models and Antiquity*. Lawrence, Kans.: Coronado Press.

Carter, Warren
1994   *Households and Discipleship: A Study of Matthew 19–20*. JSOTSup 103. Sheffield: Sheffield Academic Press.

Case, Shirley J.
1927   *Jesus, A New Biography*. Chicago: University of Chicago Press.

Chadwick, Henry
1980   *Origen, Contra Celsum*. Cambridge: Cambridge University Press.

Charlesworth, James H.
1992   From Messianology to Christology: Problems and Prospects. Pp. 3–35 in his *The Messiah: Developments in Earliest Judaism and Christianity*. Minneapolis: Fortress Press.

Chilton, Bruce
1984   *The Kingdom of God in the Teaching of Jesus*. Philadelphia: Fortress Press.

Chow, John K.
1992   *Patronage and Power: A Study of Social Networks in Corinth*. JSOTSup 75. Sheffield: Sheffield Academic Press.

Chronis, H. L.
1982   The Torn Veil: Cultus and Christology in Mark 15:37–39. *JBL* 101:97–114.

Cohen, Boaz
1977   Letter and Spirit in Jewish and Roman Law. Pp. 138–64 in Henry A. Fischel, ed., *Essays in Greco-Roman and Related Talmudic Literature*. New York: KTAV.

Cohen, David
1989   Seclusion, Separation, and the Status of Women in Classical Athens. *GR*
            36:3–15.

1991   *Law, Sexuality, and Society: The Enforcement of Morals in Classical
            Athens.* Cambridge: Cambridge University Press.

1995   *Law, Violence, and Community in Classical Athens.* Cambridge: Cam-
            bridge University Press.

Cohen, Shaye J. D.
1979   *Josephus in Galilee and Rome.* Leiden: E. J. Brill.

Cohn-Sherbok, D. M.
1981   Jesus' Defense of the Resurrection of the Dead. *JSNT* 11:64–73.

Collins, Adela Yarbro
1994   From Noble Death to Crucified Messiah. *NTS* 40:481–503.

Collins, John J.
1995   *The Scepter and the Star: The Messiahs of the Dead Sea Scrolls and
            Other Ancient Literature.* New York: Doubleday & Co.

Collins, John N.
1990   *Diakonia: Re-interpreting the Ancient Sources.* Oxford: Oxford Uni-
            versity Press.

Cope, O. Lamar
1976   *Matthew: A Scribe Trained for the Kingdom of Heaven.* CBQMS 5.
            Washington, D.C.: Catholic Biblical Association of America.

Corley, Kathleen E.
1993   *Private Women, Public Meals: Social Conflict in the Synoptic Tradition.*
            Peabody, Mass.: Hendrickson.

Corrigan, Gregory M.
1986   Paul's Shame for the Gospel. *BTB* 16:23–27.

Cox, Patricia
1983   *Biography in Late Antiquity: A Quest for the Holy Man.* Berkeley,
            Calif.: University of California Press.

Crossan, John Dominic
1973   Mark and the Relatives of Jesus. *NovT* 15:81–113.

1991   *The Historical Jesus: The Life of a Mediterranean Jewish Peasant.* San
            Francisco: Harper.

Daley, Brian E.
1993   Position and Patronage in the Early Church: The Original Meaning of
            "Primacy of Honour" *JTS* 44:529–53.

D'Angelo, Mary Rose
1992a   Abba and "Father": Imperial Theology and the Jesus Traditions. *JBL* 111:611–30.

1992b   Theology in Mark and Q: Abba and "Father" in Context. *HTR* 85:149–74.

Danker, Frederick W.
1981   The Endangered Benefactor of Luke-Acts. *SBLSP* 1981:39–48.

1982   *Benefactor: Epigraphic Study of a Graeco-Roman and New Testament Semantic Field*. St. Louis: Clayton Publishing House.

1988   Bridging St. Paul and the Apostolic Fathers: A Study in Reciprocity. *CurTM* 15:84–94.

1992   Purple. *ABD* 4:557–60.

Daube, David
1959   A Prayer Pattern in Judaism. *SE* 1 (= TU 73): 539–45.

1973   *The New Testament and Rabbinic Judaism*. New York: Arno Press.

1982   Shame Culture in Luke. Pp. 354–72 in M. Hooker and S. Wilson, eds., *Paul and Paulinism*. London: SPCK.

Dautzenberg, G.
1981   Ist das Schwurverbot Mt 5:33–37; Jak 5:12 ein Beispiel für Torakritik Jesu? *BZ* 25:47–66.

Davies, W. D.
1966   *The Setting of the Sermon on the Mount*. Cambridge: Cambridge University Press.

Davies, W. D., and Dale Allison
1988   *The Gospel according to Saint Matthew*. Edinburgh: T. & T. Clark.

Davis, John
1973   *Land and Family in Pisticci*. London: Athlone Press.

1984   The Sexual Division of Labour in the Mediterranean. Pp. 17–50 in Eric Wolf, ed., *Religion, Power and Protest in Local Communities: The Northern Shore of the Mediterranean*. Berlin: Mouton, 1984.

Deissmann, A.
1909   *Bible Studies*. Rev. ed. Edinburgh: T. & T. Clark.

Delaney, Carol
1986   The Meaning of Paternity and the Virgin Birth Debate. *Man* 21:494–513.

1987   Seeds of Honor, Fields of Shame. Pp. 35–48 in David D. Gilmore, ed., *Honor and Shame and the Unity of the Mediterranean* (American Anthropological Association special publication no. 22). Washington, D.C.: American Anthropological Association.

1991   *The Seed and the Soil: Gender and Cosmology in Turkish Village Society*. Berkeley: University of California Press.

Delling, G.
1968   πλεονέκτης. *TDNT* 6:266–70.

1977   Die Bezeichnung "Söhne Gottes" in der jüdischen Literatur der hellenistisch-römischen Zeit. Pp. 18–28 in J. Jervell and W. Meeks, eds., *God's Christ and His People*. Oslo: Universitetsforlaget.

Derrett, J. Duncan M.
1971   The Parable of the Two Sons. *ST* 25:109–16.

1973   Relationship and Prestige. Pp. 38–45 in his *Jesus' Audience: The Social and Psychological Environment in Which He Worked*. New York: Seabury Press.

1977   The Zeal of the House and the Cleansing of the Temple. *DR* 95:79–94.

1982   The Merits of the Narrow Gate. *NTS* 15:20–29.

1983a   Binding and Loosing (Matt 16:19; 18:18; John 20:23). *JBL* 102:112–17.

1983b   Peace, Sandals and Shirts (Mark 6:6b–13 par.). *HeyJ* 24:253–65.

1985   Taking Up the Cross and Turning the Cheek. Pp. 61–78 in A. E. Harvey, ed., *Alternative Approaches to New Testament Study*. London: SPCK.

1986   A Camel through the Eye of a Needle. *NTS* 32:465–70.

1987   Birds of the Air and Lilies of the Field. *DR* 105:181–92.

1988   Christ and Reproof (Matthew 7:1–5/Luke 6:37–42). *NTS* 34:271–81.

deSilva, David Arthur
1995   *Despising Shame: Honor Discourse and Community Maintenance in the Epistle to the Hebrews*. SBLDS 152. Atlanta: Scholars Press.

1966a   Exchanging Favor for Wrath: Apostasy in Hebrews and Patron-Client Relationships. *JBL* 115:91–116.

1996b   The Wisdom of Ben Sira: Honor, Shame and the Maintenance of the Values of a Minority Culture. *CBQ* 58:433–55.

Detienne, Marcel, and Jean-Pierre Vernant
1991   *Cunning Intelligence in Greek Culture and Society*. Chicago: University of Chicago Press.

Dewey, Arthur J.
1985   A Matter of Honor: A Socio-Historical Analysis of 2 Corinthians 10. *HTR* 78:209–17.

Dewey, Joanna
1980   *Marcan Public Debate: Literary Technique, Concentric Structure, and Theology in Mark 2:1–3:6*. Chico, Calif.: Scholars Press.

Di Bella, Maria Pia
1992   Name, Blood, and Miracles: The Claims to Renown in Traditional Sicily. Pp. 151–66 in J. G. Péristiany and Julian Pitt-Rivers, eds., *Honour and Grace in Anthropology*. Cambridge: Cambridge University Press.

Dietzfelbinger, C.
1979   Die Antithesen der Bergpredigt im Verständnis des Matthäus. *ZNW* 70:1–15.

Dillon, Richard J.
1995   "As One Having Authority" (Mark 1:22): The Controversial Distinction of Jesus' Teaching. *CBQ* 57:92–113.

Dodds, E. R.
1951   From Shame-Culture to Guilt-Culture. Pp. 28–63 in his *The Greeks and the Irrational*. Berkeley, Calif.: University of California Press.

Donahue, John R.
1973   *Are You the Christ?* SBLDS 10. Missoula, Mont.: University of Montana Press.

1976   Temple, Trial, and Royal Christology (Mark 14:53–65). Pp. 61–79 in Werner H. Kelber, ed., *The Passion in Mark: Studies on Mark 14–16*. Philadelphia: Fortress Press.

1986   The "Parable" of the Sheep and the Goats: A Challenge to Christian Ethics. *TS* 17/1:3–31.

Donaldson, T. L.
1985   *Jesus on the Mountain: A Study in Matthean Theology*. JSNTSup 8. Sheffield: JSOT Press.

1991   The Mockers and the Son of God (Matthew 27:37–44): Two Characters in Matthew's Story of Jesus. *JSNT* 41:3–18.

Donlan, Walter
1969   A Note on Aristos as a Class Term. *Philologus* 113:268–70.

1973a   The Origin of Kalos Kagathos. *AJP* 94:365–74.

1973b   The Tradition of Anti-Aristocratic Thought in Early Greek Poetry. *Historia* 22:145–54.

1979   The Structure of Authority in the Iliad. *Arethusa* 12:51–70.

1980   *The Aristocratic Ideal in Ancient Greece*. Lawrence, Kans.: Coronado Press.

1982   Reciprocities in Homer. *CW* 75:137–75.

Döring, K.
1979   *Exemplum Socratis*. Wiesbaden: Steiner.

Douglas, Mary
1966   *Purity and Danger*. London: Routledge & Kegan Paul.

1977   *Rules and Meanings*. Harmondsworth: Penguin Books.

Dover, K. J.
1974   *Greek Popular Morality in the Time of Plato and Aristotle*. Berkeley,
        Calif.: University of California Press.

1978   *Greek Homosexuality*. London: Duckworth.

1983   The Portrayal of Moral Evaluation in Greek Poetry. *JHS* 103:35–48.

Downing, F. Gerald
1992   The Ambiguity of "The Pharisee and the Toll-Collector" (Luke 18:9–
        14) in the Greco-Roman World of Late Antiquity" *CBQ* 54:80–99.

Drees, Ludwig
1968   *Olympia: Gods, Artists and Athletes*. New York: Frederick A. Praeger.

Droge, Arthur, and James Tabor
1992   *A Noble Death: Suicide and Martyrdom among Christians and Jews in
        Antiquity*. San Francisco: Harper.

Dubish, Jill
1986   *Gender and Power in Rural Greece*. Princeton: Princeton University
        Press.

1995   *In a Different Place: Pilgrimage, Gender, and Politics in a Greek Island
        Shrine*. Princeton: Princeton University Press.

DuBoulay, Juliet
1974   *Portrait of a Greek Mountain Village*. Oxford: Clarendon Press.

1984   The Blood: Symbolic Relationships between Descent, Marriage, Incest
        Prohibitions and Spiritual Kinship in Greece. *Man* 19:533–56.

Duff, Paul Brooks
1988   Honor or Shame: The Language of Processions and Perception in 2 Cor.
        2:14–6:13; 7:2–4. Dissertation, University of Chicago.

Duke, Paul D.
1985   *Irony in the Fourth Gospel*. Atlanta: John Knox Press.

Duling, Dennis
1975   Solomon, Exorcism, and the Son of David. *HTR* 68:235–52.

1978   The Therapeutic Son of David. *NTS* 24:392–410.

1985a   Insights from Sociology for New Testament Christology: A Test Case.
        SBLSP 24:351–68.

1985b   The Eleazar Miracle and Solomon's Magical Wisdom in Flavius Jose-
        phus' *Antiquitates Judaicae* 8.42-48. *HTR* 78:1–25.

1987   Binding and Loosing: Matthew 16:18; Matthew 18:19; John 20:23. *Forum* 3/4:3–31.

1990   Against Oaths: Crossan Sayings Parallels 59 [Matt 5:33–37]. *Forum* 6/2:99–138.

1991   "[Do not swear . . .] by Jerusalem because it is the City of the Great King (Matt 5:35)." *JBL* 110:291–309.

1992   Matthew's Plurisignificant "Son of David" in Social Science Perspective: Kinship, Kingship, Magic and Miracle. *BTB* 22:99–116.

1993   Matthew and Marginality. *SBLSP* 1993:642–71.

1995   Matthean Brotherhood and Marginal Scribal Leadership. Pp. 159–82 in Philip Esler, ed., *Modelling Early Christianity: Social-Scientific Studies of the New Testament in Its Context*. London: Routledge.

Dumézil, Georges
1943   *Servius et la Fortune: Essai sur la fonction sociale de louange et de blâme sur les éléments indoeuropéens du cens romain*. Paris: Gallimard.

Dungan, David L., and David R. Cartlidge
1974   *Sourcebook of Texts for the Comparative Study of the Gospels*. Missoula, Mont.: Scholars Press.

Dupont, Florence
1989   *Daily Life in Ancient Rome*. Oxford: Blackwell.

Dupont, Jacques
1973   *Les Béatitudes*. Paris: J. Gabalda.

Eck, Ernest van
1995   *Galilee and Jerusalem in Mark's Story of Jesus: A Narratological and Social Scientific Reading*. Hervormde Teologiese Studies Supplementum 7. Pretoria: University of Pretoria Press.

Eddy, G. E. G.
1992   Transformed Values of Honor and Shame in Luke 18:1–14. *Proceedings of the Eastern Great Lakes and Midwest Biblical Society* 12:117–29.

Edelman, R.
1987   *The Psychology of Embarrassment*. New York: Wiley.

Eickelman, Dale
1989   *The Middle East: An Anthropological Approach*. Englewood Cliffs, N.J.: Prentice-Hall.

Eisenstadt, S. N., and L. Roniger
1984   *Patrons, Clients and Friends: Interpersonal Relations and the Structure of Trust in Society*. Cambridge: Cambridge University Press.

Elliott, John H.

1988 Patronage and Clientism in Early Christian Society. *Forum* 3/4:39–48.

1990 Paul, Galatians, and the Evil Eye. *CurTM* 17:262–73.

1991a Temple versus Household in Luke-Acts: A Contrast in Social Institutions. Pp. 211–40 in Jerome H. Neyrey, ed., *The Social World of Luke-Acts: Models for Interpretation*. Peabody, Mass.: Hendrickson.

1991b The Evil Eye in the First Testament: The Ecology and Culture of a Persuasive Belief. Pp. 147–59 in David Jobling, Peggy Day, and Gerald Sheppard, eds., *The Bible and the Politics of Exegesis: Essays in Honor of Norman K. Gottwald on His Sixty-fifth Birthday*. Cleveland: Pilgrim Press.

1992 Matthew 20:1–15: A Parable of Invidious Comparison and Evil Eye Accusation. *BI* 22:52–65.

1993 *What Is Social-Scientific Criticism?* Minneapolis: Fortress Press.

1994 The Evil Eye and the Sermon on the Mount. *BI* 2:51–84.

1995 Disgraced Yet Graced: The Gospel According to 1 Peter in the Key of Honor and Shame. *BTB* 25:166–78.

Elshtain, Jean Bethke

1981 *Public Man, Private Woman: Women in Social and Political Thought*. Princeton: Princeton University Press.

Epstein, Louis M.

1967 *Sex Laws and Customs in Judaism*. New York: KTAV.

Epstein, V.

1964 The Historicity of the Gospel Account of the Cleansing of the Temple. *ZNW* 55:42–58.

Esler, Philip F.

1987 *Community and Gospel in Luke-Acts: The Social and Political Motivations of Lucan Theology*. SNTSMS 57. Cambridge: Cambridge University Press.

1994 *The First Christians in Their Social Worlds: Social-Scientific Approaches to New Testament Interpretation*. London: Routledge.

1995 *Modelling Early Christianity: Social-Scientific Studies of the New Testament in Its Context*. London: Routledge.

Evans, Craig

1989 Jesus' Action in the Temple: Cleansing or Portent of Destruction? *CBQ* 51:237–70.

Fantham, Elaine, Helene Foley, Natalie Kampen, Sarah Pomeroy, and Alan
    Shapiro, eds.
1994   *Women in the Classical World: Image and Text*. Oxford: Oxford University Press.

Faraone, Christopher A.
1991   The Agonistic Context of Early Greek Binding Spells. Pp. 4–32 in C. A. Faraone and Dirk Obbink, eds., *Magica Hiera: Ancient Greek Magic and Religion*. Oxford: Oxford University Press.

Feldman, Louis
1976   Josephus as an Apologist to the Greco-Roman World: His Portrait of Solomon. Pp. 69–98 in Elisabeth Schüssler Fiorenza, ed., *Aspects of Religious Propaganda in Judaism and Early Christianity*. Notre Dame: University of Notre Dame Press.

1982   Josephus' Portrait of Saul. *HUCA* 53:45–99.

1984   Abraham the General in Josephus. Pp. 43–49 in Frederick Greenspahn, ed., *Nourished with Peace: Studies in Hellenistic Judaism in Memory of Samuel Sandmel*. Chico, Calif.: Scholars Press.

1987   Hellenizations in Josephus' *Jewish Antiquities*: The Portrait of Abraham. Pp. 133–53 in Louis Feldman and Gohei Hata, eds., *Josephus, Judaism and Christianity*. Detroit: Wayne State University Press.

1988   Josephus' Version of Samson. *JSJ* 19:171–214.

1989   Josephus' Portrait of Jacob. *JQR* 79:101–51.

1992a   Josephus' Portrait of David. *HUCA* 60:129–74.

1992b   Josephus' Portrait of Hezekiah. *JBL* 111:597–610.

1994   Josephus' Portrait of Jehoram, King of Israel. *NovT* 36:1–28.

Ferguson, John
1958   *Moral Values in the Ancient World*. London: Methuen & Co.

Fiensy, David A.
1991   *The Social History of Palestine in the Herodian Period: The Land Is Mine*. Lewiston, N.Y.: Edwin Mellen Press.

Finley, Moses I.
1973   *The Ancient Economy*. Berkeley, Calif.: University of California Press.

1977   *The World of Odysseus*. 2d ed. London: Chatto & Windus.

Finley, Moses I., and H. W. Pleket
1976   *The Olympic Games: The First Thousand Years*. New York: Viking Press.

Fischel, Henry
1973   *Rabbinic Literature and Greco-Roman Philosophy.* SPB 21. Leiden: E. J. Brill.

Fisher, Loren
1968   Can This Be the Son of David? Pp. 82–97 in F. T. Trotter, ed., *Jesus and the Historian.* Philadelphia: Westminster Press.

Fisher, N. R. E.
1976   *Hybris* and Dishonour, I. *GR* 23:177–93.

1979a   *Hybris* and Dishonour, II. *GR* 26:32–47.

1979b   *Hybris: A Study in the Values of Honour and Shame in Ancient Greece.* London: Aris & Phillips.

Fitzgerald, John T.
1988   *Cracks in an Earthen Vessel.* SBLDS 99. Atlanta: Scholars Press.

1996   *Friendship, Flattery, and Frankness of Speech: Studies on Friendship in the New Testament World.* Leiden: E. J. Brill.

Fitzmyer, Joseph A.
1981   *The Gospel according to Luke.* AB 28. Garden City, N.Y.: Doubleday & Co.

1989   Another Look at ΚΕΦΑΛΗ in 1 Corinthians 11.3. *NTS* 35:503–11.

Foley, Helene P., ed.
1981   *Reflections on Women in Antiquity.* New York: Gordon & Breach.

Fontenrose, Joseph
1968   The Hero as Athlete. *California Studies in Classical Antiquity* 1:73–104.

Forbes, Christopher
1986   Comparison, Self-Praise, and Irony: Paul's Boasting and the Conventions of Hellenistic Rhetoric. *NTS* 32:1–30.

Forbis, E. P.
1990   Women's Public Image in Italian Honorary Inscriptions. *AJP* 111:493–512.

Forkman, Göran
1972   *The Limits of the Religious Community.* Lund: C. W. K. Gleerup.

Foster, George M.
1965   Peasant Society and the Image of Limited Good. *American Anthropologist* 67:293–315.

1972   The Anatomy of Envy: A Study in Symbolic Behavior. *Current Anthropology* 13:165–86.

Freed, E. D.
1987   The Women in Matthew's Genealogy. *JSNT* 29:3–19.

Friedlander, Gerald
1969   *The Jewish Sources of the Sermon on the Mount.* New York: KTAV.

Friedrich, Paul
1977   Sanity and the Myth of Honor: The Problem of Achilles. *The Journal of Psychological Anthropology* 5:281–305.

Frier, Bruce
1982   Roman Life Expectancy: Ulpian's Evidence. *HSCPh* 86:213–51.

1983   Roman Life Expectancy: The Pannonian Evidence. *Phoenix* 37:328–44.

Frymer-Kensky, Tikva
1980   Tit for Tat: The Principle of Equal Retribution in Near Eastern and Biblical Law. *Biblical Archaeologist* 43:230–34.

Gadd, C. J.
1948   *Ideas of Divine Rule in the Ancient East.* London: Oxford University Press.

Garnsey, Peter
1970   *Social Status and Legal Privilege in the Roman Empire.* Oxford: Clarendon Press.

Geertz, Clifford
1973   *The Interpretation of Cultures.* New York: Basic Books.

1983   *Local Knowledge: Further Essays in Interpretive Anthropology.* New York: Basic Books.

Gellner, E., and J. Waterbury
1977   *Patrons and Clients in Mediterranean Societies.* London: Duckworth.

Gerhardsson, Birger
1966   *The Testing of God's Son (Matt 4:1–11).* ConBNT 2.1. Lund: Gleerup.

1967   Jésus livré et abandonné d'après la Passion selon saint Matthieu. *RB* 76:206–27.

1973   Gottes Sohn als Diener Gottes. *ST* 27:73–106.

Giblin, C. H.
1971   "The Things of God" in the Question Concerning Tribute to Caesar. *CBQ* 33:510–27.

1980   Suggestion, Negative Response and Positive Action in St. John's Portrayal of Jesus (John 2:1–11; 4:46–54; 7:2–4; 11:1–44). *NTS* 26:197–211.

Guijarro, Santiago
1997   The Family in First-Century Galilee. Pp. 42–65 in Halvor Moxnes, ed., *Constructing Early Christian Families: Family as Social Reality and Metaphor*. London: Routledge.

Gilmore, David D.
1982   Anthropology of the Mediterranean Area. *Annual Review of Anthropology* 11:175–205.

1987a   *Aggression and Community: Paradoxes of Andalusian Culture*. New Haven, Conn.: Yale University Press.

1987b   *Honor and Shame and the Unity of the Mediterranean*. American Anthropological Association special publication no. 22. Washington: American Anthropological Association.

1990   *Manhood in the Making*. New Haven, Conn.: Yale University Press.

Gilmore, Margaret, and David D. Gilmore
1979   "Machismo": A Psychodynamic Approach (Spain). *Journal of Psychological Anthropology* 2:281–300.

Gilsenan, Michael
1976   Lying, Honor and Contradiction. Pp. 191–219 in Bruce Kapferer, ed., *Transaction and Meaning: Directions in the Anthropology of Exchange and Symbolic Behavior*. Philadelphia: Institute for the Study of Human Issues.

Giovannini, Maureen J.
1987   Female Chastity Codes in the Circum-Mediterranean: Comparative Perspectives. Pp. 61–74 in David D. Gilmore, ed., *Honor and Shame and the Unity of the Mediterranean*. American Anthropological Association special publication no. 22. Washington: American Anthropological Association.

Gnilka, Joachim
1986   *Das Matthäusevangelium*. Freiburg: Herder.

Gould, John
1980   Law, Custom and Myth: Aspects of the Social Position of Women in Classical Athens. *JHS* 100:38–59.

Gouldner, Alvin W.
1965   *Enter Plato: Classical Greece and the Origins of Social Theory*. New York: Basic Books.

Gray, Rebecca
1993   *Prophetic Figures in Late Second Temple Jewish Palestine: The Evidence from Josephus*. Oxford: Oxford University Press.

Grudem, Wayne
1985   Does κεφαλή Mean "Source" or "Authority Over" in Greek Literature? A Survey of 2,336 Examples. *Trinity Journal* 6:38–59.

Grundmann, Walter
1964   δύναμις. *TDNT* 1: 284–317.

1968   *Das Evangelium nach Matthäus*. Berlin: Evangelische Verlagsanstalt.

Guelich, Robert A.
1973   Mt 5,22: Its Meaning and Integrity. *ZNW* 64:39–52.

1976   The Matthean Beatitudes: "Entrance-Requirements" or Eschatological Blessings? *JBL* 95:415–34.

1977   The Antitheses of Matthew V.21–48: Traditional and/or Redactional? *NTS* 22:444–57.

1982   *The Sermon on the Mount: A Foundation for Understanding*. Waco, Tex.: Word.

Gundry, R. H.
1967   *The Use of the Old Testament in St. Matthew's Gospel*. NovTSup 18. Leiden: E. J. Brill.

Haacker, K.
1971   Das hochzeitliche Kleid von Mt 22,11–13 und ein palästinisches Märchen. *Zeitschrift des deutschen Palästina-Vereins* 87:895–97.

Hadas, Moses, and Morton Smith
1965   *Heroes and Gods: Spiritual Biographies in Antiquity*. New York: Harper & Row.

Hagner, Donald A.
1993   *Matthew 1–13*. Word Biblical Commentary 33a. Dallas: Word Books.

1995   *Matthew 14–28*. Word Biblical Commentary 33b. Dallas: Word Books.

Hall, Edward T.
1976   *Beyond Culture*. New York: Doubleday & Co.

Halpern, David, John Winkler, and Froma Zeitlin, eds.
1990   *Before Sexuality: The Construction of Erotic Experience in the Ancient Greek World*. Princeton, N.J.: Princeton University Press.

Hamel, Gildas
1990   *Poverty and Charity in Roman Palestine, First Three Centuries C.E.* Berkeley, Calif.: University of California Press.

Hands, A. R.
1968   *Charities and Social Aid in Greece and Rome: Aspects of Greek and Roman Life*. Ithaca, N.Y.: Cornell University Press.

Hanson, K. C.
1989a   The Herodians and Mediterranean Kinship, part I: Genealogy and Descent. *BTB* 19:75–84.

1989b   The Herodians and Mediterranean Kinship, part II: Marriage and Divorce. *BTB* 19:142–51.

1990   The Herodians and Mediterranean Kinship, part III: Economics. *BTB* 20:10–21.

1994   Transformation on the Mountain: Ritual Analysis and the Gospel of Matthew. *Semeia* 67:147–70.

1996   "How Honorable! How Shameful!" A Cultural Analysis of Matthew's Makarisms and Reproaches. *Semeia* 68:81–112.

Hare, A. Paul
1969   Groups: Role Structure. *IESS* 6:283–88.

Hare, D. R. A.
1967   *The Theme of Jewish Persecution of Christians in the Gospel according to St. Matthew*. SNTSMS 6. Cambridge: Cambridge University Press.

Harrington, Daniel J.
1991   *The Gospel of Matthew*. Collegeville, Minn.: Liturgical Press.

Harris, Marvin
1976   The History and Significance of the Emic/Etic Distinction. *Annual Review of Anthropology* 5:329–50.

Hauck, Friedrich
1967   μοιχεύω. *TDNT* 4:729–35.

1968   πτωχός. *TDNT* 6:885–87.

Hauck, Friedrich, and Siegfried Schulz
1968   πραΰς. *TDNT* 6:645–51.

Harvey, A. E.
1976   *Jesus on Trial: A Study of the Fourth Gospel*. Atlanta: John Knox Press.

Hawley, Richard, and Barbara Levick
1995   *Women in Antiquity: New Assessments*. London: Routledge.

Held, Heinz Joachim
1963   Matthew as Interpreter of the Miracle Stories. Pp. 165–299 in Günther Bornkamm, ed., *Tradition and Interpretation in Matthew*. Philadelphia: Westminster Press.

Henery, K. H.
1954   Land Tenure in the Old Testament. *PEQ* 86:5–15.

Hengel, Martin
1971   *Was Jesus a Revolutionist?* Philadelphia: Fortress Press.

1975   Proseuche und Synagoge: Jüdische Gemeinde, Gotteshaus und Gottes-
        dienst in der Diaspora und in Palästina. Pp. 27–54 in Joseph Gutmann,
        ed., *The Synagogue: Studies in Origins, Archaeology, and Architecture.*
        New York: KTAV.

1976   *The Son of God.* Philadelphia: Fortress Press.

1977   *Crucifixion.* Philadelphia: Fortress Press.

1987   Zur matthäischen Bergpredigt und ihrem jüdischen Hintergrund. *ThR*
        52:327–400.

Hertz, Robert
1960   *Death and the Right Hand.* Glencoe, Ill.: Free Press.

Herzfeld, Michael
1980   Honour and Shame: Problems in the Comparative Analysis of Moral
        Systems. *Man* 15:339–51.

1982   *Ours Once More: Folklore, Ideology, and the Making of Modern
        Greece.* Austin, Tex.: University of Texas Press.

1985a   *The Poetics of Manhood: Contest and Identity in a Cretan Mountain Vil-
        lage.* Princeton, N.J.: Princeton University Press.

1985b   Gender Pragmatics: Agency, Speech and Bride-Theft in a Cretan Moun-
        tain Village. *Anthropology* 9:25–44.

1986   Within and Without: The Category of "Female" in the Ethnography of
        Modern Greece. Pp. 215–33 in Jill Dubisch, ed., *Gender and Power in
        Rural Greece.* Princeton, N.J.: Princeton University Press.

1987   "As in your own house": Hospitality, Ethnography, and the Stereotype
        of Mediterranean Society. Pp. 75–89 in David Gilmore, ed., *Honor and
        Shame and the Unity of the Mediterranean.* American Anthropological
        Association special publication no. 22. Washington: American Anthro-
        pological Association.

Herzog, William R.
1994   *Parables as Subversive Speech: Jesus as Pedagogue of the Oppressed.*
        Louisville, Ky.: Westminster John Knox Press.

Hester, D. A.
1977   To Help One's Friends and Harm One's Enemies: A Study in the Oedi-
        pus at Colonus. *Antichthon* 11:22–33.

Hill, D.
1976   False Prophets and Charismatics: Structure and Interpretation in
        Matthew 7,15–23. *Bib* 57:327–48.

1980   Son and Servant: An Essay on Matthean Christology. *JSNT* 6:2–16.

1985   Matthew 27:51–54 in the Theology of the Evangelist. *IBS* 7:76–87.

1986   The Conclusion of Matthew's Gospel: Some Literary Critical Observations. *IBS* 8:54–63.

Hock, Ronald F.
1980   *The Social Context of Paul's Ministry: Tentmaking and Apostleship.* Philadelphia: Fortress Press.

Hock, Ronald F., and Edward N. O'Neil
1986   *The Chreia in Ancient Rhetoric,* volume I: *The* Progymnasmata. Atlanta: Scholars Press.

Hoffner, Harry A.
1966   Symbols for Masculinity and Femininity: Their Use in Ancient Near Eastern Sympathetic Magic Rituals. *JBL* 85:326–34.

Hollenbach, Paul W.
1979   Social Aspects of John the Baptizer's Preaching Mission in the Context of Palestinian Judaism. *ANRW* II.19.2: 850–75.

1982   The Conversion of Jesus: From Jesus the Baptizer to Jesus the Healer. *ANRW* II.25.2: 196–219.

1985   Liberating Jesus for Social Involvement. *BTB* 15:151–57.

1987   Defining Rich and Poor Using Social Sciences. *SBLSP* 1987:50–63.

1993   Help for Interpreting Jesus' Exorcisms. *SBLSP* 1993:119–28.

Horsley, G. H. R.
1981   *New Documents Illustrating Early Christianity.* Vol. 1. North Ryde, New South Wales: The Ancient History Documentary Research Centre, Macquarie University.

Horsley, Richard A.
1987   *Jesus and the Spiral of Violence: Popular Jewish Resistance in Roman Palestine.* San Francisco: Harper & Row.

1989   *Sociology and the Jesus Movement.* New York: Crossroad.

Horsley, Richard A., and John S. Hanson
1985   *Bandits, Prophets and Messiahs: Popular Movements at the Time of Jesus.* Minneapolis: Winston Press.

Hubbard, Benjamin J.
1974   *The Matthean Redaction of a Primitive Apostolic Commissioning: An Exegesis of Matthew 28:16–20.* SBLDS 19. Missoula, Mont.: Scholars Press.

Hufford, E. W.
1978   The Parable of the Friend at Midnight: God's Honor or Man's Persistence. *ResQ* 21:154–60.

Hui, C. Harry, and Harry C. Triandis
1986   Individualism-Collectivism: A Study of Cross-Cultural Researchers. *Journal of Cross-Cultural Psychology* 17:225–48.

Hui, C. Harry, and Marcelo J. Villareal
1989   Individualism-Collectivism and Psychological Needs: Their Relationships in Two Cultures. *Journal of Cross-Cultural Psychology* 20:310–23.

Hummel, Reinhart
1966   *Die Auseinandersetzung zwischen Kirche und Judentum im Matthäusevangelium.* 2d ed. Munich: Chr. Kaiser.

Humphreys, S. C.
1969   History, Economics, and Anthropology: The Work of Karl Polanyi. *History and Theory* 8:165–212.

1978   *Anthropology and the Greeks.* London: Routledge.

1993   *The Family, Women and Death: Comparative Studies.* Rev. ed. Ann Arbor: University of Michigan Press.

Ibrahim, Abdullahi Ali
1992   *Assaulting with Words: The Sociopoetics of the Rubatab Evil Eye Metaphors.* Chicago: Northwestern University Press.

Jackson, Bernard S.
1973   The Problem of Exod. XXI 22–25 (Ius Talionis). *VT* 23:273–304.

Jackson, H. M.
1987   The Death of Jesus in Mark and the Miracle from the Cross. *NTS* 33:16–37.

Jacobson, Arland D.
1995   Divided Families and Christian Origins. Pp. 361–80 in Ronald A. Piper, ed., *The Gospel behind the Gospels: Current Studies on Q.* NovTSup 75. Leiden: E. J. Brill.

Jay, Nancy
1992   *Throughout Your Generations Forever: Sacrifice, Religion, and Paternity.* Chicago: University of Chicago Press.

Jeremias, Joachim
1966   *The Eucharistic Words of Jesus.* London: SCM Press.

1968   ρακά. *TDNT* 6:973–76.

1971   *New Testament Theology.* New York: Charles Scribner's Sons.

Johnson, M. D.
1969   *The Purpose of the Biblical Genealogies with Special Reference to the Setting of the Genealogies of Jesus.* NTSMS 8. Cambridge: Cambridge University Press.

Juel, Donald
1977   *Messiah and Temple.* SBLDS 31. Missoula, Mont.: Scholars Press.

Just, R.
1975   Conceptions of Women in Classical Athens. *Journal of the Anthropological Society of Oxford* 6:153–70.

Kautsky, John H.
1982   *The Politics of Aristocratic Empires.* Chapel Hill, N.C.: University of North Carolina Press.

Kayama, H.
1990   The Doxa of Moses and Jesus (2 Cor. 3:7–18 and Luke 9:28–32). *Bulletin of the Christian Research Institute, Meiji Gakuin University* 23:23–48.

Kee, Howard C.
1968   The Terminology of Mark's Exorcism Stories. *NTS* 14:242–56.

1990   The Transformation of the Synagogue after 70 C.E.: Its Import for Early Christianity. *NTS* 36:1–24.

Kekes, John
1988   Shame and Moral Progress. Pp. 282–96 in Peter French, T. Uehling, and H. Wettstein, eds., *Midwest Studies in Philosophy*, volume 13: *Ethical Theory: Character and Virtue.* Notre Dame, Ind.: University of Notre Dame Press.

Kelber, Werner, ed.
1976   *The Passion in Mark: Studies on Mark 14–16.* Philadelphia: Fortress Press.

Kelly, J. M.
1976   "Loss of Face" as a Factor Inhibiting Legislation. Pp. 93–111 in his *Studies in the Civil Judicature of the Roman Republic.* Oxford: Clarendon Press.

Kennedy, George A.
1963   *The Art of Persuasion in Greece.* Princeton, N.J.: Princeton University Press.

1972   *The Art of Rhetoric in the Roman World, 300 B.C.–A.D. 300.* Princeton, N.J.: Princeton University Press.

1980   *Classical Rhetoric and Its Christian and Secular Tradition from Ancient to Modern Times.* Chapel Hill, N.C.: University of North Carolina Press.

1983   *Greek Rhetoric under Christian Emperors*. Princeton, N.J.: Princeton University Press.

Kennedy, John G.
1966   "Peasant Society and the Image of Limited Good": A Critique. *American Anthropologist* 68:1212–25.

King, G. B.
1924   The Mote and the Beam. *HTR* 17:393–404.

1933   A Further Note on the Mote and the Beam (Matt VII.3–5; Luke VI.41–42). *HTR* 26:73–76.

Kingsbury, Jack Dean
1974   The Composition and Christology of Matt 28:16–20. *JBL* 93:573–84.

1975   *Matthew: Structure, Christology, Kingdom*. Philadelphia: Fortress Press.

1977   *Matthew*. Philadelphia: Fortress Press.

1978   Observations on the "Miracle Chapters" of Matthew 8–9. *CBQ* 40:559–73.

1986   *Matthew as Story*. Philadelphia: Fortress Press.

1987   The Developing Conflict between Jesus and the Jewish Leaders in Matthew's Gospel. *CBQ* 49:57–73.

Kinstrand, J. F.
1986   Diogenes Laertius and the "Chreia" Tradition. *Elenchos* 7:217–43.

Kitto, H. D. F.
1951   The Greek Mind. Pp. 169–76 in his *The Greeks*. Baltimore: Penguin Books.

Kloppenborg, John
1986   Blessing and Marginality: The "Persecution Beatitude" in Q, Thomas and Early Christianity. *Forum* 2/3: 36–56.

1990   Alms, Debt and Divorce: Jesus' Ethics in Their Mediterranean Context. *TJT* 6:182–200.

1992   Exitus Clari Viri: The Death of Jesus in Luke. *TJT* 8:106–20.

Klose, A.
1938   Altrömische Wertbegriffe (*honos* und *dignitas*). *Neue Jahrbücher für Antike und deutsche Bildung* 1:268–78.

Knoppers, Gary N.
1992   "There Was None Like Him": Incomparability in the Books of Kings. *CBQ* 54:411–31.

Köhler, K.
1920   Zu Mt 5,22. *ZNW* 19:71–95.

Konstan, David
1995   *Greek Comedy and Ideology*. Oxford: Oxford University Press.

Krauss, Samuel
1966   *Talmudische Archäologie*. Hildesheim: Georg Olms.

Kurke, Leslie
1991   *The Traffic in Praise: Pindar and the Poetics of Social Economy*. Ithaca, N.Y.: Cornell University Press.

Lambrecht, Jan
1974   The Relatives of Jesus in Mark. *NovT* 16:241–58.

Lausberg, Heinrich
1973   *Handbuch der literarischen Rhetorik: Eine Grundlegung der Literaturwissenschaft*. Munich: Max Hüber.

Lee, Thomas R.
1986   *Studies in the Form of Sirach 44–50*. SBLDS 75. Atlanta: Scholars Press.

Lenski, Gerhard E.
1966   *Power and Privilege: A Theory of Social Stratification*. Chapel Hill: University of North Carolina Press.

Lewis, N.
1983   *The Compulsory Public Services of Roman Egypt*. Florence: Edizioni Gonnelli.

Leyerle, Blake
1993   John Chrysostom on the Gaze. *JECS* 1:159–74.

Lieberman, Saul
1942   Oaths and Vows. Pp. 115–43 in his *Greek in Jewish Palestine*. New York: Jewish Theological Seminary of America.

Llewelyn, S. R.
1994   The Development of the System of Liturgies. *New Documents Illustrating Early Christianity* 7:93–111.

Lloyd, G. E. R.
1966   *Polarity and Analogy: Two Types of Argumentation in Early Greek Thought*. Cambridge: Cambridge University Press.

Lohse, Eduard
1963   *Martyrer und Gottesknecht*. Göttingen: Vandenhoeck & Ruprecht.

1971   συνέδριον. *TDNT* 7:860–71.

Louw, Johannes P., and Eugene A. Nida
1988   *Greek-English Lexicon of the New Testament Based on Semantic Domains*. New York: United Bible Societies.

Love, Stuart
1987   Women's Roles in Certain Second Testament Passages: A Macrosociological View. *BTB* 17:50–59.

Lowry, Todd
1979   Recent Literature on Ancient Greek Economic Thought. *Journal of Economic Literature* 17:65–86.

Luck, Ulrich
1974   φιλανθρωπία. *TDNT* 9:107–12.

Luz, Ulrich
1989   *Matthew 1–7*. Minneapolis: Fortress Press.

1994   *Matthew in History: Interpretation, Influence and Effects*. Minneapolis: Fortress Press.

Lyons, George
1985   *Pauline Autobiography: Toward a New Understanding*. SBLDS 73. Atlanta: Scholars Press.

MacDonald, Dennis R.
1987   Aretê (2 Peter 1:5). *Iliff Review* 44:39–43.

Mack, Burton L.
1989   Elaboration of the Chreia in the Hellenistic School. Pp. 31–67 in Burton L. Mack and Vernon Robbins, eds., *Patterns of Persuasion in the Gospels*. Sonoma, Calif.: Polebridge Press.

1994   Persuasive Pronouncements: An Evaluation of Recent Studies on the Chreia. *Semeia* 64:283–87.

Mack, Burton L., and Vernon Robbins
1989   *Patterns of Persuasion in the Gospels*. Sonoma, Calif.: Polebridge Press.

MacMullen, Ramsay
1980   Women in Public in the Roman Empire. *Historia* 29:208–18.

Magie, David
1950   *Roman Rule in Asia Minor*. 2 vols. Princeton: Princeton University Press.

Malbon, Elizabeth Struthers
1986   *Narrative Space and Mythic Meaning in Mark*. San Francisco: Harper & Row.

Malherbe, Abraham J.
1986   *Moral Exhortation: A Greco-Roman Sourcebook*. Philadelphia: Westminster Press.

Malina, Bruce J.
1980   What Is Prayer? *TBT* 18:214–20.

1981   The First-Century Personality: The Individual and the Group. Pp. 51–70 in Bruce Malina, *The New Testament World: Insights from Cultural Anthropology*. Atlanta: John Knox Press.

1982   The Social Sciences and Biblical Interpretation. *Int* 36:229–42.

1986a   "Religion" in the World of Paul. *BTB* 16:92–101.

1986b   *Christian Origins and Cultural Anthropology*. Atlanta: John Knox Press.

1986c   Interpreting the Bible with Anthropology: The Case of the Poor and the Rich. *Listening* 21:148–59.

1987   Wealth and Poverty in the New Testament and Its World. *Int* 41:354–67.

1988   Patron and Client: The Analogy behind Synoptic Theology. *Forum* 4/1:2–23.

1989a   Christ and Time: Swiss or Mediterranean. *CBQ* 51:1–31.

1989b   Dealing with Biblical (Mediterranean) Characters: A Guide for U.S. Consumers. *BTB* 19:127–41.

1991a   Interpretation: Reading, Abduction, Metaphor. Pp. 253–66 in David Jobling, Peggy Day, and Gerald Sheppard, eds., *The Bible and the Politics of Exegesis: Essays in Honor of Norman K. Gottwald on His Sixty-fifth Birthday*. Cleveland: Pilgrim Press.

1991b   Reading Theory Perspective: Reading Luke-Acts. Pp. 3–23 in Jerome H. Neyrey, ed., *The Social World of Luke-Acts: Models for Interpretation*. Peabody, Mass.: Hendrickson.

1993a   *The New Testament World: Insights from Cultural Anthropology*. 2d ed. Louisville: Westminster/John Knox Press.

1993b   Love. Pp. 110–14 in John J. Pilch and Bruce J. Malina, eds., *Biblical Social Values and Their Meanings: A Handbook*. Peabody, Mass.: Hendrickson.

1993c   Grace/Favor. Pp. 83–85 in John J. Pilch and Bruce J. Malina, eds., *Biblical Social Values and Their Meanings: A Handbook*. Peabody, Mass.: Hendrickson.

1993d   Authoritarianism. Pp. 11–17 in John J. Pilch and Bruce J. Malina, eds., *Biblical Social Values and Their Meanings: A Handbook*. Peabody, Mass.: Hendrickson.

Malina, Bruce J., and Jerome H. Neyrey

1988   *Calling Jesus Names: The Social Value of Labels in Matthew*. Sonoma, Calif.: Polebridge Press.

1991a   Honor and Shame in Luke-Acts: Pivotal Values of the Mediterranean World. Pp. 25–65 in Jerome H. Neyrey, ed., *The Social World of Luke-Acts: Models for Interpretation*. Peabody, Mass.: Hendrickson.

1991b   First-Century Personality: Dyadic, Not Individual. Pp. 67–96 in Jerome H. Neyrey, ed., *The Social World of Luke-Acts: Models for Interpretation*. Peabody, Mass.: Hendrickson.

1996   *Portraits of Paul: An Archaeology of Ancient Personality*. Louisville, Ky.: Westminster John Knox Press.

Malina, Bruce J., and Richard L. Rohrbaugh

1992   *Social-Science Commentary on the Synoptic Gospels*. Minneapolis: Fortress Press.

Malina, Bruce J., and Chris Seeman

1993   Envy. Pp. 55–59 in John J. Pilch and Bruce J. Malina, eds., *Biblical Social Values and Their Meanings: A Handbook*. Peabody, Mass.: Hendrickson.

Malul, Meir

1985   More on *pahad yishaq* (Genesis xxiv 42, 52) and the Oath by the Thigh. *VT* 35:192–200.

1987   Touching the Sexual Organs as an Oath Ceremony in an Akkadian Letter. *VT* 37:491–92.

Manning, C. E.

1973   Seneca and the Stoics on the Equality of the Sexes. *Mnemosyne* 26:170–77.

Marcus, Michael A.

1987   "Horsemen Are the Fence of the Land": Honor and History among the Ghiyata of Eastern Morocco. Pp. 49–60 in David D. Gilmore, ed., *Honor and Shame and the Unity of the Mediterranean*. American Anthropological Association special publication no. 22. Washington: American Anthropological Association.

Marrou, H. I.

1956   *A History of Education in Antiquity*. New York: New American Library.

Marshall, I. Howard

1978a   The Meaning of "Reconciliation." Pp. 117–32 in Robert A. Guelich, *Unity and Diversity in New Testament Theology*. Grand Rapids: Eerdmans.

1978b   *The Gospel of Luke*. Grand Rapids: Eerdmans.

Marshall, Peter
1983   A Metaphor of Social Shame: θριαμβεύειν in 2 Cor. 2:14. *NovT* 25:303–17.

1987   *Enmity at Corinth: Social Conventions in Paul's Relations with the Corinthians.* Tübingen: J.C.B. Mohr (Paul Siebeck).

Martin, Dale B.
1990   *Slavery as Salvation: The Metaphor of Slavery in Pauline Christianity.* New Haven, Conn.: Yale University Press.

1995   *The Corinthian Body.* New Haven, Conn.: Yale University Press.

Martin, Josef
1974   *Antike Rhetorik: Technik und Methode.* Munich: C. H. Beck.

Martyn, J. Louis
1979   *History and Theology in the Fourth Gospel.* Rev. ed. Nashville: Abingdon Press.

Matera, Frank J.
1986   *Passion Narratives and Their Gospel Theologies: Interpreting the Synoptics through Their Passion Stories.* New York: Paulist Press.

Matsen, Patricia, Philip Rollinson, and Marion Sousa
1990   *Readings from Classical Rhetoric.* Carbondale, Ill.: Southern Illinois University Press.

Matthews, Victor H., and Don C. Benjamin
1991   The Stubborn and the Fool. *TBT* 29/4:222–26.

1992   The Virgin and the Prince. *TBT* 30/1:42–46.

1994   Female Voices Upholding the Honor of the Household. *BTB* 24:8–15.

May, David M.
1990   Leaving and Receiving: A Social-Scientific Exegesis of Mark 10:29–31. *Perspectives in Religious Studies* 17:141–54.

McCarren, Vincent P.
1980   *Michigan Papyri.* Chico, Calif.: Scholars Press.

McCasland, S. V.
1932   Portents in Josephus and the Gospels. *JBL* 51:323–35.

McCown, Chester C.
1928   Ο ΤΕΚΤΩΝ. Pp. 173–89 in S. J. Case, ed., *Studies in Early Christianity.* New York: Century Co.

McKelvey, R. J.
1969   *The New Temple: The Church in the New Testament.* Oxford: Oxford University Press.

McKenzie, D. A.
1964   Judicial Procedure at the Town Gate. *VT* 14:100–105.

Meier, John P.
1979   *The Vision of Matthew*. New York: Paulist Press.

1991   *A Marginal Jew: Rethinking the Historical Jesus*. New York: Doubleday & Co.

Mertner, E.
1956   Topos and Commonplace. Pp. 178–224 in G. Dietrich and F. W. Schultze, eds., *Strena Angelica*. Halle: M. Niemeyer.

Michalson, Jon D.
1991   *Honor Thy Gods*. Chapel Hill, N.C.: University of North Carolina Press.

Mikliszanski, J. K.
1947   The Law of Retaliation and the Pentateuch. *JBL* 66:295–303.

Milavic, Aaron
1995   The Social Setting of "Turning the Other Cheek" and "Loving One's Enemies" in the Light of the *Didache*. *BTB* 25:131–43.

Milgrom, Jacob
1983   Of Hems and Tassels. *BARev* 9:61–65.

Miller, David L.
1971   *Empaizein*: Playing the Mock Game (Luke 22:63–64). *JBL* 90:309–13.

Miller, Patrick D.
1994   *They Cried to the Lord: The Form and Theology of Biblical Prayer*. Minneapolis: Fortress Press.

Moline, Jon N.
1989   Aristotle on Praise and Blame. *Archiv für Geschichte der Philosophie* 71/3:283–302.

Momigliano, Arnaldo
1971   *The Development of Greek Biography*. Cambridge, Mass.: Harvard University Press.

Montefiore, H. W.
1960   Josephus and the New Testament. *NTS* 4:139–60.

Morris, Leon
1992   *The Gospel according to Matthew*. Grand Rapids: Eerdmans.

Most, G. W.
1989   The Strangers' Strategem: Self-Disclosure and Self-Sufficiency in Greek Culture. *JHS* 109:114–33.

Mott, Stephen C.
1975   The Power of Giving and Receiving: Reciprocity in Hellenistic Benev-
        olence. Pp. 60–72 in G. F. Hawthorne, ed., *Current Issues in Biblical
        and Patristic Interpretation—Studies in Honor of Merrill C. Tenney.*
        Grand Rapids: Eerdmans.

Moxnes, Halvor
1988a   *The Economy of the Kingdom: Social Conflict and Economic Relations
        in Luke's Gospel.* Philadelphia: Fortress Press.

1988b   Honour and Righteousness in Romans. *JSNT* 32:61–77.

1988c   Honor, Shame and the Outside World in Paul's Letter to the Romans. Pp
        207–18 in Jacob Neusner, ed., *The Social World of Formative Chris-
        tianity and Judaism.* Philadelphia: Fortress Press.

1991   Patron-Client Relations and the New Community of Luke-Acts. Pp.
        241–68 in Jerome H. Neyrey, ed., *The Social World of Luke-Acts: Mod-
        els for Interpretation.* Peabody, Mass.: Hendrickson.

1995a   The Quest for Honor and the Unity of the Community in Romans 12
        and in the Orations of Dio Chrysostom. Pp. 203–30 in T. Engberg-Ped-
        erson, ed., *Paul in His Hellenistic Context.* Minneapolis: Fortress Press.

1995b   "He Saw That the City Was Full of Idols" (Acts 17:16): Visualizing the
        World of the First Christians. Pp. 107–31 in David Hellholm, Halvor
        Moxnes, and Turid Karlsen Seim, eds., *Mighty Minorities? Minorities
        in Early Christianity—Positions and Strategies.* Oslo: Scandinavian
        University Press.

1996   Honor and Shame. Pp. 19–40 in Richard L. Rohrbaugh, ed., *The Social
        Sciences and New Testament Interpretation.* Peabody, Mass.: Hendrick-
        son.

1997   *Constructing Early Christian Families: Family as Social Reality and
        Metaphor.* London: Routledge.

Muenchow, Charles
1989   Dust and Dirt in Job 42:8. *JBL* 108:597–611.

Mullins, Terence Y.
1980   *Topos* as a New Testament Form. *JBL* 99:541–47.

Muñoz Iglesias, Salvador
1958   El génaro literario del Evangelio de la Infancia en San Mateo. *Estudios
        Biblicos* 17:243–73.

Nadeau, Ray
1952   The Progymnasmata of Aphthonius in Translation. *Speech Monographs*
        19:264–85.

Nagy, Gregory
1979   *The Best of the Achaeans*. Baltimore: Johns Hopkins University Press.

Nagy, Joseph Falaky
1981   The Deceptive Gift in Greek Mythology. *Arethusa* 14:191–204.

Nestle, E.
1908   They Enlarge the Borders of Their Garments. *ExpT* 20:188.

Newbold, Ronald F.
1984   Personality Structure and Response to Adversity in Early Christian Ha-
            giography. *Numen* 31:199–215.

Neyrey, Jerome H.
1982   The Thematic Use of Isaiah 42,1–4 in Matthew 12. *Bib* 63:457–73.

1985   *The Passion according to Luke*. New York: Paulist Press.

1986   Body Language in 1 Corinthians: The Use of Anthropological Models
            for Understanding Paul and His Opponents. *Semeia* 35:129–170.

1990a   *Paul, In Other Words: A Cultural Reading of His Letters*. Louisville,
            Ky.: Westminster/John Knox Press.

1990b   Acts 17, Epicureans, and Theodicy: A Study in Stereotypes. Pp. 118–34
            in David Balch, Everett Ferguson, and Wayne Meeks, eds., *Greeks, Ro-
            mans, and Christians*. Minneapolis: Fortress Press.

1991a   The Symbolic Universe of Luke-Acts: "They Turn the World Upside
            Down." Pp. 271–304 in his *The Social World of Luke-Acts: Models for
            Interpretation*. Peabody, Mass.: Hendrickson.

1991b   "Without Beginning of Days or End of Life" (Hebrews 7:3): Topos for
            a True Deity. *CBQ* 53:439–55.

1993a   Clothing. Pp. 20–25 in John J. Pilch and Bruce J. Malina, eds., *Bible So-
            cial Values and Their Meaning: A Handbook*. Peabody, Mass.: Hen-
            drickson.

1993b   Equivocation. Pp. 59–63 in John J. Pilch and Bruce J. Malina, eds.,
            Bible Social Values and Their Meaning: A Handbook. Peabody, Mass.:
            Hendrickson.

1993c   Nudity. Pp. 119–25 in John J. Pilch and Bruce J. Malina, eds., *Bible So-
            cial Values and Their Meaning: A Handbook*. Peabody, Mass.: Hen-
            drickson.

1993d   *2 Peter, Jude*. AB 37C. New York: Doubleday & Co.

1994a   "What's Wrong with This Picture?" John 4, Cultural Stereotypes of
            Women, and Public and Private Space. *BTB* 24:77–91.

1994b Josephus' *Vita* and the Encomium: A Native Model of Personality. *JSJ* 25:177–206.

1995 Loss of Wealth, Loss of Family and Loss of Honour: The Cultural Context of the Original Makarisms in Q. Pp. 139–58 in Philip F. Esler, ed., *Modelling Early Christianity: Social-Scientific Studies of the New Testament in Its Context*. London: Routledge.

1996a Luke's Social Location of Paul: Cultural Anthropology and the Status of Paul in Acts. Pp. 251–79 in Ben Witherington, III, ed., *History, Literature, and Society in the Book of Acts*. Cambridge: Cambridge University Press.

1996b "Despising the Shame of the Cross": Honor and Shame in the Johannine Passion Narrative. *Semeia* 68:113–37.

1996c Clean/Unclean, Pure/Polluted, and Holy/Profane: The Idea and the System of Purity. Pp. 80–106 in Richard L. Rohrbaugh, ed., *The Social Sciences and New Testament Interpretation*. Peabody, Mass.: Hendrickson.

1996d Meals, Food, and Table Fellowship. Pp. 159–82 in Richard L. Rohrbaugh, ed., *The Social Sciences and New Testament Interpretation*. Peabody, Mass.: Hendrickson.

Nickelsburg, G. W. E.
1972 *Resurrection, Immortality, and Eternal Life in Intertestamental Judaism*. Cambridge, Mass.: Harvard University Press.

1980 The Genre and Function of the Markan Passion Narrative. *HTR* 73:153–84.

Nineham, D. E.
1976 The Genealogy in St. Matthew's Gospel and Its Significance for the Study of the Gospel. *BJRL* 58:421–44.

Nissen, Andreas
1974 *Gott und der Nächste im antiken Judentum: Untersuchungen zum Doppelgebot der Liebe*. WUNT 15. Tübingen: J.C.B. Mohr [Paul Siebeck].

Nolan, Brian M.
1979 *The Royal Son of God: The Christology of Matthew 1–2 in the Setting of the Gospel*. Göttingen: Vandenhoeck & Ruprecht.

Oakman, Douglas E.
1985 Jesus and Agrarian Palestine: The Factor of Debt. *SBLSP* 1985:57–73.

1986 *Jesus and the Economic Questions of His Day*. Lewiston, N.Y.: Edwin Mellen Press.

1988 Rulers' Houses, Thieves, and Usurpers: The Beelzebul Pericope. *Forum* 4/3:109–23.

1991a   The Countryside in Luke-Acts. Pp. 151–79 in Jerome H. Neyrey, ed., *The Social World of Luke-Acts: Models for Interpretation*. Peabody, Mass.: Hendrickson.

1991b   The Ancient Economy in the Bible. *BTB* 21:34–39.

1992   Was Jesus a Peasant? *BTB* 22:117–25.

1994   Cursing Fig Trees and Robbers' Dens: Pronouncement Stories within Social-Scientific Perspective; Mark 11:12–25 and Parallels. *Semeia* 64:253–72.

O'Collins, Gerald G.
1992   Crucifixion. *ABD* 1:1207–10.

Oepke, Albrecht
1967   ὄναρ. *TDNT* 5:220–38.

Olyan, Saul M.
1966   Honor, Shame, and Covenant Relations in Ancient Israel and Its Environment. *JBL* 115:201–18.

Osiek, Carolyn
1992   *What Are They Saying about the Social Setting of the New Testament?* Rev. ed. New York: Paulist Press.

Osiek, Carolyn, and David Balch
1997   *Families in the New Testament World: Households and House Churches*. Louisville, Ky.: Westminster John Knox Press.

Overman, J. Andrew
1990   Heroes and Villains in Palestinian Lore: Matthew's Use of Traditional Jewish Polemic in the Passion Narrative. *SBLSP* 1990:592–602.

Parker, Robert
1983   *Miasma: Pollution and Purification in Early Greek Religion*. Oxford: Clarendon Press.

Parsons, Talcott
1969   *Politics and Social Structure*. New York: Free Press.

Patai, Raphael
1983   *The Arab Mind*. Rev. ed. New York: Charles Scribner's Sons.

Patterson, Orlando
1982   Honor and Degradation. Pp. 77–101 in his *Slavery and Social Death*. Cambridge, Mass.: Harvard University Press.

Pease, Arthur S.
1926   Things without Honor. *CP* 21:27–42.

Pedersen, J.
1991   Honour and Shame. Pp. 213–44 in his *Israel: Its Life and Culture*, vol.
        1. Atlanta: Scholars Press.

Pelling, Christopher, ed.
1990   *Characterization and Individuality in Greek Literature*. Oxford: Claren-
        don Press.

Péristiany, J. G., ed.
1966   *Honour and Shame: The Values of Mediterranean Society*. Chicago:
        University of Chicago Press.

Péristiany, J. G., and J. Pitt-Rivers
1992   *Honour and Grace in Anthropology*. Cambridge: Cambridge University
        Press.

Pervo, Richard I.
1985   Wisdom and Power: Petronius' *Satyricon* and the Social World of Early
        Christianity. *ATR* 67:307–328.

Pfuhl, E. H.
1980   *The Deviance Process*. New York: Van Nostrand Reinhold Co.

Picirelli, Robert
1975   The Meaning of "Epignosis." *EvQ* 47:85–93.

Pickard-Cambridge, Arthur
1988   *The Dramatic Festivals of Athens*. 2d ed. Oxford: Clarendon Press.

Pike, Dana M.
1992   Names, Theophoric. *ABD* 4:1018–19.

Piker, Steven
1966   "The Image of Limited Good": Comments on an Exercise in Descrip-
        tion and Interpretation. *American Anthropologist* 68:1202–11.

Pilch, John J.
1985   Healing in Mark: A Social Science Analysis. *BTB* 15:142–50.

1986   The Health Care System in Matthew: A Social Science Analysis. *BTB*
        16:102–6.

1988   A Structural Functional Analysis of Mark 7. *Forum* 4/1:31–62.

1989   Reading Matthew Anthropologically: Healing in Cultural Perspective.
        Listening 24:278–89.

1991   Sickness and Healing in Luke-Acts. Pp. 181–210 in Jerome H. Neyrey,
        ed., *The Social World of Luke-Acts: Models for Interpretation*. Peabody,
        Mass.: Hendrickson.

1992a   Lying and Deceit in the Letters to the Seven Churches: Perspectives
        from Cultural Anthropology. *BTB* 22:126–35.

1992b   Understanding Healing in the Social World of Early Christianity. *BTB*
         22:26–33.

1993a   "Beat His Ribs While He Is Young" (Sir 30:12): A Window on the
         Mediterranean World. *BTB* 23:101–13.

1993b   Insights and Models for Understanding the Healing Activity of the His-
         torical Jesus. *SBLSP* 1993:154–77.

1994   Secrecy in the Mediterranean World: An Anthropological Perspective.
         BTB 24:151–57.

1995   The Transfiguration of Jesus: An Experience of Alternate Reality. Pp. 47–
         64 in Philip F. Esler, ed., *Modelling Early Christianity: Social-Scientific
         Studies of the New Testament in Its Context*. London: Routledge.

Pilch, John, and Bruce J. Malina, eds.
1993   *Biblical Social Values and Their Meanings: A Handbook*. Peabody,
         Mass.: Hendrickson.

Pitt-Rivers, Julian
1961   *The People of the Sierra*. Chicago: University of Chicago Press.

1965   Honour and Social Status. Pp. 19–78 in J. G. Péristiany, ed., *Honour
         and Shame: The Values of Mediterranean Society*. London: Weidenfeld
         & Nicolson.

1968a   Honor. *IESS* 6:503–11.

1968b   Pseudo-Kinship. *IESS* 8:408–13.

1968c   The Stranger, the Guest, and the Hostile Host. Pp. 13–30 in J. G. Péris-
         tiany, ed., *Contributions to Mediterranean Sociology*. Paris: Mouton.

1975   The Kith and the Kin. Pp. 89–105 in J. Goody, ed., *The Character of
         Kinship*. Cambridge: Cambridge University Press.

1977   *The Fate of Shechem, or The Politics of Sex: Essays in the Anthropology
         of the Mediterranean*. Cambridge Studies in Social Anthropology 19.
         Cambridge: Cambridge University Press.

Pobee, John
1970   The Cry of the Centurion—A Cry of Defeat. Pp. 91–102 in Ernst Bam-
         mel, ed., *The Trial of Jesus*. Naperville, Ill.: Alec R. Allenson.

Pomeroy, Sarah B.
1984   Women's Roles in the Economy. Pp. 148–73 in her *Women in Hel-
         lenistic Egypt: From Alexander to Cleopatra*. New York: Schocken
         Books.

1994   *Xenophon, Oeconomicus: A Social and Historical Commentary*. Ox-
         ford: Clarendon Press.

Powell, Mark Allan
1990   The Plot to Kill Jesus from Three Different Perspectives: Point of View in Matthew. *SBLSP* 1990:603–13.

Qviller, Bjørn
1981   The Dynamics of Homeric Society. *Symbolae Osloenses* 56:109–55.

Ramlot, L.
1964   Les généalogies bibliques, un genre oriental. *BVC* 60:53–70.

Rapske, Brian
1994   The Shame of Bonds. Pp. 283–312 in his *The Book of Acts in Its First Century Setting*, volume 3: *Paul in Roman Custody*. Grand Rapids: Eerdmans.

Reinhold, Meyer
1970   *History of Purple as a Status Symbol in Antiquity*. Brussels: Latomus.

Reumann, John
1982   *"Righteousness" in the New Testament*. Philadelphia: Fortress Press; New York: Paulist Press.

Riggs, F. W.
1969   Bureaucratic Politics in Comparative Perspective. *Journal of Comparative Administration* 1:5–9.

Robbins, Vernon K.
1983   Pronouncement Stories and Jesus' Blessing of the Children: A Rhetorical Approach. *Semeia* 29:43–74.

1985   Pragmatic Relations as a Criterion for Authentic Sayings. *Forum* 1/3:35–63.

1989a   Chreia and Pronouncement Story in Synoptic Studies. Pp. 1–29 in Burton Mack and Vernon Robbins, eds., *Patterns of Persuasion in the Gospels*. Sonoma, Calif.: Polebridge Press.

1989b   *Ancient Quotes and Anecdotes*. Sonoma, Calif.: Polebridge Press.

1992a   *Jesus the Teacher: A Socio-Rhetorical Interpretation of Mark*. Minneapolis: Fortress Press.

1992b   The Reversed Contextualization of Psalm 22 in the Markan Crucifixion: A Socio-Rhetorical Analysis. Pp. 1161–83 in F. Van Segbroeck et al., eds., *The Four Gospels: Festschrift Frans Neirynck*. Louvain: Leuven University Press.

1993   Rhetoric and Culture: Exploring Types of Cultural Rhetoric in a Text. Pp. 443–63 in Stanley Porter and Thomas Olbricht, eds., *Rhetoric and the New Testament: Essays from the 1992 Heidelberg Conference*. JSNTSup 90. Sheffield: JSOT Press.

1994a   The Ritual of Reading and Reading a Text as a Ritual. Pp. 385–401 in David Jasper and Mark Ledbetter, eds., *In Good Company: Essays in Honor of Robert Detweiler*. Atlanta: Scholars Press.

1994b   Socio-Rhetorical Criticism: Mary, Elizabeth and the Magnificat as a Test Case. Pp. 164–209 in Elizabeth Struthers Malbon and Edgar V. McKnight, eds., *The New Literary Criticism and the New Testament*. JSOTSup 109. Sheffield: JSOT Press.

1994c   Introduction: Using Rhetorical Discussions of the Chreia to Interpret Pronouncement Stories. *Semeia* 64:vii-xvii.

Roberts, J. H.

1991   *Thaumazô*: An Expression of Perplexity in Some Examples from Papyri Letters. *Neot* 25:109–22.

Roberts, John M.

1967   Oaths, Autonomic Ordeals, and Power. Pp. 169–95 in Clellan S. Ford, ed., *Cross–Cultural Approaches: Readings in Comparative Research*. New Haven, Conn.: HRAF Press.

Robinson, James M.

1957   *The Problem of History in Mark*. Studies in Biblical Theology 21. London: SCM Press.

Robinson, Rachel Sargent

1981   *Sources for the History of Greek Athletics*. Chicago: Ares Press.

Rogers, K.

1959   The Emperor's Displeasure—*amicitiam renuntiare*. *TAPA* 90:224–37.

Rohrbaugh, Richard L.

1978   *The Biblical Interpreter: An Agrarian Bible in an Industrial Age*. Philadelphia: Fortress Press.

1984   Methodological Considerations in the Debate over the Social Class Status of Early Christians. *JAAR* 52:519–46.

1987   Social Location of Thought as a Heuristic Construct in New Testament Study. *JSNT* 30:103–19.

1991   The Pre-Industrial City in Luke-Acts: Urban Social Relations. Pp. 125–49 in Jerome H. Neyrey, ed., *The Social World of Luke-Acts: Models for Interpretation*. Peabody, Mass.: Hendrickson.

1993a   The Social Location of the Marcan Audience. *BTB* 23:114–27.

1993b   The Social Location of the Markan Audience. *Int* 47:380–95.

1993c   A Peasant Reading of the Parable of the Talents/Pounds: A Text of Terror? *BTB* 23:32–39.

1995   Legitimating Sonship—A Test of Honour: A Social-Scientific Study of Luke 4:1–30. Pp. 183–97 in Philip F. Esler, ed., *Modelling Early Christianity: Social-Scientific Studies of the New Testament in Its Context.* London: Routledge.

1996   *The Social Sciences and New Testament Interpretation.* Peabody, Mass.: Hendrickson.

Rosenberg, Roy A.
1972   The "Star of the Messiah" Reconsidered. *Bib* 53:105–9.

Rousseau, John J.
1993   Jesus, an Exorcist of a Kind. *SBLSP* 1993:129–53.

Rowe, Galen O.
1993   The Many Facets of *Hybris* in Demosthenes' *Against Meidias. AJP* 114:397–406.

Russell, D. A.
1980   Progymnasmata. P. 883 in *The Oxford Classical Dictionary.* 2d ed. Oxford: Clarendon Press.

1991   Childhood and Personality in Greek Biography. Pp. 213–44 in Christopher Pelling, ed., *Characterization and Individuality in Greek Literature.* Oxford: Clarendon Press.

Russell, D. A., and Nigel Wilson
1981   *Menander Rhetor.* Oxford: Clarendon Press.

Saldarini, Anthony J.
1988   *Pharisees, Scribes and Sadducees in Palestinian Society: A Sociological Approach.* Wilmington, Del.: Michael Glazier.

1991   The Gospel of Matthew and Jewish-Christian Conflict. Pp. 38–61 in David L. Balch, ed., *Social History of the Matthean Community: Cross-Disciplinary Approaches.* Minneapolis: Fortress Press.

1994   *Matthew's Christian-Jewish Community.* Chicago: University of Chicago Press.

Saller, R. P.
1982   *Personal Patronage under the Early Empire.* Cambridge: Cambridge University Press.

Sanday, Peggy Reeves
1981   Plans for the Sexual Division of Labor. Pp. 76–90 in her *Female Power and Male Dominance: On the Origins of Sexual Inequality.* Cambridge: Cambridge University Press.

Sanders, E. P.
1985   *Jesus and Judaism.* Philadelphia: Fortress Press.

Schaberg, Jane
1982   *The Father, the Son and the Holy Spirit: The Triadic Phrase in Matthew 28:19b*. SBLDS 61. Chico, Calif.: Scholars Press.

1987   *The Illegitimacy of Jesus: A Feminist Theological Interpretation of the Infancy Narratives*. San Francisco: Harper & Row.

Schaps, David
1977   The Woman Least Mentioned: Etiquette and Women's Names. *CQ* 27:323–30.

Schlier, Heinrich
1965   κεφαλή. *TDNT* 2:673–82.

Schmidt, K. L.
1965   ἐκκλησία. *TDNT* 3:501–36.

Schmidt, Steffen W., James Scott, Carl Landé, and Laura Guasti
1977   *Friends, Followers, and Factions: A Reader in Political Clientelism*. Berkeley, Calif.: University of California Press.

Schmidt, Thomas E.
1987   *Hostility to Wealth in the Synoptic Gospels*. JSNTSup 15. Sheffield: Sheffield Academic Press.

Schneider, Jane
1971   Of Vigilance and Virgins: Honor, Shame and Access to Resources in Mediterranean Societies. *Ethnology* 10:1–24.

Schneider, Johannes
1968   ὅρκος. *TDNT* 5:457–67.

1972   τιμή. *TDNT* 8:169–80.

Schneider, Peter
1969   Honor and Conflict in a Sicilian Town. *Anthropological Quarterly* 42:130–54.

Schoeck, Helmut
1970   *Envy, a Theory of Social Behavior*. New York: Harcourt, Brace & World.

Schottroff, Luise
1975   Gewaltverzicht und Feindesliebe in der urchristlichen Jesustradition (Mt 5, 38–48; Lk 6, 27–36). Pp. 197–221 in G. Strecker, ed., *Jesus Christus in Historie und Theologie*. Tübingen: J.C.B. Mohr (Paul Siebeck).

1978   *Essays on the Love Commandment*. Philadelphia: Fortress Press.

1986   *Jesus and the Hope of the Poor*. Philadelphia: Fortress Press.

Schrenk, Gottlob
1964   εὐδοκέω. *TDNT* 2:738–51.

Schur, Edwin M.
1971   *Labeling Deviant Behavior: Its Sociological Implications.* New York: Harper & Row.

1980   *The Politics of Deviance: Stigma Contents and the Uses of Power.* Englewood Cliffs, N.J.: Prentice-Hall.

Schweizer, E.
1972   Vorgeschichtliches zu den Seligpreisungen Jesu. *NTS* 19:121–26.

1975   *The Good News according to Matthew.* Atlanta: John Knox Press.

Seeley, David
1989   *The Noble Death: Graeco-Roman Martyrology and Paul's Concept of Salvation.* Sheffield: JSOT Press.

Segal, Charles
1971   *The Theme of the Mutilation of the Corpse in the Iliad.* Leiden: E. J. Brill.

Senior, Donald
1975   *The Passion Narrative according to Matthew: A Redactional Study.* BETL 39. Louvain: Leuven University Press.

1977   The Death of God's Son and the Beginning of the New Age. Pp. 31–51 in A. Lacomara, *The Language of the Cross.* Chicago: Franciscan Herald Press.

1984a   The Struggle to Be Universal: Mission as Vantage Point for New Testament Investigation. *CBQ* 46:63–81.

1984b   *The Passion of Jesus in the Gospel of Mark.* Wilmington, Del.: Glazier.

1985   *The Passion of Jesus in the Gospel of Matthew.* Wilmington, Del.: Glazier.

1989   *The Passion of Jesus in the Gospel of Luke.* Wilmington, Del.: Glazier.

1991   *The Passion of Jesus in the Gospel of John.* Collegeville, Minn.: Liturgical Press.

Shuler, Philip L.
1982   *A Genre for the Gospels: The Biographical Character of Matthew.* Philadelphia: Fortress Press.

Sim, D. C.
1990   The Man without the Wedding Garment (Matthew 22:11–13). *HeyJ* 31:165–78.

Sinclair, Alison
1993   *The Deceived Husband*. Oxford: Clarendon Press.

Smith, J.
1990   The Discourse Structure of the Rape of Tamar (2 Sam 13:1–22). *Vox Evangelica* 20:21–42.

Smith, Jonathan Z.
1975   The Social Description of Early Christianity. *Religious Studies Review* 1:19–25.

Smith, Richard
1988   Sex Education in Gnostic Schools. Pp. 345–60 in Karen King, ed., *Images of the Feminine in Gnosticism*. Philadelphia: Fortress Press.

Stanford, W. B.
1964   *The Ulysses Theme: A Study in the Adaptability of a Traditional Hero*. 2d ed. New York: Barnes & Noble.

Stansbury, Harry Adams
1990   Corinthian Honor, Corinthian Conflict: A Social History of Early Roman Corinth and Its Pauline Community. Dissertation, University of California at Irvine.

Stansell, Gary
1992   Honor and Shame in the David Narratives. Pp. 94–114 in *"Was ist der Mensch?" Beiträge zur Anthropologie des Alten Testament*. Munich: Chr. Kaiser.

1996   Honor and Shame in the David Narratives. *Semeia* 68:55–79.

Stanton, Graham N.
1992   *A Gospel for a New People: Studies in Matthew*. Louisville, Ky.: Westminster/John Knox Press.

Stark, Rodney
1991   Antioch as the Social Situation for Matthew's Gospel. Pp. 189–210 in David L. Balch, ed., *Social History of the Matthean Community: Cross-Disciplinary Approaches*. Minneapolis: Fortress Press.

Stendahl, Krister
1962   Hate, Non-Retaliation, and Love (QS X,17–20 and Rom 12:19–21). *HTR* 55:343–55.

1968   *The School of St. Matthew and Its Use of the Old Testament*. Philadelphia: Fortress Press.

Sterling, Gregory E.
1994   "Athletes of Virtue": An Analysis of the Summaries in Acts (2:41–47; 4:32–35; 5:12–16). *JBL* 113:679–96.

Steward, Frank Henderson
1994   *Honor*. Chicago: University of Chicago Press.

Strecker, Georg
1970   Die Makarismen der Bergpredigt. *NTS* 17:255–75.

1978   Die Antithesen der Bergpredigt (Mt 5,21–38). *ZNW* 69:37–72.

1988   *The Sermon on the Mount: An Exegetical Commentary*. Nashville: Abingdon Press.

Stegeman, Wolfgang
1985   Die Versuchung Jesu im Matthäusevangelium: Mt 4, 1–11. *EvQ* 45:29–44.

Stuart, Duane Reed
1928   *Epochs of Greek and Roman Biography*. Berkeley, Calif.: University of California Press.

Sweet, Waldo E.
1987   *Sport and Recreation in Ancient Greece: A Sourcebook with Translations*. Oxford: Oxford University Press.

Synnott, Anthony
1987   Shame and Glory: A Sociology of Hair. *British Journal of Sociology* 38:381–413.

Talbert, Charles H.
1977   *What Is a Gospel: The Genre of the Canonical Gospels*. Philadelphia: Fortress Press.

1978   Biographies of Philosophers and Rulers as Instruments of Religious Propaganda in Mediterranean Antiquity. *ANRW* II.16.2: 1619–51.

1980   Prophecies of Future Greatness: The Contributions of Greco-Roman Biographies to an Understanding of Luke 1:5–4:15. Pp. 129–41 in James Crenshaw, ed., *The Divine Helmsman: Studies on God's Control of Human Events*. New York: KTAV.

1988   Once Again: Gospel Genre. *Semeia* 43:53–74.

1996   The Acts of the Apostles: Monograph or "Bios"? Pp. 58–72 in Ben Witherington, III, ed., *History, Literature and Society in the Book of Acts*. Cambridge: Cambridge University Press.

Tannehill, Robert
1979   The Gospel of Mark as Narrative Christology. *Semeia* 16:57–95.

Taylor, G.
1985   *Pride, Shame, and Guilt*. Oxford: Clarendon Press.

Thackeray, H. St. J.
1913   A Study in the Parable of the Two Kings. *JTS* 14:389–99.

Theissen, Gerd
1979   Gewaltverzicht und Feindesliebe (Mt 5, 38–48/Lk 6, 27–38) und deren
        sozialgeschichtlichen Hintergrund. Pp. 160–97 in his *Studien zur Sozi-
        ologie des Urchristentums*. WUNT 19. Tübingen: J.C.B. Mohr [Paul
        Siebeck].

1983   *The Miracle Stories of the Early Christian Tradition*. Philadelphia:
        Fortress Press.

1991   *The Gospels in Context: Social and Political History in the Synoptic
        Tradition*. Minneapolis: Fortress Press.

1992   Nonviolence and Love of Our Enemies. Pp. 115–56 in his *Social Real-
        ity and the Early Christians*. Minneapolis: Fortress Press.

Thompson, William G.
1971   Reflections on the Composition of Mt 8,1–9,34. *CBQ* 33:365–88.

Thomson, G. H. P.
1960   Called-Proved-Obedient: A Study in the Baptism and Temptation Nar-
        ratives of Matthew and Luke. *JTS* 11:1–12.

Tigay, Jeffrey H.
1979   On the Term Phylacteries (Matt 23:5). *HTR* 72:45–52.

Tilborg, Sjef van
1986   *The Sermon on the Mount as an Ideological Intervention*. Assen: Van
        Gorcum.

1993   *Imaginative Love in John*. Leiden: E. J. Brill.

Triandis, Harry C.
1990   Cross-Cultural Studies of Individualism and Collectivism. Pp. 41–133
        in Richard A. Dienstbier and John J. Berman, eds., *Nebraska Sympo-
        sium on Motivation 1989*. Lincoln: University of Nebraska Press.

Trilling, Wolfgang
1969   *The Gospel according to Matthew*. New York: Herder & Herder.

Turner, Terence S.
1968   Parsons' Concept of "Generalized Media of Symbolic Interaction" and
        Its Relevance for Social Anthropology. *Sociological Inquiry* 38:121–
        34.

Twelftree, Graham H.
1993   *Jesus the Exorcist: A Contribution to the Study of the Historical Jesus*.
        WUNT 2/54. Tübingen: J.C.B. Mohr [Paul Siebeck].

Ullendorf, E.
1979   The Bawdy Bible. *Bulletin of the School of Oriental and African Stud-
        ies* 42:426–56.

Unnik, Willem C. van
1980   Die Rücksicht auf die Reaktion der Nicht-Christen als Motiv der altchristlichen Paränese. Pp. 307–22 in his *Sparsa Collecta*. Vol. 2. Leiden: E. J. Brill.

Vaage, Leif E.
1992   "Like Dogs Barking": Cynic *Parrêsia* and Shameless Asceticism. *Semeia* 57:25–39.

1994   *Galilean Upstarts: Jesus' First Followers According to Q*. Valley Forge, Pa.: Trinity Press International.

Van Seters, J.
1987   Love and Death in the Court of David. Pp. 121–24 in J. H. Marks and R. M. Good, *Love and Death in the Ancient Near East*. Guilford, Conn.: Four Quarters.

Vermeulen, A. J.
1981   Gloria. *RAC* 11:196–225.

Vernant, Jean-Pierre
1988   *Myth and Society in Ancient Greece*. New York: Zone Books.

Vermes, Geza
1973   *Jesus the Jew: A Historian's Reading of the Gospels*. Philadelphia: Fortress Press.

Verner, David C.
1983   *The Household of God: The Social World of the Pastoral Epistles*. SBLDS 71. Chico, Calif.: Scholars Press.

Versnel, H. S.
1970   *Triumphus: An Inquiry into the Origin, Development and Meaning of the Roman Triumph*. Leiden: E. J. Brill.

Veyne, Paul
1989   "Humanitas": Romani e noi. Pp. 385–414 in Andrea Giardina, ed., *L'Uomo Romano*. Bari: Laterza.

Wainwright, Elaine Mary
1991   *Towards a Feminist Critical Reading of the Gospel according to Matthew*. BZNW 60. Berlin: Walter de Gruyter.

Walcot, Peter
1970   The Concepts of Shame and Honour. Pp. 57–76 in his *Greek Peasants, Ancient and Modern: A Comparison of Social and Moral Values*. Manchester: Manchester University Press.

1978   *Envy and the Greeks: A Study in Human Behaviour*. Warminster: Aris & Phillips.

1991   On Widows and Their Reputation in Antiquity. *Symbolae Osloenses* 66:5–26.

Wallace-Hadrill, Andrew, ed.
1989   *Patronage in Ancient Society*. London: Routledge.

Weaver, Dorothy Jean
1992   Power and Powerlessness: Matthew's Use of Irony in the Portrayal of Political Leaders. *SBLSP* 1992:454–66.

Weber, Hans-Ruedi
1978   *The Cross: Tradition and Interpretation*. Grand Rapids: Eerdmans.

Weeden, Theodore J.
1976   The Cross as Power in Weakness (Mark 15:20b–41). Pp. 115–34 in Werner H. Kelber, ed., *The Passion in Mark: Studies on Mark 14–16*. Philadelphia: Fortress Press.

Weise, M.
1958   Mt 5,21f—ein Zeugnis sakraler Rechtsprechung in der Urgemeinde. *ZNW* 49:116–23.

Westermann, Claus
1980   *The Psalms: Structure, Content and Message*. Minneapolis: Augsburg.

White, L. Michael
1991   Crisis Management and Boundary Maintenance: The Social Location of the Matthean Community. Pp. 211–47 in David L. Balch, ed., *Social History of the Matthean Community: Cross-Disciplinary Approaches*. Minneapolis: Fortress Press.

White, Leland J.
1986   Grid and Group in Matthew's Community: The Righteousness/Honor Code in the Sermon on the Mount. *Semeia* 35:61–88.

Whitehead, David
1985   Competitive Outlay and Community Profit: ΦΙΛΟΤΙΜΙΑ in Democratic Athens. *Mediaevalia* 34:55–74.

Wikan, Unni
1984   Shame and Honor: A Contestable Pair. *Man* 19:635–52.

Wilckens, Ulrich
1972   ὑποκρίνομαι. *TDNT* 8:559–71.

Wilken, Robert
1983   *John Chrysostom and the Jews: Rhetoric and Reality in the Late Fourth Century*. Berkeley: University of California Press.

Williams, Bernard
1993   *Shame and Necessity*. Berkeley: University of California Press.

Williams, James G.
1988   Parable and Chreia: From Q to Narrative Gospel. *Semeia* 43:85–114.

Williams, Sam K.
1975   *Jesus' Death as Saving Event: The Background and Origin of a Concept.* HDR 2. Missoula, Mont.: Scholars Press.

Wilson, Robert R.
1975   The Old Testament Genealogies in Recent Research. *JBL* 94:168–89.

1977   *Genealogy and History in the Biblical World.* New Haven, Conn.: Yale University Press.

Wink, Walter
1992   Beyond Just War and Pacifism: Jesus' Nonviolent Way. *RevExp* 89:197–214.

Winkler, John J.
1990   Laying Down the Law: The Oversight of Men's Sexual Behavior in Classical Athens. Pp. 171–209 in David M. Halperin, John J. Winkler, and Froma Zeitlin, eds., *Before Sexuality: The Construction of Erotic Experience in the Ancient Greek World.* Princeton: Princeton University Press.

Winter, Bruce W.
1988   The Public Honouring of Christian Benefactors. Romans 13.3–4 and 1 Peter 2.14–15. *JSNT* 34:87–103.

Winterbottom, Michael
1964   Quintilian and the *Vir Bonus*. *JRS* 54:90–97.

Wire, Antoinette Clark
1991   Gender Roles in a Scribal Community. Pp. 87–121 in David L. Balch, ed., *Social History of the Matthean Community: Cross-Disciplinary Approaches.* Minneapolis: Fortress Press.

Witherington, Ben, III
1995   *Conflict and Community in Corinth: A Socio-Rhetorical Commentary on 1 and 2 Corinthians.* Grand Rapids: Eerdmans.

Witherup, Ronald D.
1987   The Death of Jesus and the Raising of the Saints: Matthew 27:51–54 in Context. *SBLSP* 1987:574–85.

Wuellner, Wilhelm
1990   The Argumentative Structure of 1 Thessalonians as a Paradoxical Encomium. Pp. 117–36 in Raymond Collins, ed., *The Thessalonian Correspondence.* BETL 87. Louvain: Leuven University Press.

Wurmser, L.
1981   *The Mask of Shame.* Baltimore: Johns Hopkins University Press.

Yaghjian, Lucretia B.
1996   Ancient Reading. Pp. 206–30 in Richard L. Rohrbaugh, ed., *The Social Sciences and New Testament Interpretation*. Peabody, Mass.: Hendrickson.

Yarnold, E.
1968   *Teleios* in St. Matthew's Gospel. *SE* 4 (= TU102):269–73.

Zeid, A. M. Abou
1965   Honour and Shame among the Bedouin of Egypt. Pp. 245–59 in J. G. Péristiany, ed., *Honour and Shame: The Values of Mediterranean Society*. Chicago: University of Chicago Press.

Zerbe, G. M.
1993   *Non-Retaliation in Early Jewish and New Testament Texts: Ethical Themes in Social Context*. Journal for the Study of the Pseudepigrapha Supplement 13. Sheffield: Sheffield Academic Press.

Index of Scripture and Other Ancient Sources

Index of Subjects and
and Ancient Authors